WORD IMAGE

Series Editors
Leo Hoek and Peter de Voogd

In collaboration with

Studies in comparative literature 22

Series Editors
C.C. Barfoot and Theo D'haen

Text and Visuality

Word & Image Interactions 3

Edited by Martin Heusser, Michèle Hannoosh,
Leo Hoek, Charlotte Schoell-Glass & David Scott

Rodopi

Amsterdam - Atlanta, GA
1999

Cover design: Hendrik van Leeuwen

ISBN: 90-420-0736-2 (bound)

The paper on which this book is printed meets the requirements
of 'ISO 9706:1994, Information and documentation
- Paper for documents - Requirements for permanence'.

BOOKS, TYPOGRAPHY AND OTHER MEDIA

ACKNOWLEDGMENTS

_____

The essays collected in this volume are a selection of the papers given at the *Fourth Triennial International Conference on Word and Image Studies,* 11-17 August, 1996.

My sincere thanks are due to my co-editors, Michèle Hannoosh, Charlotte Schoell-Glass and David Scott for their excellent editorial work. I also wish to thank the Department Secretary, Theres Lutz, and Maya Huber, my assistant, for helping me getting the camera-ready copy done. Fred van der Zee at Rodopi and Cedric Barfoot (University of Leiden) have made valuable suggestions in typographical and editorial matters.

University of Zurich, English Department

Martin Heusser

Theoretical Considerations

Basic Instincts and Their Discontents

Mieke Bal

> The point, then, is not to heal the split be-
> tween words and images, but to see what
> interests and powers it serves.
> W. J. T. Mitchell

When Paul de Man, in a famous 1979 essay, deconstructed the opposition between semiology and rhetoric, he could only do so because he first set it up.[1] And that he could only do because he assumed, like most people, that the realm of words is unquestionably primary and unique. In this paper I will take issue with some common assumptions regarding what is visual and what is verbal, and discuss how even elementary semiotic concepts can enhance our understanding of "what goes on" in cultural interaction through artifacts. As de Man among many others demonstrates, assumptions not only *that* language is different from the visual, but *how* these media differ, are so common that they seem axiomatic, "basic", and in no need to be spelled out, but can be acted upon, as if "instinctively".

These assumptions and their discontents can be examined through a kind of popular-culture representation of the word/image combination. If I call all artifacts "texts", it is not to reduce them to language but, on the contrary, to re-activate the etymological riches of the notion that artifacts are fabricated, complex, and structured; that they have a complex "surface" that matters like a sophisticated fabric; a texture. The cartoon, the comic strip, the emblem, but also film, tenaciously refuse the reduction our disciplinary boundaries have enforced. This cartoon (fig. 1, overleaf) was presented by the American Germanist Gerd Gemunden in a discussion of the reception of American popular culture within contemporary German culture as it is today struggling to liberate its self-image from the burden of history.[2] I wish to juxtapose it to an anecdotal example in the essay "Semiology and Rhetoric" by Paul de Man which opens his book *Allegories of Reading*. de Man uses an incident from the American satirical television series *All in the Family* to question the easy continuity between semiotics (the term I will use for his "semiology") and rhetoric in literary studies, as well as, in the end, the distinction or indifference between them.

Figure 1. Cartoon from *Tom,* Thomas Körner, Berlin: Jochen Enterprises 1993.

De Man recalls how the main character of that series is confronted with the vagaries of language:

> Asked by his wife whether he wants to have his bowling shoes laced over or laced under, Archie Bunker answers with a question: "What's the difference?" Being a reader of sublime simplicity, his wife replies by patiently explaining the difference between lacing over and lacing under, whatever this may be, but provokes only ire. "What's the difference" did not ask for difference but means instead "I don't give a damn what the difference is". (9)

Indifferent to the importance of Bunker's indifference to difference, de Man goes on to argue that the misunderstanding is really liable to provoke an existential crisis, for what is at stake is the problem of meaning. He explains:

> A perfectly clear syntactical paradigm (the question) engenders a sentence that has at least two meanings, of which the one asserts and the other denies its own illocutionary mode. [...] (10)

De Man has no other help to offer than the "intervention of an extra-textual intention". Strikingly enough, this appeal to extra-textual intention intervenes in the very argument against the opposition between internal and external criticism. But then, the description of such a possible intention shows where de Man's allegiance lies, for he continues:

> ... such as Archie Bunker putting his wife straight; but the very anger he displays is indicative of more than impatience; it reveals his despair when confronted with a structure of linguistic meaning that he cannot control and that holds the discouraging prospect of an infinity of similar future confusions ... (10)

Figure 2. From television sitcom *All in the Family*, V.P.R.O. July 31, 1988.

De Man uses this example as an entrance into a discussion that ends up giving the poets the last word in the matter, as the most profound, or encompassing, philosophers of language and meaning. How can Bunker be cast as such a wise poet? Archie Bunker is, of course, a textual figure, and the signs in the filmic text that make it much less ambiguous – his flabbergasted face, his shrugging, even his intonation that helps to tell the rhetorical from the literal question – are part of a text that does not allow such a distinction. The very look of contempt on his face as well as the over-zealous seriousness of his wife Edith, as well as *her* despair over her husband's failure to acknowledge her as a subject, are part of the semiotic system that produced this text (fig. 2).

De Man ignores the visual nature of the object he is looking at, as well as the bodily nature of speech. What he calls semiotic is avowedly just grammar; but that reduction is mobilized for the sake of establishing an opposition that he can then deconstruct in favour of ambiguity. The gesture, seemingly highly theoretical, is in the end anti-theoretical, playing as it does in the hands of those who have the "gut-instinct" that semiotics is reductive.[3]

What happened in the episode de Man takes on is something that would considerably complicate his view of language and of semiotics if he had taken the television show for what it was: a representation that does not allow the distinction between word and image, between verbal and visual behaviour and representation. But my association between this example and the cartoon in turn simplifies the same issue, by focusing on the speech acts and their mishandling by the characters, Archie and Edith Bunker. It is not so sure to me that Edith is the one who "misunderstood" Archie's rhetorical question for a literal one. For underneath that issue lies the issue of relevance.[4] The question is rhetorical only if one knows that there is no difference, but since for Edith there clearly is, the ambiguity de Man signals in the exchange becomes even more layered. In a considerably more complex interpretation than de Man would have it – a "multimedia" one, which considers body language and facial expression as part of the message – but in the same spirit of demonstrating ambiguity, I would suggest Archie's misfiring is taking a real question for an implicit demonstration – of subservience; and Edith misfires by taking a rhetorical question for a real one, believing against all odds that she will be taken seriously as a reward for her care. Nor, I will suggest, can we be so sure who, of the two figures in the cartoon analyzed below, is misfiring.[5]

A woman sitting at a desk asks a man standing before her what his nationality is: "Nationalität?" The man, his left hand with pointed finger at the seam of his trousers, his body straight up, has taken a military pose of obedience to a higher officer, and answers: "Jawoll!" In an open book case are rows of dossiers, but also a tea pot; on top of the case is a plant, a cactus, over which hangs a picture of a dog. On the window sill, a vase with flowers; beyond, a view of sky scrapers. The two figures are both caricatures. The woman has empty eyes, a moustache. She also sports a towering hairdo with a fish bone in it – the cartoonist signature detail – and net stockings. These two elements place her in the hippie era. The man has a large belly, a potato nose, a neck thicker than his head, a mouth occupying most of his face, and looks dumb in the combination of merry misfiring, military pose, and eagerness to please.

The cartoon seems a much simpler case than a television series: there is no movement, the visual image is simplified by stylized drawing, and there is only one very short speech by each character. The woman, fulfilling a bureaucratic function, is asking what the man's nationality is. The man answers the question as if it were an order; this is a misfiring different from the one that made Archie Bunker rebuff his wife rather than taking up on her offer of endless caring. The obvious context – Germany and nationalism – provides the joke with its deep meaning. The German man misfires in that he responds to the very topic of nationality – according to the view suggested by the cartoon, a painful one in Germany today – by stepping back into the national identity of the past that produced the problem of national identity in the present in the first place: the blind obedience and submission to authority that caused so much unspeakable grief. He misfires by acting out instead of stating the answer. The joke, then, seems to be at his expense. But this is only half the message. For in his very act of misfiring he states a truth of a more important and more contemporary nature: that nationalism backfires. If you ask the question of nationality, you set yourself up for getting the "wrong" answer – the question solicits the emergence of nationalism. Thus, unawares, the man here has the word of wisdom in today's debate on multiculturalism. Over against the woman's bureaucratic practice, his answer offers an "analysis" of the causes of nationalism.

Connecting the question of felicitousness of speech acts with that of relevance, as the Archie Bunker example suggested, we now get a different picture from de Man's predicament. The "truth" of the act of misfiring – which makes the misfiring man an adequate speaker on another level – is that the questions that bureaucracy asks are inappropriate, irrelevant, even harmful. We have learned that long ago from Althusser: in his essay on the work of ideology, he proposed the important concept of *interpellation* to take linguistics one step beyond itself, and provide the analytical philosophy of language with a logic it could not quite accommodate: a logic that inferred, from speech act theory's insistence that the success or failure of a speech act constitutes language's essence, the notion that the "second person" addressed by speech acts is shaped by them.[6]

Althusser thus gave an important turn to linguistic theory. Especially in the tradition of Emile Benveniste this theory had argued that the "second person", the "you" to whom every speech act is addressed, constitutes the subject in language.[7] I will return to the conclusion Benveniste drew from this, namely, that the essence of language is deixis, not reference. Althusser argued that this function of address, this "you" that constitutes the subject, is available and, in fact, a privileged function for ideology to work with. The policeman saying "you" makes *you*, specifically, into *me*, that is, turn around, feeling addressed at the same time as I feel unsettled, taken out of myself, already in fear of prison. Just so, the very fact that his nationality is asked, thus made relevant, makes the German character fall back into the kind of nationality that ideology has staked out for him. He is made to respond as the authoritarian personality as which he is addressed. In terms of nationality, and in the context of Germany, a flash of memory surfaces, of national-socialism and its ideological state apparatuses. But by thus submitting to ideology, the man-as-figure, or as sign, unwittingly also sets the woman straight, critiquing *her* submission; if he is acting out German nationality, she is acting out the result of her interpellation by the state that turned her into a willing instrument of such forms of interpellation: she acts her part as an ideological state apparatus. He interpellates her as much as she does him. Thus, just the words alone, the represented exchange, the two speech acts of question and answer become not only acts of oppression – the one that bases privileges on nationality – and submission – of the subject subjecting himself. They also become together, as text, a historical analysis of the past as Germany carries it along in the present.

This is how the cartoon is political, geared toward critique of and intervention in, today's German culture.

Thus the speech acts already challenge the distinction between inside and outside of language that is a precondition for the analysis of words alone in a multimedia text. Archie Bunker's rhetorical question, I argued, is clearly rhetorical if we take the visual representation of his body as part of his speech act. But while such a more broadly semiotic instead of literary analysis makes the speech acts less ambiguous, it makes the delimitation of the speech acts from one another more ambiguous. In the cartoon, the visual dimension of the text also considerably qualifies the linguistic aspect.

For me as a non-German and with my own historical burden, this cartoon seemed primarily a representation of three stereotypes: Germanness, "bureaucraticness", and gender: male victim and female bitch. But since the overt topic of the text is the meaning of nationality, it deserves pointing out that the image does a lot of work to complicate nationality further. The sky-scrapers outside the window recall the postwar Americanization of European cities. The outrageous appearance of the female bureaucrat with blinded eyes and a moustache, with a fish bone in her hair and netted stockings, also alludes to a certain kind of stereotype of "Americanness" in popular European culture of the fifties and sixties.

Other "symptoms" in the image further elaborate on the fact that this scene is set, not in America, but in the imaginary America German popular culture has been eying to improve its own national self-image. The antennae on the roofs of the skyscrapers signify that the scene is "Manhattan on the Rhine", a fake, enviously copied Americanness. The enthusiastic Americanization of Western European culture after the war is placed under critical siege, hopelessly betrayed by the failure of the bureaucratic management of immigration to extirpate the nationalism that ravaged history before. Against this background – or through the "screen" of this visual foreground – the verbal exchange becomes even more poignant: by answering "Jawoll!" the man implies that the question really is: "you *are* German, I hope?" and thus, he cuts right through the pretence of bureaucracy of being open to foreigners – an openness that the question, allowing for a potential variety of answers, overtly suggests – by giving the authority figure the answer she wants to hear: thank God, yes, I am "one of us". But at the same time it plays on the assumed critique of Americans against German nationalism by making the man look too dumb to be allowed in, too dumb for words. Thus the critical edge cuts both ways, and aims the joke's point beyond Germany alone.

The point is, once we admit, as I think we should, that the speech acts as quoted do not enable us to delimit what is linguistic and what is not, then the visual continues this expansion and hence, the very attempt to distinguish words from image falls flat. I am not saying there is no difference; just that in this case, Bunker's rhetorical question takes hold: what difference does it make?

De Man's argument about an irreducible tension between rhetoric and semiotics is really about rhetoric and grammar, and it is really epistemological.[8] Interestingly, in his attempt to put semiotics in its place he appeals to Peirce. But it is Peirce's concept of the *interpretant* as a necessary element of signification that, precisely, brackets the sign-object relation as semantic and the sign-sign relation as syntax. And it is the sign-interpretant relation that is at stake, not only in the Archie Bunker episode and the German cartoon, but in all language use; the notion of the direction taken by the chain of interpretants, in other words, the notion of relevance cannot be discarded, and each speech act is embedded in the framework set up by the one preceding it and that it further expands.

Both examples also demonstrate that this feature of language, *within the domain of language itself*, blocks any attempt to separate "inside" from "outside" of language. As a consequence, even if one held a totally language-centred view of semiotics, one would be forced to "step out" of this self-assigned "prison house of language". Then, the seemingly simple sign, read here as a one-word "symptom of Germanness" ("Jawoll" as a response to a question of nationality) gets "thickened" by such seemingly futile details as the tea pot in the file cabinet, the bee in the embedded picture of the dog – a detail in the detail –, and the wood varnish of the desk as an index of "surface" that underscores that surface matters, to further fill in the values of homeliness that underlie it. These are not just details, not visual "fillers", but answers to further questions about the stakes of nationalism including a certain homeliness, in turn raising new questions concerning ideological pressures surrounding the family; in other words, they are part of the conversation, and in that sense, they, too, as visual signs, function like "speeches".

Taking the visual elements of this mixed-media text seriously does neither imply a denial of a distinction between the media of language and visual representation, nor an argument for equal attention to both. Instead, the point I would like to make is the relevance of a semiotic perspective that takes its clues from a speech act theory that does not close its borders to what its logic permits to couch into rules. This perspective, which is inevitably derived from Peirce's concept of the sign as "moving", from one interpretant to the next, would have as its primary focus that which defines speech acts most keenly: the primacy of the "second person". This primacy takes texts out of a formalist and autonomist idealization and takes the text as dynamic. Simultaneously semiotics also privileges meaning and the ways in which meaning is produced, considering aspects and details as signs rather than forms or material elements only.

If I started with the exchange between speakers, it was because these examples complicated the delimitation *of* language already *within* language, and thus proclaimed the "natural" expansion of the domain of meaning production. But I had a second reason. Both the homely exchange between Archie and Edith, and the political one between the bureaucrat and the German subject, could only be effective because they were acts of "second-personhood". The speeches, the signs, would have neither purpose nor meaning outside of the situation in which the second person who is addressed "reflects" the signs "back" provided with an interpretant, a new, "more developed sign" as Peirce would have it.

In my experience, it never hurts to reiterate Peirce's famous definition of the sign:

> A sign, or *representamen,* is something which stands to somebody for something in some respect or capacity. It addresses somebody, that is, creates in the mind of that person an equivalent sign, or perhaps a more developed sign. That sign which it creates I call the *interpretant* of the first sign. The sign stands for something, its *object.* It stands for that object, not in all respects, but in reference to a sort of idea, which I have sometimes called the *ground* of the representamen.[9]

"The sign stands to somebody" means more than the need for the concept of the *interpretant.* I would like to take it literally, or visually if you like, so that it first turns 90 degrees and then another 90 degrees so that it becomes reversible. Second-personhood, then, is installed, not, or not only, within the imagetext but between sign and viewer. The confrontation of "to stand to", or before some *body* recalls the position of the German character, standing there at the mercy of bureaucracy as a sign of his troubled nationality. She does not bother to look at him, but we do: and in my reading he stands *to us* as a sign of "Germanness". But thus he sets us as viewers up as subjects whose looking includes stereotyping; as subjects somehow "defined" by the stereotyping we do; as the bodies to whom he stands in for the absent object. *We* are the second persons, that is to say, as Teresa De Lauretis's phrase has it: "the body in whom and for whom semiosis takes effect".[10] Thus this represented body "speaks" to us, critically addressing how we tend to read him "in a flash" as the German while tending to forget that we, our bodies, are involved in such stereotyping.

Caravaggio's painting *The Raising of Lazarus* of 1609, on which Louis Marin, that master of word and image studies, ended his book *Détruire la peinture* ("To Destroy Painting"), can be seen as an allegory of that fundamental principle of semiotics.

To be sure, this image cannot be "read" without appeal to the pre-established text it is supposed to "illustrate", but nor can it be reduced to that function. Marin points out how the image, uniquely for the visual medium, represents two moments, each narrated by the gesture of a hand: "*a gesture of pointing and an answer to it* captured in the same moment, as if in a snapshot" (166, emphasis in text).[11] But if Lazarus's opened hand, dropping the skull that he was clutching as an index of his state of deadness, is an answer to Jesus's pointed finger, then there is a third moment following, during which the skull has been dropped to the floor and the hand has been raised so as to catch the light that shows it.

But the ways in which visual images can narrate do not concern me here. I take this image as an aggrandized example, an allegory, of the shift *within* visual narration that the earlier examples also demonstrated. In other words, I take it as a shifter of narrative from *iconic* representation to indexical pointing, but specified as *deictic*. The freeze-like representation that, Marin argues, has all the signs of a carved low-relief freeze on a tombstone, thus changes from a sign of death to a sign of life, both for the figures and in its mode of signification.

The symptom of that shift is the obscurity, the invisibility even, of Jesus's face. It changes the concept of agency involved. What matters in this story, what constitutes the agency, is the line established between his hand, his body, and Lazarus's hand which initiates his return to life, thus starting a new life cycle, a new narrative. But not only does Jesus give life to Lazarus with his pointing finger, his embodied index; he also *receives* from Lazarus's response confirmation of his divine status. In other words, the story that develops in time from the left to the right side of this image "argues" for the importance, in narrative, of the contact, the constituting complementarity between first and second person. But, specifying indexicality as a general code connecting contiguous items, this contact emanates from, and reaches the bodily coordinates of the figures who do the "speaking" or who are otherwise engaged in semiosis. Thus, the definition of the sign can flesh out Benveniste's view, and expand it: the subject is shaped by the sign it is to others. This makes every sign a position in the "I"/"you" exchange that defined language. It gives the idea of a visual language a dimension we didn't know it had.

Since I started with words overflowing into images, I can now as well start at the other end and look at how images overflow into words: a painting by Caravaggio, depicting a well-known, traditional scene (fig. 3). We see Judith slicing the sword through Holophernes's neck, the blood spurting from him as a halo around his horrified face.[12] The image is clearly not unified; it is unequal in its treatment of the protagonists. Art historian Mary Garrard suggests an incapacity on the part of the painter to identify strongly enough with a woman character to flesh her out with the same level of human interest; as a result, she alleges, Judith is not dramatically involved in the scene:

> Caravaggio's rendering of such aesthetically imbalanced types – the female conventional, the male real – is less likely to be explained by Renaissance art theory

Figure 3. Caravaggio, _Judith Beheading Holophernes_, 1595-96. Roma, Collezione Copi.

or Jesuit theology than by the influence of gender on the practice of an artist who happened to be male. (291)

This statement projects an essentialist, anatomy-based view of gender on artistic subjectivity through a realist argument: although the phrase used is "aesthetically imbalanced types", the measure of this imbalance is realism: "the female conventional, the male real". Semiotics can help overcome this realism-cum-essentialism.

To that effect, I propose we make more of a pictorial detail that I consider as a sign in order to see how that helps me read the image. The sign I am alluding to is a visual sign, not a word – but it is discursive in Benveniste's sense in that it will trigger a response. It consists of the blood spurting out of the victim's neck. It is a powerful sign, because it is a conjunction of icon, index and symbol. The red colour is iconic, imposing the similitude between paint and blood. The direction is indexical: it comes out of the victim's body, is part of him. The symbolic nature of the association red/blood increases the effect and strengthens the realistic illusion. Yet, this realism is immediately undermined. This blood draws implausibly straight stripes of red set off emphatically on the flesh of the body, then on the white pillow and sheet. The blood is so emphatically detached from the body it could be expected to soil, that the spurts leave a shadow on the neck.

The decision to take these stripes as a sign is ours, or just mine. It has been pointed out that this could have been "proof" that Caravaggio had actually witnessed an execution.[13] But today we accept that realism does not entirely have to dictate how we read, accepting, that is, that images circulate today even if we are not necessarily aware of nor interested in how sixteenth-century people in Rome looked upon beheadings. If, instead, we look at the centre of this image and are struck by these strange stripes, then we "enter" the realm of semiotics.

This sign – the shadow, index of its "origin", the blood, as well as of the light that it begs to differ from, and sign of distance from cause to effect – works by means of perspective: the severing of image from picture plane, and the distinction between planes, suggesting, in turn as a sign, that there is a route to be travelled from foreground to background, from the eye of the viewer to the depth of the image. Perspective, usually taken to signify, if not to embody, to be, "real" vision, is, semiotically speaking, the irreducible index of the viewer. In spite of perspective's attempt to eliminate, purify the viewer from the image so that it can become an objective, "third person" representation, the "I"/"you" of discourse are inexorably signified.[14]

This image is importantly a "text": a structured, complex, meaningful surface. Whereas this shiny white of the bed linen rhymes with the immaculate bodice of the heroine, the red gush that crosses the whiteness out echoes the curtain behind him. But most importantly, the red spurts alliterate with the sword which is slightly behind them. And this order of things matters. The insistent layering of blood first, sword next, becomes indexical of the act of looking as a route, a voyage; it turns looking at this image into a semiotic event, perhaps a narrative, and makes the sign *stand to* the viewer for something else.

"Logically", realistically that is, the blood *follows* the sword as its consequence; this is so obvious one tends to take it as the natural and inevitable meaning. Visually, however, according to the eye's itinerary into the representation, being closer to the picture plane, the blood precedes the sword, as its visual "cause": *because* we see the blood, we subsequently see the sword. This seems an irresistible reminder of the deconstruction of pin and pain, rendered classical by Jonathan Culler's use of it as primary example.[15] The viewer is not just the royal first person, the "I" who dominates the image, but stands before, to, the image as a sign, a "you" whose "first-personhood" depends on how the other "I"/"you" confirms his or her subjectivity in terms of involvement in this text.

Challenging causality, the sign thus questions the stories of origin through which we culturally construct responsibility and guilt. The difference between Judith's statuesque quality and Holophernes' dramatic one, striking indeed, is not caused by stereotypical gender positions, but questions these. Each char-

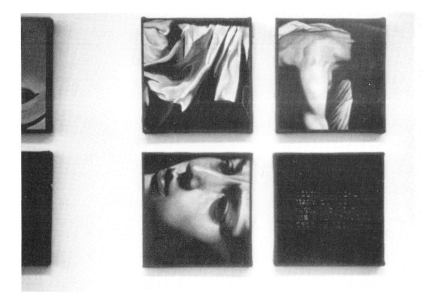

Figure 4. Dotty Attie, *A Violent Child,* 1988. Collection Cheryl and Henry Welt, New York (detail).

acter is objectified, but which objectification precedes, or causes, the other is now an open, disturbing question.

This sign helps to read the image. Following its lead into the far-reaching realm of theoretical allegory, I would like to take Judith as a figure who repre-sents a challenge, not so much to faith and chastity, nationality and group solidarity, but to our assumptions, the certainties that reign our academic work, about what it is and how it is we can know, including, about visual images, and the place of language therein, or outside of it. This is what the work has to "say" about semiotics, and its relation to disciplinary dogma. Using ancient readings of "Judith", and folding these into today's projections of essentialist identity, then, is an escape from the discursive impact of the image *as such;* not from the language behind the image but from the image *as* "language": as a semiotic text that has something to "say".

Contemporary artist Dotty Attie challenged stereotypical responses to the figure of "Judith" and to Caravaggio's representation of the topos.[16] In her work *A Violent Child* (1988) she has fragmented, copied, and rearranged that famous work, and added a narrative to it through which, in art critic Max Kozloff's words, "instead of casting the visual narrative in words, she whispers a counternarrative" (fig. 4).[17] The work consists of 40 small square canvasses, 6" x 6" each, on which details of the Caravaggio are meticulously painted, and arranged in ten rows, each row ending on a panel on which a sentence of text is stencilled. The very fragmentation, in addition to being a superb lesson in detailed looking, "argues" the inherent qualities of detailing: violence, cutting up, as well as deploying, specifying.

The narrative that is juxtaposed to the images does not illustrate these. Instead, it does what the images do, in its own medium, so as to converge in a coherent work that respects the properties of each medium but demonstrates the common semiotics of deixis in as many ways as could possibly be mustered. At first, and if read in isolation as obviously we should not do, the words suggest, in a perversely gossipy mode of intertextual allusiveness, that "Caravaggio" had a violence in him "from the start", which originated not in him but in his master. But the mode of narration, the gossipy, whispering half-truths, points in a direction even more closely related to the problem of origin, or causality, posed in the blood spurts of Caravaggio's painting. First I will focus on a feature of Attie's reworking of the painting that is a primary sign: her positioning of Judith as reclining in the lower row of panels. Thus, she becomes the victim of violence. The statuesque quality of Caravaggio's figure suddenly lights up as a sculpture on an ancient tombstone, and becomes an index, a memorial to innumerable victims of violence.

More specifically, the same figure "Judith", the topos of the heroic/wicked woman, signifier of nationalism in the one interpretation and of male dread of women in the other, is here represented as a sign of her very sign-status. The statuesque quality that Caravaggio gave her, here comes to mean that, as a representation, she is "always-already" dead. She is a monument to her own reification as a focus or token of "woman", either sanctified as heroine or vilified as treacherous, but never allowed to "live". Attie took this element from Caravaggio's painting and turned it into the ultimate or meta-sign, a sign of sign-ness, as radically different from an object or person. There is no Judith in this painting, only a "Judith", as sign, according to Peirce's definition, that stands in for the absent referent, to some body – you.

There is no better lesson in semiotics than the one this imagetext by Attie offers. It proclaims that Caravaggio was able to overcome the compulsive unification of representation that would refute elements that do not appear to "fit", and offered instead a "text" composed of a variety of signs that only on one level can be unified into a story, while also moving in different directions: self-portraiture, sculpture, and, most importantly for scholars in the Humanities, cultural critique. Thus, Attie's work proclaims in its whispering voice that a semiotic perspective on art as culturally active is indispensable.

Attie's art history lesson as semiotic also proclaims the after-effect of painting, something that Michael Holly would call prefiguration: that Caravaggio's work already inscribed, in this differentiating semiotic, the attempts to reunify his works and how these would fail – a failure whose symptom is the criticism of his female figure.[18] Finally, Attie proclaims that her own status as an artist includes a status as a superior art critic and art historian: reversing the cliché of venerating old masters, she demonstrates that it is crucial to understand contemporary art in order to understand the art of the past. She underscores the *present-ness* of cultural artifacts. And she does all that by way of a sign, which in this latter interpretation becomes a typical Saussurian sign, one that signifies by differentiation. By just turning the head 45 degrees, its meaning has changed forever.

But the work *whispers* all these arguments, the proclamation is never "loud", explicit. It is *as* a predominantly visual imagetext that it strikes us with these messages, not as message but as effect. Mindful of Francis Bacon's warning, "and the moment the story is elaborated, the boredom sets in; the story talks louder than the paint",[19] the work demonstrates that intelligence and thought, philosophy and critique, are not bound to language or to any particular medium. This is why semiotics as a theory of understanding regardless of the medium is so important.

This lesson in a semiotics of culture is further thickened by the linguistic text. I will now argue that its mode of narration is structurally iconic of the story of creation in Genesis 1-3. Further, in that capacity it emphatically evokes problems of origin; the origin of evil conjugated through the origin of the human condition; but also, of story-telling, and of the very mode of narration that is deployed before us. As I have argued elsewhere, the creation story consists of an unfolding or gradual deployment not of chronology but of differentiation and distanciation; in other words, specification.[20]

This reading can accommodate, without resorbing it, the difference between the two accounts of the creation of humanity, usually read as a clumsy conflation of sources. In the first, humanity is created in God's likeness; in the second, that abstract, or androgynous, being is further "split", literally and in a sense violently, into the two "kinds" we call sexes. The creation story can thus be read as an allegory of Ferdinand de Saussure's definition, not of the sign but of the combination of signs, of syntagmas, sentences, semiotic wholes, texts.

Here is the text:

1. Born in the small town of Caravaggio, Michelangelo Merisi, after a placid and contented infancy, became a violent child

2. The early death of his father, to whom he was much attached, was often cited for this change

3. A more likely source of his uncertain temper was his experiences when apprenticed, while still a boy, to a Milanese painter who liked to call himself a pupil of Titian

4. This artist had a passion for anatomical precision in the human and animal form

5. A secluded room away from the studio was reserved for physiological experiments on any subject safely made available

6. Small carcasses were abundant, but larger examples proved more difficult to acquire

7. Occasionally, an agreement would be made with the local surgeon, who often found the indigent of the town left on his hands after a fatal or severe illness

8. Young Merisi's many duties included helping his master in the special room

9. It was here that he learned to react quickly and mercilessly at the slightest surprise or difficulty

10. Once learned, this lesson was never forgotten

If you read Attie's sentences one after another as juxtaposed to the fragmentation of the image and the violence of each of these fragments, the gossipy mode of narration "in the third person", about Caravaggio, while – importantly – remaining active, is doubled by an ongoing specification that doubles the threat, involving the viewer/reader.

The first sentence has it all; the story is complete. Importantly, no narrative sequence, no chronology is developed throughout the ten sentences. The second offers an explanation, infusing the story with psychology. The third specifies psychological explanation further by taking the case out of the commonplace of the nuclear family structure, too general, to a specific "fact" of biography, while simultaneously taking the child out of it to become more specific, namely, an apprentice painter to another apprentice painter, thus establishing a genealogy of a biblical nature. Meanwhile, the word "source" indicates the search for origin as the narrative project explicitly.

Number 4 introduces this artist as a full participant in the story, by describing him psychologically. Simultaneously, the violence itself, the predicate of the story, is further specified, yet no more, here, than as vaguely sadistic. Number 5 fleshes the narrative out by introducing the category of space, and introduces the secret, secluded ("away from the studio") room of evil. It also introduces the genre of the fairy-tale, of Bluebeard. But the violence is here still contained, as the subjects are qualified as "*safely* made available", although "made available" is an ominous allusion to objectification. Number 6 suggests, however, a further division in small and large subjects, the latter being "more difficult to acquire;" not impossible though, which makes us rush on to the next, in order to know more. The inclusion of humans among the subjects of dissection and experiment specifies the innocent child's game and the scientist's experiments as dangerous and potentially sadistic, introduces a third character, and specifies the victims according to class, uncannily suggestive of a possible generalization to later times, including our own.

The eighth sentence is the one that I want to draw special attention to, because it accompanies the row of paintings that comprises the reclining Judith. Merisi – Caravaggio the future violent man and stunning painter – was *obliged*

to help with these sadistic games. The origin of complicity, of the secret violence done together and the bond between master and pupil, is stipulated
here. They locked themselves into the secret room that no one was to enter.
What exactly happened there? Gossip thrives on suggestion; as between 6 and
7, the "fact" itself is not stated. Nowhere in this tale is the allusion to art-
historical gossip about Caravaggio's murderous act ever stated. But he learned
something whose origin recedes back into the recesses of gossip; into ancient
culture.

By writing her superbly effective narrative in paint, in lose sentences not
ended by a colon, Attie opens up each element – each sign – to an infinitude
of further interpretations, seen as specifications. In a complementary relationship to the fragmented image that has nothing of the illustrative usually assumed in word and image relations, the narrative text embodies the rich, complex, dynamic and reader-oriented definition of the sign that we find in Peirce,
and at whose centre is the interpretant. Holding our breath from sentence to
sentence, she mercilessly carries on the work of the interpretant, offering each
time a decisively "more developed" sign. Take for example, in text panel 7, the
words "fatal *or* severe illness": something decisive happens in the space opened
by "or". From agent of a still relatively nonviolent, albeit disrespectful, disposal of the bodies of the poor, the surgeon becomes a murderer when the
bodies result from illnesses that are not by definition fatal. The small shock
that results reminds us of the work of semiosis: its dynamics *between* sign and
reader; our collusion in the production of meaning.

Indeed, the work both Caravaggio and Attie do on the relation between
imagetext and viewer, demonstrating the reversibility of "I"/"you" also in visual
terms, ties in with moral philosophy's discussions about the limits of the subject's autonomy, and epistemological discussions of objectivity. A semiotic reading of Caravaggio's work focusing on signs as working against coherence, turned
the subject into an epistemological figure questioning causality, hence, the
objectivity of knowledge, which Attie then qualified as concerning
objectification. She does that by two totally different plays on the notion of
objectivity: in the images, by turning Judith into a monument to victimhood,
and in the text, by making the evil men in the secret room perform experiments on people, killed, or perhaps not yet dead. Both objectifications are
murderous, but they "work" differently to achieve that semantic convergence.

The visual play "objectifies" the figure by underlining the statuesque quality of the figure in turning it into a dead body, then a marble relief.[21] This is
accomplished by the isolation of the detail, the changing which differentiates
it significantly – according to Saussure – and the concomitant address to the
viewer who cannot *not* notice, interpret, and judge this change. Thus it
foregrounds the interpretant as the shifter between image and viewer as between first and second person. The language text also evolves around the rela-

tion between objectivity and objectification, but with different means, bound up with narrative modes. The objectifying mode of narrative, "third-person" narration, is maintained but modelled on the specifying, not the chronological mode, so as to emphasize within *its* medium how objectivity leads to objectification. Both the gossipy and the specifying modes of narration, respectively, vulgarly social and loftily biblical, while speaking *about* the guilty objectification of subjects in the story, speak *to* the complicity of the reader/listener in the construction of guilt.

By foregrounding the mobility of the interpretant, the importance of the index, and the further specification of that sign by the reversible, bodily, deictic "I"/"you" relation, then, Attie's work in both its visual and its verbal elements foregrounds how Caravaggio's painting, in its very dis-unified modes, colludes in stereotypical reading while also critiquing it. But just as it took Attie's special art to do such a reading of the Caravaggio, just so it takes our own semiotic perspective to do justice not only to Attie's subtle and complex work – in both senses of that term – but to the interaction between the two media she deploys. An interaction that, I contend, a semiotic perspective enables us to understand.

But, enabling as this perspective may be, it can only be intellectually satisfactory if it is more than just a "device", another tool, to be used for an instrumental view of theories and disciplines, if not, just another "jargon". Obviously, I think it is more. Dynamic as the semiotic is, as per its key-concept of the interpretant, it gains itself more specificity from each encounter with objects whose subject-status it dictates. It can be argued, then, that the semiotic perspective as I have deployed it by focusing on indexicality, by engaging with the linguistic concept of deixis and the narratological, then philosophical issue of "person", also helped to set up a small incident of interdisciplinary exchange that "thickened" the reach of each participant. And that includes the imagetexts discussed. In this sense, semiotics is less a method, or worse, a "device" – one may question the need for yet more jargon, more terms – than a perspective that questions both the unity-within, the coherence, and the outside boundaries of participating disciplines, media, and works.

In other words, a perspective that is also a caution, against the kind of realism that takes commonplace assumptions for basic instincts, about disciplines, media, genders, national identities alike. In this capacity, semiotics, I submit, "touches" us all, just like the caricature figure who misfires by saying "Jawoll", thus stating a truth that is the more important as we may not like it at all.

Notes

1   Paul de Man, "Semiology and Rhetoric".
2   During a session of the Humanities Institute "Cultural memory and the Present" at Dartmouth College, Spring 1996.
3   Note Mitchell's stabbing at semiotics in *Picture Theory*.
4   Cf. Sperber and Wilson.
5   On the concept of misfiring (a speech act) see in particular Shoshana Felman's masterful *Literary Speech Acts*.
6   Althusser, Louis. *Lenin and Philosophy and Other Essays*.
7   Emile Benveniste, *Problèmes de linguistique générale*, I and "L'appareil formelle de l'énonciation".
8   It starts out from a statement by Richard Ohlman that makes it look simple but actually points the issue out quite nicely: "But whereas the rules of grammar concern the relationships among sound, syntax, and meaning, the rules of illocutionary acts concern relationships among people". The centrality of rules in Ohlman's argument ties in with Althusser's qualification of interpellation, what others have called "second-personhood". Richard Ohlman. "Speech, Literature, and the Space in Between". On "second-personhood" see Lorraine Code. *What Can She Know?*
9   The most accessible source for this famous quote is Charles Sanders Peirce. "Logic as Semiotic".
10   *Alice Doesn't. Feminism, Semiotics, Cinema.*
11   This painting is hard to see in black and white reproduction. The reader is referred to Louis Marin, *Détruire la peinture*.
12   In my book *Double Exposures* I commented on this work at length; I will briefly summarize and refocus this interpretation.
13   Françoise Bardon "Le giclement vermeil du sang de l'artère a l'évidence du réel. Caravage a dû voir quelque scène de décapitation" (6n).
14   Erwin Panofsky, "Die Perspektive als 'symbolische Form'". For an incisive critique of Panofsky's remnant realism, see Hubert Damisch, *L'origine de la perspective*. For an introduction to and context for Damisch's ideas, see Ernst van Alphen. "Moves of Hubert Damisch: Thinking about Art in History".
15   Jonathan Culler, *On Deconstruction.*
16   Attie's work was brought to my attention by Lisa Corrin's superb show *Going for Baroque*, held in Fall 1995 in The Walters, Baltimore. See Lisa G. Corrin, "Contemporary Artists Go For Baroque", 17-33.
17   Max Kozloff, "The Discreet Voyeur".
18   Michael Ann Holly, *Past Looking: Historical Imagination and the Rhetoric of the Image.*
19   Quoted by Van Alphen, *Francis Bacon and the Loss of Self.*
20   Mieke Bal, *Lethal Love.*
21   I have no space to develop here the other element that contributes to the liberation of Judith from her gendered position of trickster and murderer of men, the replacement

of Holophernes' head, a self-portrait, by that other self-portrait, *Medusa,* in turn also turned by Attie into a reclining position.

REFERENCES

Althusser, Louis. *Lenin and Philosphy and Other Essays.* London: New Left Books, 1971. [Translated by Ben Brewster].

Bal, Mieke. *Lethal Love. Literary Feminist Readings of Biblical Love Stories.* Bloomington,: Indiana University Press, 1987.

———. *Double Exposures: The Subject of Cultural Analysis.* New York: Routledge, 1996.

———. and Norman Bryson. "Semiotics and Art History". *Art Bulletin* LXXIII, 2 (1991): 174-208.

Bardon, Françoise. *Caravage ou l'expérience de la matière.* Paris: PUF, 64: 1978.

Benveniste, Emile. *Problèmes de linguistique générale.* I. Paris: Gallimard, 1966.

———. "L'appareil formelle de l'énonciation". Langage 17 (1970): 12-18. [English: "Problems in General Linguistics". Trans. Mary Elizabeth Meek. Coral Gables: University of Miami Press, 1971].

Code, Lorraine. *What Can She Know? Feminist Epistemology and the Construction of Knowledge.* Ithaca and London: Cornell University Press, 1991.

Corrin, Lisa G. "Contemporary Artists Go For Baroque". *Going for Baroque: 18 Contemporary Artists Fascinated with the Baroque and Rococo.* Lisa G. Corrin and Joaneath Spicer, eds. Baltimore, MD: The Contemporary and The Walters, 1995.

Culler, Jonathan. *On Deconstruction. Theory and Criticism After Structuralism.* Ithaca: Cornell University Press, 1983.

Damisch, Hubert. *L'origine de la perspective.* Paris: Flammarion, 1987. [Engl. *The Origin of Perspective.* Trans. John Goodman. Cambridge, MA: MIT Press 1994].

De Lauretis, Teresa. *Alice Doesn't. Feminism, Semiotics, Cinema.* London: Macmillan, 1983.

De Man, Paul. "Semiology and Rhetoric". *Allegories of Reading: Figural Language in Rousseau, Nietzsche, Rilke, and Proust.* New Haven and London: Yale University Press, 1979: 3-19.

Felman, Shoshana. *Literary Speech Acts.* Ithaca: Cornell University Press, 1983.

Garrard, Mary. *Artemisia Gentileschi: The Image and the Female Hero in Italian Baroque Art.* Princeton: Princeton University Press, 1988.

Holly, Michael Ann. *Past Looking.* Ithaca and London: Cornell University Press, 1996.

Kozloff, Max. "The Discreet Voyeur". *Art in America* 100-106 (1991): 137 (106).

Marin, Louis. *Détruire la peinture.* Paris: Éditions Galilée, 1977. [English: *To Destroy Painting,* trans. Mette Hjort. Chicago: University of Chicago Press , 1995].

Mitchell, W. J. T. *Picture Theory.* Chicago and London: Chicago University Press, 1994.

Ohlman, Richard. "Speech, Literature, and the Space in Between". *New Literary History* 4, 1972.

Panofsky, Erwin. "Die Perspective als 'symbolische Form'". *Vorträge der Bibliothek Warburg* 1924-1925. Leipzig/Berlin, 1927.

Peirce, Charles Sanders. "Logic as Semiotic". *Semiotics: An Introductory Anthology.* Edited with Introductions by Robert E. Innis. Bloomington: Indiana University Press, 1984.

Sperber, Dan and Deirdre Wilson. *Relevance: Communication and Cognition.* Oxford: Blackwell, 1995.

Sternweiler, Andreas. *Die Lust der Götter: Homosexualität in der italienischen Kunst von Donatello zu Caravaggio.* Berlin: Rosa Winkel GmbH, 1993.

Van Alphen, Ernst. *Francis Bacon and the Loss of Self.* London: Reaktion Books, 1992.

——. "*Moves* of Hubert Damisch: Thinking about Art in History". Hubert Damisch. *Moves.* Rotterdam: Museum Boymans-Van Beuningen, 1997.

One Surface Fits All: Texts, Images and the Topology of Hypermedia

Hanjo Berressem

> The history of the voice and its writing is
> comprehended between two mute writings
> (...) relating to each other as the natural and
> the artificial: the pictogram and algebra.
>
> Jacques Derrida

One of the more fascinating aspects of the postmodern, hypermedial 'docuverse'
is that its negotiation calls for the development and the use of completely new
navigatory strategies. These strategies address modes of finding one's way in
an overwhelming mass of data; in a semiotic network in which all points are
interconnected. A good figure for such a hypermedial topology, which runs
counter to the idea of one great linear narrative, is Gilles Deleuze and Félix
Guattari's image of the rhizome; a root that has a much more 'tangled' structure than that of a tree, and which looks somewhat like Ako-Pads. As Deleuze
and Guattari state,

> the principal characteristics of a rhizome: unlike trees or their roots, the rhizome
> connects any point to any other point, and its traits are not necessarily linked to
> traits of the same nature; it brings into play very different regimes of signs, and
> even nonsign states. The rhizome is reducible neither to the One nor the multi-
> ple ... It is composed not of units but of dimensions, or rather directions in
> motion. It has neither beginning nor end, but always a middle (*milieu*) from
> which it grows and which it overspills. It constitutes linear multiplicities with *n*
> dimensions having neither subject nor object, which can be laid out on a plane of
> consistency, and from which the One is always subtracted (*n*-1) ... The rhizome
> operates by variation, expansion, conquest, capture, offshoots ... the rhizome
> pertains to a map that ... is always detachable, connectable, reversible, modifi-
> able, and has multiple entryways and exits, and ... lines of flight ... the rhizome is
> *an acentered nonhierarchical, nonsignifying system without ... an organizing memory*
> or central automaton, defined solely by a circulation of states ... all manner of
> "becomings" (Deleuze and Guattari 21, emphasis added).[1]

The small, local and delinearized narratives that can grow in such a rhizome
have become commonplace motifs in poststructuralism at least since Lyotard.

Although they are in themselves ordered, this order can always, because of the topology of the rhizome, be broken up again, so that there is a constant movement of composition and decomposition. Although "[t]here exist tree or root structures in rhizomes; conversely, a tree branch or root division may begin to burgeon into a rhizome" (15). As a result, "rhizome lines oscillate between tree lines that segment and even stratify them, and lines of flight or ... rupture that carry them away" (506). In what follows, I will take this general delinearization for granted and concentrate on some aspects of the new alignment of words and images in a hypermedial environment.

In texts, from medieval manuscripts to postmodern fiction, visuals – as images or ornaments – are mostly used as supplemental illustrations that are spatially (although not contextually) separated and framed off from the body of the text. Yet they also, as in such diverse forms as dada, concrete poetry or experimental fiction, enter the textual space itself. In medieval manuscripts, such intrusions happen when the signifier itself is illuminated – when it is directly intertwined with an ivy of visual arabesques, grotesques and embellishments. If on the page such illuminations were operative on the very materiality of the signifier, in hypermedia, the illumination has become general. The function of the golden, divine light that serves as a background to so many illuminated manuscripts, has been taken over, in hypermedia, by an electronic light that comes from behind the computer screen. This electronic light can come to stand as a metaphor of a once more 'divine intervention'; the – some would say relentless – digitalization of the various codes and media; the transfer of images, sounds and texts into a digital mode. Because hypermedia, as a fully digital universe, rests, if not on a universal substance, then on a universal code, or structure, texts, images and sounds can be mapped *onto* and inserted *into* each other. They can be unproblematically and seemingly endlessly transferred, transposed and translated, because the medial shifts or, as Julia Kristeva calls them, "transposition[s]" (59) do no longer have to overcome a structural gap. The various media are no longer framed *in* and thus framed *off* from each other. Once digitalized, they can literally melt or morph into one another. The universe of hypermedia, therefore, is fluid, without any one hierarchy between the various media. In this digital universe, the new channels of communication are fiber-optic cables; cables that are, in the words of the protagonist of Ian McDonald's science-fiction novel *Scissors, Cut, Paper, Wrap, Stone* "burning, writhing with visible information" (29).

The shift from material gold to electronic light also heralds a shift from materiality to immateriality, which is, in turn, the precondition for the characteristic that the "writing surface" (Bolter 3) of hypermedia – the surface of the computer-screen that the text is scrolled across – differs decisively from the surface of the written page. The hypermedial topology is characterized by a conflation *of* and oscillation *between* surface and depth, because although the textual traces always appear *superficially* on the user's screen [the apt German term for 'desktop' is *Benutzeroberfläche;* 'user surface'], hypermedial space consists of a multiplicity of levels and layers that are successively folded onto this surface that is, furthermore, used for both reading and writing purposes and that thus conflates not only surface and depths but also the active and the passive onto one spatial plane. Hypertexting, in this light, can be understood as an intricate textual origami.

In these textual foldings, the inherently membranic computer screen does no longer function as a *material* carrier of information – as the page does – but as a disembodied, *immaterial* plane of realization or actualization. It is a surface onto which any number of equally virtual texts – both verbal and visual – are projected.[2] Across it, textual chunks and images are scrolled and then, as on Freud's 'mystic writing pad', erased or re-produced. One might even read the burning of the characters into the screen as a postmodern version of the invisible traces left on the mystic writing pad. It is precisely its own, as well as the immateriality of the texts that allows the screen to be both spatially and temporally "flexible" (2). In fact, it is defined by a fundamental "impermanence and changeability" (3).

In a fully digital, hypermedial environment, then, one surface does indeed fit all media. It can – through a mere mouseclick – be transformed from a page to a canvas, to a movie-screen or even, although here the metaphor begins to break down, to the membrane of a loudspeaker. This protean quality is why in describing a hypermedia environment, one has to take recourse to a wide, and somewhat fuzzy concept of writing, such as the Derridean one, which includes "all that gives rise to an inscription in general (...) cinematography, choreography (...) pictorial, musical, sculptural 'writing'" (Derrida 9). Gregory Ulmer's concept of a "picto-ideo-phonographic writing" (Ulmer 17) is a variation of such a Derridean notion of writing.

In all of its various realizations and manifestations, the computer screen comes to function as what Deleuze and Guattari call a plane of consistency; an a-subjective and in itself meaningless plane on which writings can morph from one format to the next; a plane that gives space to any number of movements happening on it.[3] Of course, the constant folding and refolding of writing(s) upon and into each other also changes the alignment of word and image. For one, they can no longer be thought of as supplemental to each other. Rather, their relation is constantly shifting. The conflation of *inside* and *outside* caused by the folding(s) creates a dynamics that makes it, at any given moment, undecidable whether the inside of a specific text has just been folded onto the outside of another one or *vice versa*. Similarly, it is undecidable whether the inside of a text has just been folded onto the outside of an image or the other way around.[4] It is on the background of this new topology that hypermedial relationships between text and image have to be thought.[5]

Although they have become structurally equivalent, in a hypermedial environment, texts and images still retain specific (I would almost say traditional) functions. Additionally, one has to differentiate between environments such as the World Wide Web and the Internet, which are still predominantly verbal, and 'real' cyberspace (virtual reality), which is predominantly visual – although, increasingly, these two tend to overlap. It is with a number of such functions that I now want to deal in more detail. In this investigation, I will refer to a number of science-fiction novels, because they can function as projections of a present state of things into a more fully developed future, and because the visions they develop might become inspirations for a yet-to-be-programmed reality.

Agents of the Textual Unconscious

Inside the computer screen there are endless vistas of information. Entering this space allows the user to enter an informational rhizome and to find out its topology from within. Since William Gibson's novel *Neuromancer*, this virtual and visual data-space has been defined by one basic principle; the imaging of data. Ultimately, in fact, the virtual 'datascape' relies on nothing more than the breaking-down of informational structures into visual analogs, or data-Gestalten. An early form of such imaging is the diagram. The new twist is that this abstract visual analog is turned into a reality of its own; the docuverse, the metaverse, the "oneirochronon" (Williams 10), as it is called in Walter Jon Williams' novel *Aristoi* or, to use the most general term 'invented' by Gibson and then developed in real life, cyberspace – a dynamic landscape of diagrams, whose matrix and currency is information. In cyberspace, stacks of data have turned into disembodied informational landscapes. These land- and more often cityscapes are peopled by programs that are also visual analogs; mostly analogs of users out in real space; their outfit and ration of verisimilitude representing the user's "programming skills" (12-13). As the protagonist states in *Aristoi* about a virtual personality, he "found himself admiring the program that had created the liquid depths of her eyes" (50). In general, the visual simulations

> had to be not simply real, but finer, more real, than reality itself ... The careful programming put into Gabriel's appearance, the slight exaggeration built into its visual and tactile dimensions, was meant to give it an impact somewhat greater than the real – the Realized – thing (13).

The fact that the real world is called 'Realized World' implies that the docuworld is considered as an immaterial, derealized one. The navigation in such a simulated universe relies heavily on the indexing function of images; their property of being able to serve as data-clusters and as data-compressors. Such compressions are one of the most relevant possibilities in a hypermedia environment. In what follows, I will deal with one specific visual concept that functions as more than a data compressor and that is an integral part of hypermedia and cyberspace navigation. This concept is based on programs developed to make the internet and cyberspace user friendly; the installation of browsers such as Mosaic, Netscape Navigator or the Internet Explorer. These man-machine interface programs allow access to search-engines which comb the databanks for links and for information. In Gibson's novel *Idoru*, one of the protagonists, Colin Laney, is a 'human search-engine', whose job it is to "locate key data in apparently random wastes of incidental information" (38). This ability has to do with how he processes "low-level, broad spectrum input. Something to do with pattern-recognition" (38). In choosing and ordering information from the unlimited data pool search-engines become, somewhat like Maxwell's Demon, agencies that allow for the temporary structuration and ordering of the rhizomatic informational web. While in real life, these programs remain anonymous programs, in cyber-fiction – to denote the strand of science-fiction that is set in cyberspace – they take on the form of (real or virtual) human beings, who literally point towards important or relevant information. They can be human beings, human beings whose personalities have been transferred into cyberspace, as in some of Gibson's data-constructs, or they are program-generated navigators, as in Neal Stevenson's novel *Snow Crash*. In the latter, in which cyberspace is understood as a universal library, the program relies on a cultural stereotype:

> The Librarian daemon looks like a pleasant, fiftyish, silver-haired, bearded man with bright blue eyes, wearing a V-neck sweater over a work shirt, with a coarsely woven, tweedy-looking wool tie ... Even though he's just a piece of software [and thus a piece of digital programming], he has reason to be cheerful; he can move through the nearly infinite stacks of information in the Library with the agility of a spider dancing across a vast web of cross-references ... the only thing he can't do is think (107).

A similar function is taken over by the "reno[s]" (13) in *Aristoi*. While his lover has given her reno a name – "Mine is named Caroline. I even gave her an appearance. She looks like my sister, if I had a sister – and we're great friends" (71) – the protagonist of the novel, who suffers from a positive form of Multiple Personality Disorder, tells her that "I call mine Reno, and it acts like a machine. I find that refreshing – I've got quite enough personalities in my head as it is" (71). In a theoretical context, this function is taken over by what is called the 'agent' in Gregory Ulmer's book *Heuretics: The Logic of Invention*.

In Ulmer's project of a hypermedial didactics, agents represent certain fields of data. Ulmer draws on the premise that "learning in hyperrhetoric is conducted more with memory than with argument or narrative" (189). In this context, he relates the function of the agent back to "mnemonic picture writing" (191) and to the memory palaces in mnemonics; virtual architectures that were also used to store and compress data. In order to memorize a large amount of information, the speaker would imagine to be walking through a number of rooms, each of which represented a specific topic. These rooms were filled with objects, each of which figured a sub-set of further data, the objects would have parts that would relate to further aspects of the narrative and so, recursively, on, until the last mote of dust in the palace had been semiotized. While talking, the rhetorician would follow a specific route through the palace; a route that would figure a specific line of argument.

Navigating a hypermedial environment – whether 'the Internet' or 'cyberspace' – in which texts and images are linked to other texts and images through mere mouseclicks, is, in many ways, like strolling through such a memory palace. The difference, however, is that the palace has been turned inside out. While in the classical memory palace a personal memory is 'instilled' into images and bound by them, in the hypermedial memory palace, memories are extracted from a cultural memory that serves as an endless storehouse of – always overdetermined – information. Of course, one can visualize individual data-banks within the net as classical memory palaces *within* the universal palace formed by the net itself, and in Bruce Sterling's novel *Holy Fire* a former lover does indeed bequeathe his individual, highly secured virtual memory palace, with all the information that it contains, to the protagonist. While the information is limited in such a classical palace – even if it is embedded in the net – in the palace formed by the net itself, the amount of information is 'infinite'. The hypermedial palace has an 'infinite' number of rooms and objects and an 'infinite' connectivity, which means that every room and every object is connected to every other room and to every other object. As there is no hierarchy in its rhizomatic architecture, there is no longer a linear narrative and thus no longer one specific route through the palace. Rather, there are sudden jumps, surprising mappings and complex superimpositions, secret passages and surprising vistas – endless corridors that loop back onto each other.

Still, according to Ulmer, "[t]he practice of oratorical mnemonics – conceived of as travel or navigation through an information landscape, (...) literaliz[es] the metaphor of [learning] as a journey" (192). According to this analogy, "the electronic citizen may negotiate the data environment of cyberspace the same way an orator memorizes immense quantities of written material" (192). In both cases, then, images are used to compress and store data. While the first journey, however, is one of representation, the second one is one of invention – an expedition.

According to Ulmer, agents which would function as mnemotic sorting devices could be included in a database. These would be "[p]ersonifiable as residents of the environment", and they might operate as "guide, coach, tutor, to help the user manage the overload of information" (219). It is important, however, that, as in the example from *Aristoi*, "[t]he choice of personification is specific to each user" (219), because "[t]he function of the guide is to cull the information environment for items *relevant* to the user's projects" (221). An agent should not only excavate knowledge from the databanks, this information should be relevant to the user. The user, in turn, would trust the filtering of information through the agent as somebody with whom it is possible to identify and who is entrusted with the ability to make the relevant choices.

The question, of course, is that about relevance. What kind of relevance? What kind of memories are searched for? Ultimately, Ulmer's answer is, they are unconscious ones. Yet these unconscious memories are not buried in the depths of the user's mind. Rather, they are buried in, or better spread out over, the exterior data-pool. Through the personalized interface between the datapool and the user, in fact, the user's "memory is automated" (226) and exteriorized. Through this exteriorization, the agent becomes a "liaison with the symbolic order" (221), which is similarly – if only seemingly – exterior to the subject. Through such agents, the symbolic order – of which the agents are representatives, for instance as super-egos or alter-egos, as with the imaginary sister of the lover of the protagonist in *Aristoi* or the librarian in *Snow Crash* – can come to operate in the data pool and they "indicat[e] how stereotypes and celebrities take on a cognitive role in an electronic apparatus" (219).

Ulmer's project, then, does not consist of giving a voice to an a-textual unconscious through a text, but to search for and figure a textual unconscious by drawing on a data-pool to which one is related through stereotyped agents. Through these agents, the database, as a storehouse of overdetermined meaning, comes to "include ... a computerized unconscious" (38). All this, of course, presupposes that one proceeds, and Ulmer does, from the Lacanian premise that, to quote Lacan, "*the unconscious is structured like a language*" (20). The idea is to design and to find agents whose "'judgement[s]' or intuitions of relevance include the [user's] unconscious in its psychoanalytic ... as well as in its connectionist sense" (221). In Ulmer's own case Gary Cooper functions as such an "agent of (...) [the] unconscious" (203).

The textual unconscious is realized by hypermedially connecting key terms with other key-terms of the data-bank regardless of a pre-programmed, conceptual path. Through the free association of the user's *other* (the agent) the

user begins to drift in the rhizome, similar to the way that the patient does
during an analysis. In this state, the strategy is no longer, to use another
Deleuzian and Guattarian juxtaposition, that of 'tracing' but that of 'mapping'. In the hypermedial rhizome, the connections are both unconscious and
a-logical; based on material or conceptual similarities ('mapping') rather than
on logical connections ('tracing'). In this context, it is important that the cus-
tomized agents search according to metaphors, but also, because their mode
of search is based on the identity of signifiers, according to the logic of puns.
These puns, which act as machines of invention "may be visual as well as
verbal" (228). Theoretically, this drift is a result of a "dissatisfaction precisely
with abstraction itself [and, as such, with abstract (textual) machines] – a concern with the remainder that is lost or excluded in abstractive reasoning" (93).

Such a dissatisfaction with abstraction also underlies the developments I
want to deal with in the final part of the paper, which will bring me back to
the concept of picto-ideo-phonographic writing.

CYBERGLYPHS

Apart from compressing and figuring complex information into memorable
Gestalten, images have always held a potential for affective power and for the
generation of emotion and emotional response. In recent cyber-fiction – and
this is to a large degree the result of its amalgamation of Eastern and Western
cultures (the manga and the detective novel or western) – the concept of combining images and texts into a once more more powerful form of writing is a
predominant motif. In *Aristoi*, the recombination of text and image is expressed in the form of what might be called cyberglyphs. An elite learns an
artificially developed ideography. This language is developed from "age-old
Chinese characters but adapted for modern grammar, vocabulary, and expression" (56). It is "based on the notion that writing had the greater impact the
more senses it evoked" (55). The most evolved version of this visual language
is 'Involved Ideography:'

> These intricate hieroglyphs, based on ... ideas about the wiring of the human
> mind and its relationship to information, were another step toward complexity
> and many levels higher in symbolism. Looking like a peculiarly convoluted in-
> corporation of *baroque Mayan glyphs and circuit diagrams*, the Involved Ideogra-
> phy's radicals, modalities, and submodalities were designed to involve as much of
> the reasoning cortex as possible. They required intense mental concentration to
> use or read, but were unexcelled *in packing complex information into small pack-
> ages* (56, emphases added).

As a cross between the poetical force and character of Chinese script, which had already fascinated and inspired Ezra Pound, and the imaging of complex data, the cyberglyphs become miniature memory palaces. In fact, in the novel there is a virtual room that is itself the 3-D realization of such a miniature memory palace because it is shaped like "the Involved Ideographic glyph for *dance*. ... The room is shaped like a three-dimensional representation of the glyph for movement, and the paths are arranged in the patterns for *joyful, rhythm, music*" (129-30). In *Scissors, Cut, Paper, Wrap, Stone*, one protagonist develops similarly evocative virtual universes; universes that are structured according to a specific programmed matrix, such as a Boccioni-verse which is created by a Futurist overlay:

> Planes and shafts of stabbing color, curves, angles, all connected by rushing lines of force, of velocity. (...) vibrant vortices of movement. He could *see* the energy (...) as a rush of images, time dependent action compressed into static timelessness. A discarded bottle opened up into spirals and planes of stored power; a crumpled newspaper became a whirling concatenation of information and vertigo. (28)

In the novel, something comparable to an Involved Ideographics is developed by a group of young computer scientists. The new script is "the ultimate authoritarian typeface" (41). Like Involved Ideographics, the script is highly, in fact, dangerously, affective. It is based on "visual entities (...) that the conscious mind can't process, that slip past our powers of rationality and discrimination and stimulate direct, physical responses. Like joy, or anger, or religious ecstasy" (41). These *"fracters"* (53) are culled from the data-pool, such as the fractal "Hod", which is a compression of the meanings and connotations of the divine. As the creator of the fracter states, "I accessed the National Gallery's datacore for religious art and icons and set the program parameters to flag me every time it came on something that corresponded to my definition of the spiritual, the numinous, the irrational" (45).

If these cyber-fictions point anywhere at all, it might be towards a future in which the image – in a trajectory that has been theorized from Marshall McLuhan to Guy Debord – will become more and more important both as a data-compressor and as a carrier of affective information. Effects of such an affectation in the context of learning and teaching can be seen in Ulmer's hypermedial didactics. These images, however, will be assembled from the same code from which words are assembled; a digital code that allows for the constant permutation of formerly separated media. For better or worse, and Jean Baudrillard is one of the most ardent critics of this universal code, there is now only one medium, and many variations of it. From ones and zeros bloom words and images alike.

NOTES

1   See also: "any point of a rhizome can be connected to anything other, and must be" (7). Ultimately, "[t]here are no points or positions in a rhizome, such as those found in a structure, tree or root. There are only lines" (8). Mnemonically, "short-term memory is of the rhizome or diagram type, and long-term memory is arborescent and centralized" (16).

2   On this superficial screen, a textual layering can be represented as texts that are either "tiled" or "stacked" (*Bolter* 69).

3   If Euclidean space and teleological time are the spatio-temporal frameworks of the text, hypermedia are defined through a dynamic field in which the spatio-temporal borders of discourse are dissolved. Hypermedia function according to the concept of a fully "open-bordered text" (*Landow* 61).

4   Whereas "[t]he kind of text that permits one to write, however incorrectly, of insides and outsides belongs to print" (*Landow* 42), hypermedia rather "blurs the distinction between what is 'inside' and what is 'outside'" (63).

5   Similar to the way that hypertext liquifies discursive space, it liquifies discursive time. Because the text is in a "perpetual state of reorganization" (*Bolter* 9) and becoming, its metamorphoses are defined by a *serial* rather than a *sequential* temporality. As it has neither origin nor fixed direction, from Aristotle's 'beginning, middle and end' only the middle survives. In fact, the kinetics of these "lines of force, and this movement" are what constitute "the meaning of the text" (202) in the first place. As Deleuze and Guattari state, "[i]n a multilinear system, everything happens at once" (297).

REFERENCES

Bolter, Jay David. *Writing Space: The Computer, Hypertext, and the History of Writing.* Hillsdale: Lawrence Erlbaum, 1991.

Deleuze, Gilles and Félix Guattari. *A Thousand Plateaus: Capitalism and Schizophrenia.* Trans. Brian Massumi. Minneapolis: University of Minnesota Press, 1987.

Derrida, Jacques. *Of Grammatology.* Tr. Gayatri Chakravorty Spivak. Baltimore: Johns Hopkins University Press, 1976.

Gibson, William. *Neuromancer.* Ace Books, New York, 1984.

———. *Idoru.* New York: Putnam's, 1996.

Kristeva, Julia. *Revolution in Poetic Language.* Trans. M. Waller. New York: Columbia University Press, 1984.

Lacan, Jacques. *The Four Fundamental Concepts of Psycho-Analysis.* New York: Norton, 1978.

Landow, George P. *Hypertext: The Convergence of Contemporary Critical Theory and Technology.* Baltimore: Johns Hopkins University Press, 1992.

McDonald, Ian. *Scissors Cut Paper Wrap Stone.* Bantam, New York, 1994.

Sterling, Bruce. *Holy Fire.* London: Millenium, 1996.

Stephenson, Neal. *Snow Crash*. Bantam, New York, 1993.

Ulmer, Gregory L. *Heuretics: The Logic of Invention*. Baltimore: Johns Hopkins University Press, 1994.

Williams, Walter Jon. *Aristoi*. New York: Tor, 1993.

The Rhetoric of Interdisciplinarity

Hugo Caviola

I

Today interdisciplinarity is generally understood as the cooperation of scientists belonging to different disciplines. The result of such cooperation usually amounts to an accumulation, or addition, of disciplinary contributions to a specific subject. Round table discussions or colloquia held on topics such as racism, cancer, AIDS, environmental pollution, hunger, etc. represent typical examples of this kind of interdisciplinarity. The outcome, however, often barely deserves the name of interdisciplinarity. Cooperation alone does not guarantee a *synthesis* of disciplinary perspectives. It would therefore be more appropriate to call such an accumulation of disciplinary knowledge pluridisciplinarity. Pluridisciplinarity does not necessarily exclude a synthesis, but it leaves it to the audience, the students, the readers of interdisciplinary proceedings to draw their own conclusions, to reach a personal synthesis. But how is he or she supposed to accomplish this? Although pluridisciplinarity might overcome the deplorable isolation of researchers or teachers, it does not overcome the fragmentation of knowledge, the problem that lies at the heart of all interdisciplinary endeavors. To understand the whole means more than to know the sum of its components.

Stanley Fish has recently suggested that since we cannot escape the disciplinary system, we ought to try to "become more sensitive to the 'made up' quality of knowledge" and adopt an ironical attitude toward the results the disciplines bring forth (18). Irony might be the way to make disciplinary limitations tolerable. But who would be willing to be ironical when it comes to questions of truth? We are quite ready to accept irony as an element of rhetoric. And we are equally ready to accept rhetorical truth in the realm of literature. But as scientists we feel viscerally reluctant to accept rhetoric as a constituent of scientific knowledge. What if scientific truth were a matter of rhetoric, if it were not exactly ironical, but something close to it: metaphorical, based on images rather than discursive language?

II

I want to develop my argument from a closer look at the practical difficulties faced by an interdisciplinary approach that attempts to go beyond a mere addition of disciplinary perspectives. In order for science to attain clear results and facts, it has to break down a phenomenon into aspects and integrate them into disciplinary contexts of language and methods. Georg Picht has suggested a simple example to illustrate how this functions in detail (88f). Suppose I take a piece of chalk and write on the blackboard: A=A. Pointing to what I have written I may get four possible scientific analyses:

   1) White lines before a black background
   2) An arrangement of chalk particles
   3) Three signs
   4) The theorem of identity

Obviously, what we have here are four different scientists at work. Statement 1) could be from an art historian, 2) from a chemicist or physicist, 3) from a semiotician, 4) from a philosopher or mathematician. Already at this basic stage of scientific analysis we can observe how every discipline creates its own object of inquiry. Along with this goes a certain hermeticism of the disciplinary discourses which open up next to each other. A direct combination of two disciplinary observations becomes impossible. To say, for example, that this is the theorem of identity before a black background, or to talk of the chalk particles of signs sounds absurd, poetic at best. A direct combination of disciplinary perspectives creates a conglomerate of discourses without a common denominator on a higher level of abstraction. Obviously the only common denominator of the four perspectives remains the original object of investigation: the enigmatic phenomenon A=A.

The problem reminds me of the question that has inspired Michel Foucault's famous essay *The Order of Things*. He starts his argument from a passage in a story by Borges in which the author quotes a certain Chinese encyclopaedia claiming that animals "are divided into the following categories: (a) animals belonging to the emperor, (b) animals that are embalmed, (c) that are tame, (d) sucking pigs, (e) sirens, (f) fabulous, (g) stray dogs, (h) included in the present classification, (i) frenzied, (j) innumerable, (k) drawn with a very fine camelhair brush, (l) et cetera". Facing a taxonomy that denies any common ground of its elements Foucault suggests the term *heteroclite* or *heterotopia,* an "unthinkable space" (XVii). The problems we are facing in interdisciplinary work are obviously just the same as the ones with which we are presented in Borges' Chinese encyclopaedia: a heterotopia, a space that does not distribute the multiplicity of things into combinations that make it possible for us to name, speak, and think coherently. Interdisciplinarity obviously reaches beyond the bounds of discursive language. If we want to attain a level of abstraction accommodating several disciplinary perspectives, we obviously have to go beyond words. Communicating in words a knowledge that reaches beyond words leads us into the field of rhetoric and images. The question I want to raise here is whether rhetoric and images can build bridges across the discursive voids between the disciplines.

III

As I have mentioned above there seems to be something poetic about these formulations. A sentence like "the theorem of identity before a black background" echoes modernist nonsense poetry by poets such as Christian Morgenstern or Ernst Jandl. What is it that makes them poetic? It is the levelling of two planes of abstraction, an abstract notion (here: the theorem) and a physical reality (here: the black background), the conflation of two widely separate elements based on shifting ground, on the fact that they both define the enigmatic 'thing' A=A and yet do not grasp it entirely.

The integration of two elements on the basis of both difference and similarity defines the structure of metaphor. Metaphor is a rhetorical figure that allows us to talk about one thing in terms of another. According to Max Black's seminal theory, metaphors have an interactive power, a power to bridge discursively distinct universes. To say, for example, that a flower smiles is a metaphorical statement. In scientific language flowers do not smile. In botany they unfold petals, they bloom, they wither. Scientific terminology eschews metaphorical language because metaphors do not denote items properly. They do not lead to judgments that are "clear and distinct" as Descartes required them for positive science: in that they name one thing (here the human face) in terms of another (a flower) they systematically tamper with the borderlines of disciplines. The simultaneous validity and nonvalidity of metaphorical predication, its deficient discursive quality, has led theorists to name metaphors "images" (Plato, *Symposion* 215 A and Aristotle *Rhetorics* 1412 B30). It goes without saying that not *all* metaphors have an imageable quality. But as a rule metaphor allows us to understand complex abstract subject matters in terms of more concrete graphic correlatives linked to sensory perception. This has to do with the nature of understanding. Both linguistic and psychological studies of metaphor have brought forward some evidence that understanding, in its basic forms, is imagery oriented (Paivo and Walsh 307-328) and that most of our fundamental concepts, including time, are organized in terms of spatialization metaphors (Lakoff and Johnson 17 and Lakoff in Ortony 202-251). Susanne Langer has made an observation of particular importance to our present purpose when she claimed that "metaphor is our most striking evidence of abstractive seeing" (14). 'Abstractive seeing' by means of a metaphor combines two preconditions that seem essential to interdisciplinary thinking: (a) abstraction from disciplinary limitations (b) the possibility of seeing (visualizing?) properties shared by several disciplines.

IV

If we compare the structure of divergent disciplinary discourses to the structure of metaphor, we discover a shared logic between them. We discover that the relation between different scientific approaches to an object is structured metaphorically. The white lines before a black background relate metaphorically to the arrangement of chalk particles, and the arrangement of chalk particles relates metaphorically to the theorem of identity, etc. All these different approaches are metaphorical descriptions of the same 'thing'. But subject to multiperspective, this 'thing' is no longer an object that can be grasped in clear-cut terms. It is an object projected into an heterotopian space where discursive language fails. It is a space where metaphorical and thus interdisciplinary relations abound, an aesthetic space where knowledge is (temporarily) suspended from evidence and held in a delicate balance of probability. It is where scientific knowledge reveals its artificiality, it is, in other words, the space of constructivist philosophy.

While a constructivist view of science allows a playfulness in the production of metaphors, it leaves open the question of the limits and legitimacy of metaphorical connections. Ultimately, almost anything can be linked under the heading of metaphorical similarity. There may be occasions when not only flowers but also cars and buildings may seem to smile at us. The question is to what extent science can control its metaphors and make constructive use of them.

V

Metaphors play an important role in the constitution of theories. So-called root metaphors, or absolute metaphors, frequently constitute the basic ontological commitments of theories. New theories and models by nature map a cognitive field that was previously uncharted, or charted differently. In order to integrate such a *terra incognita* into the field of knowledge scientists use analogies and metaphors. That is, they name the unknown in terms of the known. Bohr's atom model is a case in point. In order to understand, hypothetically, the nature of matter he transferred Kepler's macrocosmic model of the solar system – planets rotating around the sun – to the microcosm suggesting that electrons rotate around the atomic nucleus. By doing so, Bohr drew on the metaphor's inherent interdisciplinary potential. As we can talk about flowers in terms of smiles he chose to talk about the microcosm in terms of the macrocosm.

Obviously, in some cases science sanctions the most extravagant transfer of metaphors. What initially may seem a gratuitous 'poetic' metaphor can later be elevated to the status of accepted scientific terminology. Take the successful transfer of computer metaphors to cognitive psychology suggesting that the brain can be understood in terms of computer technology. Take metaphors such as 'system' and 'feed-back' that, once exported from cybernetics, have made successful careers in ecology, sociology, education, economics, computer science, etc. Take the successful import in art history of terms borrowed from narratology and discourse analysis, metaphors that make it possible today to talk about the graphic arts in terms of literature. Obviously, interdisciplinarity functions by metaphorical exchange. The question is what the rules are that regulate such exchange.

Although scientific language negates the metaphorical nature of its basic assumptions it cannot escape the metaphysics hidden in their uncontrolled implications. Our root-concepts are always metaphor-ridden. It does not matter whether we think of the world in terms of the mechanical metaphor as a clockwork, or of nature as an energy-processing machine, or if we compare the members of primitive societies with neurotics or children, whether we think of human drives and passions in terms of the pressure and counter-pressure principle of a steamboiler, of memory as stored in a container or as impressed in wax, or whether we conceive of the brain as an information-processing machine: we are caught in images that direct our thinking with the power of myths. Metaphors manifest their manipulative nature when their hypothetical nature gets lost, when we use them without being aware that we are using them. There is a difference between using a metaphor and being used by it. The one is to *make* believe that something is the case. The other is to *believe* it. This is when models and metaphors become myths.

Max Black has pointed out the manipulative power of such metaphor-myths with the following example:

> Suppose I am set the task of describing a battle in words drawn as largely as possible from the vocabulary of chess ... The enforced choice of the chess vo-

cabulary will lead some aspects of the battle to be emphasized, others to be neglected ... the chess vocabulary filters and transforms: it not only selects, it brings forward aspects of the battle that might not be seen at all through another medium. (42)

The chess metaphor highlights the element of playfulness, of tactics, of free disposal and it suppresses the aspects of cruelty, misery and of meaningless death caused by war.

One reason why the myth-making function of metaphor in science tends to be overlooked lies in the concept of scientific progress that prevails today. It is a commonsense assumption among many scientists that by the accumulation of individual discoveries and inventions scientific progress has taken us from mythical beginnings to the predominance of logos. According to this concept of development-by-accumulation the history of science is seen as a progress from superstitions, out-of-date beliefs and errors to truth. Conversely, if we accept the view that all basic scientific commitments are metaphorical in nature, the notion of progress from myth toward logos becomes precarious. This is in short the position Thomas Kuhn sets forth in his seminal work *The Structure of Scientific Revolutions* (1962). According to Kuhn the history of science does not progress from superstition to science. It is characterized instead by successions of paradigms. Paradigms function precisely like the chess metaphor. They regulate the questions raised and the methods used and thus determine the state of normal science for the scientific community of a historical period. They become products of a scientific community's collective insight and tend to be transferred, in part unconsciously, from one discipline to the other. It is, I think, due to the fixation of many historians of science on the accretion concept of the history of science that the interdisciplinary potential of such basic metaphors has long been overlooked. If an entire period can be dominated by one (or a few) shared metaphor(s) it must be possible to lay them bare and thus integrate seemingly disparate discourses synchronically. In order to see such metaphorical ramifications, however, the history of science would have to give up its obsession with sequence and chronology. Instead, it would have to open its perspective on the intra- and extrascientific resonance such paradigmatic metaphors have.

VI

Let me illustrate this by an example. A multitude of cultural manifestations of Modernism can be comprised under the analogy of the opening up of a previously closed form, or in other words: the penetration of inside and outside.

The image simplifies and generalizes. But it is precisely this schematic nature that makes the metaphor function as a paradigm to include fields as divergent as the ones presented in the following. The example illustrates that it is the conceptual openness of the metaphor that allows it to develop both intra- and extrascientific resonance pervading the entire period: Sociology describes Modernism as a breakdown of social hierarchies in the cities of the second part of the nineteenth century. Modern city life is defined by the rise of the masses that integrate individuals regardless of their social class.

At the same time modern urban centers develop suburban belts that erode the previous borderline between city and countryside. Life in suburbia combines a natural environment with an urban culture.

In the course of the nineteenth century a number of European countries abolish passport requirements. National boundaries become more porous so that travellers and transports can cross them with greater ease (France 1848, Belgium 1861, Germany 1867, Italy 1889).

Similarly, some technological innovations entail an opening up of form. The telephone functions as an electronic window penetrating the line between the private and the public sphere. Simultaneously electric light begins to blur the borderline between day and night. Industrial worktime can be extended into nighttime, and an entire generation of artists (Flaubert, Proust) cultivate a lifestyle of daytime sleep and nighttime work.

In architecture new supporting steel frames and walls of glass make it possible to open up the closed form of traditional brick architecture. Frank Lloyd Wright's domestic architecture called for a radical opening of interior living space. Long horizontal sweeps of windows created what he called "outdoor living", "the 'inside' becoming 'outside'". The same phenomenon is manifest in the construction of the Eiffel Tower (1889). Traditional distinctions of inside and outside are useless to describe its skeleton structure.

In modern medicine the invention of the x-ray penetrated the opacity of the body, opening up to vision the human skeleton. Similarly, modern physics 'opens up' the form of matter. Under the assault of relativity physics the nucleus of matter disintegrates and matter is defined as a function of energy. What used to be a stronghold of materialism is dematerialized and transformed into dynamics.

In analogous fashion Freud's psychoanalysis disintegrates the nucleus of the individual psyche. The integrity of the bourgeois self is broken up into conflicting functions. Thinking, feeling and behavior become transparent for subconscious impulses. The self is dominated by the other.

In the image of man promulgated by Modernism the borderline between man and animal is eroded. The animalization of man is one of the prevailing motifs of modern art, especially of Expressionism and Dadaism.

In literature, new narrative techniques break down the traditional form of the novel. Multiperspective and stream-of-consciousness technique celebrate a fusion of an interior world and a public reality. Grammar and semantics fail to be stable factors of representation. The borderline between language and silence is broken down. Radical language skepticism, for example in Joyce, Beckett, Musil or Hofmannsthal, produces what could be termed an aesthetics of silence. Moments of mystical insight are stylized as wordless statements. Silence begins to speak.

A similar transformation can be observed in the plastic arts. Alexander Archipenko's sculpture *Woman Combing Her Hair* (1915) shows a phenomenon reminiscent of the Eiffel Tower. It shows a woman who presents an impressive flourish of hair while her face is represented by a gaping hole allowing us to look through her head. A distinction of inside and outside has become obsolete. Space is no longer a background phenomenon but a constituent element of the work. What used to be background in traditional sculpture is now transformed into foreground representing an essential element such as the figure's face. What we can see in Archipenko's sculpture as a radical opening of form has already been adumbrated by Impressionism in a more moderate fashion: outlines, the material integrity of physical forms, are dissolved. Similarly, Cubist multiperspective gives up the separation of inside and outside. Along with this goes the obsolescence of the picture frame.

Modern theater participates in the opening up of form. Around the turn of the century, some daring playwrights and designers try to eliminate the sharp separation between stage and audience. In 1905 the German Max Reinhardt is the first stage director to bring the performers out into the audience over bridges and ramps. Stage fiction and audience reality mingle.

In modern philosophy we can observe a denial of closed systems of thought in Nietzsche and William James. In both philosophies multitude and movement of experience are more real than the closed forms of transcendental concepts.

METAPHOR: OPENING UP OF FORM / PENETRATION OF INSIDE AND OUTSIDE

Sociology	• social hierarchies
	• city and countryside
Politics	• national boundaries
Technology	• telephone (private-public)
Lifestyle	• daytime – nighttime
Architecture	• F.L. Wright's "outdoor living"
	• Eiffel Tower
Medicine	• x-ray penetrates body
Physics	• relativity theory dematerializes matter
Psychoanalysis	• disintegrates the self
	• man and animal
Literature	• multiperspective, stream-of -consciousness, language
	• silence
Plastic Art	• background – foreground
Theater	• stage and audience
Philosophy	• denial of closed systems

What are we to make of such a morphological image of Modernism? Should we conclude from it that we have now discovered what Modernism really is: opening up of form? Certainly not in a literal sense. The interdisciplinarity I am proposing here does not claim its reduction to be absolute. Metaphorical exchange is based on analogy. And there is no conceptual rigor in analogy. Analogy is an aesthetic, not a rational category. Consequently, such interdisciplinary synchronic cuts produce an essentially unstable form of evidence. The image remains flickering, hypothetical. No doubt, there is some evidence that we have found a powerful paradigm of Modernism – this does not exclude the existence of others. There are studies on Modernism that have revealed different and equally pervasive period metaphors such as waves, lines and streams (Asendorf). They interact with the opening up of form in various ways. And they serve to remind us that metaphorical truth remains ultimately tentative.

The many facets of Modernism have taken us back to a heterotopian plurality of worlds that can no longer be united under a common denominator that is 'clear' and distinct'. The example confirms our initial intuition that interdisciplinary thinking has to go beyond the bounds of discursive language. The fact that the paradigm 'opening up of form' happens to be a spatial metaphor ties in with our observation (in Section III) that both basic understanding and abstraction tend to favor imagery oriented metaphors. Psychological studies of metaphor provide further evidence for this predominance of spatial

representations: Paivio and Walsh have observed that imageable metaphors
are more likely than verbal strings to facilitate abstraction because they allow
greater speed in the search for relevant combinations. At the same time they
tend to be more coherent and holistic than language-initiated representation
and more easily remembered (307-28).

VII

In conclusion, let me summarize the import of rhetoric in interdisciplinary
thinking. The role of metaphor in interdisciplinarity ties in with its function
in science in general. If we accept the assumption that at some fundamental
level both literary and scientific language are inextricably metaphorical in nature, then scientific inquiry is bound up with rhetoric. This is manifest in the
theory-constitutive metaphors that regulate the basic questions and assumptions of scientific inquiry. Once the metaphorical – and hence hypothetical –
nature of theories is forgotten they tend to elude disciplinary control and dis-
seminate synchronically across intrascientific and extrascientific borderlines.
This is when the interdisciplinary potential of metaphor is unleashed.

   The interdisciplinarity that I am suggesting here goes against the grain of
diachronic historiography and against the assumption that science advances
from myth to logos. Instead, it calls for a historiography of synchronic cuts
across the borderlines of established disciplines. The image of Modernism that
I have sketched is such an example of synchronic historiography that attempts
to lay bare a period metaphor. It suggests a synthesis of disciplinary perspectives that is poetic and rhetorical in nature. And it is rhetorical because scientific inquiry itself is ultimately built on rhetorical ground.

   I believe that if we had more studies of this sort, studies that attempt to lay
bare the macro-rhetoric characteristics of historical periods, we would have a
more coherent understanding of the past. And at the same time we would gain
a keener awareness of the metaphors that underlie our present culture and the
scientific inquiry we pursue in it.

REFERENCES

Asendorf, Christoph. *Ströme und Strahlen. Das langsame Verschwinden der Materie um 1900.*
      Berlin: Anabas, 1989.
Black, Max. *Models and Metaphors. Essays in Language and Philosophy.* Ithaca, NY: Cornell
      University Press, 1962.

Fish, Stanley. "Being Interdisciplinary Is So Very Hard to Do". *Profession* (1989): 15-22.

Foucault, Michel. *The Order of Things*. Vintage: New York, 1973.

Lakoff, George. "Contemporary Theory of Metaphor". *Ortony* (1993): 202-51.

Lakoff, George and Mark Johnson. *Metaphors we Live By*. Chicago and London: The University of Chicago Press, 1980.

Langer, Susanne. *Philosophy in a New Key*. Cambridge, MA: Harvard University Press, 1942.

Ortony, Andrew, ed. *Metaphor and Thought*. 2nd enlarged ed. Cambridge: Cambridge University Press, 1993.

Paivo, Allan and Mary Walsh. "Psychological Process in Metaphor Comprehension". *Ortony* (1993): 307-28.

Picht, Georg. "Bildung und Naturwissenschaft". In: Clemens Münster and Georg Picht, *Naturwissenschaft und Bildung*. Würzburg: Werkbund Verlag, 1953. 75-102.

Bernard Noël: Espace, Regard, Sens

Andrew Rothwell

'Un trait après l'autre, une image sort du corps par la main' (*Journal du Regard* [henceforth 'JR'] 29): one of Bernard Noël's aims as an art writer is to trace the physical process underlying the production of pictures, and responses to them. This is part of a wider enterprise, begun in *Extraits du corps* of 1958, to construct a materialist poetics able to counteract the mentalistic slant of Surrealism, Existentialism and the Western intellectual tradition as a whole, giving priority to the body as locus of production of thought, emotion and other mental attributes: hence Noël's close attention to the gestures of painters, prior to any reference to intention (in *Onze romans d'œil* in particular). His approach to the 'mind-body problem' (how is it that a physical organism can produce high-order mental phenomena such as consciousness?) is essentially metaphorical. He treats body, mind and external world as communicating and interacting spaces, and on this basis develops a web of metaphors in which to capture and examine the mechanisms of perception and artistic creation/reception. These metaphors deconstruct and reconfigure our understanding of thought and imagination, art and reality, shifting our assumptions about the primacy of the mental resolutely towards physicality and so questioning the very notion of identity.

Since the late 1970s Bernard Noël has written numerous catalogue prefaces for contemporary artists, as well as major monographs on figures as diverse as Gustave Moreau, Magritte, David, Olivier Debré, Géricault, Matisse, and Masson. Although these texts all relate to specific artists, they also work together to articulate an overall view of how art functions, a dual focus exemplified by the re-use of many extracts in the prize-winning *Journal du Regard* (1988).

Before investigating the space of the picture, Bernard Noël explores the spatiality of perception in general, rejecting the Cartesian view of sense-impressions as unmediated:

> La vue n'est pas un constat, c'est une lecture. Nous lisons le visible tout en croyant regarder la réalité. (JR 23)

Seeing, whether in everyday life or when we look at art, involves interpretation, a generally unconscious process of abstracting and making sense, as if there were 'dans l'œil une sorte de pré-mentalité' (JR 27). We move around inside a spatialized image, every aspect of which carries a name tag, meaning, or function, and so have no direct contact with reality:

> Nous ne sommes pas au monde mais dans l'espace d'une image volumineuse dont chaque élément est moins présent que son explication. (JR 74)

> L'espace du regard est le visible. Et le visible est notre lecture du monde: nous voyons moins du monde que du sens. (*L'Espace en demeure* [henceforth 'ED'], n.p.)

Seeing is reading, reading for sense, familiar patterns, accustomed relationships: things 'in their place'. The ethical task of art, for Noël, is to make this process visible and call into question our automatic 'construction' of reality, making possible a fresh vision which is existentially defining: 'il nous faut déchirer ces images pour VOIR – et pour venir au monde' (JR 37).

Corresponding to this external image is the internal imaging space of the mind, the 'volume' of our mental interiority:

> Le sentiment d'intériorité n'est-il pas le simple report, derrière l'œil, du volume du regard? (JR 24)

> Dedans n'est-il pas l'autre espace, celui où le visible s'inverse et devient vision ? Ce qui est derrière les yeux ne ressemble-t-il pas à ce qui est devant? (ED; cf. *Poèmes 1*, 284)

> Dedans n'est que l'espace inversé, et là le visible se métamorphose en son image. (JR 56)

Here the eye is the point of articulation between external world and mental 'space', and the physical act of seeing, of carrying over from outside to inside the head, has a foundational role in creating our image of self, our very identity. This process is however more complex than the words 'simple report' would suggest. The two spaces may have equivalent geometry, but their contents are non-identical: although linked by *ressemblance*, the image is inverted ('le visible s'inverse'), and inversion is only one of the distorting, transforming mechanisms which affect perception:

> Il n'y a rien dans l'expérience intérieure ..., mentale ..., qui ne soit du dehors, mais inversé, inverti, permuté, travaillé ... (Deblé, *Mille fois dedans,* 36)

Such reconfigurations create a gap between 'le visible' and our 'vision' of it which defines our identity, but which generally goes unrecognised because of our naive belief in unmediated perception. For Bernard Noël, art must draw attention to this gap, opening it up as a space of alternative representation to be explored by artist and onlooker in mutual self-definition.

This perceptual model, in which the lens of the eye marks the boundary between the visible outer world and its inverted internal image, has the optical configuration of a camera. However, Noël's account of what happens to the image inside the head rejects the modern instrument's connotations of intricacy and mechanical precision, returning to the ancient *camera obscura* as metaphor for the dark, inscrutable depths of the body, by definition 'invisibles':

> L'invisible est derrière nos yeux, c'est l'épaisseur du corps. Nous sommes ainsi des machines obscures: le noir en quelque sorte d'une chambre noire. (JR 19)

> Le visible, c'est la chambre blanche où tout se donne à voir, lumineusement. L'invisible, c'est la chambre noire qui, en moi, transforme tout ce qui est hors de moi en visible. (JR 27)

Within the dark 'épaisseur' of the flesh and its deep-seated urges occurs the 'travail' which physically transmutes 'le visible' of an exterior 'chambre blanche' into mental images with their own visibility. Linking the two 'chambres' is our 'regard', which spills out to fill them like a fluid (in the case of the 'chambre noire', photographic developing fluid):

> Nous avons deux regards, l'un qui se répand au dehors, où il crée le visible, et son volume; l'autre qui se répand à l'intérieur, soit pour y développer le visible, soit pour y voir qu'il ne voit rien que la coulée bruissante de l'air noir. L'imagination nage dans cet air-là et s'y révèle comme l'image dans la chambre obscure. (*Fred Deux* 4)

If no interpretable (recognisable) inner image 'develops', when for instance we look at non- or semi-figurative painting (although in the case of the quasi-organic drawings of Fred Deux, the mind hovers disturbingly on the verge of recognition), imagination takes over and 'develops' not an image from outside, but an image of itself and its own activity ('s'y révèle comme image'): it allows us to see ourselves seeing and working to interpret what we see.

Perhaps most interesting in the above extract is the *air* metaphor, a central plank in Bernard Noël's account of perception and a bridge to his art criticism proper. The 'coulée bruissante de l'air noir' inside the head both signals the absence of any identifiable referent, and constitutes 'dark air' as the fluid, mobile medium of imagining activity. Air is also, as many other extracts make clear, the element in which 'le regard' itself 'swims' ('l'air … comme l'eau du regard' [JR 42]), whether it be directed out into the light 'air' of reality or in towards the 'chambre noire', and as such forms a further figural link between them:

> Le regard est la substance même de la rencontre: substance aérienne qui est réciproquement l'air de la tête et l'air du monde. (JR 37)

Air, as the poet Pierre Reverdy discovered when elaborating his own model of Cubist representation around the year 1918 (Rothwell, *Textual Spaces* 36-44), is a richly suggestive metaphor for perception, 'le regard', but also for thought, or what Reverdy called 'la conception'. Material but intangible, it stands midway between physical phenomenon and mental concept; life-giving and essential, it has the force to displace objects; fluid and translucent, it invisibly bathes everything we see, filling the gaps between things and linking them together:

> Le voyant ne voit pas seulement les choses, il voit l'air qui est entre les choses, c'est-à-dire l'espace, qui est à la fois leur lieu et leur lien, donc la matière même de leur rapport. (JR 74)

Noël's latter-day 'voyant' is no mystic, but someone (artist, poet, viewer, reader) able to perceive his or her own perception, sensitive less to visible phenomena than to the space (physical and mental) in which they exist (their *lieu*), and its various configurations (the *liens* it supports between them). *Air* thus becomes a figure of the sense relations we all construct to link things together in the inner world of the imagination, for in this mental environment, 'nous sommes dans le sens comme nous sommes dans l'air' (JR 90).

What distinguishes artists from the rest of us, for Bernard Noël, is their ability not only to perceive the 'air' of their own looking, but particularly to externalise and spatialize it. In his 1983 book *Matisse* (henceforth 'M'), he pays particular attention to the painting *La Desserte rouge* (1908), in which he sees Matisse as freeing himself from the 'espace contraint' (M 12) of realism, the mimetic reproduction of an external space through such devices as local colour and single-point perspective. In *La Desserte rouge,* 'l'espace pictural existe pour lui-même' (M 14); colour invades and liberates space, objects are no longer present mimetically but as signs and ornamental patterns (the various arabesques, from the trees in the 'garden' to the blue branches and flowers on wallpaper and tablecloth):

> l'espace est rouge, d'un rouge carmin. Cette couleur n'est pas un fond, elle est visiblement l'air du tableau. Les divers éléments du sujet sont plongés dans ce rouge comme ils seraient plongés dans l'air de la réalité ... (M 14)

Quoting Matisse's own writings in which he expresses the intention of creating 'un espace spirituel' (M 15), governed by a 'perspective de sentiment' (M 17) rather than the geometrical perspective of realism, Bernard Noël sees this picture, with its 'unreal' but harmonious red atmosphere, as marking the shift in modern art towards the expression of mental rather than physical space.

Pictorial space, and the air metaphor which allows it to be related to the 'bodily' imagination of the artist so that the picture becomes an account of the process of seeing, is even more important in Bernard Noël's readings of abstract art. Exemplary in this regard are his two fine texts on Vieira da Silva, both originally catalogue prefaces subsequently reprinted in *Poèmes 1* (1983): 'L'Espace en demeure' of 1978 and 'Les États de l'air', written for a 1982 exhibition with the evocative title 'Perspective labyrinthe, dessins'. The latter poem in particular picks up the characteristic criss-cross cellular layout of the artist's work, suggestive of complex planar structures receding in depth, to revisit and reconfigure the spatial metaphors of mind and vision explored earlier. The first two stanzas establish the existential role of vision in constructing our mental 'domain' ('le pays' [l. 3]), and its structure as the inverted image of an external 'profondeur'. As with Fred Deux's drawings, the absence of a clear referent from the external world fills the apparently empty pictorial depth with air ('les parois de vent/ce vide' [ll. 2-3]), the mental *air* of the imagination which turns our vision back on itself ('renverse/le regard sur soi' [ll. 4-5]) and makes us see ourselves seeing ('nous fait sauter dans nos yeux' [l. 6]). In six short lines da Silva's abstract picture-space has thus become, with the active collaboration of the poet-critic, a mental landscape which is simultaneously a portrait of the viewer. The medium and agent of this specular reversal, developed in the rest of the poem as a to-and-fro oscillation between pictorial and mental space ('toujours le va et vient/le vu et le non vu' [ll. 7-8]), is the intangible 'vent' of line 2, passing from one space to the other unhindered by referential obstacles and linking 'l'air du monde' with 'l'air de la tête'. As we look, we graft our own mental reality ('le non vu', '[le] pas là' [ll. 8, 9]) onto the visible, pictorial cues until our eye, in an image reminiscent of Baudelaire's 'thyrse', entwines itself around the picture's airy scaffolding ('le bâti d'air' [l.15]) and our visual explorations of its labyrinth become 'tant de passages/en nous-même s'ouvrant' (ll. 11-12).

Through this pictorial labyrinth our eye follows a 'chemin d'air/semé de cailloux d'encre' (ll. 22-3), guided towards a personal 'reading' of it by the poetic text which itself is composed of 'islands' of ink (a negative inversion of the 'petits cailloux blancs' used in "Hansel and Gretel" to mark a path) distributed amid the 'air' of the white page. Thus the poem becomes in addition a verbal-visual analogue of the drawings it evokes, a *transposition d'art* functioning on the basis of common spatial metaphors. Both poem and drawings act like a mirror in which we see the 'moon' of our own pupil, shining (again in inverted, negative image) 'au ciel de papier' (l. 31), and upon the surface of which we 'breathe' our own meanings, which Noël suggests are at the same time universal ('chacun retourne au tout' [l. 37]), in a 'buée de traces' (l. 35). The paper sky, the blank physical 'support' of both drawings and poem, thus acquires great semiotic and existential resonance from the 'air' metaphor, which allows the flat page to expand into infinite depth and become a space where our thought can take flight and soar at will, like a bird: 'une part d'air/page pour battements/quand la pensée s'envole' (ll. 32-4).

'Le Dehors mental', the earlier text on da Silva, uses a different configuration of the same euphoric image, contrasting the effectiveness of the mental 'wing' in ensuring flight (shades of both Baudelaire and Mallarmé) with the absence of any trace of its activity:

> L'espace de l'œuvre est analogue au trajet de l'aile
> qui n'inscrit pas son vol tout en volant   (ll. 21-2; cf. *Poèmes 1*, 289)

Matisse uses the same metaphor to stress the need for painting to escape from mimetic constraints, what Noël calls 'le déjà-vu', and become 'le support d'une ouverture, un appel à sortir [de la ressemblance], à s'envoler hors de sa limite' (M 14). In 'Les États de l'air', the 'envol' achieved by the onlooker is a mental expansion or projection, as the inner space of the head literally follows the 'regard' into the receding pictorial depth and occupies it:

> chaque limite appelle
> le regard s'y dépasse
> la tête est ce là-bas
> où elle le rejoint   (ll. 46-9)

The spatial conflation of 'regard' and 'tête' is mirrored here by the criss-crossing relationship between the pronouns in the last line and their antecedents, initially difficult to untangle. The next stanza hints that this a not just a mental phenomenon, but also produces a new physical image of the looking self ('alors dans l'œil allé/le corps se voit venir/où le mental s'aère' [ll. 50-52]) which is displaced into alterity, so that the picture allows us to encounter a different, perhaps less reassuring, image of ourselves. Thus in each of these cases the 'air/aile' metaphor links an aesthetic and technical rejection of realism to a proposed new ethical and existential function for art based on the physical act of looking.

The idea of a physical rather than purely mental involvement with pictorial space takes on greater prominence in Noël's 1993 book *André Masson* (henceforth 'AM'), significantly subtitled 'La Chair du regard'. Many of the same metaphorical structures are used to relate the viewer's gaze to the picture, but with a physical twist appropriate to the violent, erotically-charged atmosphere of Masson's work. On the first page, Noël characterises his own experience of looking at automatic pictures in terms of a dynamic, aggressive interaction between pictorial and mental spaces which penetrates deep into the viewer's physical unconscious. The pictorial line, the product of what he defines, in a crucial correction of Breton's canonical definition, as an 'automatisme *physique* pur' (AM 35), seems to spring directly from the viewer's gaze, so strongly is he compelled to follow it by the sensual curiosity it arouses in him, 'cet appétit venu soudain au bout de votre vue' (AM 7). Picture space becomes a medium of exchange of unconscious desires and impulses, never still and inviting contemplation like a da Silva drawing, but writhing and twisting with 'saccades' and 'pulsions', literally attacking the viewer's *mentalité* and undermining his certainties and self-image:

> l'air, contaminé par ce tourbillon, ne laisse pas même tranquille le volume que votre tête, jusque là, prenait pour son intérieur. (ibid.)

Masson's semi-figurative work is so disturbing, according to Bernard Noël, because it brings about in the viewer a 'rencontre de la chose vue et d'un appétit intérieur' (AM 145), revealing to him his own violent and sexual impulses. At the moment of looking and attributing meaning the (male) viewer is drawn into committing a sexual act, as he 'traite la vue comme une ouverture vulvaire où sa sombre énergie s'active' (AM 149), bringing about a 'glissement sexuel d'un autre contenu sous la peau des choses' (ibid.). Now, the function of the 'regard' and the mental/pictorial space in which it operates is to mediate an explicitly copulatory exchange of pulsions between mind and world, to be 'le "milieu" naturel où s'accouplent ce que nous projetons vers le monde et ce que le monde projette en nous' (AM 146). This is no doubt why, unlike a da Silva drawing where picture space is light and airy and invites an initially mental occupation, the gaze that encounters a Masson floats in a darker, more sinister fluid: 'la nuit figure l'espace où l'œil s'en va nager dans son propre regard vers l'illimité' (AM 146). What the eye sees, however, is its own gaze doubled back, and although the 'trace de chair et de violence' (AM 7) left in the mind is ultimately the viewer's own, in a final inversion the air metaphor re-asserts its priority to suggest that this cathartic release of physical pulsions leads once again to a liberating mental 'ouverture': 'l'œuvre se retourne et passe des états de la sève et du sang aux états de l'air' (AM 162).

I hope that this brief excursion into Bernard Noël's art writing has given a taste of an original and compelling theory of pictorial production and reception which is both illuminating in general terms, and flexible enough to capture the specificity of artists as diverse as Matisse, da Silva and Masson (to say nothing of the dozens of others, contemporary and canonical, on whom he has written at greater or lesser length). Crucial to sustaining this balance is Noël's deployment of spatial metaphors to develop a rich textual construct which both mirrors the formal characteristics of its object and analyses their effects. His premise that good art contains 'un air à travers lequel jamais encore nous n'avions regardé' (JR 113) is an attractive and ethically satisfying one, as is the notion that the artist's function is to 'ranimer la relation du regard et de la chose' ('De beaux hybrides' 3), allowing the viewer to 'toucher de l'œil le monde' (JR 95). These phrases can in fact appropriately be turned back on Bernard Noël's own art writings, which in their turn contribute significantly to sustaining and stimulating 'la jeunesse du regard' (JR 113).

REFERENCES

Deblé, Colette. *Mille fois dedans: 69 dessins accompagnés de 2 entretiens avec Bernard Noël*. Paris: Borderie (La Bibliothèque oblique), 1979.

Kelly, D. and J. Khalfa (eds). *The New French Poetry*. Newcastle upon Tyne: Bloodaxe Books, 1996.

Noël, Bernard. *André Masson: la chair du regard*. Paris: Gallimard, 1993.

————. 'De beaux hybrides'. Preface to *Lüpertz Peintures*. *Repères* (Cahiers d'art contemporain) 56 (1989). Paris: Galerie Lelong. 3-8.

————. *David*. Paris: Flammarion ('Maîtres de l'art moderne'), 1989.

————. *Extraits du corps*. Paris: Editions de Minuit, 1958. Cf. revised version in *Poèmes 1*, 29-73.

————. *Fred Deux: l'expérience extérieure*. Paris: Galerie Jeanne Bucher, 1983 (catalogue of an exhibition of 11 large drawings by Fred Deux, Sept.-Oct. 1983).

————. *Géricault*. Paris: Flammarion ('Maîtres de l'art moderne'), 1991.

————. *Gustave Moreau*. Paris: Editions Fernand Hazan, 1979.

————. *Journal du Regard*. Paris: P.O.L, 1988.

————. 'Les États de l'air'. *Vieira da Silva: Perspective labyrinthe, dessins*. Paris: Galerie Jeanne Bucher, 1982 (n.p.). Cf. *Poèmes 1*: 299-304 and Kelly and Khalfa: 222-5 (including English translation by Peter Collier).

————. *L'Espace en demeure* (Nevelson, Vieira da Silva, Abakanowicz). Paris: Galerie Jeanne Bucher, 1978 (n.p.). Cf. revised version, 'Le Dehors mental', in *Poèmes 1*, 281-290.

————. *Magritte*. Paris: Flammarion ('Maîtres de l'art moderne'), 1977.

————. *Matisse*. Paris: Hazan, 1983 (revised 1987 edition cited).

————. *Olivier Debré*. Paris: Flammarion ('Maîtres de l'art moderne'), 1984.

————. *Onze romans d'œil*. Paris: P.O.L, 1988.

————. *Poèmes 1*. Paris: Flammarion, 1983.

Rothwell, Andrew. *Textual Spaces: the Poetry of Pierre Reverdy*. Amsterdam: Rodopi, 1989.

Pour l'amour d'un plaisir sévère: Following Louis Marin

Nigel Saint

In a radical text of 1929 entitled "Léonard et les philosophes", which weaves through aesthetic considerations about the arbitrary and the necessary, the intuitive and the structured, Paul Valéry wonders what really makes us return to philosophers:

> Quand nous nous mettons à les lire, n'est-ce pas avec le sentiment que nous nous soumettons pour quelque durée aux règles d'un beau jeu? Qu'en serait-il, de ces chefs-d'œuvre d'une discipline invérifiable, sans cette convention que nous acceptons pour l'amour d'un plaisir sévère? Si l'on réfute un Platon, un Spinoza, ne restera-t-il donc rien de leurs étonnantes constructions? Il n'en reste absolument rien, *s'il n'en reste des œuvres d'art.* (141)

The distinction Valéry makes between the rules of a system and its aesthetic quality is subverted further by the work of the French theorist and historian of representation Louis Marin (1931-1992). Marin seeks pleasure in the philosophical systems of the classical period by investigating the rules of their games. There is no project to verify discourses of Classicism, but their working principles and rhetoric can be explored in order to increase the potential of our enquiry. My direction in reading Marin's work here, however, may still be compared to Valéry's "plaisir sévère", namely for a theory of neutrality in the interpretation of Poussin.

I begin with Marin's early work on Poussin around 1970, where he establishes a method of enquiry into the structure and discourse of Poussin's landscapes, which was to culminate in the theoretical "rêverie" of *Détruire la peinture.* Then I move ahead to a crucial period in Marin's work on Poussin, around 1980-81, when the beginning of two trajectories may be located. In the first case, the question of the power of classical representation is investigated through the idea of the sublime, in other words by considering how classical representation can indicate both Nature's excess, in a painting where a storm drives the narrative, and its own impossible aspiration to completeness as a theory of representation. This first trajectory leads us to Marin's articles of 1990-1992 on the sublime and the limits of representation in Poussin. The second path in Marin's work, operating in counterpoint leads from the same starting-point around 1980-1981 to later articles on the process of metamorphosis, or the

Figure 1. Nicolas Poussin, *Landscape with a Man Killed by a Snake*. London, National Gallery; reproduced by courtesy of the Trustees, The National Gallery, London.

birth and death of looking: how the spectator becomes engaged in the dynamics of looking presented in a mythological painting and is thereby constituted as a subject in and before the painting. This leads us to Marin's reflections on the status of the subject in *The Arcadian Shepherds* in the Louvre collection. With reference to his posthumously published work on Philippe de Champaigne, what I propose to re-work as a theory of neutrality can be seen to emerge as a way of reading these two strands together.

In "La description de l'image", an article of 1970 on Poussin's *Landscape with a man killed by a snake* (fig. 1), Marin places the spectator within the web of the different directions of looking presented in the painting. Plotting these lines of sight enables Marin to set out how this painting indicates the disruption and alarm caused by the death in the peaceful landscape. Marin argues that spatial proximity of the figures in the picture does not necessarily imply narrative continuation – "le contigu n'est pas le continu" (46) – and that the tracing of visual affects causes the picture to move, as if able to stage movement. Here Marin uses the theory of reading a painting he outlined in "Le discours de la figure": the task of the reader is to detach the implied meaning of a figure from the figure, to pursue the network of the signifiers rather than the signified. Hence, in this case, the painting avoids the reduction of the narrative to one action, the killing of the man by the snake. However, the replacement of one implied discourse by another is to be resisted, so Marin does not consecrate the signifier:

A la limite, on pourrait dire que la sémiologie du tableau se développe sur un manque essentiel: elle ne peut parcourir et posséder la totalité de l'espace qu'elle recouvre et en effectuer la fermeture épistémologique. (54)

This is not a weakness, since the painting may then be understood as the space in which the oscillation between signifier and signified is played out. One eludes the other, which is why Marin speaks in his analysis of a game. Therefore, in the Poussin landscape, in the National Gallery, London, the pursuit of signs leads the spectator to find that the polyvalence of the picture lies in the need to repeat any attempt at verbal description. The exchanges of looking and interpretation in the painting are therefore explored, opening up the way to the recognition of the traces and displacements of desire, on the part of the artist and the spectator, in this representation of death, alarm and horror.

Already, in "Le discours de la figure", Marin seeks further ways of thinking around this question of visual pleasure. The simulacrum of a representational painting leads him to consider the otherness of the space presented. The figure of utopia is here invoked to indicate the space which is not a place, not space and other to space; in this utopia appears the visualized structure of the relevant myth; the structures of the story and the painting are aligned in order to try to bring word and image as close together as possible. This allows Marin to posit the idea of a space released in the painting when the distance from Myth is recognised:

Une des lectures du tableau de Poussin consistera donc à constituer, à partir du texte du récit, son utopie qui est, en fin de compte, le signifiant présent et dérobé du savoir mythique qui s'est implicité dans l'espace figuratif. (54)

The Arcadian Shepherds (fig. 5, below) would provide Marin with his principal example for further investigation of this figurative space, where History and Myth are inscribed and presented on the canvas. I will return to this utopian space during my discussion of the second strand of Marin's work on Poussin in the 1980s.

In *De la représentation* we learn that narcissism was on Marin's mind in 1980: he wished to get beyond the situation of seeing his own act of looking at a painting (200-3). Narcissism is the starting-point for the two trajectories which may be traced in Marin's later interpretations of Poussin, leading him to offer two theories for the status of the spectator-subject looking at Poussin. The problem of narcissism is tackled in an article of 1981 on Poussin's *Landscape with Pyramis and Thisbe* (fig. 2). In a detailed account of the attempts by pictorial representation to figure the time and space of the upheaval and drama of a storm, Marin argues that the lightning acts as a supplement to the narrative, its presence in the painting figuring the rupture caused by excessive light. The unrepresentable seems to be represented: we see the simultaneous effects

Figure 2. Nicolas Poussin, *Landscape with Pyramus and Thisbe.* Frankfurt am Main, Städelsches Kunstinstitut. Reproduced by kind permission of the Städelsches Kunstinstitut. © Photograph: Ursula Edelmann.

of the storm as we could never see them outside this representation, since a series of sudden moments is brought together in one time and place. Yet Marin is puzzled by the calm lake, unaffected by the storm, which therefore appears to undermine Poussin's narrative. The response to this dilemma is that the lake represents the spectator in the story of the storm and of the human drama, a spectator who at the end of looking is able to remain detached from the system of representation. The spectator is taken outside the structure of the painting, released from the signs of the sublime, while also realising that the serenity of the lake is made possible by the painting. Hence the problem of narcissism is here overcome by Poussin's art:

> Entre les deux, un miroir d'eau calme, celui de Narcisse – mais où, loin d'en mourir par stupéfaction de son propre désir de voir, le regard du sage se contemple dans la figure de son œil, en contemplant, apaisé, l'œuvre de peinture, dans sa présentation « indifférente » à ce qu'elle représente. (105)

The lake is clearly crucial to the representation, but in this version of the enigma Marin uses what he knows historically of the aesthetic discourse of painting. The fact that in his work Marin returned several times to the figure of the calm lake may be explained by the persistent problem that we are considered to be wise readers of the story, placed both inside and outside the picture. Knowledge of seventeenth-century art theory – signified knowledge – may at times distract us from the visual.

In a paper from 1983, "Le sublime classique", Marin departs from the idea of the detached spectator in order to emphasize the theoretical significance of the lake. The spectator is more firmly placed in the context of the system of representation, recognising the presence of the theory of painting in the depiction of the storm, even if this recognition indicates its very fallibility:

> ... l'œil du sage, l'œil du peintre n'hésitera pas à inscrire au prix d'une incohérence majeure où bienséance, convention, vraisemblance s'effondrent, la figure de la théorie, celle de l'apathie théorique de son regard dans la fiction d'un lac dont les eaux reflètent, inchangées, les choses bouleversées qui l'environnent. (149)

Marin works on the idea that the absence or negative trace of the storm is part of the strategy of representing the excess of the sublime. In "Déposition du temps dans la représentation peinte", the negative figure of theory is found to operate by syncope in the time of its recognition (299-300). For Marin here we have the full potential of seeing, which painting can represent at the ultimate test of its powers. The subject, named specifically in "Déposition", has its power to contemplate and to theorize surpassed by the explosion of the sublime. Now that the subject has been theoretically overwhelmed, we can ask if any trace remains of the spectator, and one way of enquiring is to consider whether there is anything left of the spectator's body.

A second trajectory in Marin's later work on Poussin leads first to another article of 1983: "A l'éveil des métamorphoses: Poussin (1625-1635)". Looking at depictions of sleeping figures, Marin asks "Comment peut-on parler sur un corps endormi? Quelle puissance donner au langage pour dire ce qui est apparemment sans puissance?" (161). Looking at a sleeping figure in a copy made by Poussin of Heintz's *Diana and Actaeon,* Marin notes that the spectator is in effect protected from metamorphosis by being able to see the sleeping figure, while the other figures cannot see her. The absence "represented" by a figure asleep leads Marin to consider otherness, in the form of his own inaccessible body when asleep:

> ... mon corps s'endormant sera toujours – comme inexorablement – le corps d'un autre, le corps autre de l'autre que le corps éveillé du langage dans les premiers gestes de la parole n'effleura jamais que de l'extérieur pour le dire, l'écrire, le décrire? Mots glissant, à leur tour, à sa surface, un peu au-dessus, sans l'éveiller. (163)

Words caress the exterior and the surface of the painting. The same process occurs when Marin looks at the sleeping figures in *Venus and Adonis* in the

Figure 3. Nicolas Poussin, *Venus and Adonis.* Museum of Art, Rhode Island School of Design; Walter H. Kimball, Georgianna Sayles Aldrich, Mary B. Jackson, Edgar J. Lowness and Jesse Metcalf Funds.

Providence collection (fig. 3), except that in this case he finds that the activities of the *putti* to the left of the sleepers may be observed as if they enact the dreams of the sleepers, as if he is magically able to cross the footlights and look at a scene which he can in reality neither see nor relate.

Consistent with his aim of determining the status of the spectator-subject in this act of looking, Marin realizes that his motivation is anticipated by the picture:

> Oui, mais il y a le désir ... de connaître déjà cette contemplation silencieuse, en repos, et qui cependant guette des signes qui le saisissent comme autant d'insinuations de ce secret, qui montrent, dans leur brièveté – ou semblent montrer – qu'il y a un secret à atteindre et qui, peut-être, créent sa présence pressentie : l'autre en un mot, miroir de soi qui me permet d'imaginer une étrange puissance sans pouvoir. (166)

The outcome of looking is the dawn of a condition between representative mastery and powerlessness, where the distance between spectator and scene is

Figure 4. Nicolas Poussin, *Echo and Narcissus.* Paris, Louvre. Reproduced by kind permission of the Museum.

traversed endlessly without resolving the mystery, and also, therefore, without being placed outside the painting. Throughout these reflections, Marin is concerned with the status of the subject as an embodied self, and the nature of the experience of looking, at and on the surface of Poussin's paintings.

The question of narcissism is commemorated and bypassed in the final stage of Marin's study of the processes of metamorphosis, where he studies the representation of life and death in *Echo and Narcissus* (fig. 4) in the Louvre collection. The spectator is drawn into a picture at the point when the artifice of representation suggests the re-awakening of the dying figures. The act of looking involves waiting for the meaning of the metamorphosis to emerge. The rock figures the possibility of the birth of a statue and the return from sleep of an echo of his other voice, his prior involvement in the story related. This otherness, now at the surface of the painting, repeats the silent poem of the painting. The emergence of the voice of the spectator is considered a space or opening:

> Et c'est ainsi que parfois, par une grâce qui est la beauté dans ses effets sensibles, il advient entre sommeil et éveil, silence et parole, que le regard trouve sa fin dans une voix et celle-ci, à son tour, dans un visible, par une incessante métamorphose où s'ouvre l'espace du sujet et d'où émerge de sa réserve endormie le moi. (174)

Figure 5. Nicolas Poussin, *The Arcadian Shepherds.* Paris, Louvre. Reproduced by kind permission of the Museum.

Following Marin across the threshold, into the painting, the subject comes to rest at a place that is an intermediary position between self and double, beyond any sexual difference, occupying the space of the surface which is the painting. The theory of this space is the framework for articulating the fate of the subject looking at Poussin.

Marin's aim is to explore how the painting by Poussin, how its "effets sensibles", can be thought to constitute, instead of the neutralised, annihilated space of *Détruire la peinture*, rather a neutral and potential space where the desires of the spectator do not control interpretation, a space with the scope for visual encounter suggested earlier in relation to the structure of Myth. In the depiction of the death of Narcissus, he finds that the desire to understand the way the painting stages the process of metamorphosis involves the vulnerable self undergoing change as it is invited to contemplate what he calls the poignant opaqueness of painting, where, however, the attentive "moi naissant" can revel in the challenge of perception. Here the subject experiences the "plaisir sévère" of contemplating Poussin.

This position is also reached when the death of the subject is represented by Poussin in a different guise and the "effets visuels" are again negotiated. In *The Arcadian Shepherds* in the Louvre (fig. 5), discussed in a paper from 1986 entitled "Le tombeau du sujet en peinture", Marin concentrates on the significance of EGO, noting that the visual sign of the tomb is appropriated by everyone in the painting. Death cannot be known; in this painting Marin finds that the word EGO indicates a double lack: the artist/spectator and the voice emerging from the tomb, both subjects of the enunciation of the text, "Et in Arcadia Ego". Thus the tomb acts as a double metaphor for the effacement of death. At the beginning of the article Marin sets out the meaning of death for representation, not in terms of images of death which we can see represented, but death itself:

> ... cette autre mort qui non seulement suspendrait toute représentation d'elle-même, mais encore neutraliserait toute présentation de l'imagination dans l'indéfini du neutre, du ni l'un ... ni l'autre, à égale et infinie distance de toute position et de toute négation, de toute détermination. (267)

Marin locates the particular power of this neutralisation precisely in the meeting of the shadow cast by the sun and the written sign of the epitaph, at the neutral place of death on the surface of the painting, where at the centre of the painting the focal points of perspective are annulled. The mythical origin of painting is present in the shadow on the tomb; the tomb of the artist figures origin, time and death in the same shadow. The neutralisation of the subject by death figures its birth, life and death in this representation. However, does this neutralisation allow for a space of contemplation?

The theoretical display by Marin still anchors the spectator firmly in the activity of looking at the painting. Marin resumes his discussion of the painting in "Aux marges de la peinture : voir la voix". In view of the spatial arrangement of the figures and tomb, it may seem that the voice of the shepherd is given the power of visibility and legibility. The painting has been able to represent its own original power. But when the surface of the painting is considered, the shadow cast by the shepherd reminds the spectator that the scene represented comes after the voice that utters the original words; the anterior voice was always there, whereas the voice of the shepherd is a visual artifice, created by Poussin for contemplation. The original voice emerges just before:

> Et c'est alors que dans cet intervalle infiniment mince, dans cet interstice infime, entre deux figures dans le plan, survient la voix-d'un-dire au voir, une voix antérieure à l'articulation de l'énoncé immémorial gravé dans la pierre, une voix qui serait l'origine de ce dit. (336)

The patience of the spectator of the signs of representation is finally rewarded by this realization of the mythical resonance of this interstice of origin, life and death. Formerly just a neutralised point, following the annulment of perspective, the spectator now "hears" the voice of Myth at the surface of the painting. Such a voice does not resonate phenomenologically from the sur-face: its severity lies in its indication of the distance between ourselves and Myth.

The figure of the *neutre,* discussed in Marin's *Utopiques, jeux d'espaces* as a figurative space between contradictions, is the condition of the subject during this alternative passage through Marin's writings on Poussin. In *The Arcadian Shepherds,* death displaces the EGO into an unfixed space between stories of birth and death. The realisation that the spectator undergoes a metamorpho-sis in this space comes when a new space of contentment is discovered and when the visual power of painting provides theory's pleasure at the surface. In one of his early pieces on *The Arcadian Shepherds,* "... Et", Marin's text con-cludes its discussion of the emergence of the story of the myth by not fixing the spectator at any set point, although the presence of the shadow is unavoid-able; nowhere but mortal, looking, at the surface.¹ For Marin, in this account of Poussin's representation (and theorisation) of the status of the subject, the dynamics of interpretation at the surface of the painting figure the human condition.

Marin's exploration of the position of the spectator at the surface of repre-sentations of Myth allows for Pascalian agility without a lapse into the anaes-thetised art history which the work of the theorist Mieke Bal also resists. One reading of Marin's work on the sublime could see it as the recuperation of Poussin's art for an immanent view of the world. On the other hand, the surfaces of Poussin are more difficult to recuperate than those, for example, of Philippe de Champaigne, whose work figures, for Marin, the hidden presence of God according to Port-Royal and Pascal. There the signifiers suffice for the exegesis; the divinity makes a sign. In the case of Poussin's paintings, which kept on calling dangerously at Louis Marin, the turn to theology to assist interpretation is not similarly invited. In Marin's late work, notably in *De l'entretien,* the theorisation of the dialogue continues the work on the time and space of the *neutre,* since thinking about the infinite approaches of the critic to the image shifts the focus from theories of representation to the search for the plenitude of affect offered by systems of representation, while at the same time preserving their specificity (28-9). Therefore what persists in the work of Louis Marin is not only an enquiry into the subject's transcendence by representation but also a search for a mode of interpretation that will con-stantly explore how the audience and the representation engage in a dialogue, with its surprises, recurrences and uncanny logic.

REFERENCES

Marin, Louis. "Le discours de la figure" (1969). In: *Etudes sémiologiques. Ecritures, Peintures.* Paris: Klinksieck, 1971. 45-60.

———. "La description de l'image" (1970). In: *Sublime Poussin.* Paris: Le Seuil, 1995. 35-70.

———. *Utopiques, jeux d'espaces.* Paris: Minuit, 1973.

———. *Détruire la peinture.* Paris: Galilée, 1977.

———. "... Et" (1977). In: *Sublime Poussin.* 106-7.

———. "Les fins de l'interprétation, ou les traversées du regard dans le sublime d'une tempête" (1980). In: *De la représentation.* Paris: Gallimard-Le Seuil, 1994. 179-203.

———. "La description du tableau et le sublime en peinture" (1981). In: *Sublime Poussin.* 71-105.

———. "A l'éveil des métamorphoses : Poussin (1625-1635)" (1983). In: *Sublime Poussin.* 161-74.

———. *De la représentation.* Paris: Gallimard-Le Seuil, 1994.

———. "Le sublime classique: les 'tempêtes' dans quelques paysages de Poussin" (1983). In: *Sublime Poussin.* 126-50.

———. *Sublime Poussin.* Paris: Le Seuil, 1995.

———. "Le tombeau du sujet en peinture" (1986). In: *De la représentation.* 267-81.

———. "Aux marges de la peinture : voir la voix" (1988). In: *De la représentation.* 329-41.

———. "Déposition du temps dans la représentation peinte" (1990). In: *De la représentation.* 282-300.

———. *Philippe de Champaigne ou la présence cachée.* Paris: Hazan, 1995.

———. *De l'entretien.* Paris: Minuit, 1997.

Valéry, Paul. "Leonard et les philosophes" (1929). In: *Introduction à la méthode de Léonard de Vinci.* Paris: Gallimard, 1992.

Entre le texte et l'image: une pragmatique des limites

Áron Kibédi Varga

Áron Kibédi Varga

TEXTE ET IMAGE EN QUATRE TERMES

Lorsque l'on veut étudier les rapports entre texte et image, montrer ce qui les rapproche et ce qui les distingue, et tracer ainsi une pragmatique des limites, il faut commencer par distinguer clairement les différentes significations de ces deux termes.

Le mot *texte* peut avoir deux sens. Le texte oral – qu'il s'agisse d'une épopée, d'un discours politique ou d'un sermon – fait partie d'une performance visuelle continue qui a ses lois propres, lois de la pragmatique et lois de la grammaire. Celui qui parle est ici un exécutant, comme le musicien qui joue à partir d'une partition, devant un public. Contrairement au texte écrit, le texte oral nous entraîne, tout retour en arrière est difficile: on risque de perdre le fil du discours si l'on s'arrête sur ce qui vient d'être dit. Parallèlement, le mouvement linéaire inexorable impose une simplicité relative de la syntaxe et du style ainsi que de nombreuses répétitions. Le texte chanté est une variante du texte oral; il comporte quelques contraintes supplémentaires. Tout cela est bien connu.

La pragmatique du texte *écrit* est différente: l'aspect performatif et la visibilité du texte semblent réduites à un minimum, le lecteur est devenu lui-même l'exécutant. Il n'y a plus d'interactivité entre un ou plusieurs exécutants professionnels et un public, seules existent la page et l'écriture telles qu'elles sont perçues par le lecteur solitaire. Tout se décide au niveau de la lecture individuelle, qui n'est pas nécessairement continue: on peut ralentir ou accélérer le contact avec les mots qui se suivent et on peut feuilleter, c'est-à-dire revenir en arrière, tout ceci selon les nécessités de la compréhension. De par sa typographie, le texte écrit menace de se rapprocher de l'image;[1] la lecture efficace privilégie donc la typographie la plus conventionnelle pour résister au potentiel iconique des lettres.

Le mot *image* peut revêtir à son tour deux significations tout à fait opposées.[2] L'image *mobile*, que l'on rencontre au théâtre et au cinéma, se présente en général dans un cadre immuable, écran ou scène dans une salle obscure. À l'intérieur de ce cadre contraignant, les images successives évoluent selon une syntaxe précise de la continuité: chaque image est déterminée par un rapport métonymique avec celles qui précèdent et qui suivent. L'image mobile néces-

site, comme le texte oral, des exécutants; ceux-ci, les acteurs, obéissent strictement aux instructions du metteur en scène. La production réussit ainsi, dans
le cas de l'image mobile, à déterminer largement la réception, qui a toujours
lieu de manière collective: rien n'est laissé au hasard lors de la "lecture" d'un
film ou d'une représentation théâtrale.[3]

En revanche, l'image *fixe* de la peinture a un cadre moins contraignant: le
musée (l'église, le château) est un espace qui accorde plus de libertés au spectateur individuel que la salle obscure au public collectif. Son regard peut s'arrê-
ter sur tel détail, passer rapidement sur tel autre. La 'lecture' d'un tableau est
aléatoire. Le spectateur peut même, ici, se servir de son corps, par exemple en
s'éloignant et en se rapprochant du même tableau plusieurs fois de suite.

D'une manière générale, ces quatre catégories ont été étudiées séparément.
Le texte oral est devenu l'objet d'études de l'anthropologie et de l'analyse du
discours, l'image mobile celui des spécialistes du théâtre et du cinéma: historiens, sémioticiens, narratologues. Enfin, le texte écrit et l'image fixe – "la
poésie et la peinture" dans la tradition antithétique de Lessing – sont étudiés
de manière comparée depuis des siècles, mais plus particulièrement de nos
jours, par les historiens[4] et notamment par les historiens de l'art et de la littérature. Cette distinction classique ne peut, bien entendu, s'établir que dans les
communautés ayant abandonné l'oralité: elle est post-orale.

Lecture du texte, lecture de l'image

Au premier abord, il semble que le texte oral et l'image mobile soient les deux
terrains d'études les plus prometteurs et les plus passionnants: ils font appel à
une sémiotique multimédiale qui détermine le fonctionnement parallèle et
complémentaire des paroles, des sons, des couleurs et des gestes: quels sont les
sons, quels sont les gestes qui accompagnent de préférence telle parole, quelles
sont les paroles et les gestes les plus appropriés à tels sons, et ainsi de suite.[5]

En revanche, la rivalité séculaire de la poésie et de la peinture, l'immense
bibliographie du *paragone*,[6] nourrie par les réflexions de nombreux artistes et
critiques, de Léonard de Vinci à nos jours, suppose une opposition irréducti-
ble entre le texte écrit et l'image fixe. L'étude comparée peut paraître par con-
séquent particulièrement ardue: comment rapprocher, voire intégrer, ce qui
s'oppose? En disant ceci, on oublie cependant une chose: l'opposition est en
général postulée, on le voit, du côté de la production, c'est-à-dire par les créateurs qui s'inscrivent, qu'ils le veuillent ou non, dans une vieille tradition culturelle. Mais ces mêmes rapports se présentent tout à fait autrement si on les
envisage du côté de la réception, c'est-à-dire du point de vue du public, le
lecteur et le spectateur.

Malgré le désaccord de nombreux artistes et historiens de l'art et de la littérature – qui persistent dans la tradition de Lessing – la recherche en psychologie cognitive semble en effet montrer que, du côté de la réception, la séparation entre la lecture du texte et celle de l'image est beaucoup moins étanche qu'on ne le croyait.[7] Plusieurs décennies après les travaux classiques de Buswell (1935) et de Yarbus (1967) sur la manière dont l'œil perçoit un tableau, la psychologie cognitive découvre des analogies troublantes entre la manière de regarder et la manière de lire: la lecture d'un texte ne possède pas la linéarité que les lignes imprimées suggèrent; l'œil saute les mots faciles, s'arrête sur les mots difficiles, revient en arrière. La syntaxe aléatoire des saccades et des fixations pendant la lecture ressemble étrangement à celle qui préside notre regard devant un tableau, la durée des fixations suit les mêmes lois sémantiques que celles qui déterminent le regard: la lecture comme le regard passent vite sur les endroits et les mots qui sont facilement assimilables, qui n'offrent aucune résistance à la compréhension et ils s'arrêtent en revanche plus longuement sur les endroits essentiels d'un tableau, respectivement sur les mots dont le sens apporte le plus d'information nouvelle.

Autrefois, comparer texte et image signifiait, du point de vue de la réception, que l'on comparait deux activités radicalement différentes, celle du lecteur accumulant dans le temps son savoir progressif selon une continuité linéaire imperturbable et celle du spectateur embrassant d'un seul coup d'œil un ensemble d'éléments dans l'espace; aujourd'hui, l'étude des rapports entre texte et image doit se faire sous un tout autre jour. Il ne s'agit plus d'établir des analogies entre deux terrains que tout semble opposer, mais, au contraire, de marquer les spécificités du texte et de l'image, deux artefacts dont la réception ressemble étrangement. Pour bien voir ce qui les distingue, il faut commencer par l'étude des phénomènes les plus difficiles; non pas de cas d'opposition radicale donc simple, comme celle d'un texte philosophique opposé à un tableau abstrait, pour montrer ainsi la nature peu "imagée" de tel texte de Kant et la nature peu "textuelle" de tel tableau de Mondrian. Au contraire, il faut commencer précisément par l'étude des cas où la distinction fait problème, où les frontières semblent s'effacer. Où tracer les *limites* qui séparent le texte et l'image, où entrevoir le seuil qui permet de passer de l'un à l'autre?

Je laisse donc de côté les rapports de *complémentarité,* c'est-à-dire les cas où le texte apporte à l'image ou, inversement, l'image au texte, un complément d'information, jugé utile par le destinateur: – que celui-ci soit le peintre qui ajoute un titre à son tableau (soit pour aider soit pour dérouter le spectateur), l'éditeur qui commande des illustrations pour les ajouter au roman ou au recueil de poèmes qu'il entend publier ou enfin le fabriquant qui veut combiner, dans la publicité de sa marchandise, les effets rhétoriques de l'objet représenté et du slogan textuel qui permet de la particulariser. Le texte est complémentaire à l'image dans le cas du titre traditionnel, l'image est complémentaire au texte quand il s'agit de l'illustration et la complémentarité fonctionne dans les deux sens pour la publicité. Ce qui caractérise la complémentarité dans tous ces cas, c'est que, malgré le rapport de dépendance de l'un des deux éléments vis-à-vis de l'autre, les deux éléments se laissent toujours nettement séparer.

LES LIMITES: LA COÏNCIDENCE PARTIELLE

Pour étudier les limites, c'est-à-dire la séparation minimale entre texte et image, il faut se tourner du côté des rapports de *coïncidence,* c'est-à-dire des cas où la forme des deux artefacts est inséparable; j'en distinguerais principalement trois: coïncidence partielle, coïncidence entière et coïncidence cachée.

Une coïncidence *partielle* a lieu lorsqu'une partie d'un texte peut être détachée du reste dans la mesure où elle constitue, aussi, une image. La partie détachée est à la fois texte et image. L'image qui se superpose au texte est en général utilisée, non pas pour décorer celui-ci, mais pour imposer au spectateur-lecteur une autre, une seconde lecture, qui tantôt ajoute au texte une information nouvelle tantôt en renforce le sens rhétoriquement, par une espèce de pléonasme. L'exemple le plus connu de coïncidence partielle est sans doute la figure de l'*acrostiche*. La typographie voyante des initiales nous invite à une deuxième lecture (partielle) du poème, la lecture verticale de ces initiales qui livre le nom de l'auteur, Villon, dans la *Ballade des contre vérités,* ou celui des femmes courtisées, chez le poète hongrois Balassa (1554 -1594).

Les 28 pages du manuscrit *De Laudibus Sanctae Crucis* que Raban Maur, un moine de Fulda a écrit et "illustré" vers 810, nous offrent un autre exemple de coïncidence partielle. La Sainte Croix, métonymie de la souffrance du Christ et du salut des croyants, est un symbole éminemment visuel et il s'imposait de ne pas en faire la louange uniquement en paroles. Sur la méditation poétique en latin des mystères de la Sainte Croix[8] se superposent donc chaque fois un ou plusieurs dessins qui délimitent un ensemble de lettres et cet ensemble constitue des mots qui renforcent, rhétoriquement et iconiquement, la louange de la Croix. Ainsi, la troisième figure (ill. 1) introduit neuf dessins, neuf lettres majuscules[9] superposées au texte et qui constituent les deux mots SALUS CRUX, mais qui forment en même temps une croix, désignant ainsi le lieu du salut. Les neuf figures-lettres ainsi détachées dans le texte contiennent les noms des neuf ordres d'anges[10] – séraphins, chérubins, trônes, archanges, anges, puissances, pouvoirs, principautés et dominations – invités à "louer ensemble la victoire du Roi éternel".

La série de méditations encomiastiques, menées selon la tradition théologique, se termine, à la 28e page, par un vœu personnel (ill. 2). Agenouillé

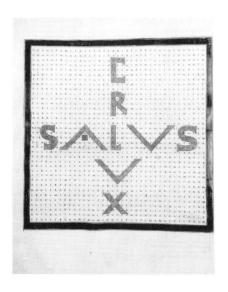

Illustration 1.

Illustration 2.

devant la croix, l'auteur révèle son identité. Les lettres inscrites dans la croix disent: "O bois, je t'implore, toi qui es autel, et j'implore d'être emporté sur ton autel" et les lettres inscrites dans la figure du moine agenouillé: "O Christ, dans ta clémence, je t'en prie, protège-moi, Raban, au jour du Jugement".

Chez Raban Maur, la coïncidence est partielle. Sur le texte de base sont surimposés des tracés formant soit des caractères, lettres plus grandes que celles du texte de fond, soit des images (le moine agenouillé). Grâce à cette iconisation d'une partie du texte, l'attention du lecteur est retenue plus longtemps: elle passe du regard initial rapide à la lecture, puis les dessins l'obligent à passer à une deuxième lecture. Les lettres qui se trouvent, elles, à l'intérieur des contours lui livrent l'essentiel: un résumé de la page.

Il est curieux de constater que la coïncidence partielle ne se pratique pas dans le sens inverse. Détacher par la typographie certaines lettres ou tracer un contour autour de quelques-unes, voilà deux procédés qui permettent d'iconiser partiellement un texte, d'introduire dans un texte mobile l'immobilité de l'image. Des procédés analogues ne sont guère utilisés pour transformer une partie de la représentation mimétique en texte, pour inviter le spectateur à abandonner momentanément le mouvement du regard pour celui de la lecture. La présence – pour ne citer qu'un exemple – de lettres et de mots dans les tableaux cubistes de Braque, de Picasso, de Juan Gris, ne vise jamais cet effet: les mots ne se superposent pas à l'image, ils en font partie, on les regarde.[11] En revanche, la peinture du XXe siècle offre, de Kandinsky à Twombly et à la poésie concrète, de nombreux exemples d'illusion textuelle: le spectateur se trouve au premier moment dérouté, croyant avoir affaire à des lettres, à une écriture, à un texte, pour découvrir aussitôt que ce qu'il voit n'est ni idéogramme ni alphabet mais un ensemble de figures iconiques qui leur ressemble.[12]

LES LIMITES: LA COÏNCIDENCE ENTIÈRE

Les procédés signalés jusqu'ici ont en commun d'"iconiser' des lettres – séparément ou en groupes – plutôt que d'offrir une véritable image mimétique. Dans les cas de coïncidence *entière,*[13] c'est-à-dire là où image et texte sont absolument inséparables, la *lettre* iconisée (ou réiconisée) joue de nouveau un rôle important: ce procédé est l'effet soit de réflexions théologiques soit de réflexions pédagogiques. La calligraphie répandue dans les pays islamiques peut être mise en rapport avec l'interdiction théologique de représenter mimétiquement des êtres humains, en particulier le Prophète lui-même: le verbe est sacré, donc il peut être simultanément esthétisé, mais l'auteur ou le médiateur de ce verbe est irreprésentable, donc doit rester invisible.[14] Certains manuels scolaires présentaient autrefois des *alphabets iconisés,* dont les lettres ressemblent à des objets ou à des êtres humains, à des images familières aux élèves;[15] pour les enfants, il semble en effet difficile au début de faire une distinction entre l'activité du regard et celle de la lecture, les lettres leur apparaissant avec la même valeur iconique que les images.

La coïncidence complète au niveau du *texte* peut prendre trois formes: le poème figuratif, le poème visuel et la peinture textuelle. L'auteur du poème figuratif est en général un homme de plume – écrivain, poète, savant – , celui de la peinture textuelle, qui est une invention moderne, est en général un peintre, tandis que peintres et poètes se disputent le terrain du poème visuel.

LE POÈME FIGURATIF

Les "carmina figurata" ont une tradition séculaire,[16] on les rencontre dès le Moyen Âge et plus particulièrement à l'époque baroque et au XXe siècle. Le *poème figuratif,* ou calligramme, représente ce qu'il dit, il figure ce qu'il permet ensuite de lire. Il prend la forme d'un objet représentable, il ressemble à un oiseau, à une rose, à des gouttes de pluie. Mais le texte du poème figuratif ne répète presque jamais exactement ce que la figure a laissé voir: le texte ne confirme pas purement et simplement l'image. L'écart entre les deux peut prendre plusieurs formes, qui constituent autant de traits distinctifs du texte. Nous en distinguerons ici trois.

Les *Calligrammes* de Guillaume Apollinaire offrent une riche variété de poèmes figuratifs. La figure dessinée de la couronne contient le poème suivant: "les rois qui meurent tour à tour renaissent au cœur des poètes", celle d'une flamme renversée 'dit': "mon cœur est pareil à une flamme renversée".[17] Le rapport entre texte et image est soit métonymique – la couronne renvoie aux rois qui 'appellent', selon une connotation culturelle très ancienne, les poètes[18] – soit métaphorique, comme dans le deuxième cas. En outre, la répartition, dans le recueil d'Apollinaire, des poèmes figuratifs parmi les autres, imprimés de manière traditionnelle, a encore une autre fonction, plus globale: l'image détruit la continuité de la lecture, d'une page à l'autre, elle impose au lecteur un arrêt momentané, un effort plus ou moins synesthésique: "Entends nager le Mot poisson subtil", demande Apollinaire.[19]

La coïncidence entière entre texte et image n'exclut donc pas pour autant, du côté du texte, certaines variations subtiles que l'image ignore. Le poème "Rose" de Heinrich Trier, publié en 1718, présente la forme d'une rose, mais le texte ne décrit pas simplement la fleur, elle constitue une longue allégorisation chrétienne sur le symbole de la rose, toujours entourée d'épines: l'image dénote, se situe au niveau du sens propre, là où le texte connote, renvoie au sens figuré traditionnel et familier au lecteur chrétien. La connotation du texte rejaillit ensuite, bien entendu, sur l'image: celle-ci connote là où elle renvoie à une doxa, à un texte.[20]

Explicitation métaphorique de l'image, passage du sens propre au sens figuré, et enfin, une troisième variante de la spécificité textuelle: celle du passage du général au particulier. Le poème "Biography in 100 Words" de Thomas Kabdebo se présente au regard comme un homme, n'importe quel homme, que le texte particularise ensuite: "Born on a planet called earth..." etc. et se termine par: "My name is Thomas George J. Kabdebo".[21] Une fois de plus, la coïncidence est entière mais elle permet de dégager une particularité du texte dont l'image est démunie: celle-ci ne saurait particulariser.[22] On sait que, en peinture, le tableau d'histoire et le portrait ont besoin d'un titre pour que le spectateur non-initié sache de quelle scène ou de quelle personne il s'agit: la généralité n'est dépassée que grâce au texte, au titre.

Quel est le rapport qui relie l'image et le texte dans le calligramme? Parler, comme l'a fait Michel Foucault,[23] de rapport tautologique n'est exact que dans la mesure où l'on considère que, en fait, le même objet 'se lit' deux fois: la première fois, le calligramme semble 'parler' sans détour, déictiquement: "voici une couronne", "voici une flamme renversée", "voici une rose" "voici un homme", mais la deuxième fois il parlera des poètes-rois, d'un cœur amoureux, du bien et du mal, du réfugié politique.

La poésie figurative étant le fait d'écrivains, l'aspect iconique de leur œuvre reste en général assez schématique: il s'agit de dessins noir et blanc, aux tracés facilement identifiables. Leurs auteurs cherchent rarement à dépasser un mimétisme traditionnel et banal.[24]

LA POÉSIE VISUELLE

La deuxième catégorie de coïncidence entière concerne la *poésie visuelle,* c'est-à-dire des poèmes dont l'arrangement spatial n'obéit pas à des règles de mimétisme iconique. Les mots et les phrases ont une figure ou une typographie variable qui met en valeur ce qui les entoure: le blanc de la page, la salle de musée. Le spectateur-lecteur est doublement dérouté, d'abord, comme dans le cas des poèmes figuratifs, par l'impossibilité d'entamer immédiatement la lecture, et ensuite parce que, contrairement au poème figuratif, rien ne lui indique le sens de cette lecture, le début et la fin du texte étant devenus affaire de choix, à opérer par le lecteur.

Ainsi, *Le coup de dés* de Mallarmé peut être lu de différentes façons (ill. 3): en niant la pertinence des blancs, on peut aller selon les conventions consa-

Illustration 3.

crées, de gauche à droite et de haut en bas; ou, au contraire, le ralentissement iconique de la lecture peut être saisi comme une invitation au respect des blancs, à de multiples arrêts, à une lecture aux mouvements irréguliers, selon le vœu même de Mallarmé;[25] ensuite, on peut lire ensemble, en sautant d'une page à l'autre, les mots imprimés selon la même typographie; mais nous savons combien la poésie garde, bien plus que la prose, les traces de l'oralité: le changement de la typographie peut donc tout aussi bien suggérer au lecteur de pratiquer une lecture sonore, chaque changement de l'imprimé ayant alors pour effet un changement de la voix.

La poésie visuelle n'apparaît pas seulement dans les livres, mais aussi dans des installations. Cet objet de Bruce Nauman (ill. 4), qui date de 1981-1982,[26] possède à la fois plusieurs caractéristiques de l'image et du texte, en particulier du texte poétique. Il est image: 1. parce que les mots qui le composent ne se suivent pas mais se trouvent disposés dans l'espace et 2. parce que chaque mot se présente, non pas en noir et blanc mais en couleur, principalement en deux couleurs simultanément: jaune et rouge, vert et orange, rouge et bleu. Il est poème: 1. parce que les trois mots représentés s'associent grâce à un jeu très étroit de sonorités – *Violins Violence Silence* sont reliés par trois *a-i*, tandis que le passage de *v* à *s* qui aurait pu rompre leur unité, se trouve compensé, dans les deux derniers mots, par la répétition exacte de *e-n-s;* et 2. parce que chaque mot est répété une fois, les deux premiers séparément, le troisième en boustrophédon. Les jeux de sonorité (rimes internes et finales) se combinent avec la répétition et constituent ainsi, dans une image, l'exact équivalent d'un poème traditionnel, tel que, par exemple, Jakobson les définit.

Une interprétation de cet objet de Bruce Nauman doit nécessairement s'appuyer à la fois sur son aspect iconique et son aspect textuel: preuve supplé-

Illustration 4.

mentaire, s'il en est besoin, de la coïncidence totale du texte et de l'image ! La disposition spatiale semble suggérer une architecture éclatée, grâce aux deux mots *violins* et *violence* que l'on peut lire de gauche à droite, il est vrai, mais en montant puis en descendant: "la musique nous permet de monter, la violence détruit", c'est-à-dire fait (re)descendre. Les deux mots se trouvent ensuite, de gauche à droite, répétés, mais à l'envers: la disposition architecturale gagne là un deuxième sens: "la musique élargit, s'envole, la violence par contre est une implosion". Contrairement aux deux autres mots, le mot *silence* ne se lit pas une seule fois nettement, de gauche à droite: les lettres se surimposent dans les deux sens et se lisent sens dessus-dessous, c'est-à-dire qu'elles sont illisibles, elles ne se liraient que s'il était possible de renverser l'installation. 'Le silence, ici, n'est pas synonyme de sagesse et d'harmonie, il est l'effet de la violence, c'est le silence de la peur et de la mort qui s'installe après la destruction de la musique'. En outre, le sens de la lecture des deux premiers mots et le renversement du troisième semble demander une interprétation narrative: les trois mots suggèrent dans cet ordre un déroulement temporel, ils représentent les trois étapes principales d'un événement dramatique.[27]

LA PEINTURE TEXTUELLE

La troisième catégorie de coïncidence entière entre texte et image, la peinture textuelle, présente des textes sur un tableau; l'aspect iconique est limité, l'objet n'en garde souvent que les traces. On peut considérer la genèse de la peinture textuelle comme l'ultime et logique conséquence du *paragone*. Au 18e siècle, la rivalité entre peinture et poésie demandait que les peintres fassent des tableaux qui intègrent le mouvement, des tableaux d'histoire donc, et – simultanément – que les poètes décrivent aussi exactement que possible les champs de blé, les animaux, les montagnes, c'est-à-dire que leurs poèmes s'approchent des paysages peints. À ce parallélisme paradoxal – peinture narrative vs. poésie descriptive – en correspond un autre au 20e siècle: certains poètes présentent, comme on a vu, des poèmes figuratifs, des poèmes qui ont la forme d'une image – et en même temps se font de plus en plus nombreux les peintres qui 'écrivent' des tableaux, qui inscrivent des textes sur la toile.

Ces mots et ces phrases se présentent sous une forme typographique conventionnelle, peu iconique: ils sont parfaitement lisibles. On pense à certaines œuvres de Bruce Nauman, de Cy Twombly,[28] de Lawrence Weiner, de Jenny Holzer.[29] Souvent l'image n'est plus qu'évoquée, elle n'est présente que métonymiquement: par le cadre ou par l'endroit où cet objet nous est présenté. Le cadre remplace le découpage des pages d'un livre, les textes apparaissent sur un tableau ou sur plusieurs tableaux juxtaposés, dans un musée ou dans une salle de galerie. Les phrases possèdent tantôt une force de suggestion poétique – "One Hundred Live and Die", dit le titre d'une installation de Bruce Nauman, "Wilder Shore of Love", lit-on sur un tableau de Cy Twombly – tantôt elles traduisent une volonté aphoristique, une volonté de transmettre un message, des vérités que l'image est incapable d'exprimer: ainsi, il n'est pas impossible de tirer des textes de Jenny Holzer une philosophie morale sophistiquée, nourrie d'intertextualité contestataire, qui accepte et critique à la fois le 'American way of life' de nos jours, exactement comme on peut déduire des maximes de La Rochefoucauld une philosophie morale du désenchantement à l'époque de Louis XIV en France.[30]

Les peintres en question entendent-ils ainsi dénoncer le medium qu'ils se sont choisis et qui serait incapable de communiquer certaines valeurs auxquelles ils sont attachés ? Ce qui est certain, c'est que la peinture textuelle se trouve à l'extrême limite de ce qu'on appellerait une coïncidence du texte et de l'image. D'une manière générale, lorsque nous nous trouvons en présence d'un poème figuratif ou d'un poème visuel, l'objet en question fait appel à nous en tant que spectateur et ensuite seulement en tant que lecteur: le regard précède toujours la lecture. Par contre, dans la poésie textuelle, seul le lieu choisi fait penser à un tableau, mais en réalité c'est tout de suite le lecteur qui s'active, on peut sauter la phrase préalable du regard; la peinture textuelle annonce, déjà, une forme de coïncidence cachée.

LA COÏNCIDENCE CACHÉE.

Certains textes littéraires, on le sait, ont été conçus en fonction d'images, ils renvoient clairement à des tableaux, à certains genres picturaux: l'ekphrasis au tableau d'histoire,[31] le portrait littéraire au portrait peint.[32] Ces tableaux ne sont pas nécessairement présents au moment de la lecture: *on se les imagine*. Le problème se pose alors, d'une manière beaucoup plus générale, de la faculté imaginative du lecteur. Deux questions complémentaires pour notre propos: est-il possible de lire un texte littéraire quelconque sans que des images surgissent ? et: est-il possible de voir une image qui ne soit pas l'illustration virtuelle d'un texte ?

Il me semble que la réponse à la première question ne puisse être que négative: notre faculté imaginante est infinie, le moindre texte ayant des propriétés fictionnelles (description, narration) génère immédiatement et inlassablement des images dans notre esprit. Toutefois il ne s'agit plus de coïncidence, de rapports, entre deux artefacts, les textes ouvrant ici sur une tout autre catégorie d'images, celle des images mentales.

Retournons maintenant la question: y a-t-il toujours un texte derrière une image? L'histoire de l'art aussi bien que l'expérience quotidienne de chacun montre que d'innombrables images sont en fait des *illustrations* cachées. Elles ont un rapport de complémentarité avec un texte, elles ne sont pas indépendantes, elles demandent à être commentées, éclairées. Les tableaux d'histoire des siècles classiques illustrent un texte, la culture verbale dominante de l'époque, même lorsqu'ils ne renvoient pas à tel passage précis de la Bible, d'Homère, des *Métamorphoses* d'Ovide ou de Tite-Live. De même, au 20e siècle, tel tableau issu du courant du réalisme socialiste restera l'illustration d'un discours.

Ce tableau de Filatov ("Octobre") (ill. 5) ne représente pas simplement une conversation entre plusieurs hommes, il met en relief, un homme de la ville, en cravate, que tout distingue des autres. Tous les regards se tournent vers lui et il est impossible au spectateur de se contenter de ce que le regard lui offre, il a besoin d'un récit qui le renseigne sur l'identité du personnage central, Lénine en l'occurrence. Ce tableau n'est pas autonome en tant que tableau, il exige un texte.

Mais en est-il de même de tous les tableaux ? La dépendance textuelle de la peinture a toujours été particulièrement forte pour les genres picturaux qui représentent des êtres humains. Notre curiosité tient à particulariser ces êtres mortels, hommes et femmes du passé, là où elle se contente en général de l'anonymat pour les animaux ou les rivières. Grâce, aussi, au changement progressif des sujets choisis, ce caractère illustratif de la peinture s'estompe de plus en plus au cours du 19e siècle. Pour celui qui regarde un paysage impressionniste, le renseignement fourni par le titre est un supplément agréable mais non

Illustration 5.

pas nécessaire. Le regard déclenche certes des activités mentales: plaisir sensuel des couleurs, souvenirs d'enfance, mais celles-ci ne nécessitent aucune information supplémentaire de nature textuelle. Après plusieurs siècles de domination logocentrique, l'image s'émancipe, elle déclare son autonomie par rapport au texte.

Concluons. L'étude de la pragmatique des limites, de la coïncidence entre texte et image au niveau de la réception, nous amène à proposer deux thèses. Premièrement, nous constatons que coïncidence formelle ne veut pas dire simultanéité réceptive. Le caractère iconique inévitable de l'écriture reste un obstacle à la perception simultanée de l'image et du texte (ce qui ne pose aucun problème pour la parole sonore: au cinéma, au musée, son et image nous parviennent en même temps). Mais ici les opérations du regard et de la lecture se distinguent, le seuil étant le moment précis de la transformation, celui où le regard est relayé par la lecture qui particularise, qui intègre l'image dans notre savoir, conventionnel et textuel.

Deuxièmement, nous constatons une curieuse asymétrie. D'une part, le seuil qui sépare texte et image n'est pas aussi souvent franchi dans les deux sens. Dans le cas de la coïncidence entière, un texte peut prendre la forme d'une image, se cacher derrière une figure mais une image ne se transforme jamais en texte. D'autre part, pour l'imagination du destinataire, la coïncidence cachée caractérise tous les textes – tous suscitent des images mentales – mais non pas toutes les images – toutes ne renvoient pas à un texte. Le regard précède la lecture, mais il n'est pas nécessaire que la lecture suive. On n'a pas encore suffisamment mesuré les effets radicaux de l'autonomie de l'image: cette autonomie engendre un nouveau type de savoir qui réussit à se passer du verbe.[33]

NOTES

1 L'écriture a – aussi bien que son corollaire, la lecture, dont il sera question un peu plus loin – un statut ambigu entre parole et image. Cf. Anne-Marie Christin, *L'image écrite*, Paris, Flammarion, 1995.

2 Je laisse de côté les autres significations possibles, en particulier les images verbales (ex.: métaphore) et mentales (ex.: rêve). Cf. W.J.T. Mitchell, *Iconology*, University of Chicago Press, 1988, chap. 1. Pour les images mentales, voir Klaus Sachs-Hombach, éd., *Bilder im Geiste*, Amsterdam, Rodopi, 1995.

3 La présentation d'un film à la télévision modifie considérablement, bien entendu, certaines conditions de la pragmatique de l'image mobile.

4 Cf. Francis Haskell, *History and its Images, New Haven, Yale University Press, 1993; Karl F. Morrison, History as a visual art in the 12th Century*, Princeton University Press, 1990. Pour l'intérêt historique de l'image mobile, voir Rainer Rother, éd., *Bilder schreiben Geschichte: der Historiker im Kino,* Berlin, Klaus Wagenbach Verlag, 1991.

5 Cf. Patrice Pavis, *Problèmes de sémiologie théâtrale*, Montréal, Presses de l'Université du Québec, 1976; Ion Whitmore, *Directing Postmodern Theater,* Ann Arbor, University of Michigan Press, 1994; Jan-Dirk Müller, éd., *'Aufführung' und 'Schrift' im Mittelalter und früher Neuzeit*, Stuttgart, Metzler, 1996; *Language and Beyond*, Actes du colloque d'Anvers (à paraître); etc.

6 Cf. Lauriane Fallay d'Este, *Le Paragone – le Parallèle des arts,* Paris, Klincksieck, 1992.

7 Voir à ce sujet en particulier la remarquable synthèse de Sabine Gross (*Lese-Zeichen, Kognition, Medium und Materialität im Leseprozess,* Darmstadt, Wissenschaftliche Buchgesellschaft, 1994) qui s'appuie essentiellement sur des recherches américaines.

8 *La Légende dorée* donne de nombreux épisodes au sujet des miracles intervenus autour de la Sainte Croix; ce sujet a inspiré entre autres le grand fresque de Piero della Francesca à Arezzo (L'Exaltation de la Sainte Croix).

9 Le *De Laudibus* comporte une composition numérique complexe, au symbolisme évident. Cf. Raban Maur, *Louanges de la Sainte Croix,* édition présentée par Michel Perrin, Paris, Berg International, 1988, 20-3.

10 Denis l'Aréopagyte semble être à l'origine de la distinction courante des anges en trois fois trois catégories. Voir par exemple le catalogue de l'exposition *Le Retour des anges,* Paris, Union Latine, 1996.

11 Cf. Robert Rosenblum, "Picasso and the Typography of Cubism", in: *Art Bulletin,* 1981, pp. 34-47. – Plusieurs expositions ont retracé, ces dernières années, l'histoire des rapports entre peinture et écriture, entre mots insérés dans des tableaux et textes visualisés, en particulier au XXe siècle: Utrecht 1991, Anvers 1992, Marseille 1993, Vienne-Francfort 1993-1994.

12 Par exemple Kandinsky, *Succession,* 1935. Cf. Francis Edeline, "Manipulation du graphème chez les poètes concrets". In: *Art & Fact*, (Liège), 3, 1984, 134-5.

13 La coïncidence entière de deux images, respectivement de deux textes, existe aussi. Dans le premier cas, on parle de figure équivoque ("Umspringfigur"): il s'agit de dessins noir et blanc dont les silhouettes peuvent être interprétées de deux manières différentes: comme une vase ou comme deux têtes rapprochées, comme un lapin ou

comme une oie (voir là-dessus E. H. Gombrich, *Art and Illusion,* Oxford, Phaedon Press, 5e éd., 1977, 4; et les remarques critiques de Flint Schier, *Deeper into Pictures, an Essay on Pictorial Representation,* Cambridge University Press, 1986, 8 et 144). Dans le deuxième cas, il faut distinguer les lettres et les sons. La même série de lettres ne peut jamais donner deux textes différents (la figure du palindrome n'est en fait que la double lecture d'un même texte), mais la même prononciation peut engendrer, grâce au jeu des homonymies, deux phrases ayant des sens différents. Voici un exemple pris dans les Grands Rhétoriqueurs: "Gal, amant de la reine, alla, tour magnanime, / Galamment de l'arène à la Tour Magne, à Nîmes".

14 Alain Besançon, *L'image interdite, une histoire intellectuelle de l'iconoclasme,* Paris, Fayard, 1994.

15 Cf. Sabine Gross, *op. cit.,* 50. – L'alphabet corporel a pu être la base de certaines chorégraphies baroques; cf. Mark Franko, *Dance as Text – Ideologies of the Baroque Body,* Cambridge University Press, 1993. – Pour l'iconisation (symbolique ou non) des lettres, voir aussi "The Word on the Page", no. sp. *Word & Image,* janvier-mars 1996.

16 Les deux ouvrages fondamentaux sont Giovanni Pozzi, *La parola dipinta,* Adelphi, Milano, 1981, et Jeremy Adler und Ulrich Ernst, *Text als Figur – Visuelle Poesie von der Antike bis zur Moderne,* Weinheim, 1988. Pour l'Espagne, voir Fernando R. de la Flor, *Emblemas,* Alianza, Madrid, 1995, 209-32, pour la Hongrie: Pál Nagy, *Az irodalom új müfajai,* Institut de littérature hongroise, Université de Budapest, 1996.

17 "Cœur couronne et miroir", in: *Œuvres poétiques,* Paris, Gallimard, Bibliothèque de la Pléiade, 197. Pour une interprétation complète de cette page, ce 'cœur' et cette 'couronne' devraient être, bien entendu, mis en rapport avec le 'miroir' qui figure sur la même page.

18 Il s'agit du vieux topos selon lequel les Grands doivent leur immortalité aux poètes: "Ce que Malherbe écrit dure éternellement".

19 *Op. cit.,* 223. Tous ces textes se trouvent bien entendu dans le recueil *Calligrammes.*

20 Pour une interprétation détaillée de ce poème, dédié à une dame à la cour du duc de Braunschweig, voir Adler-Ernst, *op. cit.,* 130-1.

21 Cité d'après Sabine Gross, *op. cit.,* 75.

22 La non-individuation de l'image est un sujet souvent débattu dans l'esthétique moderne (Gombrich, Böhm, etc.).

23 *Ceci n'est pas une pipe,* Montpellier, Fata Morgana, 1973, chap. 2.

24 Le poème figuratif présente en général une seule figure, mais on trouve parfois des constructions plus complexes: chez Apollinaire, ("Voyage", *Calligrammes,* 198-9, où le titre même exclut une représentation mimétique simple) ou encore chez Marinetti ('parole en libertà').

25 "Préface", in: *Œuvres complètes,* Paris, Gallimard, Bibliothèque de la Pléiade, 1945, 455. Pour une étude sérieuse de ce texte, il faut cependant avoir recours à la seule édition du *Coup de dés* qui soit conforme à la volonté du poète. Elle ne fut réalisée qu'en 1980 (!) par Mitsou Ronat et Tibor Papp (Paris, Change errant/d'atelier, avec un essai important de Mitsou Ronat).

26 Bruce Nauman, *Exhibition catalogue and catalogue raisonné,* Walker Art Center, Minneapolis, 1994, 155.

27   Les couleurs demanderaient une interprétation supplémentaire: plus encore que les
      lignes, elles introduisent le style individuel, c'est-à-dire ce qui dépasse le caractère
      dénotatif de l'image.

28   Cy Twombly constitue un cas particulier parce que ses tableaux ne (re)présentent pas
      des caractères imprimés mais une écriture personnelle. Roland Barthes souligne à
      juste titre ici l'importance du *geste* corporel dans son rapport avec l'écriture (*L'obvie et
      l'obtus – Essais critiques III,* Paris, Seuil, 1982, 145-62).

29   Pour les artistes cités ici, voir les catalogues mentionnés à la note 11.

30   À côté d'installations lumineuses, Jenny Holzer propose souvent des maximes pré-
      sentées selon une typographie extrêmement simple et dont l'ordre alphabétique n'est
      pas sans rappeler l'acrostiche. Voici quelques exemples pris au hasard: *Decadence can
      be an end in itself – Humanism is obsolete – It is heroic to try to stop time – Labor is a life-
      destroying activity – Morals are for little people – People are boring unless they are extremists
      – Private property created crime – Sin is a means of social control – You must know where
      you stop and the world begins.* Pour une interprétation de cette œuvre, voir p. ex. le
      catalogue de l'exposition de Düsseldorf, présenté par Marie Luise Syring (1990) ou
      le livre de Michael Auping (*Jenny Holzer,* New York, Universe, 1992).

31   Je pense ici bien entendu à l'ekphrasis classique, celle de Philostrate, qui décrit pres-
      que uniquement des scènes mythologiques, c'est-à-dire des narrations.

32   Voir Jacqueline Planchié, *La mode du portrait littéraire en France, 1641-1681,* Paris,
      Honoré Champion, 1994.

33   Pour l'autonomie de l'image, voir entre autres Gottfried Böhm, "Zu einer Hermeneutik
      des Bildes", in: Hans-Georg Gadamer & Gottfried Böhm, éds., *Die Hermeneutik
      und die Wissenschaften,* Francfort, Suhrkamp, 1978, 444-71; et Hans Holländer, "Bilder
      als Texte, Texte und Bilder", in: J. Zimmermann, éd., *Sprache und Welterfahrung,*
      Munich, 1978, 269-300.

The Ekphrastic Figure of Speech

Tamar Yacobi

Ekphrasis is generally considered a literal mimesis of its art-object. In practice, however, ekphrasis often doubles as a figure of speech (a metaphor, a simile, etc.), thus compounding various levels and modes of representation. "The woman smiles like the Mona Lisa", is an everyday case in point. Here the ekphrastic source, Leonardo's famous painting, is not only re-presented in the verbal medium. It also operates as a vehicle within a simile, representing a first-order world, namely, the woman who smiles enigmatically. In the ekphrastic figure of language, then, ekphrasis and figurality meet, as do the corresponding fields of research.

The question is what such an intersection entails, signifies, performs within the literary text or its reading. Where, for example, does the composite whole overlap or exploit, where does it outshine, either of its components? What does the ekphrasis gain in assuming the shape of a figure? Conversely, how can the figure profit from an ekphrastic (rather than purely verbal) analogue to its subject?

To take the clearest type of figuration, simile is a two-term analogy in which a subject or "tenor" is explicitly compared to a "vehicle": "My love" as tenor in Burns, to "a red, red rose", as vehicle; "the woman [who] smiles" in my simple example, to "the Mona Lisa". Among the constants involved here, note the form's ontological dualism. Though tenor and vehicle are coupled in the given language, they do not refer to the same "world", the same domain of existence. Existentially, the tenor is part of the (fictive) reality presented in the text; while the vehicle, qua figure *of speech,* belongs to another reality, one introduced only by, for, and through the comparison, i.e. as part of the intentionality and discourse of the simile-maker. Thus "My love" and "the woman [who] smiles" exist within the worlds of Burns and my example, respectively; while the "the red, red rose" or "the Mona Lisa" are brought to bear on them, as a matter of discursive similitude, from without the represented reality. But in the reading, we are invited to draw each pair into unity.

Like the simile, ekphrasis entails a relation between domains, with a fundamental variance in both the domains and their relation. Here, first of all, the two domains (the representing vs. the represented) belong to two media (verbal vs. visual), or two art-forms (literary vs. graphic). These ekphrastic constraints contrast with the figure's representational license, whereby both the tenor and the vehicle remain open slots: anything may be compared to anything, including cabbages and kings. The opposition in the freedom of choice extends to the medium. Where the figure boasts semiotic unity, ekphrasis entails semiotic bi-polarity. The one is essentially all language, the other is language replacing and "crossing" a sign-system outside language.

Second, even the figure's two-worldness, or what I called its ontological duality, recurs here with a multiple difference. In simile, one domain (e.g. the red rose's) is introduced to represent another domain (e.g. that of "My love"), which counts as basic or first-order – brute reality, so to speak, within the poem's context. In ekphrasis, however, the represented as well as the representing domains are representations of an object: Keats' ode, for instance, in rendering the Grecian Urn, renders afresh what the Grecian Urn has supposedly rendered already, by its own pictorial means and for its own aesthetic ends. By appeal to Meir Sternberg's comprehensive theory of "quotation" as discourse about discourse ("Polylingualism", "Proteus", "Point of View" and "How In-direct Discourse Means"), we can precisely trace the ekphrastic chain of mimesis: the ode does not so much represent (simile fashion) as re-present, cite, allude to what and how the Urn *im*-mediately represents. Like all "quotation", therefore, ekphrasis bundles together no less than three, rather than two, domains: one first-order, strictly "represented"; one second-order, "representational" in the visual mode; one third-order, "re-presentational" in the linguistic discourse.

This distinctiveness of ekphrasis stretches to part-whole relations. The visual source transforms in verbal re-imaging from a self-contained whole into a part of another whole, hence from end to means. Thereby it comes to signify in a new way and to serve new purposes, determined by the writer's frame of communication. Even if Keats' re-presentation of his Grecian Urn extended to every word of the poem and to every feature of the object, the title "Ode" would nevertheless be enough to subordinate the givens to distinctively literary coordinates of meaning, e.g. thematic or generic, just as the shift in medium would impose on them the (re-)presentational features and resources of language. By contrast, in the unquoted figure, no matter how subordinate the vehicle is to the tenor – the "red rose" to the "love" – both still essentially remain parts of a single and all-linguistic whole.

We can now begin to appreciate what happens in the ekphrastic figure, where the assorted lines of divergence all twist round into convergence. For example, the intersemiotic image doubles as a speech-"image", the target as tenor and the inset source as vehicle, the allusive re-presentation as a figurative representation, complete with the suitable priorities of meaning and effect. The intersection thus opens new issues of ekphrasis as it underlines and revitalizes more familiar ones. What, to repeat my opening questions, does the ekphrastic allusion gain from its restructuring within the frame of a similitude? How does the simile benefit from an ekphrastic vehicle?

Elsewhere I already outlined some answers, e.g. regarding the ways the ekphrastic figure crosses pictorial vividness with verbal density ("Verbal Frames"). Here I want to show how literature can multiply such figures in order to compound these and other effects, especially through the multiple interplay of opposites unified: repetition vs. variation, similarity vs. sequentiality, space vs. time, descriptiveness vs. narrative development. Such compound effect may result from a variety of sequential developments. Observe how a figure of speech evolves in concert along two lines: toward ever-greater ekphrastic salience and narrative functionality.

In Isak Dinesen's tale 'The Monkey,' a matchmaking old lady angrily comments on the heroine's rejection of her nephew and protégé:

> "What is it she wants to be? .... A stone figure upon a sarcophagus – in the dark, in silence, for ever?" (137)

The metaphor "A stone figure upon a sarcophagus" generalizes the re-presented object to the lower limit of ekphrasis. "A stone figure" is so indefinite as to leave it uncertain whether the "figure" is human, let alone whether it is male or female, allegorical or imitative of whoever is buried underneath. To underline the visual source of the metaphor, Dinesen indeed anchors the figure in a thicker spatio-temporal context: "upon a sarcophagus – in the dark, in silence, for ever". The reader, however, is still "in the dark", for a statue hidden beyond contact loses its raison d'être as art-object. But this paradox of hidden visuality, I will argue, is also the first stage in the evolution of this figurative "figure" into a richer ekphrastic life as well as into multiple psychological and narrative functionality.

The very marked absence of both visual and auditory contact, "in the dark, in silence", suggests that such divorce need not, or will not, be "for ever". The figure's vehicle evokes the motif of the artwork which, buried with its generation, has disappeared from sight; and its tenor amounts to the proverbial heart of stone. Two topoi in one, at one, on different levels of existence and meaning. By their joint rationale, therefore, the lost object may always be retrieved, the stony heart melt, in the narrative future. Our expectations accordingly spring to life, nor is their narrative potential confined to the mere foreshadowing of plot reversal. The suggestiveness of the figure of the buried art-object extends to a more visual drama: for how would its re-appearance affect its prospective viewers, the rejected suitor above all?

Even as it brings home the meagreness of ekphrastic detail, the question opens up visual possibilities for the narrative future. These are actualized in a later scene that repeats the metaphor with certain variations, including an ascent in definiteness. The rejected suitor, Boris, surprises the girl, Athena, in her bedroom, and a deadly struggle ensues. Athena, who has been brought up like a young man, fights back, to the verge of victory. Then Boris inadvertently touches her lips with his, and, as if thunderstruck, she falls down unconscious. In the eyes of her assailant

> She was indeed now like a stone effigy of a mail-clad knight, felled in battle.
> (Dinesen 154)

Formally, the interworld analogy entailed by the device rises in explicitness: from metaphor to simile between the fictional human agent ("She") and the artwork ("like ..."). Quantitatively, compared with the earlier "stone figure", the vehicle of similitude is more detailed. Therefore, in genre, it also grows more determinately ekphrastic, because the catch-all "figure" has narrowed down into an "effigy": a replica or portrait, which is further defined by its humanity, maleness, profession, attire, and fate. If all ekphrasis re-presents a representation and if all analogy likens separate domains, then the vehicle of figurative likeness now re-re-presents in sharper detail an artwork that claims representational likeness to *its* object. Furthermore, the second ekphrastic analogy carries over the stone and death attributes, with cumulative results. All the more so because the recurrence doubles as a narrative sequence: the old lady's "What is it she wants to be?" stands to the nephew's "she was indeed" as a rhetorical question to an enacted answer, a foreshadowing to a fulfilment. In organized linear perception, therefore, we mount the effigy of the simile "upon the sarcophagus" of the earlier metaphor.

Given the evolving figuration of the stone "figure", this twofold pictorial montage is relatively specific. Even so, the reference is not to a particular artwork, but to what I call an *ekphrastic model:* the common denominator of several visual artworks (Yacobi, "Pictorial Models"). Here, the model rests on a sculptural cliché, the statue of a dead hero. All too familiar, the "stone effigy of a mail-clad knight" on the tomb is meant to signify the essential characteristics and story of the buried knight: his valor and death in battle. However, the more continuous, elaborate and stereotyped the ekphrastic vehicle, the more incongruous the figuration seems. For why would an unconscious girl, who has just been attacked by a rejected suitor, be compared so insistently to a dead male knight in his tomb, let alone to "a stone figure/effigy" of one *upon* the tomb?

In context, the reader is less surprised. Not only has Athena fought courageously, like a knight. The ekphrastic simile is also in character. As implied by her mythological name, she has been brought up to deny her femininity, to live and fight like a man. When Boris touches her lips, he forces on her an unprecedented awareness of her sexuality, and she faints with rejection and disgust. Her male animus has fallen in the battle, and since she would not acknowledge her femininity, she has turned – figuratively – into stone. Thus the repetition and amplification of the figure of similitude helps us to equate her denial of marriage with her denial of her born self. Hence also the recourse to ekphrastic rather than first-order similitude, to the knight's stone "figure/ effigy" rather than his bloody corpse: unlike him, who has fulfilled himself and now lies petrified in perpetuity after a suitable death to gain an afterlife, she has never been alive, so far at least. Unity goes with variety, similarity across worlds brings out diversity. As typical of complex literary figuration, the analogy implies more or other than it says – and precisely due to its ekphrasticness.

For a related general lesson, notice how the present ekphrastic analogy counters the value-laden *interart* analogy drawn by theorists like Murray Krieger and Wendy Steiner: the frozen stasis of the visual art-object, they believe, is envied and imitated in literary ekphrasis. Our ekphrastic figuration disconfirms in miniature this imagined ekphrastic law, for it rather emphasizes the negative aspects of stasis (for elaboration see Yacobi, "Pictorial Models" 615-17). Athena's unconscious body, analogized to a stone effigy, is the icon of physical defeat and psychological repression, of overall death *in* rather than after life. Further, the stasis is here momentary, if not illusory, because of its multiple latent narrativity. Even the vehicle of the fallen knight smuggles into the given static picture the whole story of his valor, battle, injury, and death, all prior to the setting of his effigy on his tomb. (Were it not a figure of speech, the effigy could be said to envy the narrativity of language.) Once we turn from vehicle to tenor, from the effigy of the dead knight to the unconscious girl, the supposed stasis bristles with dynamic narrative implications for the future as well as for the past. Most immediately, when Athena wakes up, how will she react? And how will both the insight gained into her nature and the sight of her response affect the dramatic viewer, as suitor and/or subject? For these developments, I refer you to the tale itself; but wherever they lead, it is certainly towards my counter-rule of ekphrasis, here encapsulated: precisely because the ekphrastic simile is a figure of speech, later events may always "resurrect" its tenor.

Multiple narrative evolution is only one way of turning the recurrent or composite ekphrastic figure to rich literary account. Such figures may also group together to complicate each other's effect in tense juxtaposition. The focus of my second point, accordingly, shifts from the dynamics of sequence along a figurative chain to the play of equivalence and difference within a figurative cluster. An example would be how the combination of an ekphrastic with an ordinary figure of speech enriches the meaning and impact of a short poetic stretch.

Here is Browning's dying Bishop begging his so-called nephews to carry on his plan for the ornamentation of his tomb. They are to place between the knees of his effigy

> Some lump, ah God, of *lapis lazuli*,
> Big as a Jew's head cut off at the nape,
> Blue as a vein o'er the Madonna's breast ...
> (Browning, 1951:113)

The formal structure is that of a double closed simile ('a' is like 'b$_1$' in bigness, and like 'b$_2$' in blueness). The doublet, however, conjoins two modes of similarity on different levels of representation: the one standard, first-order, the other ekphrastic, second-order. Their criteria for analogy, or comparability, also seem to vary, in the degree of shock effect they tolerate. The ekphrastic analogy between the colors of a semi-precious stone and of a detail within a religious painting – "a vein o'er the Madonna's breast" – is somewhat odd, if not blasphemous, especially for a Bishop; the use of "a Jew's head cut off at the nape" as a vehicle and measure of the "lump's" size appears simply outrageous in its brutality.

This first impression of multiple incongruity among the terms of likeness is true, yet limited, since it ignores part/whole relations. Globally, we have to take into account the twofold communicative structure of the monologue, with the Renaissance Bishop addressing his relatives in the fictional arena, and Browning silently affecting his nineteenth century readers from his authorial vantage point behind the Bishop's back. Locally, the oppositions in value are complicated through the juxtaposition of the two similes within one intricate figurative whole.

To start with the fictional hero-speaker, his characteristics in both roles motivate the composite simile. To describe his magnificent stone with due exactitude, the Bishop resorts to figuration, showing himself either blind or indifferent to the offensiveness of his vehicles. This is suggested in the extreme formal symmetry of the couplet,

> Big as a Jew's head cut off at the nape,
> Blue as a vein o'er the Madonna's breast ...

The two lines begin with a stressed voiced labial sound, "Big", "Blue", whose sensuousness is in context almost expressive of a kiss. Notice also the syntactic near-identity of the couplet, down to particulars. Moreover, the chiasm of "Jew's head" and "Madonna's breast" underlines how their similarity extends to the semantics, as terms that co-refer to parts of the human body.

Coming from the epicurean Bishop, all these formal harmonies imposed on sharp existential disharmony signify his exclusive concern with the beauty and size of his lovely stone. Either simile is developed to capture another aspect of the stone. For the Bishop, "Big as a Jew's head cut off at the nape" primarily serves to express magnitude: the anti-semitic undertone gets thrown in as a fringe benefit, with no ideological any more than ethical strings attached. Nothing impedes, therefore, the transition to the ekphrastic model, either, in quest of a color term: "Blue as a vein o'er the Madonna's breast ..." An apparent jump from the enemy's camp to his own, the follow-up simile is a return to his only true adoration: beautiful *objets d'art*. His choice of vehicle from a conventional sacred painting relates to his obsessive fixture throughout the monologue on having his tomb decorated. Focusing on a painterly detail, the Bishop elevates the manner above the religious subject-matter. The eye of a connoisseur – and the Bishop is one – would judge the realism of a painting by the rightness of the blue that depicts the vein under the finely transparent skin; and so would this eye judge the beauty of the *lapis lazuli* upon the tomb.

The sacredness of the whole visual model matters as little to the simile-maker as did either the heresy or the humanity of the Jew in the twin analogy. And as with value schemes, so with representational levels: direct mimesis and ekphrasis, life's world and art's, are yoked together by violence, not so much thoughtlessly as single-mindedly. Small wonder he reduces the antagonism of Judaism and Christianity to the neat linguistic chiasm of two bodily synecdoches. And that chiasm in its turn becomes his means for conveying the material attributes of the envisioned lapis lazuli. It is due to vignettes such as this couplet that Browning was praised by Ruskin for embodying in his Bishop "the Renaissance spirit, – its worldliness, inconsistency, pride, hypocrisy, ignorance of itself, love of art, of luxury, and of good Latin".

So, within the monologue's overall communication structure, the dramatic monologist gets characterized by his ways of characterizing the stone. However, behind the Bishop's back and in contact with his own audience, ourselves, Browning makes the same representational choices, but for a different rhetorical purpose. His goal is to complicate the reader's reaction to the versatile speaker, to disable a black-and-white effect, whereby the complacent reader judges an immoral prelate. Indeed, the intricacy of the desired attitude motivates the intricacy of our double simile.

Reconsider the first simile from the authorial perspective. The line opens with an anti-semitic stereotype descriptive of the lump's size ("Big as a Jew's head"). But the sequel "cut off at the nape" adds information that is novel, vivid, shocking, and redundant all at once – so much so as to give an impression that the beheading is executed now, while we read the second half of the line. Browning thus exploits the temporality of language to foreground the decapitation and accordingly the callousness of the speaker. If Robert Langbaum defines the dramatic monologue by its balance of sympathy and judgment, then surely at this point judgment outweighs sympathy. Yet not for long, because right at this point the ekphrastic Christian simile joins the cavalierly anti-semitic. In linear conjunction, the first part of the second simile, "Blue as a vein", follows so hard upon the previous shocking comparison that for a moment the "*blue*" appears to be "red" with *bl*ood flowing from the "vein" of the "head cut off". With this further development of the repulsive likeness, the Bishop's image seems to go from bad to worse. Learning, however, that the "vein" is part of another human organ and body, a pictured body at that, the reader's predicament is newly defined. The ekphrastic simile conveys a familiar pictorial model: the serene Madonna, herself multiply incompatible with the anti-semitic stereotype, and thus charged with judgment. The Bishop, however, is not concerned with the pictorial model as a whole but with one subtle detail, "a vein o'er the Madonna's breast". His precise allusion, I would claim, speaks to the connoisseur in us. Our moral abhorrence of his joining the two similes together is thus tempered by our understanding – if not enjoyment – of the artist-like finesse. Aesthetics both counterpoints and counterbalances ideology: the monologue's poetics in a nutshell.

In this paper I have introduced the ekphrastic figure of speech as a distinctive, though by no means uncommon, juncture of word-image relations. At the intersection of figurality (e.g., simile) and ekphrasis, the former's analogy between two existential domains (tenor vs. vehicle) compounds the latter's trio of domains (represented object ⇒ visual representation ⇒ verbal re-presentation). With ekphrasis doubling as the simile's vehicle, and the link of similitude as part of a chain of (re)presentation, the effects join forces to match. Some of these functional interplays have been exemplified. First, a figure of speech evolves with variations along a tale by Isak Dinesen into a figurative chain, so as to compound ekphrastic with narrative dynamism. Second, the juxtaposition of an ekphrastic with a regular simile (in a passage from a Browning dramatic monologue) enables the rich play of equivalence and difference within a figurative cluster. As this play reflects the monologue's generic tension between the speaker's and the author's discourse, the ekphrastic simile here becomes a microcosm of the whole's significance, effect, and art.

References

Browning, Robert. *Selected Poetry of Robert Browning*. Ed. Kenneth L. Knickerbocker. New York: Random House, 1951.

Dinesen, Isak. *Seven Gothic Tales*. New York: Smith and Haas, 1934.

Krieger, Murray. "*Ekphrasis* and the Still Moment of Poetry; or, *Laokoön* Revisited". *Perspectives on Poetry*. Ed. James L. Calderwood and Harold E. Toliver. New York: Oxford University Press, 1968. 323-48.

Langbaum, Robert. *The Poetry of Experience*. New York: Norton, 1963.

Steiner, Wendy. *The Colors of Rhetoric*. Chicago: Chicago University Press, 1982.

Sternberg, Meir. "How Indirect Discourse Means: Syntax, Semantics, Pragmatics, Poetics". *Literary Pragmatics*. Ed. Roger Sell. London: Routledge, 1991. 62-93.

———. "Point of View and the Indirections of Direct Speech". *Language and Style* 15 (1982): 67-117.

———. "Polylingualism as Reality and Translation as Mimesis". *Poetics Today* 2 (1981): 221-34.

———. "Proteus in Quotation-Land: Mimesis and the Forms of Reported Discourse". *Poetics Today* 3 (1982):107-56.

Yacobi, Tamar. "Pictorial Models and Narrative Ekphrasis". *Poetics Today* 16 (1995): 599-649.

———. "Verbal Frames and Ekphrastic Figuration". *Interart Studies: New Perspectives*. Ed. Erik Hedling, Ulla-Britta Lagerroth and Hans Lund. Amsterdam: Editions Rodopi B.V., 1997. 35-46.

Paintings, Prints and Photographs

Le titre à l'œuvre. Manet, modernisme et institutions

Leo H. Hoek

L'hypothèse sociologique que je voudrais défendre ici est que les changements de l'art sont entraînés par des modifications institutionnelles dans le champ artistique, déclenchées à leur tour par des transformations politiques et sociales.[1] J'illustrerai cette hypothèse par l'exemple de l'intitulation des œuvres d'art.

LE TITRE COMME MARQUE D'IDENTIFICATION ET CLEF DE L'INTERPRÉTATION

Le titre d'une œuvre d'art est perçu communément comme une directive elliptique, qui complète verbalement l'information iconographique contenue dans l'œuvre. Il présenterait à lui seul tout un programme pour l'interprétation et constituerait par là un pilier central du sens attribué à l'art. Tantôt, le titre paraît en effet révéler naturellement au spectateur la signification d'un tableau, comme dans la peinture académique, tantôt, il paraît suggérer un sens déviant ou même radicalement incompatible, comme dans la peinture surréaliste ou dans l'expressionnisme abstrait, tantôt encore il semble échapper à tout effort d'interprétation, comme dans les innombrables toiles intitulées *Composition, Improvisation,* ou *Peinture.*

Les questions qui ont le plus préoccupé les historiens de l'art et les sémioticiens également, sont toutes sans exception d'ordre essentialiste et se concentrent sur la définition des traits distinctifs du titre (cf. Genette, Hoek). Rarement, on a posé la question de savoir quel est le rôle des institutions dans la production des titres et quel est le rôle institutionnel que le titre joue lui-même.

LE TITRE COMME INSTRUMENT DE CONSÉCRATION DANS LA CRITIQUE D'ART

La forme sous laquelle l'œuvre d'art apparaît dans le discours est celle du titre et le discours contextuel où le titre fonctionne est appelé critique d'art, comprise dans un sens large comme tout commentaire sur l'art contemporain ou ancien. La critique d'art joue un rôle prépondérant dans le processus de valo-

Illustration 1. Eugène Delacroix, *Hamlet et Horace au cimetière,* 1839. Paris, Musée du Louvre.

risation de l'art, parce que les critiques d'art développent et utilisent des conceptions de l'art comme instruments pour interpréter et évaluer l'art (cf. Van Rees).

    Les critiques se servent de titres pour illustrer les conceptions de l'art qu'ils veulent défendre. La citation de titres fameux est un instrument puissant pour convaincre le public de la légitimité de la conception de l'art promue. En étayant à l'aide d'une conception de l'art la valeur artistique assignée à certaines œuvres et refusée à d'autres, les critiques d'art sélectionnent des noms d'artistes et consacrent les titres des œuvres qui appartiendront au canon artistique. La citation d'un titre fonctionne ainsi comme un instrument de consécration légitimant l'œuvre d'art intitulée.

INDUSTRIALISATION ET PROFESSIONNALISATION

La pratique actuelle de l'intitulation est le résultat de progrès marqués dans l'histoire de l'édition du livre et dans la condition sociale de l'écrivain et de l'artiste. La genèse du phénomène de l'intitulation de l'œuvre d'art s'explique

Illustration 2. Jacques-Louis David, *Les Funérailles de Patrocle,* 1779. Dublin, National Gallery.

comme le résultat de deux changements profonds dans le champ social et dans le champ culturel, à deux siècles de distance, à savoir l'invention de l'imprimerie au milieu du XVe siècle et la professionnalisation du statut de l'artiste (cf. Heinich) à partir du XVIIe siècle. L'imprimerie a rendu indispensable l'identification matérielle de l'œuvre. L'institution des Académies et les expositions régulières que sont les Salons des XVIIIe et XIXe siècles, ont institué un discours sur l'art, qui s'appuie lourdement sur les titres comme instruments pour désigner, interpréter et évaluer l'art.

LE TITRE INDICE DU SUJET REPRÉSENTÉ

Dans la tradition académique, diffusée dans l'enseignement de l'École des Beaux-Arts, et contrôlée par l'Académie, le choix et l'élaboration du sujet à peindre constituaient une phase décisive dans la création de l'œuvre d'art. Le titre donné ensuite au tableau était un indice certain du sujet et du genre, facilitant la classification artistique. Aussi, les Jurys de Salon se basaient-ils sur les titres des tableaux pour classer ceux-ci parmi les différents genres traditionnels de peinture (cf. Sfeir-Semler 298). Les titres shakespeariens (*Hamlet et Horace au cimetière,* 1839, ill. 1), goethéens (*Marguerite à l'église,* Salon de 1846) ou dantesques (*Dante et Virgile,* Salon de 1822) de Delacroix sont jugés typiques de la peinture romantique et les titres évoquant l'Antiquité inscrivaient les œuvres dans la tradition académique. Jusqu'à la fin du XIXe siècle, le choix du sujet, emprunté de préférence à l'Antiquité ou éventuellement à l'histoire nationale, a gardé son importance dans le contexte académique (cf. Vaisse 71-2).

Critiquer un tableau signifiait en général critiquer son sujet, indiqué par le titre. Ce titre devait satisfaire à deux exigences contradictoires. D'une part, le titre avait pour tâche d'indiquer et de légitimer le sujet représenté sur le tableau, en référant à la tradition historique, mythique ou religieuse, propre à la 'grande peinture'. La représentation postulait une équivalence entre la réalité historique et le sujet du tableau, exprimé dans un titre comme *Les Funérailles de Patrocle* (David, 1779, ill. 2). De tels titres narratifs permettaient aux spectateurs de reconnaître les personnages représentés et d'interpréter leurs actions; aux peintres ils permettaient d'afficher le genre des tableaux et de prouver ainsi leur conformité aux exigences formelles de l'Académie ou du Salon, quitte à rebaptiser leurs œuvres après la fermeture des portes du Salon, ce qui n'était pas rare (cf. White & White 77). D'autre part, le titre, de même que l'explication dans le livret, ne devait pas être indispensable à la bonne compréhension du tableau. On critiquait sévèrement ces titres qui étaient visiblement destinés à remédier à un manque de narrativité de la toile: la peinture devait parler pour elle-même. Des titres ouvertement explicatifs témoignaient d'un manque de confiance de l'artiste dans sa propre compétence à exprimer le sujet, ou bien ils prouveraient que le sujet choisi était trop obscur pour être spontanément reconnu et ne se prêtait donc pas à la peinture. Henri de Latouche, auteur littéraire et critique d'art, écrit dans le *Constitutionnel* à propos du Salon de 1819: "La peinture est un de ces arts évidents qui doivent se passer de secours étrangers", les "écriteaux" et les "pancartes" devraient être laissés au théâtre de boulevard (cité dans Wrigley 56). Plus répréhensible encore est le peintre qui ne réussit pas à éclaircir son sujet, même en l'expliquant dans le livret. Le critique ne lui épargne pas ses sarcasmes, écrivant:

> Que me fait que l'on ait imprimé dans un Catalogue: c'est ici la veuve d'Hector, si je ne vois qu'une femme ordinaire implorant la bonté du ciel en faveur d'un moribond? Je préfère l'adresse de ce Peintre, assez connu, qui prenait la peine d'écrire lui-même sur ses Tableaux: ceci est un coq. (cité *ibid.;* cf. David, *Andromaque pleurant Hector,* 1783, ill. 3)

Pour les critiques d'art du XIXe siècle, les mots de 'sujet', 'thème' ou 'titre' étaient des équivalents parfaits: en reflétant le sujet, le titre constituerait pour un tableau une qualité aussi indispensable qu'un sujet bien choisi, comme le savait aussi Fromentin, qui écrivait:

> En France, toute toile qui n'a pas son titre et qui par conséquent ne contient pas un sujet risque fort de ne pas être comptée pour une œuvre ni conçue ni sérieuse. (132)

Voyons maintenant comment le Modernisme – et notamment un peintre comme Manet – a réussi à miner l'intitulation académique traditionnelle.

Illustration 3.   Jacques-Louis David, *Andro-
maque pleurant Hector*, 1783. Paris, Musée du
Louvre.

LE MODERNISME DE MANET

On sait que les toiles de Manet refusent au spectateur toute information sur le
sens narratif de la scène représentée ou sur les affects des personnages. Ce n'est
pas que les éléments narratifs manquent, mais la logique narrative n'y est pas
suffisamment cohérente pour qu'on puisse en distiller une anecdote vraisem-
blable. Dans la peinture de Manet, la cohérence narrative des toiles académiques a fait place pour une visualité pure, c'est-à-dire la primauté de la plasticité
dans l'absence de toute intrigue narrative. La représentation des personnages
est réduite à leur présence picturale; et s'il y a intrigue, celle-ci est purement
visuelle. Les personnages ne sont pas des éléments d'une action narrative qui
les réunirait en spectacle dramatique éloquent, comme c'était le cas sur les
tableaux académiques. Ils ne se regardent pas mais, en apparence conscients de
la présence du peintre ou du spectateur, ils semblent momentanément inter-
rompre leurs activités pour participer à une scène de pose. La présence des
personnages est réduite à leur regard, à leur désir de se montrer, à être là comme
prétexte à la peinture. La prise de conscience par les personnages met à distance le spectateur. Celui-ci s'en trouve incapable d'attribuer à la scène représentée une signification narrative quelconque. Le sujet du tableau – des per-

Illustration 4. Edouard Manet, *Le Déjeuner sur l'herbe*, 1863. Paris, Musée d'Orsay.

sonnages dans une barque, sur un balcon, dans une chambre ou en plein air – est donné directement pour être retiré aussitôt: tous les repères qui auraient pu contribuer à l'interprétation narrative de la scène sont supprimés. Il ne reste qu'une indifférence à la signification du sujet. De manière comparable à Flaubert, Manet fait 'un tableau sur rien'.

On peut constater dans la peinture de Manet des traits typiquement modernistes: la prise de conscience par les personnages, regardant 'activement' le spectateur au lieu d'être vu par lui, et l'autoréflexion de l'artiste, représenté en spectateur et parfois figé comme un personnage sur la toile. La peinture de Manet défie une lecture réaliste et impose une lecture moderniste par son imprévisibilité narrative, par la réflexion du médium pictural, par l'autoréflexion de l'artiste, et par des réflexions discursives, comme la citation (de prédécesseurs et de l'histoire du champ), la parodie, l'ironie, et la mise en abyme. Nous pouvons supposer que le modernisme aura laissé ses traces non seulement dans la peinture de Manet mais aussi dans l'intitulation de ses toiles.

LES TITRES DE MANET

Les titres choisis par Manet font ressortir une déviance typiquement moderniste par les traits suivants: une relation problématique entre le spectateur et les personnages, une représentation à la fois contemporaine et énigmatique minant la représentation traditionnelle de l'homme, et une indétermination quant à la portée et les limites de l'œuvre. Manet paraît en effet avoir choisi ses titres de telle manière que les critiques d'art auraient de la peine à s'en servir pour interpréter et classer ses tableaux d'après les principales conventions académiques. Examinons de plus près quelques titres célèbres de Manet.

Une toile comme *Le Déjeuner sur l'herbe* (1863, ill. 4) avait tout pour déconcerter les critiques. Par l'imprévisibilité des rôles narratifs des personnages représentés, ce tableau manquait de sens reconnaissable pour le critique. En outre, il ne s'inscrit dans aucune des catégories traditionnelles de l'art: la représentation est contemporaine et exclut donc le tableau d'histoire, la scène est trop peu reconnaissable pour être un tableau de genre, et le groupe est bien trop curieux pour un portrait. Il est significatif que *Le Déjeuner sur l'herbe* s'intitulait d'abord *Le Bain*. C'est non seulement un titre 'cache-sexe' (Queneau), vraisemblablisant ce que la représentation pourrait avoir de scandaleux, mais le mot 'bain' suggère aussi le nettoyage auquel Manet a soumis la peinture académique et rappelle la 'purification' du champ artistique. Cette explication devient plus probable encore, quand on se souvient de *L'Œuvre* (Zola), où Claude Lantier se plaint de la noirceur des toiles de l'ancien Salon, "cuisiné au bitume", et s'exclame:

> Nom d'un chien, c'est encore noir! J'ai ce sacré Delacroix dans l'œil. Et ça, tiens! cette main-là, c'est du Courbet... Ah! nous y trempons tous, dans la sauce romantique. Notre jeunesse y a trop barboté, nous en sommes barbouillés jusqu'au menton. Il nous faudra une fameuse *lessive* ...." (*L'Œuvre* 103, je souligne)

> "Oui, notre génération a trempé jusqu'au ventre dans le romantisme, et nous avons eu beau nous débarbouiller, prendre des *bains* de réalité vivante, la tache s'entête, toutes les *lessives* du monde n'en ôteront pas l'odeur. (*L'Œuvre* 415, je souligne)

Dès 1867, Manet a exposé son tableau sous le nouveau titre *Le Déjeuner sur l'herbe*. Il a été signalé que l'aspect provocateur des titres de Manet réside dans la transgression qu'ils opèrent par rapport à la pratique d'intitulation académique courante (cf. Lilley 168). Ainsi *Le Déjeuner,* que nous présente Manet, est au fond bien trop frugal pour mériter ce titre, car, à part quelques fruits, les personnages n'ont manifestement mangé que des huîtres. Or, ces huîtres nous mettent sur la piste d'une interprétation érotique du tableau. On présume communément que cet aliment stimule la puissance sexuelle de l'homme. La

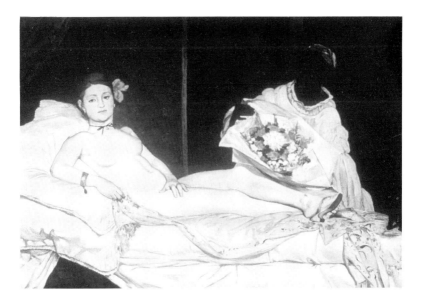

Illustration 5. Edouard Manet, *Olympia,* 1863. Paris, Musée d'Orsay.

connotation des huîtres prend du sens lorsqu'on sait que, dans un inventaire de ses tableaux et entre amis, Manet référait familièrement au *Déjeuner sur l'herbe* par *La Partie carrée*, c'est-à-dire une "relation sexuelle entre deux couples avec échange des partenaires" (*Nouveau Petit Robert* 1597), titre qui illumine tout de suite le sens érotique du tableau. Ce sens n'était pas inconnu des visiteurs du Salon des Refusés, à en juger d'après les réactions du public, rapportées par Zola dans *L'Œuvre,* où le tableau en question s'appelle *Plein air:*

> plein air, oh! oui, plein air, le ventre à l'air, tout en l'air, tra la la laire! Cela tournait au scandale... C'est cochon, oui, vous aurez beau dire, c'est cochon! (184-5)

Le titre de l'*Olympia* de Manet (ill. 5), exposé au Salon de 1865, n'était guère plus accessible à la critique contemporaine. La plupart des critiques désespéraient d'y trouver du sens narratif. La consonance classique du titre *Olympia,* désignant le sujet stéréotype de l'odalisque, le grand format du tableau et la citation implicite de Goya, Ingres et Titien devaient inciter les critiques à n'y voir qu'une de ces 'grandes machines' académiques dont le sujet était l'enjeu. Le titre est pourtant, à lui seul déjà, une infraction à cette attente: 'Olympia' (ou 'Olympe') n'est en effet pas un nom de déesse grecque mais un surnom fréquent de courtisane (cf. Clark 284-5, note 23). L'Olympia de Manet avait en effet la pose et les attributs – lit, servante, fleurs, animal de compagnie – des

Illustration 6. Edouard Manet, *Mlle V. en costume d'espada*, 1862. New York, Metropolitan Museum of Art.

nombreuses odalisques et Vénus exposées au Salon. Pourtant, le portrait d'une courtisane au lieu d'une Vénus n'était pas ce que les critiques attendaient du grand art. Le titre d'*Olympia* désinforme donc le spectateur. On a signalé aussi que des titres narratifs alternatifs ne seraient guère possibles pour l'*Olympia: Le Repos,* titre pourtant bien manettien, serait équivoque, *La Visite* serait un titre trop suggestif, *La Chatte* serait vulgaire, et *Le Bouquet* paraîtrait décentré (cf. Lilley 166). Pour une interprétation socioculturelle de l'*Olympia,* il aurait fallu un titre explicite impossible, tel que *Jeune fille moderne* ou *Portrait d'une courtisane.* C'était donc la lisibilité narrative qui posait aux critiques le plus grand problème.

Comme celui du *Déjeuner sur l'herbe,* le titre *Olympia* excelle donc par son opacité et sa neutralité narrative, tout en ayant l'air d'un titre anecdotique traditionnel.

L'autoréflexivité, cet autre trait du modernisme, se laisse lire dans plusieurs titres bien connus, qui trahissent tous la scène de pose: *Jeune femme étendue en costume espagnol* (1862), *Jeune homme en costume de majo* (Salon de 1863), *Couple en tenue de canotage* (1874), et *Mlle V. en costume d'espada* (1862, Salon de 1863, ill. 6). Au lieu d'intituler ce dernier tableau d'après le sujet représenté – une 'espada', c'est-à-dire le torero chargé de la mise à mort –, Manet nous révèle par son titre (... *en costume de* ...) qu'il a représenté non pas une espada mais un modèle, Mlle Victorine, déguisée en torero (cf. Lilley 166, Stoichita 88). Il souligne par son titre à la fois l'impossibilité de la représentation – l'espada n'étant bien sûr jamais une femme – et le rejet du sujet narratif comme enjeu de l'art – l'intérêt du tableau n'étant pas dans l'anecdote. Le tableau s'affiche dès le titre comme une mise en scène qui renvoie à la profession du peintre. Dans cette perspective, le geste élégant de l'espada, qui s'est détournée pour regarder fixement le peintre-spectateur, suggère la mise à mort non pas d'un taureau, d'ailleurs quasi absent, mais de la peinture académique périmée. En outre, l'arrière-plan du tableau est bien trop schématique pour représenter une véritable arène; Mlle Victorine pose, bien sûr, non pas dans une arène mais dans l'atelier devant l'image d'une arène, peinte d'après une gravure de Goya. Tout est faux dans ce tableau, et, cent ans plus tard Manet aurait pu appeler son tableau 'Ceci n'est pas une corrida'!

A titre de conclusion

Nous avons vu qu'au milieu du XIXe siècle l'éloquence univoque du titre académique transparent, qui "parlerait trop haut" (Mallarmé), a été remplacée par la déviance narrative du titre moderniste. L'artiste moderniste s'efforce de soustraire son œuvre à l'emprise sociale du marché tout aussi bien qu'à l'emprise institutionnelle académique. A cette fin, il abandonne progressivement la peinture anecdotique narrative et même, plus tard, toute figuration, pour adopter une peinture de plus en plus abstraite. La déviance narrative, qui marque nombre de titres modernistes, se muera dès la fin du siècle en antinarrativité résolue. Le modernisme se reflète dans l'emploi de titres moins ouvertement narratifs, voire carrément déviants, qui infirment la cohérence narrative de la représentation traditionnelle. Un peintre comme Manet a reflété le modernisme par son souci d'autoréflexion et de déviance narrative jusque dans le choix de ses titres.

Tout se passe comme si l'évolution historique des titres artistiques avait connu jusqu'à la fin du XIXe siècle deux phases: celle des Salons, marquée par la conformité des titres descriptifs et thématiques, et celle du champ artistique autonomisé, marquée par la déviance des titres modernistes. A l'origine, le titre est conforme, descriptif, thématique et révèle le sujet de la composition. Avec le modernisme le titre déviant commence à être utilisé pour désigner non seulement le sujet mais aussi la facture de l'œuvre. Les titres modernistes – impressionnistes, symbolistes et même cubistes – détournent le sens du tableau, en accentuant la déviance par rapport à la représentation apparente. L'autoréflexivité et la plasticité sont présentées dans les titres comme les véritables sujets de l'œuvre. Ces deux modes d'intitulation – par conformité ou par déviance – continuent à se référer, explicitement ou implicitement, à la représentation du contenu ou de la forme de l'œuvre d'art. Le même rapport représentatif qui existe entre le représenté et le représentant, existe aussi entre l'œuvre et le titre qui la désigne. L'évolution des modes d'intitulation, déclenchés à chaque fois par des changements institutionnels, illustre parfaitement les relations tantôt convergentes, tantôt divergentes, mais toujours passionnantes, entre les 'arts sœurs'.

NOTES

1   Pour une approche institutionnelle de l'œuvre d'art, nous renvoyons aux travaux sociologiques et anthropologiques de Pierre Bourdieu et aux travaux menés en histoire de l'art par Pierre Vaisse, Jean-Paul Bouillon, Dario Gamboni, Patricia Mainardi, Andrée Sfeir-Semler, Harrison C. White & Cynthia A. White, parmi d'autres.

LIVRES CONSULTÉS

Clark, T. J. *The Painting of Modern Life. Paris in the Art of Manet and his Followers.* Princeton (N. J.): Princeton University Press, 1984.

Fromentin, Eugène. *Les Maîtres d'autrefois.* P. Moisy éd., Paris: Garnier (Coll. Classiques Garnier), 1972.

Genette, Gérard. *Seuils.* Paris: Le Seuil, 1987.

Heinich, Nathalie. *Du peintre à l'artiste. Artisans et académiciens à l'âge classique.* Paris: Minuit, 1993.

Hoek, Leo H. *La Marque du titre. Dispositifs sémiotiques d'une pratique textuelle.* La Haye-Paris-New York: Mouton Editeur (Coll. Approaches to Semiotics 60), 1981.

Lilley, Ed "How far can you go? Manet's Use of Titles". *Word & Image* X, 2 (1994): 163-9.

Rees, Kees van. "How Conceptions of Literature are Instrumental in Image Building". Klaus Beekman ed., *Institution and Innovation.* Amsterdam-Atlanta GA: Rodopi, 1994. 103-29.

Le Nouveau Petit Robert. J. Rey-Debove & A. Rey éds. Paris: Dictionnaires Le Robert, 1994.

Sfeir-Semler, Andrée. *Die Maler am Pariser Salon 1791-1880.* Frankfurt/New York-Paris: Campus Verlag-Editions de la Maison des Sciences, 1992.

Stoichita, Victor I. "Manet raconté par lui-même". *Annales d'Histoire de l'Art et d'Archéologie de l'Université Libre de Bruxelles* XIII, 1991. 79-94.

Vaisse, Pierre. *La Troisième République et les peintres.* Paris: Flammarion, 1995.

White, Harrison C. & Cynthia A. White. *La Carrière des peintres au XIXe siècle. Du système académique au marché des impressionnistes.* Préface de J.-P. Bouillon. Paris: Flammarion (1ère éd. angl. 1965), 1991.

Wrigley, Richard. *The Origins of French Art Criticism.* Oxford: Clarendon Press, 1993.

Zola, Emile. *L'Œuvre.* Publié par A. Ehrard. Paris: Garnier-Flammarion, 1974.

The Painter Who Disappeared in the Novel:
Images of an Oriental Artist in European Literature

Shigemi Inaga

Marguerite Yourcenar's "Comment Wang-Fô fut sauvé", one of the famous episodes constituting *Les Nouvelles orientales,* ends with the supernatural disappearance of the painter into his own painting. A painted ship in a screen executed by Wang-Fô approaches the surface of the painting and finally comes out of it, flooding the hall where the screen has been set up. Wang-Fô climbs into the ship to return to the painting and finally he and the ship disappear far away into the painted sea ...

Contrary to the author's declaration, this short story is not directly based on a Chinese Taoist classic ("'Comment Wang-Fô fut sauvé' s'inspire d'un apologue taoïste de la vieille Chine") but seems to be based on a modern Japanese tale retold by Lafcadio Hearn (1850-1904). As Sukehiro Hirakawa has already pointed out (without yet being either recognized or accepted among Western scholars), Yourcenar must have read the French translation of Lafcadio Hearn's "The Story of Kwashin Koji", published in his *A Japanese Miscellany* (1901).[1] Hearn noted that the story is "related in a curious old book *Yasô Kidan*",[2] but this is misleading. Far from being an "old book", *Yasô Kidan,* or *Ghost Stories for the Night Lecture* was written by a contemporary Japanese writer Kôsai Ishikawa, and the first volume was published in 1889, the second in 1894. In Hearn's library (preserved at Toyama University) we find the second print of the first volume, republished in 1893, as well as the second volume which contains the original "Story of Kwashin Koji".

By insisting on this philological detail, I do not intend to accuse Yourcenar of concealing her real source in her post-scriptum. To pretend that Japan must be absolutely differentiated from China would be too nationalistic. Rather, I wish to elucidate the contrast in aesthetic tastes by comparing the Japanese original, Hearn's adaptation and Yourcenar's reappropriation.

I

The original Japanese text is characterized by a concision comparable to that of Chinese ghost stories such as *The Strange Stories of Liao Zhai* by Pú Sông-líng (1640-1715), by which Kôsai Ishikawa may have been inspired. Yet, we

have not discovered the Chinese source which Yourcenar claims to have con-
sulted.[3]

To give an idea of the final part of Kôsai Ishikawa's story I quote Hirakawa's
tentative literal translation from the pseudo-Chinese style Japanese in which
the story is written.

> There was a screen upon which were painted the Eight Beautiful Views of the
> Lake of Omi. A boat there was about an inch in length. Kwashin Koji then
> waved his hand, inviting it to come. The boat, wavering, drew nearer and glided
> out of the screen, and it grew as large as several feet long. At the same time, the
> water of the lake flooded the room, and all spectators were surprised, girding up
> their hakama robes in haste. They were standing up to their girdles in water.
> Kwashin Koji was now in the boat, and the fisherman calmly rowed the boat and
> they went away we know not where.[4]

The comparison with Hearn's adaptation demonstrates how Hearn amplified
this original into a vividly evocative *tableau-vivant* by carefully adding realistic
details suggesting the gradual approach of the boat such as: "Still the boat
drew nearer – always becoming larger – until it appeared to be only a short
distance away. And, all of a sudden, the water of the lake seems to overflow –
out of the picture into the room". The more realistic the depiction is, the more
supernatural the miraculous effect is. "The creaking of the single oar (and not
a pair of oars as in the West) could be heard" must be the reflection of the
visual and auditive memory of the days Hearn spent in the old Japanese town
of Matsué, on the shore of the Lake Shinji-ko. And Hearn adds what was
lacking in the original: "No sooner had the boat passed the apparent foreground of the picture than the room was dry again! But still the painted vessel
appeared to glide over the painted water – retreating into the distance, and
ever growing smaller – till at last it dwindled to a dot in the offing".

Yourcenar's reappropriation of such details, invented by Hearn, permits us
to suppose that Yourcenar read Hearn rather than referring to an unknown
Chinese original. For one thing she emphasizes the auditive effect: "Le bruit
cadencé des rames s'éleva soudain dans la distance, rapide et vif comme un
battement d'aile".[5] Then there is the sudden disappearance of the water after
the miracle: "Bientôt, ils (les courtisans) se trouveront à sec et ne se souviendront
même pas que leur manche ait jamais été mouillée". And when the boat returns to the picture, "Le niveau de l'eau diminuait insensiblement autour des
grands rochers verticaux qui redevenaient des colonnes. Bientôt, quelques rares
flaques brillèrent seules dans les dépressions du pavement de jade. Les robes
des courtisans étaient sèches, mais l'Empereur gardait quelques flocons d'écumes
dans la frange de son manteau".[6]

The main problem with Yourcenar's depiction resides in the position of

Figure 1. "Kwashin Koji, Tasogaregusa", illustration from
Yasô Kidan, vol. 2, 1894. Reproduced in Hearn (cf. n. 2).

the painting. In the first version she wrote: "Le rouleau achevé par Wang-Fô restait posé sur la table basse". But how can a ship emerge from the painting posed on a table? Confused, Machiko Tada, Japanese translator, changed the situation and described the painting as "being hung on the wall". Yourcenar herself changed this part in a later edition of 1979 in such a way that "le rouleau achevé par Wang-fô restait posé contre une tenture" (fig.1).[7]

II

In both cases, the passage from reality to the fiction of the painted world constitutes the main framework of the story. However, the reason why Hearn and Yourcenar were interested in the same plot seems divergent. Though relying on the same anecdote, the aesthetic messages are not compatible with each other.

The Kwashin Koji story is situated during the period of Tenshô civil war (1573-1591). At the beginning of the tale, Kwashin Koji shows a picture by Sôtan Oguri depicting the Buddhist hell to the Great Lord Oda Nobunaga (1534-82 – Nobunaga is one of the historical models of James Clavel's popular novel *Shôgun*).[8] "When Nobunaga saw the kakemono he was not able to conceal his surprise at the vividness of the work" explains Hearn, faithfully retelling the original story, "the demons and the tortured spirits actually appeared to move before his eyes; and he heard voices crying out of the picture;

and the blood there represented seems to be really flowing – so that he could not help putting out his finger to feel if the painting was wet [this is Hearn's invention]. But the finger was not stained – for the paper proved to be perfectly dry" (214).

After the demonstration, when Kwashin Koji leaves the palace, Arakawa, one of Nobunaga's retainers, secretly follows the old man. Taking the chance, he draws his sword, kills him, and takes the picture. "The next day Arakawa presented the kakemono to Oda Nobunaga, who ordered it to be hung forthwith. But when it was unrolled, both Nobunaga and his retainer were astonished to find that there was no picture at all – nothing but a blank surface". Accused of smuggling, Arakawa is confined. Scarcely has Arakawa completed his term of imprisonment, when the news is brought to him that Kwashin Koji was exhibiting the famous picture in the grounds of Kitano Temple. Arakawa can hardly believe his ears, but several days later, he finally succeeds in capturing the old man, who willingly follows Arakawa to be examined in court.

Examined by the chief officer at the court of the palace, Kwashin Koji makes the following strange declaration:

> In any picture of real excellence there must be a ghost; and such a picture, having a will of its own, may refuse to be separated from the person who gave it life, or even from its rightful owner. There are many stories to prove that really great pictures have souls. It is well known that some sparrows, painted upon a sliding-screen (fusuma) by Hôgen Yenshin, once flew away, leaving blank the spaces which they had occupied upon the surface. Also it is well known that a horse, painted upon a certain kakemono, used to go out at night to eat grass. Now, in this present case, I believe the truth to be that, inasmuch as the Lord Nobunaga never became the rightful owner of my kakemono, the picture voluntarily vanished from the paper when it was unrolled in his presence. But if you will give me the price that I first asked – one hundred ryô of gold – I think that the painting will then reappear, of its own accord, upon the now blank paper. (219-20)⁹

On hearing of these strange assertions, Nobunaga orders the hundred ryô to be paid and comes in person to observe the result. "The kakemono then unrolled before him; and to the amazement of all present, the painting has reappeared, with all its details. But the colors seems to have faded a little; and the figures of the souls and the demons do not look really alive, as before. Perceiving this difference, the lord asks Kwashin Koji who replies: "The value of the painting, as you first saw it, was the value of a painting beyond all price. But the value of the painting, as you now see it, represents exactly what you paid for it – one hundred ryô of gold.... How could it be otherwise?"

The metamorphosis of the picture according to the price people put on it suggests that the value of the painting changes according to the attitude the beholder (or holder) takes toward it. In this sense the artistic and fictional world is not totally transcendent and isolated from the real and vulgar world. Aesthetic contemplation does not necessarily exclude the participation of the common people. Clearly, there is a mutual relationship between them. Kwashin Koji himself, who "was always dressed like a Shintô priest, but [who] made his living by exhibiting Buddhist pictures and by preaching Buddhist doctrine", is not a hermit but a rather vulgar, insolent drunken old man who earns his living by "deluding people by [his] magical practices" of hypnotism.

In contrast Wang-Fô, figured by Yourcenar, seems to be a pure and unearthly aesthete. This painter-hermit has no interest in the worldly affairs. Wang-Fô "aimait l'image des choses, et non les choses elles-mêmes, et nul objet au monde ne lui semblait digne d'être acquis, sauf des pinceaux, des pots de laque et d'encres de Chine, des rouleaux de soie et de papier de riz". And even on finding himself seized, for a reason unknown to him, Wang-Fô is simply irritated by the lack of the color harmony of the clothing of the soldiers: "Les soldats ... posèrent lourdement la main sur la nuque de Wang-fô, qui ne put s'empêcher de remarquer que leurs manches n'étaient pas assorties à la couleur de leur manteau".

It is true that Wang-Fô has a supernatural power to enliven the painting. What is painted by him has more power than the usual creatures: "les fermiers venaient le supplier de leur peindre un chien de garde, et les seigneurs voulaient de lui des images de soldats". However, the following expression reveals the source of Yourcenar's inspiration: "On disait que Wang-Fô avait le pouvoir de donner la vie à ses peintures par une dernière touche de couleur qu'il ajoutait à leurs yeux". Here Yourcenar clearly demonstrates her knowledge of an old Chinese proverb, "with the last touch of finish on the eye, the painted dragon flew up to the sky".[10]

Instead of repeating the "animistic" explanation of the mysterious "life" and "soul" of the painting, as was declared by Kwashin Koji, Yourcenar prefers to remain faithful to the European tradition and respects the irreconcilable opposition between life and art: by imitating the antithetical contrast and opposition frequent in Chinese poetry, Yourcenar gives an androgynous image to Wang-Fô's disciple, Ling.

Depuis des années, Wang-Fô rêvait de faire le portrait d'une princesse d'autrefois jouant du luth sous un saule. Aucune femme n'était assez irréelle pour lui servir de modèle, mais Ling pouvait le faire, puisqu'il n'était pas une femme. Puis Wang-Fô parla d'un jeune prince tirant de l'arc au pied d'un grand cèdre. Aucun jeune homme du temps présent n'était assez irréel pour lui servir de modèle, mais Ling fit poser sa propre femme sous le prunier du jardin".

Figure 2. Léon Cogniet, *Tintoretto peignant sa fille morte*, 1843.
Oil on Canvas, 143 x 163 cm. Bordeaux, Musée des Beaux-
Arts.

And she adds: "Et la jeune femme pleura, car c'était un présage de mort." The
last phrase is almost superfluous, as every reader of "The Oval Portrait" by
Edgar Allan Poe already has a foreboding of her death. The following phrase
only reinforces this prediction: "Depuis que Ling préférait les portraits que
Wang-Fô faisait d'elle, son visage frémissait, comme la fleur en butte au vent
chaud ou aux pluies d'été". The reader already feels a certain *déjà vu:* the
hanging of Claude in Émile Zola's *l'Oeuvre*. And indeed this expectation will
not be disappointed. In the next phrase we read "Un matin, on la trouva
pendue aux branches du premier rose: les bouts de l'écharpe qui l'étranglait
flottaient mêlés à sa chevelure". Reminiscence of *Pelleas et Mélisande,* of course,
which will be repeated when the Imperial Hall was inundated by the magical
water: "les tresses des courtisans submergés ondulaient à la surface comme des
serpents, et la tête pâle de l'Empéreur flottait comme un lotus".

Wang-Fô thus paints the dead face of Ling's wife as if he were the direct
ancestor of Tintoretto painting her dead daughter's head, as in a famous painting by Léon Cogniet (fig. 2). While Ling is busy grinding the pigments for his
master: "cette besogne exigeait tant d'application qu'il oubliait de verser des
larmes", which recalls to our mind the famous anecdote of Claude Monet,
who was frightened by his own enthusiastic concentration when drawing his
dead wife Camille's face. In short, while borrowing an oriental setting and
flavour, Yourcenar evokes the European fin de siècle literary topos of artistic
fictional world living on the sacrifice of the real life, as is repeated in Oscar
Wilde's *The Picture of Dorian Gray.*

The invention of Ling as homosexual and androgynous disciple of Wang-Fô makes Yourcenar's separation from Hearn's interpretation decisively clear. When Ling was suddenly decapitated by the order of the Emperor (a happening which is also predictable), "Wang-Fô désespéré, admira la belle tache écarlate que le sang de son disciple faisait sur le pavement de pierre verte" (22). Such a visual aestheticism already predicts Yourcenar's affinity with Yukio Mishima's self-aestheticizing bloodshed and dramatization of the severed head as sacrifice and ordeal destined for European audience.[11]

In Hearn's story, it was Kwashin Koji who, by his own magic survived the attack by Arakawa. While in Yourcenar's version, it is Ling, who is miraculously resuscitated and appears as the boatman from inside of the painting: "c'était bien Ling ... Mais il avait autour du cou une étrange écharpe rouge". And hereafter, the relation between master and disciple is in a sense overturned. Ling seems to be already initiated to the secret of the fictional world in the painting to which Wang-Fô is apparently not yet accustomed. Once again, in Yourcenar's *œuvre romanesque* the absolute superiority of the artistic world over the real world is highlighted by the role of Ling who is dead in reality but alive – accordingly – in the painting.

Moreover, the reason why Wang-Fô was honored by a death sentence from the Emperor, "le Maître Céleste", was that his paintings was more beautiful than the real world in which the Emperor reigns, and that the Emperor, as a child, took Wang-Fô's painting for the real world:

> [T]u m'as menti, Wang-Fô, vieil imposteur: le monde n'est qu'un amas de taches confuses, jetées sur le vide par un peintre insensé, sans cesse effacées par nos larmes. Le royaume de Han n'est pas le plus beau des royaumes, et je ne suis pas l'Empereur. Le seul empire sur lequel il vaille la peine de régner est celui où tu pénètres, vieux Wang, par le chemin des Mille Courbes et des Dix Mille Couleurs. Toi seul règnes en paix sur des montagnes couvertes d'une neige qui ne peut fondre, et sur des champs de narcisses qui ne peuvent pas mourir. (21)

III

Such was Yourcenar's pseudo-oriental aestheticism and escapist retreat into an isolated fictional world of art. Do the Japanese contemporary comic creators try to deliver the same message in their reinterpretation of the same plot? Let us examine briefly three examples, following Inuhiko Yomota's fine analysis.

Sampei Shirato, one of the emblematic figures in the cold-war period of Japanese comics faithfully depicts Kwashin Koji's story (fig. 3). Here, the lack of stylistic distinction in comics between the panel-painting (executed by the

 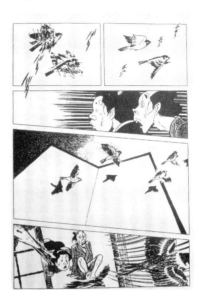

Figure 3 (left). Sanpei Shirato, "Myôkatsu" [1963], *Taima no Garo,* vol.1, Tokyo: Shôgakkan, 1992. (Source: Inuhiko Yomoda). Figure 4 (right). Kazuo Uemura, *Kyôjin kankei,* vol. 4, Tokyo: Sêrindô, 1978. (Source: Inuhiko Yomoda).

painter named Sensui) in the image and the image itself (executed by Shirato himself) blurs the demarcation between reality and fiction. As a result we do not know when the seascape in the comics is supposed to be transformed into real sea, or if the water flooding the hall belongs to reality or not as depicted in the comics. In comics, the distinction between different levels of realities can easily be erased. The depicted panel painting, for example, is no less (and no more) real than the depicted comic characters who are contemplating it. Both of them are simply ink images on paper. In this fictional framework, the supposed reality is easily confused with fictional phenomena, thus creating delusions and illusions. Readers are trapped in the *trompe l'œil* and can be manipulated at the mercy of the author's narrative strategy.[12]

The next example is taken from *Kyôjin-Kankei, [La Liaison folle]* (1978) by the late Kazuo Uemura, who pretended to be a modern ukiyo-e master and has prematurely disappeared. The story narrates Hokusaï's life as a painter. In the last scene of the story of more than one thousand pages (fig. 4), the painted birds fly away from the screen on which they have been depicted. Uemura clearly and deliberately repeats the famous anecdote of the sparrows flying away from the scroll Kwashin Koji was evoking. But their disappearance does in no sense suggest the magical power of the painting. Instead of indicating the immortality or eternity of the art, this ending simply emphasizes the mer-

Figure 5. Yoshiharu Tsuge, "Chîko", Yoshiharu Tsuge zenshû, vol. 4, Tokyo: Chikuma Shobô, 1993. (Source: Inuhiko Yomoda).

ciless mutability, fugitiveness and transient ephemerality of the floating world *(ukiyo)*.

Finally, Yoshiharu Tsuge's case (fig. 5) is a more ironic and subtle reappropriation of the same plot. "Chîko" (1966) is a story of the break-up of a young couple in *concubinage*. The paddy-bird, named "chîko" depicted here was a symbol of their tie. A poor and unsuccessful comic writer has killed the bird by accident and feels guilty of it *vis à vis* his partner. The morning following the incident, he is surprised and terrified to find the bird (as if) alive in the bush. In reality, however, the bird in question was nothing but a drawing he has made of it, which his partner has set in the bush to surprise him. Of course, the reader of the comics cannot distinguish the bird supposed to be alive in the comic from the drawing depicted in the comics itself.

But in the comic's reality, how is it possible that the characters can mistake a drawing in black and white for the real paddy bird? It becomes clear, then that "he" is not surprised by the illusion "we" are caught by; on the contrary, we recognizes now that "he" is shocked by the mischievous joke his partner has invented. And this joke was not intended for "him" at all, but, surprisingly enough, it was exclusively intended for "us", the readers of this story who are not capable of distinguishing the "real" bird from its drawing in the comics. This insolent intrusion of the fictional world into the readers' mind, provoking a sense of the uncanny (Freud's *das Unheimliche*), was the omen of the couple's approaching separation, which was also the end of the story.

This complicated double deceptive delusion, illusion and disillusion, is a device specifically elaborated in the conflict of grammar and rhetoric of the comics out of the yoke – and out of the order – of the classical Western aesthetics of *mimesis*.

To conclude, let me quote from Louis Gonse reporting in 1884 a naive

observation made by an (imaginary) Japanese commentator on the retrospective exhibition of paintings by Édouard Manet. "Je m'imaginais au premier
moment que les personnages prenaient corps et allaient sortir de la toile pour
me parler; sensation que j'ai rarement éprouvée dans vos expositions de
peinture".[13] Can this anecdote be reduced to the Pygmalion complex? Is the
East-Asian aesthetics of *animation,* which believes in the animating and ani-
mated souls or the ghosts living in (and out of) the painting, compatible with
the aesthetics of representation, where fiction and reality seem to remain irreconcilable with, if not impenetrable to, each other, as was the case with
Yourcenar's story on Wang-Fô?[14] Did Yourcenar find something different in
her last "Tour de la prison" to the country where comics and animations refuse
to be confined to the realm of pure fiction, but incessantly transgress the limit
between truth and fiction, as was problematized by the seventeenth century
Kabuki marionette scénario writer, Monzaemon Chikamatsu? The questions
raised by these works cannot be answered here, requiring, as they do, fuller
investigation in a cross-disciplinary and cross-cultural perspective.[15]

NOTES

1   Sukehiro Hirakawa, "Animistic Belief and Its Use in Japanese Literature: The Final
     Disappearance of Kwashin Koji", in Kin'ya Tsuruta (ed.), *Nature and Self-hood in
     Japanese Literature,* Jôsai International University and Department of Asian Studies
     UBC, 1993, 79-85. The present paper is written as a reaction to Angelic Rieger's
     "*Comment Wang-fô fut sauvé* de Marguerite Yourcenar – ou le tableau qui sauve", in
     Jean-Pierre Guillerm (éd.), *Récits/tableaux,* Lille: Presses universitaires de Lille, 1994,
     201-14.

2   Lafcadio Hearn, *The Writings of Lafcadio Hearn,* Boston and New York, Houghton
     Mifflin Company MDCCCXXII, Volume X, 213 sq.

3   A similar anecdote attributed to the painter Wu Tao-Tsu in the Tang Dynasty is
     related in Arthur Waley's *Introduction to the Study of Chinese Painting,* in 1923, which
     Yourcenar could have consulted. On the political implications of the use of Chinese
     in Japan, see Naoki Sakai's paper presented at the 1996 Dublin IAWIS conference:
     "Calligraphic Aspects of eighteenth-century Japanese Writing".

4   The English translation is by Sukehiro Hirakawa. The original text is reproduced in
     the appendix of Yakumo Koizumi, *Kaidan, Kitan* (ed. by Sukehiro Hirakawa), To-
     kyo: Kôdansha Gakujutsu bunko, 1990, 425-9. It is indeed still an open question as
     to whether Kôsai Ishikawa, as a prolific commentator on Chinese classical poems of
     the Tang and Sun Dynasties (with the publication of 16 volumes on the subject),
     had not been inspired by some Chinese sources, such as the *Strange Stories of Liáo
     Zhai* by Pú Sông Líng (1640-1715), for example.

5   Marguerite Yourcenar, *Oeuvres romanesques,* Gallimard, 1982, 1143-53.

6   This could be an allusion to a famous poem by Wáng Châng Líng (698-755) which evokes a crystal heart.

7   Yourcenar also modified this part in her later edition for children. Cf. Sukehiro Hirakawa , "Kwashin-koji no shômetsu", in *Animizumu wo yomu,* Tokyo: Shinyô-sha, 1994, 86.

8   On this practice of pictorial exegesis, see Ikumi Kaminishi's paper on "Etoki: A Method of Pictorial Exegesis", presented at the 1996 Dublin IAWIS Conference.

9   One of the sources of this anecdote is attributed to the painter Kose no kanaoka (9th Century), related in *Kokonchomonjû.* See the useful compendium by Hiroshi Oonishi added at the end of the Japanese translation of *Die Legende vom Künstler,* by Ernst Kris and Otto Kurz, [1934], 1978; *Geijutsuka-Densetsu,* Tokyo: Pelican-sha, 1989.

10   The famous proverb finds its origin in Châng Sêng Yáo's anecdote in Southern Sun Dynasty, related in the *Documents on Masterpieces of Every Age,* many variants of which are widely known to exist among East-Asian cultures, including Japan.

11   By saying so, I infer that Mishima's aesthetics is not at all Japanese but a fabricated orientalist and *japonisant* image for Western consumption only, although such concern with the West (including China until the 19th century) is part of the Japanese tradition.

12   See the chapter "The magic of the paper" in Inuhiko Yomota, *Manga Genron [Prinpicia Manga-us],* Tokyo: Chikuma-shobô, 1994, 63-9; Sanpei Shirato's comic interpretation, first published in 1963, is now available in *Taima no Garo,* Tokyo: Kôdansha,1992, 284-6, where the author also combines another magical tale related to Kwashin Koji which in turn had given birth to Ryôtarô Shiba's short story "Kwashin Koji no genjutsu" [1961], now available in Ryôtarô Shiba, *Kwashin Koji no genjutsu,* Tokyo, Shinchô-sha, 1977, 8-47, where Ryôtarô Shiba evokes as a source *Kyojitsu-zôdanshû* (1625). For other related sources, see also the explanation by Hiroshi Nunomura in Yakumo Koizumi, *Kaidan, Kitan,* 347.

13   Louis Gonse "Manet", *Gazette des Beaux-Arts,* fév. 1884, 134.

14   "La Disparition d'Honoré Subrac" (1910), by Guillaume Apollinaire and "Le Passe-Muraille" (1943) by Marcel Aymée are examined by Hirakawa by way of comparison *(op. cit).* Vladimir Nabokov and Italo Calvino can be added, among others, to the list. A typical example of the simplified Western-Eastern dichotomy in aesthetics is criticized in Tomonobu Imamichi, "Mimesis and Expression: A Comparative Study in Aesthetics", in M.C. Doeser and J.N. Kraay (eds.), *Facts and Values: Philosophical Reflections from Western and Non-Western Perspectives,* Dordrecht: Martinus, Nijhoff, 1986. See also, Áron Kibédi Varga, "De Zeuxis à Warhol", *Protée,* printemps 1996, 101-9. The Zeuxis model must be confronted by Oriental counterparts, but here, of course, is not the place to do so.

15   The following task is to re-examine the theoretical reflections made by such authors as Paul Claudel, André Malraux, Donald Keen, Roland Barthes and Marguerite Yourcenar on the Japanese theatre, in reference to and by contrast with the aesthetics of *mimesis.* Cf. Patrice Pavis, "Intermédialité dans les spectacles vivants", read at the 1996 Dublin IAWIS conference, which gives suggestive insights into the problem.

A Reading of the Structures of *La Guerre* (1916) by Pierre Albert-Birot

Debra Kelly

> Et l'on commence avec les mains l'infini que l'on finit
> avec l'esprit ce cher compagnon qui sait tout faire
> jusqu'à nous-mêmes et nous conduit partout où personne
> n'ira jamais
>
> ....
>
> Et que l'on peut offrir à soi-même et à quelques autres
> dans un poème qui a l'air d'être fait de lettres
> assemblées en mots ordonnés sur du papier mais
> qui prend la forme du poète et de son infini
>
> Pierre Albert-Birot, "Huitième poème", *Poèmes à l'autre moi*

Pierre Albert-Birot (1876-1967) remains a figure largely unknown to the general reading public and neglected by the academic establishment. His work is now much better known in France due to the untiring work of his widow Arlette Albert-Birot and the Parisian publisher Jean-Michel Place[1]. Albert-Birot's artistic and poetic production covers the whole range of possible modes of expression: figurative painting and sculpture, still life, landscape, cubist and abstract canvases, experimental forms of what he called "la peinture absolue", conventional verse poetry, punctuated and non-punctuated poetry and prose, sound-generated poetry, visual poetry or "poésie plastique", translation, linear narrative in both the traditional novel and in more ambiguous form, theatre, autobiography, and criticism. The reasons for the "neglect" into which his work had fallen are multiple, although at the root seems to be Albert-Birot's own fiercely independent creative stance after the First World War, his dislike of "isms" and especially his mistrust of what would be the dominant "ism" of the period, Surrealism.[2]

The painting on which I will focus in this paper was finished in 1916, although it is clear from sketches and other productions related to the final oil on canvas that the painter/poet had been working and re-working this idea for some time in his notebooks in which he also prepared work for *SIC*. This painting is therefore produced both at a crucial point in the First World War (1916 is the year of Verdun and of the Somme and is the year in which both the military and popular perceptions of the war changed radically), and at a

Figure 1. Pierre Albert-Birot, *La Guerre,* 1916. Oil on canvas, 125.5 x 118 cm. Musée d'Art Moderne, CGP, Paris (catalogue number CAM 1977. 639).

crucial point for Albert-Birot's artistic development (he repeatedly insisted on his own "rebirth" with *SIC,* and an important element in his personal myth was his abandonment of painting for poetry after painting *La Guerre).* He had founded his literary and artistic journal *SIC* in January 1916, and this was published continuously from the beginning of 1916 until December 1919, thrusting Albert-Birot to the forefront of the avant-garde.[3] The journal was an important rallying point for the avant-garde which was frequently under attack during the war years from the artistic establishment.[4] The most frequent contributors included Apollinaire, Reverdy, Aragon, Tzara and the Italian Futurists, and the journal stood, as the poet himself has said, at the crossroads of Futurism, Dadaism and Surrealism, its pages also continuing to defend Cubism. The formative contact with Apollinaire, the great champion of Cubism, and a creative attitude developed through the visual arts, are of fundamental importance for all aspects of Albert-Birot's work. Poised between the old and new methods of creation at his disposal, it is in 1916 that the sculptor and painter completes his metamorphosis into poet. This abstract canvas, *La Guerre,* is crucial to this metamorphosis.

Albert-Birot came late to writing and poetry (he was forty in 1916) having trained as a sculptor and painter, and he continued to refer to the visual arts in his theoretical discourse on the artistic process throughout his life. If we compare *La Guerre* directly with *Grabinoulor,* the vast unpunctuated six-volume prose "epic" which is Albert-Birot's masterpiece, the two modes of expression initially appear to be totally incompatible, indeed diametrically opposed. *La Guerre* is composed of divisions and limits, of fragments, of parts, hyperstructured without constructing a whole. *Grabinoulor* is an enormous and proliferating whole, a whole that superficially refuses all division by its non-use of punctuation and its avoidance of ending, a narrative that turns back on itself. Yet despite the absence of punctuation and the apparent opportunity for completeness, nondivison, the narrative is rigorously structured, it is a linear narrative with chapters, chapter headings, volumes, rigorous syntax; division is therefore upheld within its wholeness. Somehow, however, the space and time of the narrative do not function in a linear fashion; *Grabinoulor* is, like *La Guerre,* a continual juxtaposition of disparate yet ordered elements. The narrative is also constructed as a series of concentric circles that ripple out from the body of *Grabinoulor* to encompass his apartment, the street, Paris, the world, the universe and beyond in time and space. A series of concentric circles is also part of the dynamic of the structures of *La Guerre,* as is the thrusting straight line. There is interaction both on the canvas and in the narrative between circle and straight line, and this relationship between canvas and "epic" is expressed in the language of these structuring lines.

In theory, the tools of analysis for a visual structure will permit us to read a linear text and its unfolding space, and a comparison between the two modes of expression may tell us something about the way in which the pictorial and the verbal function. The visual is therefore not considered here as imagery or theme, but as structure. This hypothesis is borne out, not only in the reading of the painting and of the narrative, but also of the poetic works. The framework I use in particular is the methodology developed by J-M Floch in *Petites Mythologies de l'Oeil et de L'Esprit* (note the allusion to Merleau-Ponty's *L'Oeil et L'Esprit*). A semiotic reading such as that elaborated by Floch to read the visual by putting in place codes of expression for images and specific visual categories allows an apprehension of the relationship between form and content. Floch therefore provided the critical tools with which to uncover the processes of the conditions of meaning in the visual (in his case an abstract work by Kandinsky, *Composition IV*). I work here within the framework offered by Floch (in isolating various elements of the canvas, for example), but I emphasize Albert-Birot's painting as a space in which the matrix of a poetics is inscribed as my original intuition and hypothesis had led me to do. In addition, I use certain discourses of psychoanalysis (particularly Sami Ali, *L'Espace imaginaire*) in order to read the dynamic of the work, and by that I mean the ways in which this 'geometry' of straight and curved line structures a space of desire.

The reception of any non-figurative canvas poses an enigma from the outset and a preliminary set of decisions must be made concerning that object in the face of the hesitancy and ambiguity it produces in the viewer/reader. Albert-Birot's *La Guerre* obviously invites speculation on a possible narrative given the thematic and ideological associations of a painting with such a title produced in 1916 by an artist/poet who had openly claimed to have found a new personal and artistic freedom. The presence of such a heavily connoted title directs the initial viewing/reading of such a message within common, shared human experience, and we can then add to that what we know of the artists's personal experience. Theoretically for Albert-Birot the war becomes the first part of the equation which will establish the regeneration of France and of French art particularly (see, for example, *SIC* 5, May 1916). Such a title also interacts with myriad other artistic creations celebrating or denigrating war in all its manifestations. Yet the viewer/reader still has to decipher the language of the abstract canvas and to do this must define the object of analysis in a less ambiguous way. If "abstraction" is intensely subjective, the expression of this subjectivity can only be apprehended by rigorous analysis, just as creation necessitates an ordering, as Kandinsky pointed out: "La création est un libre jeu de forme et de moyens d'expression à l'intérieur de règles strictes". These "rules" of creation and analysis are in no way stifling or limiting. Rather they allow both the creator and the viewer/reader a way of apprehending the conditions of creation. The procedures of semiotics assist in the apprehension of the modern work of art, providing ways to "decipher" and to posit possible "meanings", to propose a "visual poetics" (understood as a theory of the way in which a text or canvas functions) with which to read the work, to reveal the structure of the text or canvas, and the way in which meaning is constructed and produced. Possible meanings are attributable to the canvas by its title, its "name" signifying its presence in a historical, artistic and personal moment. Yet the reading of its "meanings" does not end there, and the ways in which semiotic procedure allows the uncovering of the conditions of creation and of the relationship between *La Guerre* and writing, both poetry and narrative which are to follow it, prove fundamental for the understanding of Albert-Birot's artistic universe. To quote Floch:

> On voit que la sémiotique visuelle ne fait pas sienne une lecture linéaire et continue des tableaux ou des photographies mais qu'elle essaie de mettre en place des procédures d'établissement du texte plastique en s'interrogeant sur la nature

sémiotique des différents types de contiguïté (les 'lisières' ou les 'bords') ou de non-contiguïté (les 'sauts anaphoriques' produits par les récurrences plastiques du même et de l'autre qui peuvent constituer une trame sur toute la surface plane du tableau). Ces organisations syntagmatiques peuvent ainsi rendre compte et des lectures orientées partielles et des saisies simultanées des formants ou des termes opposés d'une même catégorie dans le cas des contrastes.[5]

Before continuing with this reading of the surface structure of *La Guerre,* it is important to quote two passages from *Grabinoulor* which clearly provide an "intertext" between canvas and narrative:

> on y trouve douceur et violence et haine laideur et beauté et des tas de choses et même impalpabilité peut-être peuvent-ils les manifester et les poser sur une toile *au moyen des sept couleurs et les deux lignes mères la droite et la courbe* (V, 6, 637, my emphasis)

and:

> encore un 'abstrait' et même ajouta Grabinoulor un presque vrai en dehors de toute figure objective c'est si j'ose dire la représentation de la 'bellicité' en quelque sorte *un chaos geométrique* et en certains endroits je vois bien de telle matière surtout dans les blancs les gris et les noirs ce tableau est-il récent? point du tout je ne suis amusé à le peindre voici bientôt trente ans en un temps où la peinture 'abstraite' était nommée par Apollinaire orphique il a d'ailleurs vu celle-ci avant de mourir (IV, 13, 528, my emphasis)

The space of the canvas is created "au moyen des sept couleurs" (the seven colours of the spectrum, the field of perception of the human eye) and "les deux lignes mères la droite et la courbe". An initial division may be made between the right- and left-hand sides of the painting with an important focal point in the upper centre. The space may be divided into the visual opposi- tions of shape and the direction of these shapes: the large circular shape in the top centre, the elongated triangular shapes pointing across and up which origi- nate on the left-hand side; the broader flatter triangles which originate on the right. Further divisions are made by the series of bold, curved lines which reverberate across from the right. There is thus opposition between straight and curved lines and this division is made more complex by three straight lines which divide the canvas into four unequal parts and radically fragment the lines and shapes within them. The whole therefore emerges in disruption and movement. An initial opposition is set up between rapid fragmentation and the more unified figure suggested by the large circular mass of grey in the top centre which contrasts strongly with the sharp bright angles of the trian- gles on the left-hand side. There is movement in colour as well as structure with vibrant primary reds, yellows, and bright blues dominating the left-hand side, moving to dark blues, greens, browns and finally greys and blacks on the more muted right-hand side. These are not blocks of colour but each shape is subdivided into shades of that colour adding density to the flat planes, each space worked and re-worked, making felt the presence of the material, of matter, palpable expression of something more intangible.

The initial binary opposition in shape, then, is between circle and triangle, between straight and curved lines, a geometrical representation which speaks of something other than itself. In colour, too, there is an opposition between colour and "non-colour" (grey, black, white), between a chromatism and an anti-chromatism which also organises the space of the painting giving substance to the geometric division. This initial segmentation based on a binary opposition between forms allow us then to identify a primary set of units – right, left, centre, which are each themselves made up of smaller signifying units.[6] The central section of the canvas, where these forms meet, is more troubling for this line of enquiry since what appears to be a train of smoke, a recognizable figurative element, is introduced at the crucial point of contact and interaction between the abstract forms. This more figurative element thus poses questions concerning the modes of representation and signification within the canvas. It is also, however, another line of rupture.

Following the hypothesis that this space is a signifying whole, the contrasting organisation identifiable through the co-presence of opposing visual categories allows us to discuss a textual structure, in other words, to read beyond the apprehension of circle and triangle, curved and straight line. It is not only the meaning of the canvas which we are reading here, but the matrix of a poetics. The way in which the "poetic" space of *La Guerre* is constructed, assembled with the precision of geometry, and with the whole range of colour from primary colours and their mixtures to the "non-colours" of black, white and grey, the way in which abstract and figurative expression combine, the intense subjectivity and rigid logic at work, the interaction between "l'imaginaire" and the real, this will be the way poetry and prose in every form possible will be generated. This "language of lines", of forms, which structures Albert-Birot's canvas is both a "surface" structure and the expression of a "deep" structure underlying this canvas and the poetic production to follow. The identification of shape and colour in the composition provides a number of categories with which to read the work: curved/straight; acute/obtuse; plain/shaded; bright/muted colours; wholeness/fragmentation – which all function to constitute the deep level of expression. On the deep structural level, the functioning of the forms, these sharp-edged, acute shapes suggest *discontinuity*, division; their pointed, penetrating shape is of the immediate, the instant, the triangles susceptible to further and further fragmentation in the broad lines of the canvas's construction. Colour also is applied in segments, again connoting fragmentation and discontinuity and making that fragmentation tangible. The circle and the curved lines which reverberate across the canvas are the largest single form and the presence of the curved line looms vast, an imposing *continuous* presence. In linear terms, in the opposition between the short, straight lines of the segmented elements and the continous, curved line which constitutes the circle, there again appears to be a correlation between discontinuous and continuous, the immediate moment and the eternal, the incessantly fragmented and that which constantly endures.

The procedures of semiotic analysis enable us to understand how the visual discourse of line and colour produce a poetic discourse: there is a narrative at work within the abstract composition which we may read having apprehended its language, not a reading which exclusively refers to the external (although this is not to deny that the painting certainly represents its historical period, a confrontation between opposing forces, negative and positive, etc.), but a reading of its internal meaning. We have previously suggested that the opposition between discontinuity/continuity, immediacy/duration allows us to place the work within the perspective of the dynamism of the present moment which is to be celebrated as creation comes into being in that moment of movement and speed. Yet a greater artistic goal would be the recuperation of that present, to make it endure as an eternal moment. This double-focused relationship with time is upheld by Albert-Birot's own attitude towards the new, the dynamic and the energy of the avant-garde's experiments, which sought to achieve simultaneity of expression and to render the multiplicity of their experience of the modern world. On the other hand, the presence of the circle indicates a yearning for a transcendence of the moment which is thereby rendered eternal. The forces of the immediate and the eternal produced visually here will become the very basis of Albert-Birot's poetics: how to confer a lasting value on the present moment. On the surface level and in a perspective offered by the title, the relationship between the forms is one of opposition, of combat and conflict, and a reading with reference to a social and historical reality outside the canvas may be effected. The painting may also be read as an autobiographical and artistic statement. Albert-Birot is at war personally as he struggles to find an artistic identity, the painting representing a rupture between his "old" and "new" forms of expression and his advent to a conception of the "modern". He is also at war in defence of the avant-garde currently experiencing a backlash from the artistic establishment of the period. At the deep level of meaning the spatial structure of the canvas reveals a construction, a structuration in time. *La Guerre* is an expression of time in a visual composition working within the poles of duration and fragmentation. The composition expresses the dynamics of the present moment both in the historical context of the war and in the artistic expression of that moment, the two an instant in history. The moment is at once a part of the unfolding, eternal movement of time and a break in that movement. The irruption of war into history and of the avant-garde into artistic history injects a dynamism into the course of events. 1916 is a breaking point. The canvas is at once a celebration of the moment, of its energy and possibility, and an awareness of its nature as fragmentary – a fleeting moment in eternity. In the course of time it is a mo-ment assimilated into a greater totality, suggested by the reverberations of the circles which move across the canvas and encompass the dynamic shapes. The dual nature of time, and of events, either historical or artistic, is presented visually in their structures of continuity and discontinuity. The canvas equally presents the entrance of the individual moment that is the artist/poet into time. The self is part of the flux of history, the poetic self seeks a status which endures. What all these readings share is the structure of continuity and rup-ture in the experience of war, of the avant-garde, in individual experience, in artistic experience. This awareness of rupture and continuity are temporal struc-tures, the conflict between the present moment and the eternal which under-lies Albert-Birot's poetics. In *La Guerre* can be read the visual form of the awareness of the dynamic of the present moment and the will to recuperate it into the eternal moment of the work of art which endows the temporary with enduring status. "Chaque tableau sera un temps de la création du monde en création perpétuelle", declares Albert-Birot.

Grabinoulor is ostensibly a linear narrative, but it is constructed in the Cubist "état d'esprit", a juxtaposition of elements where past, present and future are simultaneously present. The figures of the straight and curved lines are generative forces because of the tension between them, and lead to the production of a geometric space inside the narrative. Although the constraints of this short analysis do not allow me to develop a fuller comparison of *Grabinoulor* with *La Guerre,* I will end by saying that *Grabinoulor* comes into being at the limit of external and internal space, it is a world metamorphosed by desire and coded geometrically.[7] The poet's task is to re-make the world in the shape of his desire, to pass from the experience of rupture in everyday life to a realm of continuity. The external limits of time and space dissolve in the narrative in order for another space to be constructed, where internal creation rules, the space of the imagination. Semiotic analysis provides the tools for us to read the language which governs the conditions of creation of that other space:

> Donc passez vos jours à vivre en rond, cultivez la courbe, c'est ma ligne, je n'en comprends pas d'autres; je te le dis Adam, aie peur de la droite, ligne affreuse et d'ailleurs impossible; je sais ce que je te dis, aie peur de l'angle, même obtus; le soir courbez-vous pour me remercier de vous avoir donné un jour bien arrondi. (Pierre Albert-Birot, *Les Mémoires d'Adam,* 79)[8]

NOTES

1   The Editions Jean-Michel Place have notably published in the last few years the first
      integral edition of Albert-Birot's masterpiece *Les Six Livres de Grabinoulor* (1991),
      Marie-Louise Lentengre's monograph *Pierre Albert-Birot: L'invention de soi,* two re-
      prints of the avant-garde journal *SIC* founded and edited by Albert-Birot, and the
      proceedings of the prestigious Cerisy colloquium devoted to Albert-Birot in Sep-
      tember 1995 which provided the first major overview of his work. Thanks to these
      publications and to the re-editions of the major poetry collections and the theatrical
      works by Rougerie, his work is widely available. Albert-Birot was the focus of an-
      other international conference held at the University of Nanterre-Paris X in Decem-
      ber 1996.

2   With regard to Surrealism, see Germana Orlandi Cerenza and Marie-Louise Lentengre
      in their early seminal articles respectively: "Pierre Albert-Birot: un surréaliste hors
      du 'château'", typescript translation of the article which appeared in Italian as "Pierre
      Albert-Birot, un surrealista fuori del 'Castello'", and "Grabinoulor ou le triomphe
      de l'imaginaire".

3   *SIC,* 54 issues, Paris, January 1916 to December 1919. Reprinted Paris: Chroniques
      des Lettres Françaises, 1973; Paris: Jean-Michel Place, 1980, 1993. For the poet's
      own account of the production of the journal see "Naissance et vie de *SIC* " in
      Autobiographie. He ends its publication in 1919 when he is ready to affirm his indi-
      vidual identity against the further ruptures of the avant-garde. *SIC* is simultaneously
      an artistic, historical and personal document.

4   For a convincing account of the establishment backlash against avant-garde art and
      particularly Cubism, see Kenneth Silver. *Esprit de corps* (translated into French as
      Vers le retour à l'ordre). Silver documents and discusses the effect of the war on a
      Modernism born of a group which contained members of disparate national origins.
      The artistic establishment seized the moment and delivered onslaughts against the
      "degeneration" of French Art in the pre-war years caused, they believed, by foreign
      influences.

5   J.-M. Floch. *Petites Mythologies de l'Oeil et de l'Esprit.* The title obviously acknowl-
      edges Merleau-Ponty's *L'Oeil et L'Esprit.* See Floch also in his article, "Les Langages
      planaires".

6   Cf. Floch, op. cit., 43: "on peut ainsi essayer de diviser cet espace en unités discrètes
      provisoires, grâce à quelques oppositions visuelles prises comme critères de découpage
      et produisant des ruptures de continuité dans l'étendue".

7   I have developed this more fully in my book, *Pierre Albert-Birot: A Poetics in Move-
      ment, A Poetics of Movement* and in my contribution to the Cerisy conference pro-
      ceedings, "Une lecture de *La Guerre:* la matrice d'une poétique".

8   Pierre Albert-Birot. *Les Mémoires d'Adam et les pages d'Eve.* Paris: L'Allée, 1986.

REFERENCES

Albert-Birot, Pierre. *Les Mémoires d'Adam et les pages d'Eve*. Paris: L'Allée, 1986.

———. "Naissance et vie de *SIC. Autobiographie,* suivi de *Moi à moi*. Troyes: Librairie Bleue, 1988.

———. *Poèmes à l'autre moi, Poésie 1927-1937*. Mortemart: Rougerie, 1981.

———. *Les Six Livres de Grabinoulor*. Paris: Jean-Michel Place, 1991.

———. ed. *SIC*. 54 issues. Paris, January 1916 to December 1919. Reprinted Paris: Chroniques des Lettres Françaises, 1973. Paris: Jean-Michel Place, 1980, 1993.

Cerenza Orlandi, Germana. "Pierre Albert-Birot, un surrealista fuori del 'Castello'", "Surréalisme/Surrealismo". *Quaderni del novecento francese* 2. Roma: Bulzoni. (Translated into French: "Pierre Albert-Birot: un surréaliste hors du 'château'". Paris: Nizet).

Floch, J.-M. *Petites Mythologies de l'Oeil et de l'Esprit*. Paris and Amsterdam: Hadès-Benjamin, 1985.

———. "Les Langages planaires". *Sémiotique. L'Ecole de Paris. Paris: Hachette, 1982.*

Kelly, Debra. *Pierre Albert-Birot: A Poetics in Movement, A Poetics of Movement*. London: Associated University Presses, 1997.

———. "Une lecture de *La Guerre:* la matrice d'une poétique". *Pierre Albert-Birot. Laboratoire de modernité*. Paris: Jean-Michel Place, 1997.

Lentengre, Marie-Louise. "Grabinoulor ou le triomphe de l'imaginaire", "La letteratura e l'immaginario". *Atti del XI Convengni della Società per gli studi di lingua e letteratura francese*. Verona, 1982.

———. *Pierre Albert-Birot: L'invention de soi*. Paris: Editions Jean-Michel Place, 1993.

Merleau-Ponty *L'Oeil et l'Esprit*. Paris: Gallimard, 1984.

Silver, Kenneth. *Esprit de corps. The Art of the Parisian Avant-Garde and the First World War 1914-1925*. London: Thames and Hudson, 1989. (Translated into French as *Vers le retour à l'ordre*. Paris: Flammarion, 1991).

Renouard, Madeleine, ed. *Pierre Albert-Birot. Laboratoire de modernité*. Colloque de Cerisy. Paris: Jean-Michel Place, 1997.

Poetic Painting and Picturesque Poetry: Literature and Visual Arts in the Emergence of National Symbolic Repertoires in the River Plate Area

Laura Malosetti Costa

> To excite the imagination, painting needs to be poetic as poetry needs to be picturesque. The reason for this is very clear: the idea that escapes painting, that is to say, the idea that is not picturesque or has not a certain dramatic movement, presents itself confusedly to the imagination.
>
> Bartolomé Mitre[1]

When I was a child, in Montevideo, I saw every day an image of a dying Indian in *scorzo* reproduced on the covers of my school notebooks. He was Tabare, a blue-eyed Indian son of a Spanish woman captive and a Charrua chief, who died tragically, a victim of his dual nature, divided between "civilization and barbarism". Tabare was a literary figure from a poem written in the last decades of the nineteenth century by Juan Zorrilla de San Martín, a text that became extraordinarily popular in Uruguay, to the point of being considered the "national poem". Tabare was for us, Uruguayan children, the nation itself.

Of late, the interest of historians in the emergence of modern nations and nationalism has increased. Eric Hobsbawm's conceptual framework of the "invention of traditions" for the formation of nations, and Benedict Anderson's concept of "imagined communities" are also significant for art-historical investigations into the role of mythic and iconic repertoires in the process of conformation and consolidation of national identities.[2] Within such processes, not only the strategies of the ruling classes must be borne in mind, but also the movements "from below", the fate of images – literary or visual – in the popular mind.

I propose here to focus on only one aspect of the intense mythopoetic activity both in Argentina and Uruguay in the second half of the nineteenth century, particularly since 1870, when intellectual as well as political elites committed themselves to the consolidation of the idea of nation after a long period of civil wars.[3] I will refer to the interaction of poetry and painting (or poets and painters) and the particular case of the painter Juan Manuel Blanes. Consequently, I will only consider briefly other important areas of the aesthetic-symbolic framework created then, such as narrative and essay, monumental statuary, or theatre. I will also put aside the first moment of emergence of national identities, built up around emblematic colours, anthems and public pageantry.[4]

During the nineteenth century, the appropriation and integration of Argentina's enormous territory was a permanent concern for its creole elites. The immense and flat *pampas,* also called the "desert" – almost twenty thousand square miles of extraordinarily fertile lands to the South of Buenos Aires – were populated by various nomadic "tribes" that had been expelled from their original habitat near the coast. Indian raids *(malones)* beset estates and settlements in the course of which cattle was taken away, men were killed and women and children made captives. This was the setting for the first romantic images of the nation in Argentina. Not so in Uruguay: the Oriental Band of the River, a small territory where natives had been annihilated earlier and were evoked with melancholy during the last decades of the century.[5]

In the 1830s, the so-called "second independent generation" (representing the urban bourgeoisie) introduced romanticism to the area of the River Plate. Most of them were Buenos Aires citizens but wrote from exile in Montevideo or Chile. They introduced the romantic concept of nation and liberal ideas together with an aesthetic paradigm. This generation was a vanguard both in political and aesthetic terms, founding their project on the power of the written word (Viñas). They believed in the evocative power of literature and the influence of the press. From then on literature and politics remained closely related. The major poets were also presidents, legislators, diplomats, landlords. They were also often journalists and historians, well read and well travelled.

This group set out to seek the nation's identity through historical awareness and national distinctive features. In 1837 Esteban Echeverría published *La Cautiva (The Captive),* in which he established what was to be considered the essential landscape of the nation: the pampa. In the foreword he explains that he intends to "create a national literature" and therefore will proceed to depict the desert, "our bountiful inheritance". "Our" does not, however, include the Indians, shown in the poem as the fiends victimizing Maria, the helpless captive. The poet's words conjure up land and myth to create the national landscape which inspired territorial appropriation. *La Cautiva* represents a will to "domesticate" the wild, a project from the city.

Echeverría's poem became an instant popular success. However, the author had not created it *ex nihilo.* The flat, limitless, stern and overwhelming landscape "only comparable to the sea" was already a *cliché* in the tales of travellers and explorers since the eighteenth century (Prieto, *Los Viajeros).* The ocean metaphor would shape a land the likes of which the Europeans had never seen (Malosetti and Penhos). In Echeverría's pampa there are glimpses of Byron's *Childe Harold*,[6] but also the writings of Francis Head, Samuel Haigh, Joseph Andrews, Edmond Temple and other well-known voyagers.[7]

This perspective from abroad provided by passing travellers and natives in exile came to dominate the building of the nation's image. European – mainly British – interests in the area were strong in those times of expansion and played an important role in the economic and political process.[8] The "vision from abroad", the image reflected in a European mirror – English at first – was a most significant element in the construction of an imaginary framework for the new nations.

The same is true for visual images: the albums of "picturesque visions" by the artists accompanying the expeditions (Brambila, Jean Ravenet, William Holland, Del Pozo) and by the foreign settlers in Buenos Aires and Montevideo were the visual counterparts of such reports. Emeric Essex Vidal, Henry Sheridan, Leon Palliere, among others, captured the picturesque in the appearance and customs of the Indians and the *gauchos*.[9] But the pampa was not perceived as a "landscape" by those romantic European eyes, as it was not seen as a possible subject for paintings. It could only be perceived as scenery for the human drama. The incommensurable plains, the uninterrupted horizon were empty, mute; there were no models for such landscapes.[10] Ernst Gombrich has pointed out that no artist can paint what is before his eyes without the conventions of his culture. The painted depiction of reality is made possible by the existence of a tradition, that is to say, other paintings. Only at the turn of the century – when the importance of the subject in art began to fade – would the landscape of the pampa be the focus of the artists' view.

The German romantic painter Johann Moritz Rugendas, who travelled the Argentinian pampas despite Humboldt's advice to avoid those regions so as not to "waste his talents",[11] was enthralled when he read *La Cautiva*. Although his letters reveal his admiration for Echeverría's poetic landscape, his paintings and etchings inspired by the poem reflect mainly the erotic theme of the abduction, present for centuries in European art. From then on the abduction and rape of white women in the Indian raids became a major motif in Argentinian national art (Malosetti).

The main problem facing the young nations during the first four decades after emancipation were the civil wars between antagonistic parties. Thus another topic emerges from the literature of the period: the opposition between civilization and barbarism. In 1845, Domingo F. Sarmiento published his *Facundo*, setting this polarized view of history and a theory of geographic fatality: "The ills of Argentina," he states, "are caused by vastness; the all-encompassing desert has encroached on its entrails". Equating the city to civilization, for him the barbaric desert spawns tyrants such as Facundo Quiroga, considered the paradigm of tyranny.

Civil wars raged on until the decade of 1860-70, when peace appeared to a significant part of the ruling classes as a necessary condition for modernization and development. The era of "discipline" had arrived (Barran). Local warlords and wandering gauchos had to be held in check. Estates were fenced for livestock grazing and immigrant settlers started agriculture.

In Argentina, these projects were hindered by the "Indian and gaucho problem". The "conquest of the desert" was made possible by the systematic extermination of the Pampa Indians by 1879 and the levies that banished the traditional nomadic lifestyle of the gaucho.[12] Once the gauchos ceased to exist as a danger for the "civilizing" process, their image was adopted as an archetype of national identity, reinvented as a symbol of the "traditional roots".

From this process a new poetic form was born: the gaucho poems claiming for pacification and national reconciliation, denouncing the injustices against the gauchos. *Martin Fierro,* written by José Hernández in 1872 became the cornerstone of a literary genre that would surge through the cities from the 1880s. Those cities – and particularly Buenos Aires – were dramatically transformed in the eighties by a massive European immigration that poured in and seemed to threaten this budding national identity.[13] In this context the gaucho creole discourse would become hugely popular (Prieto, *El Discurso*).

This period also gave rise to great historical narratives with the emerging figures of national heroes, establishing the historical landmarks that would help overcome partisan conflicts, emphasizing events leading to national unity, commemorated by monuments in the cities (Espantoso Rodríguez et al.).

The task of developing the fine arts began to be seen as an important means of attaining the status of a "civilized" nation. The so-called "Generation of the 80s", liberal and cosmopolitan, called for a national identity which they conceived of according to the European model. This entailed the cultivation of the arts just as in Paris or Florence.[14] But that would not be easy in the River Plate. There was no tradition, no academy from colonial times. Also political instability and civil wars had frustrated various attempts to establish art institutions (Ribera). There were no official policies promoting fine arts, no schools of art, no salons, no exhibition halls except a few odd store windows. Painters did portraits, and although some of them also painted picturesque scenes or landscapes, these were thought of as minor genre.

In this context, the Uruguayan painter Juan Manuel Blanes (1830-1901) appears as a key figure with a decisive influence on the creation of a national pictorial tradition both in Uruguay and Argentina. Blanes started his training during the civil war period, but all through his remarkable artistic career managed to avoid taking sides.[15] He produced a profusion of images that – inspired by the works of poets and historians – in turn provided inspiration to them and gave shape to the modern "re-invention" of these two nations. The positions he took up – both ideological and aesthetic – were characterized by eclecticism, accompanying the democratic and nationalistic ideals of the "progressive" sectors of our ruling class (Peluffo).

Blanes freely used the academic style he had learned from the Florence master Antonio Ciseri to attain clarity and emotional eloquence in his works. In his letters and writings he expressed the desire to become an American artist (not just Uruguayan) and stated that art should be useful and edifying, sparking high ideals. He wrote that he did not want to make "productions only for the cultured classes, so that art like the artist may become the expression of his race, his people, his land".[16] His determination to reach a "large public" did much for the advent of a "national art" whose lack so concerned men of letters.

In 1871 Blanes achieved massive acclaim when his canvas *A Yellow Fever Episode in Buenos Aires* was shown in the foyer of the Opera Theater in that city. Buenos Aires had been ravaged for six months by the plague and found in Blanes' painting the moving image of the recent tragedy. For weeks crowds of deeply moved viewers gathered every day in front of the painting. It was an unprecedented event. Poets, historians, politicians – even President Sarmiento – published long laudatory reviews in the papers. Blanes had taken his subject from a newspaper article (Amigo). However, he had turned his painting into an allegory of social solidarity personified by two prominent public figures who had also been victims of the epidemic.[17]

Blanes continued to paint large historical canvasses for Argentina, Chile and Uruguay. *The Oath of the 33 Orientals* was a huge success in Montevideo in 1878. For the first time, the public found in these paintings the likeness of their heroes, the semblance of events of their national history. In a literary contest held the next year to celebrate the Uruguayan independence, the poet Juan Zorrilla de San Martin won and was enthusiastically praised for a piece about the same subject.[18] Some years later Zorrilla would write: "for a long time the eyes of our people have only known national glory, the only life, through the lines and colours of Blanes. Many have envied us for him".[19]

Throughout his career Blanes focused on the construction of images of the American nations, and not only in his great historical canvases. He painted a number of allegorical works based on poems, some of them very popular ones. In these compositions the allegorical intention emerges more or less clearly from the new codes introduced by romanticism. The issues around which the cultured elites were constructing the nation were taken up by his paintings in an expressive way: the scourge of civil wars, the emblematic image of the gaucho, the Indian and the desert. Although in many of his smaller works Blanes maintains the vision "from abroad", stressing picturesque costume in others, (e.g. *The Defeated)* he shows his characters as victims of the civil wars. Sometimes the link with poetry is explicit, as in the paintings alluding to the unpopular Paraguay war, perceived in both countries as the last and cruel sequel of civil wars, which ended with the devastation of Paraguay and the slaughter of most of her men.[20] Both works were inspired by two very popular poems of the time.[21] *The Paraguayan* is the mourning nation weeping over her ruins. In *The Last Paraguayan* the emblematic figure is the unknown soldier who would pervade the antebellum images of the twentieth century.

Blanes shows a remarkable diversity in depicting Indians. *The Angel of the Charruas,* based on an early Zorrilla de San Martín poem, shows a lament for a vanished people. *The Abduction of a White Woman* and *Ready for the Raid* are obviously inspired by *La Cautiva:* the Indians are shown as brutish savages (Penhos). The ravishing of white women fascinated Blanes, who painted this subject many times.

Although he longed to be an American artist, Blanes became the Uruguayan national painter. Argentina had seemed ready to adopt him in the seventies, but in the eighties turned to a demand for local representatives. Several promising young painters were sent to Europe. A key moment to observe the advancement of the artistic activity in Argentina is the Continental Exhibition of 1882 in Buenos Aires. The fine arts sections of the industrial exhibitions were important opportunities to achieve success in countries without Art Salons. In this particular show, Blanes was still the dominant painter with more than 20 works.[22]

The reviews in the Buenos Aires press provide a good understanding of the way these paintings were interpreted: they were "read" as discourses.[23] The critics were not so unconditionally enthusiastic about Blanes by this time, instead they praised some of the young Argentine painters who studied in Europe, in particular Ballerini.[24] He had presented a canvas that had received high praise: *Civilization and Barbarism* – where he had painted some Indians tearing down railroad lines and telegraph poles.[25]

In 1881, the pages of *La Ilustracion Argentina,* founded by some of the most prestigious poets of the time with the express purpose of advancing "the fine arts and letters", reveal the lack of master painters in the unqualified support to very young artists, for example Ballerini, one of whose works illustrated the cover of the first issue.[26] One year later, an article of the same publication finds these young artists lacking, and offers a way to develop the arts: "Our nature, with its picturesque or grandiose scenes; our land with her past ... here is the vast flux where every artist may find light, colours, passion, beauty: all that lies at the soul of art ...."[27] Opinions were divided. Some, like the columnist, think that there is no national art because painters failed to look for inspiration in local landscape or history. Others claim that this is due to the lack of official support and access to European models to imitate.[28] These are in favour of the French "modern" school while the former still lean toward the Italian tradition.[29] Yet all of them agree that Buenos Aires has not developed "the artistic taste".

Towards the end of the century, poets discussing at the *Ateneo*[30] still demanded painters for the pampa landscape, even calling light effects to the attention of the artists.[31] Young painter and writer Eduardo Schiaffino, who later founded the first Fine Arts Museum, stated that the pampa landscape did not exist: he called it an impossible subject for painting because it was just literature, an invention of poets.[32]

At that time Blanes still painted great historical compositions like *The Conquest of the Desert* but did not arouse the earlier enthusiasm. The aesthetic paradigms were changing.

Two of those art students in Europe in 1882, surely under the influence of the *Ateneo* poets, painted two different images of the desert: Angel Della Valle in 1892 continued the poetic tradition with the touching *Return from the Indian Raid (La Vuelta del Malon)* and with it obtained public acclaim. Eduardo Sivori, at the turn of the century, for the first time painted the horizon as the only protagonist of a canvas.

Thus, throughout the nineteenth century the images of the new nations were essentially a literary creation. The national school of painting emerges under the initiative of the poet-politicians. Blanes and his followers overcame the picturesque "vision from abroad" by looking to literature. They in turn received support from poets and historians in the public acceptance of their role as national painters. Writers were the promoters of "national painting".

Notes

1   *Carta-prefacio* addressed to Domingo F. Sarmiento in his book of *Rimas* (1854). Bartolomé Mitre was President of Argentina during the period 1862-1868.

2   In this respect the works of Maurice Agulhon, Jean Starobinski, Pierre Nora and Michel Vovelle about the iconography of the French Revolution are outstanding. In recent years, several researchers both in Argentina and Uruguay have addressed this issue in our countries from different points of view (cf. e.g. Burucúa and Compagne as well as Amigo).

3   Formerly both Argentina and Uruguay were part of the Spanish Viceroyalty of the River Plate, together with Paraguay and Bolivia. Uruguay was called the "Oriental Band" of the Uruguay river.

4   Burucúa and Compagne state that the first symbols of nationality emerge around two great generic myths or *topoi* addressed to legitimate the new order: the universal revolutionary myth (each new nation as part of a general revolutionary process), and the indigenous myth: the continuity of the new nation with a past of freedom which had ceased with the arrival of Spain.

5   The last Charruas were surrounded and completely destroyed by the first Uruguayan president, Fructuoso Rivera, in 1831.

6   After his five years of studies in Paris (1825-1830) Echeverría writes to a friend that he was fascinated by Byron. In fact, Echeverría introduces his poem with some verses by Byron in English: "Female hearts are such a genial soil / For kinder feeling whatsoever their nation / They naturally pour the "wine and oil" / Samaritans in every situation".

7   At least 14 English travelers who visited the River Plate between 1820 and 1835 wrote their memories and experiences. Cf. Prieto, *Los Viajeros* (29).

8   Mary Louise Pratt (1992) has pointed out the significant role played by traveler's literature in those first decades of the nineteenth century, in relation to European expansionism. She observes a "reinvention" of South America then as landscape but also as source of richness and subject of political organization. It was a vision that intended to legitimize that expansionism as a civilizing enterprise.

9   Gauchos: the (often) mestizo roaming horsemen who lived by hunting wild cattle and trading the skins. Cf. Martínez Estrada.

10   In 1826 Miers wrote that the pampa was an "unlimited plain empty of landscape". Beaumont in 1828: "Nothing in this place can satisfy Aesthetic emotion ... the beauty and the sublime are absent from this landscape".

11   Letter from Humboldt to Rugendas. Cited by Anadon.

12   In 1879 a military expedition led by General Julio A. Roca "pacified" the desert harassing native tribes. The prestige of this general increased to the point of his being elected president of Argentina twice (1880-1886 and 1898-1904).)

13   More than a million immigrants arrived in Argentina between 1880 and 1890, many of whom could not get land grants – the prevailing latifundist scheme prevented that – and remained in Buenos Aires. Similar quantities are registered in the following decades until 1910. Cf. Romero (138 ff).

14   Cf. *La Prensa* (April 4, 1882): "We must accept that we have already to study a lot, that we have not to economize efforts in order to attain a place among the nations that cultivate the Fine Arts. We are very far from the possibility of organizing Salons of painting and sculpture to reward those who excel with their works so as to develop the instruction and culture of the masses".

15   Perhaps it is better to say that he always supported the governments, no matter who held the power. But his convictions were basically democratic, liberal and positivist.

16   Cf. Blanes, *Memoria del cuadro de los Treinta y Tres*.

17   These two men were Cosme Argerich and José Roque Perez, two well-known members of the Popular Society formed by the Freemasonry to fight the epidemic (cf. Amigo).

18   Cf. Zum Felde, Vol. 1 (268-70). The poem was "*La leyenda patria*". Zorrilla did not win the prize because his poem was too long, but was immediately considered by everybody as the real winner. Since then, Zorrilla had to recite his poem at every patriotic feast.

19   1908. Reproduced in the catalogue of the Exhibition Juan Manuel Blanes. Montevideo: Teatro Solís, 1941.

20   Argentina and Uruguay – together with Brazil – attacked Paraguay when the regime of Solano López claimed better commercial opportunities. At the beginning, some political factions and chieftains of both countries had supported Solano López.

21   "Nenia" by the Argentine poet Guido Spano and "To a Paraguayan" by the Uruguayan Sienra y Carranza.

22   The newspapers *La Prensa* and *La Patria Argentina* published various articles on Blanes between March and April 1882. Cf. *La Prensa* March 16, 1882 (1, 7): "Blanes shines. Not the ancient Blanes, the one of the *Yellow Fever* and *Rancagua,* but the modern Blanes of *The Paraguayan.* She floates in light effluvia as the image of pain flooding the world with her tears and puts in the visitor's mouth Guido's sobs of regret for his beautiful Urutaú". (Refers to "Nenia" by Guido Spano).

23   Cf. for example *La Prensa* (April 6, 1882). The columnist, who signs "A.", refers to Blanes' painting: "The last moments of Jose Miguel Carrera": "This page of our history is very instructive ... In this painting we see the consequences of civil war! The ambition, pride and hate are going to be satisfied, and also God's and the peoples' justice ...."

24   "The paintings by Ballerini and Guidice, our hope in the art of the brush, deserve special attention ..." *La Prensa* (March 16, 1882).

25   Cf. *La Ilustración Argentina* 2 (June 20, 1881) and *La Prensa* (May 12, 1882). This painting is lost.

26   *La Ilustración Argentina* 1 (June 10, 1881). The engraving reproduced an allegorical painting Ballerini had shown in a shop window (Bossi): "Argentine Republic offering her intellectual productions to Science, Literature and Fine Arts".

27   *La Ilustración Argentina* 2 (May 30, 1882).

28   Two of them were Carlos Gutiérrez and Eduardo Schiaffino.

29   Cf. Carlos Gutiérrez: *La Patria Argentina,* (April 15, 1882): "The art of painting in Buenos Aires is deeply divided between two factions. This is not only the antagonism of two schools but also the hate between two races, one of which snatches supremacy from the other".

30   Gathering of intellectuals and artists for cultural purposes (cf. Schiaffino).

31   Rafael Obligado. *Discourse at the Ateneo,* 1894. Op. cit. (55).

32   Cf. E. Schiaffino. *Discourse at the Ateneo,* 1894. (306 ff).

REFERENCES

Achugar, Hugo. *Poesía y sociedad (Uruguay 1880-1911).* Montevideo: Arca, 1985.

Amigo Cerisola, Roberto. "Imágenes para una nación. Juan Manuel Blanes y la pintura de tema histórico en la Argentina". In: *Arte, Historia e Identidad en América. Visiones comparativas. XVII Coloquio Internacional de Historia del Arte.* Mexico: UNAM, 1994.

Anadon, Ana. "Los viajes pintorescos del siglo XIX: Humboldt y Rugendas". In: *Segundas Jornadas de Teoría e Historia de las Artes.* Buenos Aires, CAIA, 1990. 43-54.

Anderson, Benedict. *Imagined Communities. Reflections on the Origin and Spread of Nationalism.* London and New York: Verso, 1983.

Andrews, Joseph. *Journey from Buenos Aires through the Provinces of Cordova, Tucuman and Salta to Potosi* (etc.). London: John Murray, 1827.

Barran, José Pedro. *Historia de la sensibilidad en el Uruguay.* Montevideo: Ediciones de la Banda Oriental, 1990.

Blanes, Juan Manuel. *Memoria del cuadro de los Treinta y Tres.* Montevideo, 1878.

Burucúa, José Emilio and Campagne, Fabián A. "Mitos y simbologías de la nación. Los países del Cono Sur". In: A. Annino, L. Castro Leiva, and F. X. Guerra, comp.: *De los imperios a las naciones: Iberoamérica.* Zaragoza: Iber Caja, 1994. 349-81.

Chiaramonte, José Carlos. "Formas de identidad en el Río de la Plata luego de 1810". In: *Boletín del Instituto de Historia Argentina y Americana "Dr. E. Ravignani".* 3rd. period No. 1, Buenos Aires: FFyL, 1989. 71-92.

Echeverría, Esteban. *La Cautiva. El Matadero.* Buenos Aires: Peuser, 1958.

Espantoso Rodríguez, Teresa *et al.* "Imágenes para la nación argentina. Conformación de un eje monumental urbano en Buenos Aires entre 1811 y 1910". In: *Arte, Historia e Identidad en América. Visiones comparativas. XVII Coloquio Internacional de Historia del Arte.* Mexico: UNAM, 1994.

Gellner, Ernest. *Nations and Nationalism.* Ithaca, New York: Cornell University Press, 1983.

Gombrich, Ernst. *Arte e Ilusión. Estudio sobre la psicología de la representación pictórica.* Barcelona: Gustavo Gili, 1979.

Haigh, Samuel. *Sketches of Buenos Aires, Chile and Peru.* London: Effingham Wilson, 1831.

Head, Francis Bond. *Rough Notes Taken During Some Rapid Journeys Across the Pampas and Among the Andes.* London: John Murray, 1826.

Hobsbawm, Eric and Terence Ranger, eds. *The Invention of Tradition.* Cambrigde University Press, 1983.

Malosetti Costa, Laura and Marta Penhos. "Imágenes para el desierto argentino. Apuntes para una iconografía de la pampa". In: *Ciudad/Campo en las artes en Argentina y Latinoamérica.* Buenos Aires: CAIA, 1991. 195-204.

Malosetti Costa, Laura. *Rapto de cauivas blancas. Un aspecto erótico de la barbarie en el siglo XIX.* Buenos Aires: FFyL, 1995.

Martínez Estrada, Ezequiel. *Radiografía de la pampa.* 1933. Buenos Aires: Losada, 1974.

Mitre, Bartolomé. *Rimas.* Buenos Aires: Imprenta de Mayo, 1854.

Peluffo, Gabriel. "Pintura y política en la significación nacional de Juan Manuel Blanes". In: *Blanes dibujos y bocetos.* Catalogue. Montevideo: Museo Municipal "Juan Manuel Blanes", 1995.

Penhos, Marta. "Indios del siglo XIX. Nominación y representación". In: *Las Artes en el debate del V Centenario. IV Jornadas de Teoría e Historia de las Artes.* Buenos Aires: CAIA FFyL, 1992 188-95.

Pratt, Mary Louise. *Imperial Eyes. Travel Writing and Transculturation.* London and New York: Routledge, 1992.

Prieto, Adolfo. *El discurso criollista en la formación de la Argentina moderna.* Buenos Aires: Sudamericana, 1988.

———. *Los viajeros ingleses y la emergencia de la literatura argentina (1820-1850).* Buenos Aires: Sudamericana, 1996.

Rafael Obligado. *Prosas.* Buenos Aires: Academia Argentina de Letras, 1976.

Ribera, Adolfo L. "La pintura". In: *VVAA. Historia General del Arte en la Argentina.* III. Buenos Aires: Academia Nacional de Bellas Artes, 1984. 113-27.

Romero, José Luis. *Breve historia de la Argentina.* Buenos Aires: Huemul, 1978. 138 ff.

Sarmiento, Domingo Faustino. *Facundo Civilización y barbarie.* 1845. Buenos Aires: Espasa Calpe, 1970.

Schiaffino, Eduardo. *La pintura y la escultura en la Argentina.* Buenos Aires: Edición del autor, 1933.

Temple, Edmond. *Travels in Various Parts of Peru. Including a Year's Residence in Potosi.* 2 vols. Philadelphia-Boston: Carey-Lilly, 1833.

Viñas, David. *Literatura argentina y realidad política. De Sarmiento a Cortázar.* Buenos Aires: Siglo Veinte, 1970. 15 -17.

Zum Felde, Alberto. *Proceso Intelectual del Uruguay y crítica de su literatura.* Montevideo: Imprenta Nacional Colorada, 1930. 3 vols.

ILLUSTRATIONS

Figure 1. Johann Moritz Rugendas, *El Malón (The Indian Raid),* ca.1848. Oil/canvas, 78 x 102 cm. Buenos Aires, private collection.

Figure 2. Juan Manuel Blanes, *Un episodio de la fiebre amarilla en Buenos Aires (An Episode of the Yellow Fever in Buenos Aires),* 1871. Oil/canvas, 230 x 180 cm. Montevideo, National Museum of Visual Arts.

Figure 3. Juan Manuel Blanes, *El Juramento de los 33 Orientales (The Oath of the 33 Orientals)*,
1877. Oil/canvas, 311 x 564 cm. Montevideo, National Museum of Visual Arts.

Figure 4. Juan Manuel Blanes, *La
Paraguaya (The Paraguayan)*, ca.1879.
Oil/canvas, 100 x 80 cm. Montevideo,
National Museum of Visual Arts.

Figure 5. Angel Della Valle, *La vuelta del malón (The Return of the Indian Raid),* 1892. Oil/canvas, 186 x 292 cm. Buenos Aires, National Museum of Fine Arts.

Figure 6. Eduardo Sívori, *El bañado (The Marsh),* 1902. Oil/canvas, 39 x 46,5 cm. Buenos Aires, National Museum of Fine Arts.

News from Plato's Cave: Jeff Wall's *A Sudden Gust of Wind* and *Dead Troops Talk*

Jürgen Müller

To give a concrete example of the possibilities of a specifically visual argument, I would like to concentrate on two works by the Canadian artist Jeff Wall.[1] What both of these works have in common is that the visual event is established in such a way that it can be read as an ironic commentary on images. In contemporary art Wall's oeuvre makes it clear that far from requiring an additional linguistic reflection, images can "argue" for themselves. In an unexpected way Wall's images combine simple everyday perceptions of the spectator with art-historical quotations. Furthermore, they dramatize media-reality and, last but not least, they try to establish a theory of visual cognition.

The first work (fig. 1, overleaf) is entitled *A Sudden Gust of Wind*. According to its dependence on the unity of space and time, it shows what we expect from a classical concept of an image. The photograph gives the impression of spontaneity, almost like a snapshot. In the foreground there are four persons who seem to be affected by the vagaries of nature. While the person on the very left loses his manuscript – it is being blown away by the wind – the man next to him is only just able to hold on to his cap. Opposite him, a man tries to spot his hat, which he has already lost in a sudden gust of wind. He is given particular prominence by his position on the vertical axis. Only the fourth man is able to keep his cap on his head. The entire composition of the foreground emphasizes the instantaneous character of the event. The attitudes of all four persons are determined by extreme postures which result from the strong wind. Two trees, bent by the force of the wind, echo the agitation of the human figures. Overall, the picture gives the impression of being completely "natural", felicitously capturing the events shown.

With another look however we begin to realize how carefully composed this image is. A group of persons is arranged on a narrow stretch in the foreground. The organization of space could be characterized in terms of almost abstract compositional lines: space is made visible and given depth by the diagonal line which starts in the left corner and leads along the shore of the canal toward the center of the image thus stressing the low horizon of the scene. This low-running horizontal line, commonly found in Dutch landscape painting, converts the sky into a screen on which this scene of upward whirling, scattered sheets of paper is projected. The manuscript sheets are trans-

Figure 1. Jeff Wall, *A Sudden Gust of Wind,* 1993. Transparency in lightbox, 229 x 337 cm.

formed into an image of movement delineated on the plane. However, the manuscript also renders visible what usually cannot be seen – that is: the movement of the wind.

The subtitle already gives an important clue for the understanding of Wall's picture: it is additionally entitled "After Hokusai". The cibachrome by the Canadian artist is a paraphrase of a coloured wood-cut (fig. 2) from Hokusai's series *36 Views of the Fuji.*[2] The inscription in the upper left part of Hokusai's picture gives the name of the region where the shrine in the middle is to be found. In Hokusai's wood-cut the same subject as in Wall's picture is depicted – an arrangement of persons who find themselves exposed to the whims of nature and a manuscript belonging to the person on the very left being caught by the wind. Now, at the very latest, it becomes obvious that Wall's rendering is an imitation modelled on Hokusai.

In fact, Wall arranged the scene with actors and probably used a wind-machine to whirl the sheets around. He also drew on the possibilities of photographic digitalization: with the help of a computer, single scenes, taken one by one, have been arranged to form a homogeneous picture. Thus the simultaneity of the scene conceals the procedure of its gradual evolution. However, even if we keep the computer-aided construction in mind the number of the different scenes cannot be perceived. This way of production seems to translate techniques used in nineteenth century history painting. What would then have been constructed by assembling several studio studies in one picture, can today be achieved by the technical possibilities of the digitalized image. Jeff

Figure 2. Hokusai, "A High Wind in Yeijiri", from *Thirty-six Views of the Fuji*, ca. 1831-3. 26 x 37 cm.

Wall's picture is a cibachrome and a large scale transparency, that is to say a medium commonly used in advertising: these transparencies are mounted in aluminium show cases which are illuminated by fluorescent tubes. Compared to common photographic techniques this intense illuminated image has a more striking effect with regard to the illusion of three-dimensionalitly. This results in the somewhat paradoxical effect of the light seemingly being emitted by the image. The hybrid character of this technique must be emphasized. It modifies the slide projection, converting a projection surface into a screen in analogy to the television screen.

THE IDEA OF SPACE AS A TRAVESTY OF TIME

One more discovery is to be made when one closely examines the figure on the far left. Judging by the clothes it seems to be a male person except for the painted hands (fig. 3 – detail), the hands of a woman cross-dressing. This is a visual clue hinting at the travesty which takes place in the picture: a travesty

Figure 3. Jeff Wall, *A Sudden Gust of Wind* (detail).

symbolising a "picture redressed". Just as the title *A Sudden Gust of Wind (After Hokusai)* refers to a point beyond the textual level and leads the viewer to question the self-explanatory character of the work, so the woman in disguise represents an inter-referential marker. Within the picture itself Wall shows us that what we took for evidence is partly already interpretation. The scene is dominated by an autumnal mood. The gust of wind takes hold of the tree's leaves and of the pages belonging to the human text alike. Wall's work transforms a nineteenth century Japanese picture into the pictorical reality of western civilization at the end of the twentieth century. The persons are dressed in a way which is more or less modern. The landscape with irrigated rice-plots shown on the coloured wood-cut is still of an agrarian character. Wall turns it into a contemporary agro-industrial scenery. To the left, different plots are marked out by white stakes. The stretch of running water beside the barren trees may be a canal under construction. In Wall's picture there is nothing purely accidental about the scenery be it the field, the trees, or the water, in fact, everything is designed by man.

There are, however, also significant differences between Wall's and Hokusai's works. For the Japanese artist there is one overruling reason to show us the scene in the foreground: he wants to contrast the transitoriness of human existence with the permanence of the mountain. In Wall's picture there is no such opposition. Mount Fuji is an abstract sign, a symbol represented by a single line. Human thought, recorded on the sheets of paper in Hokusai's print, is blown away in the face of the mountain's eternal majesty. There are different modes of depiction, too. In Hokusai's print, space is graded by curved lines, whereas Wall uses a system of graduated diagonals according to the rules of central perspective. But there is no target within this model for creating space. It leads – in spatial terms – nowhere, it is merely a principle of quantification, a means of measuring distances. Another contrast can be found regarding the sheets: while the blowing pages on Wall's picture seem to show numbers, Hokusai's are empty. The transformation of pictorial detail in the work of the Canadian artist seems to be somewhat laconic, considering that Mount Fuji finds its counterpart in the skyscraper to the left. Likewise the shinto shrine in Hokusai is echoed by the ramshackle huts on the right. Although nature is depicted in both images, it has a completely different meaning. In conclusion it might be said that the aspect of travesty, which is normally used to entertain and amuse, is transformed into a model of intercultural differences. I have chosen the term 'laconic' because of the absence of any spiritual or metaphysical context. At first sight it seemed as if Wall used the content of Hokusai's picture: the four figures, the landscape as well as the gust can be found in both. But with respect to travesty, the formal organization of the two images differ. The difference becomes even more pronounced concerning the meaning of both images. Hokusai has chosen the Fuji as a meditative sign, while Wall uses the scene for an art-theoretical message. In this context it is interesting to know that the Japanese term for photographing *shashin,* which literally means "writing down reality" can be opposed to the western term "light-drawing".

If we take a final look at Wall's picture we have to admit that the choreography is perfect: three of the figures constitute one single sequence of movements. Standing on tip-toe, the person on the far left is caught in an unsteady pose at the beginning of the movement. The second figure continues this movement by spinning around, and finally, the person in the center of the composition follows the flight of his hat like a discus-thrower watching his discus. This sequence is of interest because it can be seen not only simultaneously but also as a sequence. Only the starting-point and the end of the movement are obligatory, the pictures between these two points are optional. A similiar sequence was first put together by Edward Muybridge (fig. 4, overleaf). One can imagine a series of photographs which contains many or only a few moments of a sequential movement. The photographic image arises by stopping the movement. As for the viewer, it has to be pointed out that the idea of readability of images necessarily implies a link between time and meaning in our perception. The traditional opposition linking duration to literature and simultaneity to the pictorial arts becomes obsolete.

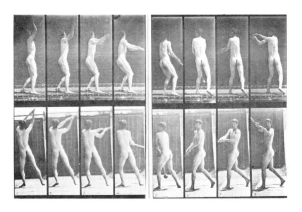

Figure 4. Edward Muybridge, *Man Swinging Bat.*

ICONOLOGY

If at first we consider this image simply as an autumnal scene, we then experience a shift in our perception as we come to recognize the integrated sequence of movements or the motif of travesty. Wall's *A Sudden Gust of Wind* is structured by irony which determines the change of our perception. In the end we find our perception of the picture completely inverted. My interpretation of Wall's image uses the iconological model of understanding pictures. Considering the current criticism of iconology, it may be helpful to ask why iconology continues to be a successful method and which future possibilities it may offer.[3] In this context, it is important to stress the close affinity between iconology and the aesthetics of perception. Both iconology and perception theory stress the productive role of the interpreter or viewer. This emphasis on the subject of visual perception in Erwin Panofsky's academic writings is closely related to his neo-Kantian position.[4] In 1932 the art historian, then in Hamburg, pointed this out in his article "Zum Problem der Beschreibung und Inhaltsdeutung von Werken der bildenden Kunst", showing that the specific virtue of visual argumentation is tied to the different degrees of readability of the different levels of the image.[5] His theory of iconology overcomes a positivistic understanding of pictures and can therefore be compared to intertextual research today. He aims to reconstruct that which is not explicitly shown by using

Figure 5. Jeff Wall, *Dead Troops Talk (A Vision After an Ambush of a Red Army Patron Near Mogor, Afghanistan, Winter 1986)*, 1992. Transparency in lightbox, 229 x 417 cm.

systems of reference associated with the concrete picture. Following Panofsky, no picture can be understood without ist context; understanding pictures is inseparably linked to the previous knowledge of the viewer. The results of interpretation will not be the same if the dependence of Wall's work on Hokusai remains in the dark.

This probably sounds easier than it really is, because meaning in an iconographic correlation is not intrinsic but differential so that the apparent evidence and identity of the picture depends on the pictorial tradition.

Each image combines iconographical and formal "ingredients". Furthermore, each picture belongs to a certain genre which also marks the necessity of a deeper interpretation. The fundamental difference between "word" and "image" cannot fully be grasped by the idea of a distinction between visual and phonetic signs. This does not become obvious before one questions the variety of the rules for linking these signs. While in written as well as in spoken language nouns are necessarily substituted by pronouns to provide a coherence of content, there are no comparable tools in the understanding of images. In most pictures there is more to be seen than is necessary to understand them. But the ability to segment perception in order to focus certain motifs within the image enables the spectator to select information continuosly. To understand an image means to have an idea of the hierarchy of information within the image.

THE THINKING IMAGE

Another of Wall's works which is of interest in this context is entitled *Dead Troops Talk* (fig. 5). We believe to be familiar with these kinds of images from news magazines. Russian soldiers were killed in an Afghan guerilla-attack. A young resistance fighter is searching a backpack for loot. A stoney slope is the background for the scene forming its overall two-dimensional impression set by two diagonal lines bracing the opposite corners of the picture. Horizontal and vertical lines lay out an almost classical construction. This strict scheme only becomes visible after a general impression of chance and accident has been established. In the upper left corner we see a wall, oil barrels and a battered piece of corrugated iron. Barely visible on the opposite side are the legs of two figures that might be two more resistance fighters. The upper part of the picture seems to end rather arbitrarily, thus emphasizing the way reporting photography cuts out a portion of reality.

Only on second glance the viewer finds that he has been taken in by a cliché – the cliché of fallen soldiers on the battlefield. For the blood-stained supernumeraries are not dead: grinning and talking to each other they rise from their poses, laughingly showing their fatal wounds – as if it were the scene after the "take". Everything was just posed, the cruel reality is fiction. One is reminded of a scene of Coppola's "Apocalypse Now", where a successful assault is being replayed for television. Furthermore the deathly pallor of battered corpses and their sinister games reminds us of the zombies as known from horror movies. The pictures of our media-reality may provide what we expect from them. The image we first suppose to be a visual stock-taking, reveals itself as an illusion. Now the crumpled paper (fig. 6 – detail) tissue and a tube of make-up or paint can be seen between the bodies. A snake is just crawling under a rock. These details are visible only if we look at the picture with a detective eye. This game with the viewer's distance to the picture reminds me of the many-figured compositions by Pieter Bruegel, which force the viewer to step closer to discover new details in an almost microscopic sphere. In this act of getting closer we move about with detailed detection. The viewer's position gets more critical or rather: more analytic. The make-up tube is tiny and can only be seen right in front of the picture. But still there is no privileged point of view. *Dead Troops* is the paradoxical combination of an obsession for detailed objects, e. g. the uniforms and the over-arrangement of this massacre with artificial blood and exaggerated poses. Wall's work is an irritation, an alienation of the supposed certainty of pictorial perception. On closer look the picture taken for a war photograph falls apart and reveals in a very unspecific way motifs from nineteenth century history painting: a soldier to the right pathetically touching his chest is a recurring motif from battle pieces. The pose of another figure reminds us of the mourning melancholic

Figure 6. Jeff Wall, *Dead Troops Talk* (detail).

father from Géricault's *The Raft of Medusa*.[6] Or the strange figure in the left foreground is similiar to a character in Delacroix' *Dante's Bark*.[7] The arrangement of the personnel inside a triangle works in a similiar way. What looks like a random arrangement at first, as in the case of the *Sudden Gust,* proves to be a formal composition. The figure seen from the rear in the left hand corner determining an entrance into the picture is a set piece of aesthetic perception: the composition rises from the lower left hand corner to the figure opposite on the right side. At the center of the composition is the vertex of the compositional triangle which is also the intersection of the diagonal lines. By means of this formal composition three soldiers form a central group enacting a grotesque scene. As if in play the "living dead" are showing each other their wounds, two soldiers aggravating a third one, by making him look into their wounds. This absurd motif condenses the narrative action of the picture: disgust and visual pleasure, sadism and exhibitionism force us to look at what we do not want to see. Yet another figure to the right seems to be rather amused by this scenario.

    Wall's cibachrome is a history painting of our time, relying equally on the pictorial tradition of both "high" and "low" culture. The large picture offers two different possibilities of perception: one that relies on distance for a total overview, another that encourages the detection of minute detail. Thus, we are confronted with two problems. How many single pictures were in fact fashioned into one unified scene? What does understanding a picture mean if one cannot rely on the evidence of the visible? Complex iconographic allusions are characteristic of most of Jeff Wall's works. It would be hard to pin-point all the references to other works of art that characterize his compositions. What is the purpose of these references? Would one misunderstand his works, if one did not take them into account? Wall's concept emphasizes the fact that any picture – whether intentionally or not – points beyond itself and can thus only be understood as one voice in a concert of many different voices. The blending of allusions into high art and with ordinary scenes brings up the problem of the relation between pictures inside and outside the museum. Some of Wall's pictures are open structures, they will find neither an identity nor a self-contained meaning. From this point of view *Dead Troops* is itself a visualised theory of the non-identical picture.

(The paper was translated by Sebastian Hackenschmidt.)

NOTES

1   de Duve, Thierry, Boris Groys, Arielle Pelenc, eds. *Jeff Wall*. London: Phaidon, 1996.

2   Hillier, J. *Hokusai*. Paintings, Drawings and Woodcuts. New York: Phaidon, 1978 [third edition].

3   Arrouye, Jean. "Archäologie der Ikonologie". Andreas Beyer, ed. *Die Lesbarkeit der Kunst, Zur Geistes-Gegenwart der Ikonologie*. Berlin: Wagenbach, 1992. 29-39.

4   Heinz Abels. "Die Zeit wieder in Gang bringen. Soziologische Anmerkungen zu einer unterstellten Wirkungsgeschichte der Ikonologie von Erwin Panofsky". Bruno Reudenbach, ed. *Erwin Panofsky. Beiträge des Symposions Hamburg 1992*. Berlin: Akademie Verlag, 1994. 213-28.

5   Erwin Panofsky. "Zum Problem der Beschreibung und Inhaltsdeutung von Werken der bildenden Kunst". Ekkehard Kaemmerling, ed. *Bildende Kunst als Zeichensystem. Ikonographie und Ikonologie*. Köln: Dumont, 1984. 185-206. [third edition].

6   Eitner, Lorenz. *Géricault's Raft of the Medusa*. London: Orbis Publishing, 1972.

7   Huyghe, René. *Delacroix*. München: C.H. Beck, 1967. 107-12.

Bruised Words, Wounded Images, in Frida Kahlo

Clara Orban

Frida Kahlo's works provide a poignant testimonial to a ravaged life. Through a series of misfortunes, she spent the majority of her adulthood undergoing dozens of painful, and often unnecessary, operations. Her canvases display her body's anguish, especially as she paints her broken flesh and bones. Since the early 1980s, Frida's work has attracted renewed interest. During most of her life she lived in the artistic shadow of her husband, the muralist Diego Rivera; current critical interest focuses intensely on her.[1] Scholars often discuss Frida's work thematically, concentrating on the abundant use of Mexican symbols, the overwhelming preference for self-portrait, and the insistence on portraying her physical ailments. The paintings which depict these shocking images often include words on the canvas. While many critical studies have noted that Frida's canvases with words resemble traditional Mexican *retablos,* or ex-voto offerings, they do not offer close analyses of the inscriptions themselves.[2] This paper studies the interaction of words and images in some of her work.

To Kahlo, inspiration was almost always mediated through the physical illness of her own broken body. At the age of six, she was stricken with polio which left her right leg weak and which probably contributed to its amputation due to gangrene when she was in her forties. As a teenager, she had hoped to study medicine. In her late teens, Kahlo was pierced through by a handrail as she was traveling on a bus which was sideswiped by a tram. The metal bar injured her spinal cord, crushed her right leg, and broke her pelvis.[3] Probably as a result of the accident, the three pregnancies she experienced were terminated, leaving her childless. She began painting as a way to relieve the boredom of her confinement. According to Hayden Herrera, "the girl whose ambition was to study medicine turned to painting as a form of psychological surgery" (74). Throughout the decades, her most frequent subject remained her fractured self.

The representational division between icon and symbol partially explains Frida's need to include words on her canvases.[4] These two ways of representing reality can work at counterpurposes when juxtaposed in a work of art, or they may complement each other. Complementary symbols imply that the void can be crossed, that wholeness can result from division. Throughout her life, Frida longed for wholeness in her body. She fulfills her wish in her art by confronting words and images on the canvas; often, both representational forms are necessary for understanding her work. Word and image come together to represent and to bridge the gap in her broken body, to make whole what is divided.

In Frida's work, the wound is often also the female, or femininity itself. Frida's miscarriages thwarted her desire for wholeness through motherhood. The vulva, a fissure reminiscent of an anatomical wound, appears prominent on canvases which depict births or miscarriages. The broken spinal column which tortured Frida for her adult life mirrors the split between saying and seeing. In *La columna rota* (*The Broken Column*, 1944), an ionic column, broken in several places, replaces her spinal column.[5] This work inverts the representational and the biological. The visual pun shifts from architectural element to damaged body part. Yet both spine and column are broken, and only the external brace which Frida often wore to support her ailing back provides support. The artistic refuge she sought in life does not provide the metaphorical support she needs. Only the machine made by the doctor can reassemble the fragments. Further, Frida's split self runs so deep that she often depicts herself as double. In *Las dos Fridas* (*Two Fridas,* 1939), Frida represents herself at two stages of life, two images of herself linked by large veins.[6] The blood supply stems from a small portrait of Rivera, whose stormy relationship with Frida was legendary. The hemostat in the young Frida's hand cannot staunch the blood. The purity of her white dress is soiled by blood, which mixes with the ornamental red flowers.

Approximately 55 of her 143 small canvases, executed in tiny, meticulous brush strokes, are self-portraits. She most often wears elaborate Mexican clothing, extravagant jewelry, and looks directly at the viewer with a calm, controlled expression. These self-portraits directly relate to the way in which the fractured body may often produce a fractured psyche. Yet not all the canvases on which Frida painted the pain of isolation and alienation are obvious self-portraits, although they do have autobiographical referents. In many instances, the artist employed words on the picture plane, along with gruesome, bloody images, to depict the fracturing of self. In *Unos cuantos piquetitos* (*A Few Small Nips,* 1935), Frida has captured the reality of a newspaper story in which a pimp, having been charged with the murder of his girlfriend, explains to the judge that "I only gave her a few small nips".[7] Frida found this *fait divers* of particular resonance since she had just discovered that her beloved sister, Cristina, had had an affair with Rivera. This betrayal, more so than Rivera's other escapades, emotionally hurt Frida. Seen in this light, the bloodied corpse of the woman can represent the psychologically wounded Frida, whose body has been rendered lifeless by this latest treason. The lover is too cruel to realize the enormity of his deed, thus rendering the inscription ironic.

However, analysis of the frame leads to a richer reading. As often is the case in paintings in which Frida disrupts the viewer with the sight of blood, the carnage does not stop at the picture frame, but invades the viewer's space. The blood on the frame seems applied by bloodied hands, leaving bloody fingerprints. This may indicate that Frida not only identifies with the scorned, murdered lover, but also fantasizes about being the assassin, avenging the hurt she feels. The blood is on Frida, it is part of her now, the hurt is hers as well. She leaves a trail of blood for the viewer.

The words on this canvas, "a few small nips", seem to hover above the picture space. This technique is reminiscent of *retablo* art. Victor Fosado writes that these traditional Mexican religious folk art paintings, often on wood or metal, are commissioned to depict a miracle cure or divine intervention. The bottom or top of the picture space typically include the words of testimonial. The top of the canvas usually shows the saint(s) who performed the miracle, and who are being thanked through the *retablo,* the ones to whom the work is dedicated. The center of the work often depicts the event, the cure, or the miracle, with the recipient of the miracle prominently featured. Fosado's analysis of Frida's work as it relates to this tradition concludes that Frida transforms herself into an image on the votive painting. She is both the saint and the beneficiary of the *retablo* (Fosado 179). Many of Frida's canvases with words display them in this *retablo* fashion. Rivera, always a keen supporter and analyst of his wife's work, noted that in Frida's *retablo*-like drawings, the Virgin, Christ and the saints disappear. What remains is the permanent miracle of life, represented by blood, the circulatory system, and internal organs on the picture plane.[8] In *A Few Small Nips,* then, Frida may be stating that life continues, even after treason, murder, and infidelity.

Another work in which words combine with images of destruction to heal the split inherent in the suffering self is *El suicidio de Dorothy Hale* (*Suicide of Dorothy Hale,* 1939).[9] Clare Booth Luce commissioned Frida to paint the work in honor of their mutual friend as a gift for Hale's mother. Yet Luce hated the work so much that she demanded Frida blot out the words on the canvas which stated her patronage. Again, the blood which drips from the lifeless corpse invades the viewer's space as though the agony refused to be contained by the frame. In this painting, in contrast to the previous one, the blood seems to seep in small rivulets from inside the frame, as though the canvas were absorbing Hale's blood. While the frame of *A Few Small Nips* contained fingerprints, traces for reading murder, here, the frame soaks the suicidal "blood"; it and the paint used to depict it, are one.

The words on this canvas provide a narrative of the event: "in the city of New York, the twenty-first day of the month of October, 1938, at six in the morning Mrs. Dorothy Hale committed suicide by throwing herself from a very high window of the Hampshire House building. In her memory, (blot),

this *retablo* was executed by Frida Kahlo". The narrative nature of the text
mimics the narrative nature of the simultaneous images, in which we see the
woman's fall in two different temporal moments, and then her lifeless body on
the pavement. The blood smear under the word "suicide" tautologically enhances the word's meaning. In *A Few Small Nips,* the words on the canvas float
above the space. They are separated from the background, as though on a
cloth, but integrated into the canvas. This distancing simulates reading words
in a newspaper, from which Frida garnered the details of the crime. The large,
bold capital letters scream recognition: words of the assassin that scream his
crime. In *Suicide of Dorothy Hale,* the neat, minuscule script mimics the neat,
minuscule brushstrokes on the canvas. The text appears in a peripheral zone,
still part of the canvas, but already becoming part of the frame. These words
stand guard between the reality of our world and the illusion of the picture
plane. Hale's foot crosses that line, transgressing the boundary. These are the
words of the artist, who confronts us with details of this death. They provide
precise, temporal frames for the event, and descriptive elements such as the
adverbial phrase "very high". Frida masks her emotional involvement in the
crime depicted in *A Few Small Nips* by using words on the canvas whose litotic
nature contrasts markedly with the hyperbolic presence of blood on the canvas. In *Suicide of Dorothy Hale,* however, she enriches her text with details to
make us part of the tragic iconographic and linguistic narrative, which stands
as an epitaph for Hale.

   If we look closely at the words, those in block letters spell the names of the
artist and of the deceased woman, connecting the two. In an ironic inversion
of the *retablo,* could it be that the name of the victim represents the one for
whom a miracle was performed, while the name of the artist is the one by
whose intercession the miracle was performed? Perhaps Hale's dead but sensual body is a metaphor for Frida herself, full of life and sensuality, but broken
and misshapen.[10]

   After 1940, Frida's life changed for the worse. Divorced, then a year later
remarried to Rivera, they lived almost separate lives in two different sections
of her "casa azúl".[11] In her forties, she had lost hope of having the child she so
longed for. Furthermore, despite numerous surgeries, her physical ailments
only worsened. During these years, self-portraits with inscriptions, along with
images of the lacerated body provide a tautology of suffering: pain is rendered
through images of wounded bodies, and through words on the canvas.

   A self-portrait from 1940 presents a symbolic sexual mutilation. *Autorretrato
con pelo cortado* (*Self Portrait With Cropped Hair*) shows Frida wearing a baggy
man's suit, with tresses of her newly shorn hair scattered around the room.[12] In
the upper portion of the canvas, words from a song: "Look, if I loved you, it
was for your hair. Now that you are bald, I do not love you anymore". These
words are spoken by a lover who will presumably abandon Frida, now that her

hair has been cut. As Robin Richmond declares, in this work Frida "looks out of the painting at Diego with a slight smirk on her face. He, too, loved her hair, and now, like him, it is gone. She has become a man without her man" (113). These words are not separated by visual means from the background of the canvas. The words and accompanying musical notes hover within the space with the lightness of background music. Two horizontal linear waves extend the words and sound waves visually to the outer edges of the canvas and beyond. These words could be spoken by Diego, or by Frida, who may be commenting on the fact that Diego was much older than she is. They are also the words of all of us, of those belonging to the culture which would recognize the lyrics of a popular song. The scissors, poised at her genitals, suggest the defiant attitude of one who has undergone sacrificial mutilation. These words and their ambiguous origin create a complexity of human relationships between viewer, canvas, and the lover.

The hair in this picture takes the place of the spilled blood in the paintings discussed earlier. They are parts of the body which are rendered in sacrifice, in pain, to the viewer. Frida's text implies an infidelity, and the images imply her way of coping with it. She destroys that part of her anatomy which renders her the most feminine, which she would spend hours adorning with ribbons, flowers, fruits, combs and jewelry: her hair. In many other portraits, Frida accentuated the masculine features of her face—her bushy eyebrows and slight mustache. In this painting, she goes one step further by destroying the feminine and donning masculine attire. Even more, the enormity of the man's suit makes it likely that she has portrayed herself wearing Diego's clothes. She destroys herself and assumes the persona of the one she castigates. To become fully herself, she must become him. The words on this canvas provide emotional healing by lifting tension through laughter.

In 1946, Frida returned to images of her surgeries in a very explicit way, and this time, added words to the canvas. *Arbol de la esperanza, mantente firme (Tree of Hope, Stand Firm)* again depicts the split Frida: on one side, the faceless body on the operating table, spinal cord broken; on the other, the healthy woman, triumphantly carrying the brace she will ostensibly no longer need.[13] The healthy Frida carries a banner, almost a revolutionary slogan, which states "tree of hope, remain firm", the title of a folk song. Not by chance does a revolutionary context loom large, given that Diego and Frida were both prominent members of the Mexican Communist party. This canvas was executed after she had undergone an unsuccessful spinal fusion at New York's Hospital for Special Surgery. The barren, desert landscape only accentuates the poignancy of these words. It is hope against hope for Frida. Her spirit retains its optimism, but she knows there is little hope left for a cure, only a revolution could provide this. Frida sees herself hoping for the revolution, for the return

Figure 1. *Yo soy la desintegración. The Diary
of Frida Kahlo. An Intimate Self-Portrait* (71).
Permission to reproduce kindly granted by
La Vaca Independiente S. A. de C. V.

to a health she had not enjoyed since childhood. The words and their placement in heraldic fashion add this revolutionary element.

Frida's paintings chronicle her shifting relationship to her body, as she
lives her shifting relationship to others. The emotional wounds others inflict
upon her become physical wounds on the bodies of women on her canvases.
At times, her relationship to her wounded body is rendered explicitly through
images of wounds and words on the same canvas. Undoubtedly, Frida's works
are among the most personal of any artist. Yet perhaps the most personal words
and images Frida ever depicted are in her diary, published in 1995, and until
then virtually inaccessible. Frida kept this diary from the early '40s until her
death in 1954. It is unusual in that it is both a veritable sketchpad and a
journal intime. As Sarah M. Lowe has noted, these texts represent private
records "written by a woman for herself" ("Essay" 25). Also, it is not a typical
sketchbook because Frida does not use it for preparatory drawings (Lowe,
"Essay" 26). It remains a repository of feelings, in words and images. It has
often been noted that Frida's self-portraits are almost antithetical to the genre.
Her defiant features stare at the viewer as though they were a mask, unrevealing
of emotion. Lowe reminds us that Frida referred to herself as "la gran
ocultadora", the great dissimulator ("Essay" 26). In this diary, her most per-

Figure 2. *Alas rotas. The Diary of Frida Kahlo. An Intimate Self-Portrait* (156). Permission to reproduce kindly granted by La Vaca Independiente S. A. de C. V.

sonal testimonial, Frida uses words and images, color, line, prose and poetry, to unmask herself.

As mentioned earlier, by 1940, Frida had reached a crisis. Her last decade was consumed with increasing pain, which led to the amputation of her foot due to gangrene. This pain, which is often clinically rendered in her paintings, appears in her diary in all its emotional horror. It is difficult to date the pages of the diary, on which she worked intermittently, but the page reproduced in Figure 1 was composed sometime between 1944 and 1947. The image of the architectural column, which recalls her earlier painting *The Broken Column*, represents her last hope of wholeness. The caption, "I am disintegration", reinforces the image of the leg/column giving way under the weight of the body. The words float about the picture, the phrase ending in mid air, suspended by punctuation. The boldest word is "desintegración", in capital letters. Those which are graphically more tenuous mark her existence: "Yo soy (la)". Being itself destructs on this page. Frida depicts herself as virtually lifeless, almost a doll impaled on a column. Falling below her body are duplicate body parts – an eye, a hand, a head. Columns are often all that remain of ruined temples from ancient civilizations; it is all that is left to support the crumbling ruin that is Frida's body. The heaviness of her flesh as she struggles to walk and stand reappears often in the diary. In characteristically optimistic terms, Frida takes on suffering as a cloak; not only does she suffer, but she becomes suffering itself. By appropriating the image of her broken self, in a way, she becomes whole. What comes apart in her body can only be restituted in her art.

In one of her last diary entries, executed after 1953, Frida unflinchingly sees the end, and, again characteristically, makes a wry pun about her deformity. In this page of the diary (fig. 2), "Are you going? No" appears on the top of the page, while the words "broken wings" appear on the bottom. Even her end will not be hastened due to her illness. The body becomes more difficult to bear as Frida realizes death is near. With this poignant farewell, Frida explores the possibility of leaving the body which has always been a burden to her. Her body, which had crumbled in the earlier drawing from her diary, disappears here; only her breasts and face remain visible. She looks directly out from a wall of what appear to be branches, with flames engulfing their roots. She may be the Phoenix, or more likely a martyr, burning, but sure to rise again. Even in the sad realization that her wings cannot offer her flight, she depicts herself as a figure of hope and courage. Her metaphorical wings, her wholeness, live through her art.

In his introduction to the diary, Carlos Fuentes wrote that Mexicans differ from Europeans in that, while Europeans conceive of death as a finality, Mexicans "descend from death [they] are children of death [. . .] death is [their] companion" (23). He understands Frida's work in the light of this quintessential "Mexicanness": her ability to greet death as though she had always known it. Perhaps she had. Her diary, that most personal testimonial, continues to join words and images on the page as a way of exploring the existential rupture of the self.

NOTES

1   Renewed critical interest in Frida's work can be traced to Hayden Herrera's 1983 biography, which offered a compilation of the painter's life. In the same year, another book on Frida appeared, written by her friend, Raquel Tibol. One of the most penetrating studies of Frida's art is Sarah Lowe's 1991 text. Frida has become a virtual cult figure, and several artists have created works inspired by her style.

2   Several of the works cited here are among those to which I refer.

3   See Herrera (45) and following, for more information on the accident.

4   Much debate centers around the nature of this separation, whether or not it remains an uncrossable divide.

5   For illustration, see Richmond (21).

6   For illustration, see Richmond (111).

7   For illustration, see Richmond (69). In this paper, I have translated words on the canvas from the Spanish.

8   This reference can be found in *Museo Frida Kahlo* (11).

9   For illustration, see Richmond (114).

10 Many critics have commented on the sensual nature of the corpse, its outspread legs, and its gaze, as though living, looking directly at the viewer,

11 This "blue house" is where Frida was born in 1907 (although she liked to state her birthday was 1910, so her birth would coincide with the Mexican Revolution). Her family was experiencing financial problems when Frida became engaged to the successful Rivera, who offered to pay off the mortgage on the property. Frida inherited the house, which the two artists shared. This same building today houses the Frida Kahlo Museum.

12 For illustration, see Richmond (112).

13 For illustration, see Hayden Herrera, Figure XXX (290 ff.).

References

Fosado, Victor. "Les tableaux votifs – les alliés de Frida". In: *La casa azúl*. The Hague: Museum Palaeis Lange Voorhout, 1993.

Fuentes, Carlos. "Introduction". *The Diary of Frida Kahlo. An Intimate Portrait*. New York: Abrams, 1995.

Herrera, Hayden. *Frida. A Biography of Frida Kahlo*. New York: Harper and Row, 1983.

Kahlo, Frida. *The Diary of Frida Kahlo: An Intimate Self-Portrait*. Introduction by Carlos Fuentes, essays and commentaries by Sarah M. Lowe. New York: H. N. Abrams; Mexico: La Vaca Independiente S.A. de C.V., 1995.

Lowe, Sarah M. *Frida Kahlo*. New York: Universe, 1991.

———. "Essay". *The Diary of Frida Kahlo. An Intimate Portrait*. New York: Abrams, 1995.

Museo Frida Kahlo. Mexico City: Universidad Autónoma del México, 1955.

Richmond, Robin. *Frida Kahlo in Mexico*. San Francisco: Pomegranate, 1994.

Tibol, Raquel. *Frida Kahlo: An Open Life*. Trans. Elinor Randall. Albuquerque: University of New Mexico Press, 1983.

Pictorial *ars praedicandi* in Late Fifteenth-century Paintings

Véronique Plesch

It is as much a cliché to compare paintings to *muta praedicatio* – silent preaching – (Gougaud) as it is to call them the books of the illiterate. The relationships between preaching and the visual arts are usually taken for granted by scholars dealing with monumental and public art, especially that found in rural zones, where the level of literacy is assumed to be low. As a result of this basic assumption, the links between these two forms of expression have seldom been addressed concretely. To fully grasp the interaction between pictorial and homiletic practices, different possibilities should be considered: the relationship could be one of content; it could also be a functional one, in which the paintings are integrated into a sermon through direct references made by the preacher; or the two forms of expression could be morphologically comparable in their rhetoric and organization.

Art historical scholarship often resorts to vague references to the homiletic content of paintings, considered within a primarily logocentric framework, in which the unilateral influences go from word to image, from sermon to pictorial decoration. Some art historians, however, have addressed this relationship in more specific terms, suggesting a more fluid coexistence of the two forms of expression. In 1957, Lilian Randall linked the emergence of marginalia in manuscript illumination with the development of exempla in vernacular sermons. In the course of her study, she analyzed the relationship between sermon and images not only in terms of content and sources but also – although briefly – in terms of form and function. More recently, Michael Baxandall suggested intimate connections between the two forms of expression: "the preachers coached the public in the painter's repertory, and the painters responded within the current emotional categorization of the event" (55). Alessandro Nova explained how Lombard choir screens covered with passion scenes are closely tied to the Franciscan Observance and to Saint Bernardine's conception of preaching. Andrée Hayum, besides noting "common threads" in Mathias Grünewald's Isenheim altarpiece and contemporary sermons, considered structural links between the spoken delivery of a sermon and the strategies of appeal to an audience that Grünewald employed as a painter (104).

In order to explore further the links between homiletic and pictorial expressions, I have chosen as a case-study the mural decoration of the pilgrimage church of Notre-Dame des Fontaines, at La Brigue, some 80 km north-east of

Figure 1. Giovanni Canavesio, *Mocking of Christ.* Notre-Dame des Fontaines, La Brigue. Courtesy of the Frick Art Reference Library.

Nice. They present a privileged case indeed, for the artist who completed them in 1492, the Piedmontese Giovanni Canavesio, was also a priest. In fact, I have come to the conclusion that the messages put forth by Canavesio, as well as (and more importantly) the strategies he employed to convey meaning and to structure the viewer's experience, pictorial and grounded in tradition though they may be, are also informed by his priestly training, and that they reflect mental structures derived from one of his most important professional tools, the *ars praedicandi.*[1] At the end of the twelfth century Alan of Lille wrote the first of such preaching manuals, one that remained the "most accomplished example of the genre" and the "standard ... throughout the middle ages" (Briscoe 20, 25). In it, he defined preaching as "an open and public instruction in faith and behavior" (Alan 17). Preaching thus fulfills a two-fold purpose: to teach about faith and about behavior, or, as Alan put it "preaching sometimes teaches about holy things, sometimes about conduct" (17).

"Teaching about holy things": the first function of preaching is the teaching of the Gospel (Longère 16). Already in this sense pictorial cycles narrating the life of Christ share preaching's basic content. At La Brigue the story of Christ's life is told in 37 scenes, from his Infancy on the triumphal arch, to his Passion and Resurrection on the nave walls. Preaching could also be said to teach about conduct, for it provides the viewer with the behavioral model of

Figure 2. Giovanni Canavesio, *Crowning with Thorns*. Notre-Dame des Fontaines, La Brigue. Courtesy of the Frick Art Reference Library.

imitatio Christi. The knowledge of Christ's sufferings helps the faithful to bear their own and to sublimate them, as it expounds on the Christian equation between suffering and redemption. Christ's example can also be an encouragement to specific ascetic and penitential practices, especially during Lent, such as fasting and abstinence. Such a message is prominent at Notre-Dame des Fontaines, a pilgrimage sanctuary – that is, a building at the service of an eminently penitential practice (Dupront, Sigal). Moreover, the passion cycle presents a very detailed account of Christ's sufferings, including, besides the traditional representations of the *Mocking* (fig. 1), the *Crowning with Thorns* (fig. 2), and the *Flagellation* (fig. 3), an additional, fourth, scene of torture which takes place between the first appearance before Pilate and that before Herod. The inclusion of this episode increases the gravity of Christ's sufferings; at the same time the expiatory message is more emphatically rendered by the diversity and intensity of the tortures to which Christ is submitted, each of the henchmen being engaged in more than one action: one simultaneously blows a horn and makes an insulting gesture, the next hits, insults, and pulls Christ's beard, the third hits and spits, the fourth hits and pulls hair, and the last spits and gestures insultingly.

The cycle also develops the plots of secondary figures such as the apostles Judas and Peter, who constitute opposing behavioral exempla: Peter betrays

Figure 3. Giovanni Canavesio, *Flagellation* (left), *Denial of Peter* (right). Notre-Dame des Fontaines, La Brigue. Courtesy of the Frick Art Reference Library.

Christ by denying him, but through tears of repentance redeems himself (fig. 3) while Judas, despite regretting his betrayal and returning the 30 silver coins (fig. 4), damns himself by despairing and committing suicide (fig. 4). These figures convey an ethical message: no matter how serious the sin, in order to be saved what is important is to repent in time, and not to despair. Thus Canavesio aims at encouraging the viewer to receive the sacrament of penance. This sacrament consists of three moments: contrition, confession, and satisfaction. Contrition is the feeling the sinner experiences when he realizes that he has sinned and regrets it. He should then confess to an ordained minister of the Church, who will order him to perform penitential activities such as prayers, fasting, giving alms or masses, and, if necessary, returning ill-gotten gains (Tentler). This process is staged here (fig. 4): Judas, moved by contrition, confesses his sin to the priests – the speech act of confession is materialized by the scroll with the opening words "Pecavi" – he also returns the money, thus achieving satisfaction. Unfortunately, he nonetheless despairs of Christ's pardon.

In 1215 the Fourth Lateran council made confession obligatory at least once a year (generally at Easter time), and since then one of the main purposes of preaching has been to encourage it (Martin 386 ff, Bernstein 15, Tentler 81). For Alan of Lille a good sermon should "move the spirits of its hearers, stir up the mind, and encourage repentance" (19-20). Teaching about sins

Figure 4. Giovanni Canavesio, *Remorse of Judas* (upper register), *Nailing to the Cross and Suicide of Judas* (lower register). Notre-Dame des Fontaines, La Brigue. Courtesy of the Frick Art Reference Library.

Figure 5. Giovanni Canavesio, *Last Judgment*. Notre-Dame des Fontaines, La Brigue. Courtesy of the Frick Art Reference Library.

prepares one for confession, and so preachers defined, enumerated, and classified sins (Tentler 111-12, 233; Longère 213). In the ninth chapter of the *Rule of St. Francis,* the friars were instructed to preach "vice and virtue, punishment and glory":[2] the discourse on sins is intimately tied to their contrary, the virtues, and to their respective rewards, hell and heaven. At the same time, confession was presented as the means to escape hell, for the preachers strove to show the continuity between the actions here below and their outcome in the next world (Longère 212). So does Canavesio, who stages a varied cast of sinners, with the *Last Judgment* (fig. 5) trenchantly displaying their fate. In this monumental composition on the entrance wall, we find the proof of the effectiveness of Peter's tears of repentance, for he appears among the apostles, indeed at a place of choice, closest to Christ and on his right side. We also find Judas among the damned, under the banner of the "traditori e desperati", traitors and desperates.[3]

Of all the paintings in the chapel, the *Last Judgment* is the one most unmistakably addressing the viewer, for it is there that the ultimate and irreversible reward and punishment for one's life appears. The actuality and the proximity of the depiction are heightened by the use of vernacular Italian inscriptions to label the damned.[4] The representation also emphatically states the link between sin and penance: next to the archangel Michael, an angel blows a trumpet, with a scroll that reads: "As your sin was infinite, so should be your penance" thus expressing the implacable accountability that ties the two concepts.

Vivid and detailed descriptions of hell played an important role in penitential preaching. The Dominican Stephen of Bourbon, in his *Treatise on Different Preachable Matters,* which he compiled between 1250 and his death in 1261, devotes an important section to hell, entitled "On the fear of hell", itself divided into nine chapters (Bernstein 30 ff). Besides descriptions of hell and its torments there is a chapter on the "Benefits of meditating upon hell", which in essence are two: to avoid sin and to mitigate present suffering. At La Brigue, the accent is unmistakably on punishment rather than on reward: St. Michael and Christ both turn towards the damned and do not seem to care much about the blessed. Unlike most contemporary Last Judgments, La Brigue's damned are not labeled according to capital sins, but instead by activities, or actions, which further anchor the depiction into the here and now: we have "traitors and desperates", "thieves, deceivers and blasphemers", "hypocrites and false penitents", "procuresses and their adulterers", "usurers with false merchants", "usurers and robbers", "false witnesses" (Baschet 392). In addition we find the Jews, whose presence among the sinners is anomalous inasmuch they do not represent a specific type of sinful activity, nor a capital sin – there is indeed a strong anti-Jewish undercurrent at La Brigue. And there, too, Canavesio adopts an attitude comparable to that of contemporary preachers, who were particularly outspoken against Jews. I should also add that through an attack on Jews, Canavesio hopes to warn his public against unbelief and probably also against the Waldensian heresy. He also lobbies in favor of the founding of Christian lending institutions, the Monte di Pietà, as a means of avoiding Jewish usury.[5]

If in the *Last Judgment* Canavesio breaks with the tradition and does not include capital sins as categories of damned, these can nevertheless be found elsewhere at La Brigue. The passion cycle offers a set of figures who, by their depiction or the meaning attached to them, allude to capital sins.[6] The high priest Caiaphas tears his clothes apart during Christ's appearance, as do personifications of *ira*, the sin of anger (fig. 6). The three apostles who abandon Christ by falling asleep at Gethsemane can be seen as prey to *accidia*, sloth. *The Suicide of Judas* (fig. 4) can be interpreted as another embodiment of *ira*, often personified as a figure committing suicide. But Canavesio's rendition of the Suicide – in its own elongated frame – also calls to mind depictions of the sin of despair, such as the *Desperatio* painted by Giotto in the Arena Chapel.

Morphologically, too, the strategies Canavesio used can be compared to those recommended to preachers in the *ars praedicandi;* rules which themselves were based on classical rhetorical theory (Longère 33-4, Briscoe 56).

Figure 6. Giovanni Canavesio, *Entry into Jerusalem* (upper register), *Christ before Caiaphas* (lower register). Notre-Dame des Fontaines, La Brigue. Courtesy of the Frick Art Reference Library.

Canavesio shaped his pictorial idiom – his visual *elocutio* – in order to capture the attention of the viewer, and to involve him or her. Through the placement of figures and the way in which the action unfolds, he imparted a strong left to right motion to his depictions to guide the viewer's eye through a correct viewing sequence.[7] Canavesio strove to make the account as vivid as possible, by varying physiognomies and postures, costumes and settings. As was advised to preachers, he modulated his *elocutio*,[8] by investing the depictions with different moods and rhythms, going from quiet, dignified, and harmonious depictions, as in the *Entry into Jerusalem* (fig. 6), to jarring compositions as the *Flagellation* (fig. 3) with its confused space —which I consider as depending upon a conscious choice, aimed at expressionistic purposes, rather than the result of a technical incapacity. He thereby transposed into the pictorial realm Alan of Lille's precept to preachers, to "introduce moving words which soften hearts and encourage tears" (22, Briscoe 23). By 1492 the requirement to stir the public's emotions was more important than ever, preaching having become an extremely theatrical activity.

Through the organization of the different parts of the narrative account – the *ordinatio* – and through the treatment of individual scenes, Canavesio employed strategies which were among the means used by preachers to expand themes and which, at the same time, constitute didactic tools: these include contrary themes, resemblances, causes and effects, distinctions (Longère 198, 200-1; Briscoe 30-1). Binary oppositions, supposed to be easy to memorize, strongly structure Canavesio's paintings. They inform his pictorial idiom, with his dichotomic use of ugly and/or caricatural features and postures versus idealized ones, of profile views, reserved for Christ's enemies, versus three-quarter views for Christ's followers. They also structure single panels, such as the *Crucifixion,* with its traditional dichotomy of good characters on Christ's right and bad ones on his left – the Good Thief Dismas and the Bad Thief Gestas, an angel and a devil, St. John with the holy women and the soldiers fighting for Christ's tunic. This is also seen in the panel of Judas' *Remorse* (fig. 4), with Christ being led to his positive, redemptive death and Judas about to commit his negative, damning suicide. Oppositions also articulate counterpoints of scenes. Such is the pairing of Judas' *Suicide* with the *Crucifixion,* a powerful comment upon the sinful and redemptive death. There are also several significant instances of vertical juxtapositions between scenes in the upper and lower register. The *Washing of the Feet* and the *Denial of Peter* (fig. 3), for example, both place an emphasis on the apostle. In the *Washing of the Feet,* Peter appears in a central position and the moment depicted is the one of his dialogue with Christ, as reported by John (13:6-11), with Christ saying to Peter: "If I do not wash you, you have no part in me" and Peter replying: "Lord, not my feet only but also my hands and my head!" The following words of Christ, "You are not all clean", (John 13:11) assume, in the context created by the disposition of the scenes, the status of an anticipation of Peter's betrayal in his *Denial,* and most importantly, generate a metatext expounding on moral cleansing through penance. The *Washing of the Feet* indeed affirms the need for such a purification and reinforces the message delivered in the lower panel: Peter's successful penance through tears.[9]

We have seen, too, how protagonists in the passion cycle, such as Christ and Judas, are also opposed. And so are those who succeed in their repentance, Peter and others, such as the good thief Dismas, who are opposed to Judas, who fails by despairing. Formal analogies constitute a visual equivalent of metaphors, another important tool for the preacher. In the context of the emphasis given to penance and purification – purification through penance – the presence of maids engaged in housekeeping activities in association with the depiction of Christ's sufferings (in the *Mocking,* fig. 1, and the *Crowning with Thorns,* fig. 2) assumes its full meaning, house-cleaning being a common homiletic trope for confession (Martin 392, 448 ff, 451; Owst 35-6). Peter's successful penance after his *Denial* (fig. 3) is combined with a cluster of formal allusions to cleansing: his weeping is paired with the washing of his feet by Christ in the scene above, and the cloth he uses to wipe his tears is juxtaposed to the white cloth hanging from the balcony above him.[10] Finally, there are the springs below the chapel, whose miraculous waters are the origin of the sanctuary and a metaphor for the purification achieved through pilgrimage.[11]

As a fifteenth-century preacher, Canavesio manifested his taste for the numbering of the parts of his discourse, expressed in his use of *tituli,* Latin inscriptions that run below each scene and number and describe them. His choice of Latin for the *tituli* and for other inscriptions is also comparable to contemporary sermons, in which Latin quotations were generously interspersed throughout a vernacular discourse (Martin 269, Briscoe 52). As Alan Knight has shown for late medieval religious theater, Latin insertions functioned as markers, pointing to the homiletic character of a passage (248). In the relationship between text and image, Latin inscriptions fulfill a similar connotative role, while the paintings, as in a sermon with parts in Latin, appear as equivalents of the vernacular. Latin and vernacular stand in the same relation to each other as Scriptures and lessons drawn from them, the moral lessons to be applied in everyday life.

If the paintings' message is forcefully conveyed, it is not for all that monolithic. As was recommended to preachers, Canavesio aimed his paintings at different publics,[12] displaying behavioral examples and counter-examples, and threatening the audience with punishment in hell. He also proposed more complex theological and doctrinal messages. We find, for example, through the choice and treatment of scenes and through the importance given to figures such as Judas and Malchus, a reflection on the issue of unbelief and of its links with Judaism and heresy – two themes full of resonance to La Brigue in

1492, which then had a Jewish community and was confronted with the threat of Waldensianism (Plesch 254-62). Also, among the more sophisticated messages we find a consideration of Judas' role in the Economy of Salvation. The viewer is led to ponder whether Judas' treason was a necessary evil or not, and therefore whether it was unavoidable for Christ to die on the cross (Plesch *passim*).

Canavesio's working through the combination and adaptation of borrowed motifs – both formal and conceptual – is a creative approach he also shared with preachers, sermons being "essentiellement des montages de pièces rapportées" (Martin 243). Painter and priest, Canavesio made use of visual and verbal models to achieve a real "polyphonic textual dialogue" (to borrow Heinrich Plett's felicitous expression [10]) between the paintings and their sources. He translated verbal signs into visual ones when he rooted the subject of his depictions in a text – the Gospels. More than that, the paintings' narrative and message are a crystallization of an enduring and multifaceted tradition comprising not only the four Gospels, but also apocrypha, glosses, dramatic adaptations, and other religious texts – a common textual repository from which preachers, dramatists, and painters alike drew their inspiration and their materials (Longère 177-202). He also assimilated and transformed visual texts, incorporating elements or entire compositions from contemporary engravings, from earlier passion cycles, and from his *own* previous cycles. All these elements were processed through assimilation and transformation characteristic of the intertextual work. In order to unify these heterogeneous elements, Canavesio the painter affirmed the linearity of his new text through a visual syntax, displaying his consummate understanding of the medium. In so doing, Canavesio the priest was fulfilling William of Auvergne's requirement of "materie continuatio" – maintaining a smooth flow of ideas (Briscoe 31).

I have mentioned how binary oppositions were supposed to be easy to memorize. Indeed, memory is fundamental to the homiletic practice, and many of the precepts from the *ars praedicandi,* and Canavesio's derived characteristics I have described, have a mnemonic function. If these features can help secure the depicted events in the memories of viewers, they also constitute an aid for the preacher. The creation of memory images in the orator's mind constitutes a "pictorial script" of sorts on which he could base his speech (Enders 45). Thus the cycle could be seen as a materialization of Canavesio's own theater of memory, making it available for future use by other preachers.

NOTES

1   On Canavesio, the most recent contributions with a bibliography are Rotondi Terminiello and Algeri and De Floriani 324-48 and 499. My own study of the passion cycle at La Brigue has yielded two results which, at first, may seem contradictory. If it confirms that both stylistically and iconographically Canavesio's art is rooted in the pictorial traditions established earlier in the fifteenth century in the duchy of Savoy by artists such as Giacomo Jaquerio, it also reveals an unusual richness and complexity. In the tension created by this apparent conflict lies the main interest of this case-study. We have an artist who was a priest, and who, as such, knew at once both the medium and the messages to be conveyed and was familiar with the functions religious pictorial decoration should fulfill. Thus, Notre-Dame represents a pertinent case, one that provides us with an entry into the issues of the meanings and functions of the monumental passion cycle as a genre.

2   Quoted by John W. O'Malley in Amos (6). This goal is apparent in all the *ars praedicandi*. Alan of Lille's *Ars praedicandi* consisted of three sections: how to fight the vices (chapters 2-10), how to promote virtues and spiritual or moral behavior (chapters 11-25 and 29-37) and how to adapt preaching to different social groups (chapters 38-47).

3   Judas is also present in hell in Dante's *Divina Commedia,* at the very bottom of the *Inferno,* inside Satan's middle mouth (*Inferno,* 33:55-62): see Axton 197. There are examples of depictions of Judas in Last Judgments in Savoy, such as at the chapel of the Madonna della Neve (della Piana), at San Michele Mondovì and painted in 1484 by Jean Baleison at the chapel of San Sebastiano at Celle Macra. In both cases the representations are inspired by Dante, with Judas immediately next to Lucifer – which is not the case at Notre-Dame.

4   Latin is used throughout the chapel but in the *Last Judgment* it is reserved for Christ, for the saints and patriarchs, the angels and the devils.

5   Plesch 254-62. For another instance of artistic production linked to propaganda in favor of Monti di Pietà, see Lavin, "The Altar".

6   On capital sins in general, see Bloomfield and Katzenellenbogen.

7   On how to view pictorial narrative, see Lavin, *The Place of Narrative.*

8   For preachers being advised to modulate their delivery, see Baxandall 64.

9   On the importance of tears in the context of repentance, see Payen. Tears also appear in the semantic field of *penitentia* as analyzed by Martin in late medieval sermons (389-92).

10 Peter's wiping of his tears calls to mind the statement by Olivier Maillard, a fifteenth-century preacher, that "confession washes with tears. True contrition dries them with a linen cloth" (quoted by Taylor 127).

11 On the importance of springs in the establishment of pilgrimage sites, see Dupront 37-38.

12 See above, note 2.

REFERENCES

Alan of Lille. *The Art of Preaching.* Trans. G. R. Evans. Kalamazoo: Cistercian Publications, 1981.

Algeri, G. and A. De Floriani. *La pittura in Liguria. Il Quattrocento.* Genova: Tormena, 1992.

Amos, T. L., et al. *De Ore Domini: Preacher and Word in the Middle Ages.* Kalamazoo: Medieval Institute Publications, 1989.

Axton, R. "Interpretations of Judas in Middle English Literature". In: P. Boitani and A. Torti, eds., *Religion in the Poetry and Drama of the Late Middle Ages in England.* Cambridge: Brewer, 1990. 179-97.

Baschet, J. *Les justices de l'aud-delà: Les représentations de l'enfer en France et en Italie, XIIe-XIVe siècle.* Rome: Ecole Française de Rome, 1993 (Bibliothèque des écoles françaises d'Athènes et de Rome, 279).

Baxandall, M. *Painting and Experience in Fifteenth-Century Italy.* 2nd ed. Oxford/New York: Oxford University Press, 1988.

Bernstein, A. "The Invocation of Hell in Thirteenth-Century Paris". In: *Supplementum Festivum. Studies in Honor of Paul Oskar Kristeller.* Binghamton: Center for Medieval and Early Renaissance Studies, State University of New York at Binghamton, 1987. 13-54.

Bloomfield, M. *The Seven Deadly Sins: An Introduction to the History of a Religious Concept, with Special Reference to Medieval English Literature.* East Lansing, Michigan: Michigan State College Press, 1952.

Briscoe, M. G. *Artes Praedicandi.* Turnhout: Brepols, 1992 (Typologie des sources du Moyen Age occidental, 61).

Dupront, A. "Pèlerinages et lieux sacrés". In: *Du Sacré. Croisades et pèlerinages. Images et langages.* Paris: Gallimard, 1987. 366-415.

Enders, J. "Visions with Voices: The Rhetoric of Memory and Music in Liturgic Drama". *Comparative Drama* 24 (1990): 34-54.

Gougaud, L. "Muta praedicatio". *Revue bénédictine* 42 (1930): 168-71.

Hayum, R. *The Isenheim Altarpiece. God's Medicine and the Painter's Vision.* Princeton: Princeton University Press, 1989.

Katzenellenbogen, A. *Allegories of the Virtues and Vices in Medieval Art.* London: Warburg Institute, 1939.

Knight, A. "Bilingualism in Medieval French Drama". In: *Jean Misrahi Memorial Volume. Studies in Medieval Literature.* Ed. H.R. Runte et al. Columbia, S.C.: French Literature Publications Company, 1977. 247-64.

Lavin, M. A. "The Altar of Corpus Domini in Urbino: Paolo Uccello, Joos Van Ghent, Piero della Francesca". *Art Bulletin* 49 (1967): 1-24.

———. *The Place of Narrative. Mural Decoration in Italian Churches, 431-1600.* Chicago/London: University of Chicago Press, 1990.

Longère, J. *La prédication médiévale.* Paris: Etudes Augustiniennes, 1983.

Martin, H. *Le métier de prédicateur à la fin du moyen âge (1350-1520).* Paris: Editions du Cerf, 1988.

Nova, A. "I tramezzi in Lombardia fra XV e XVI secolo: Scene della Passione e devozione francescana". In: *Il francescanesimo in Lombardia: Storia e arte*. Milan: Silvana, 1983. 196-215.

Owst, G.R. *Literature and Pulpit in Medieval England*. 2nd rev. ed. New York: Barnes and Noble, 1961.

Payen, J.-C. *Le motif du repentir dans la littérature française médiévale (des origines à 1230)*. Geneva: Droz, 1967.

Plett, H. "Intertextualities". In: H. F. Plett, ed. *Intertextuality*. Berlin/New York: Walter de Gruyter, 1991. 3-29.

Plesch, V. *Pinctor et Presbiter: Structures of Meaning in Giovanni Canavesio's Passion Cycle at Notre-Dame des Fontaines, La Brigue (1492)*. Ph.D. diss. Princeton University, 1994.

Randall, L. M. C. "Exempla as a Source of Gothic Marginal Illumination". *Art Bulletin* 39 (1957): 97-107.

Rotondi Terminiello, G. "Giovanni Canavesio". In: *The Dictionary of Art*. Ed. Jane Turner, New York: Grove's Dictonaries, 1996. V, 601.

Sigal, P. A. "Le pèlerinage comme pénitence". In: M. Viller et al. *Dictionnaire de Spiritualité ascétique et mystique. Doctrine et Histoire*. Paris: Beauchesne, 1984. Vol. 12, cols 919-20.

Taylor, L. *Soldiers of Christ. Preaching in Late Medieval and Reformation France*. New York/Oxford: Oxford University Press, 1992.

Tentler, T. *Sin and Confession on the Eve of the Reformation*. Princeton: Princeton University Press, 1977.

Visual Representations of Political Discourse:
The Example of the French Communist Party Between the Wars

Ruth Rennie

This paper deals with perhaps the most overt kind of political use of image in examining the case of political propaganda, specifically that of the French Communist party between the wars. To set this discussion in its proper context it is first necessary to define the term "propaganda" which is to be understood here in its pre-World War Two sense, thus devoid of any suggestion of falsification of information or mental manipulation. In the inter-war period the term propaganda still retained much of the original sense of the term, coined by the Catholic church in 1622 as *Congregatio de propaganda fide,* encompassing all means by which a set of ideas is disseminated. The roots of the French Communist party's conception of propaganda, and many of its practices, may be traced back to the French Revolution when the means of dissemination of doctrine were turned to political education. Ideologically influenced by the rationalism of the Enlightenment, French revolutionary propaganda sought to obtain the reasoned adherence of the people to a political doctrine by rational argument. This overtly pedagogical form of political propaganda was adopted in the nineteenth century by the organised labour movement, increasingly influenced by Marxist Socialism which later provided the ideological basis of Communism. The "scientific" rationalism of Marxist doctrine and the predominance of intellectuals amongst the leaders of the French labour movement reinforced the pedagogical nature of political propaganda (Tartakowsky). The emphasis on rationality entrenched the dominance of text-based media (oral or written) as the preferred means of diffusion. This approach resulted in a deep suspicion within the French Socialist movement of propaganda practices considered to be demagogic in appealing to the emotions rather than to reason – a definition which included image (cf. Burrin, Nadaud).

It was this concept of propaganda that the newly formed French Communist Party (SFIC) inherited when it split from the Socialist party in December 1920. While the innovations of Leninism organised and systematised political practice within the new party, the concept of political pedagogy remained unchanged. The notion that propaganda should provide rational education remained paramount, and the principal tools of French Communist propaganda remained textual (Pey).

Despite its natural reticence towards the employment of visual images which departed from rational, textual discourse, the Communist party did produce an increasing number of propaganda images in the interwar period, chiefly motivated by the need to respond to visual propaganda produced by its adversaries on the political right wing (Buton and Gervereau). However, at least in the early part of this period, these images clearly reflect the party's adherence to rational argument as the basis of propaganda.

In order to examine Communist visual propaganda over this period I will concentrate here on illustrated posters, in particular those produced during election campaigns. The principle advantages of this selection are that these posters represent the greatest and most concentrated production of propaganda, and that they appeared at regular intervals across the period, making them particularly pertinent to an investigation of the evolution of graphic styles and their adaptation to a propagandist message.

In the first half of the interwar period, the French Communists as a revolutionary party rejected parliamentarianism and defined their objective in an electoral campaign not to win votes but to exploit the opportunity to mobilise the masses and to gain adherents to the Communist cause. The production of propaganda was therefore generally characterised by pedagogical attempts to present fundamental party doctrine in a convincing way. With the introduction of the illustrated poster to the Communist propaganda arsenal, this approach gave rise to the use of graphic compositions which were often complex, combining an abundance of elements recreating in a visual form the textual argumentation of the party's ideology.

As the efficiency of a propaganda image depends on the public's ability to identify the elements depicted and attribute to them their intended symbolic value (Ellul), the forms of image and the thematic language used in visual representations of Communist doctrine are rooted in French graphic traditions already endowed with political significance. Many elements of the visual language, like the archetypical image of the Capitalist, derive from imagery developed by the Socialist or trade union movements (Hobsbawm). An equally important set of stylistic influences was provided by caricature, and particularly the "dessin de presse" developed in the political press of all tendencies (Delporte). The adoption of visual styles with which their public was familiar maximised the legibility of the images.

This method is exemplified by the poster *Formez le bloc ouvrier-paysan* (fig. 1) produced by Jules Grandjouan for the first legislative election campaign of the interwar period in 1924. Most clearly the graphic composition of this poster revolves around a fundamental opposition, visually representing the basis of Communist doctrine – the class struggle, or the antagonism between"capital" and "labour". The graphic elements of the composition (form, colour, volume) establish visual contrasts to emphasise the relationship be-

Figure 1. French Communist Party poster for the Legislative Elections of 1924 (Jules Grandjouan). Paris: Archives Nationales.

tween the two groups as defined by Communist theory. The contrast between the workers as producers (identified by the textually labelled fruits of their labours) and the Capitalist as speculator and profiteer (visually associated with bank notes) is given specific political significance by the composition of the elements: the workers on both sides of the image, the figure of the Capitalist in the center which emphasises the power of the Capitalist based on dividing the workers. The sense of injustice and oppression is reinforced by the miserabilist depiction of the working classes – worn faces, bearing of heavy loads, and sickly blue tint – which is contrasted with the fat bodies, smiling faces and vibrant, clear, single colour of the central figure. The primary purpose of the composition is thus clearly to translate into visual terms the Communist objective to forge class consciousness by creating an awareness of oppression. However, a second level of meaning is also introduced relating the image to the specific issues addressed in the electoral campaign. In the posters establishing this link is the principal function of the text.

Here, while the central figure in this image is clearly a relatively traditional representation of Capitalism in general, the figure is also portrayed with two faces, using the ancient visual metaphor of Janus. The significance of this depiction is provided by the textual caption integrating a party political argument. The label identifies the two sides of the same figure as "Bloc national de gauche", and "de droite". A link is therefore established between the political parties and the figure of the archetypical Capitalist, stressing the Communist claim that the parliamentary system serves the interests of Capitalism and the bourgeoisie rather than the workers. Presenting these two political groupings (the Socialist/Radical-Socialist alliance, and the right wing governmental "Bloc National") as two sides of the same figure suggests that they are by nature indissociable. This reflects one of the core political arguments of the Communist party in this period – the criticism of the Socialist leaders whose belief in parliamentarianism constitutes a betrayal of the working class by engendering their collaboration with other bourgeois parties. This figure therefore combines a complex message carried by recognisable visual symbols (the figure of the Capitalist) and metaphors (the two-faced head) with textual captions establishing a link between the fundamental ideological message and the contextual political one.

In the following legislative election campaign in 1928, a change in graphic style is clearly evident. The purified style of caricature developed in both the right and left-wing press, came to dominate the poster (Gervereau). However, in the Communist poster the objective of the visual reproduction of complex argumentation remained essentially the same as in 1924.

The poster *Ne marchez plus comme en 1919 et en 1924* is characterised by the large number of visual elements it includes. One important innovation in relation to the previous posters however is that here much of the text and labelling has been dropped in favour of the use of visual symbols. Although not traditional iconographic elements, the militant significance of these symbols had often been established for the public by their extensive use in the caricatures published by the artist, the best known Communist caricaturist of the period, Raoul Cabrol, in the Communist daily paper *l'Humanité*.

The main part of the image shows a voter confronted by the three main political leaders presenting their party's electoral programme in poster form. The contextual political message is shared between the symbolically charged image and the text. The association of the parliamentary system with Capitalism is provided by the use of the archetypal figure of the Capitalist in place of the leader of the "Union Nationale" government. The criticism of the Socialist leader seen to be in alliance with other bourgeois parties, is made by the parallel positions in which the leaders are presented. The suggestion of a common anti-communism, emphasising that the parties are indistinguishable from each other in acting against the interests of the working class (which only the Communist party defends), is specified by the text on the electoral posters the leaders are presenting, labelled in each case "programme contre le communisme". In addition to this central argument, the right hand side of the poster is occupied by secondary elements relating to specific Communist political claims. Thus the figures of several government ministers are represented and associated with objects symbolising their functions and the implict danger they pose for the working class (a purse for taxation, a soldier's helmet for militarisation, and a police baton for the repression of communist and trade union activity). A third set of purely textual arguments is set out in the form of budgetary figures included in a box in the top right hand corner, which have no direct relationship to the image. Thus it is clear that, despite the purification of the graphic style of caricature, the basic approach to visual propaganda still revolved around complex compositions involving numerous elements representing textual arguments.

Figure 2. French Communist Party poster for the
Legislative Elections of 1932. (Anon). Amsterdam: IIVSG.

Communist propaganda methods began to evolve in the second half of
the interwar period, influenced by changes in both the political context and
the visual context in French society. The first real indication of a change in the
graphic conception of the propaganda image occurs in 1932.

On a technical level it is marked by the appearance of photographic images in Communist propaganda posters. In part this change reflects evolutions
in the visual context in French society as a whole. The late 1920s and early
1930s saw an explosion of visual media made possible by new technical developments. The appearance of an illustrated press based on the photo, and the
rapid expansion of cinema as a popular leisure activity had brought the photographic image to a mass audience. In addition the militant use of photography, particularly photomontage made its first appearance in French posters in
a work by Carlu in 1931 (Gervereau).

In 1932 four of the nine posters produced by the Communist party, again
for the legislative election campaign of that year, incorporated photographic
images. The composition of these posters indicates the changes in the conception of visual propaganda initiated by the introduction of photography and
photomontage into French Communist posters.

The most striking contrast between the poster *Le régime capitaliste c'est la
guerre* (fig. 2) and those that preceded it is the marked simplification in presentation and content. Rather than combining many elements to represent an

ideological argument, this poster focuses its denunciation of Capitalism on a single issue – in this case the threat of war – which it represents iconographically by a small number of elements (a plane and a tank) which symbolically embody the central idea. Moving away from the established iconography of the Socialist/Communist movement, it uses a single image with topical resonance (and therefore legible to a wide public) which acquires symbolic significance in the specific context in which it is used. The function of the text, the most evident part pared down to a simple and effective *mot d'ordre*, –*Le régime Capitaliste c'est la Guerre* is thus no longer to link an inherently ideological image to a specific political context, but to provide a visually neutral image with political significance. The second novelty of these posters is that they rely for their effect on a strong initial visual impact, and thus to an emotive reaction which precedes the rational response traditionally sought by Communist propagandists. Rational argumentation is naturally included, in the form of the rising curve of a graph accompanied with dates and figures of military expenditure, however the size and position of this text indicates that it is intended to represent only a secondary, supplementary argument.

Although these changes concern only a minority of the posters produced in 1932, the evolution begun by these innovations has important consequences for the graphic conception of French Communist propaganda posters. The first is the introduction of images involving a small number of related elements, concentrating on one issue in the political debate, rather than presenting a multifaceted argumentation. In 1935 the party produced a series of three illustrated posters, on specific themes, – unemployment, the threat of war, and Fascism – for the municipal election campaign, which reflected this new approach. The antiwar poster *Le communisme c'est la paix* re-employs the motif of the plane to embody the menace of war. While the graphic composition remains loaded with elements, the addition of falling bombs, a person in a gas mask, a frightened child, and menaced buildings amongst which we recognise the Eiffel tower, only serves to heighten the central message. The text, reduced to a short *mot d'ordre* makes explicit the political significance of the image, relating it to the fundamental denunciation of Capitalism in the slogan "Régime capitaliste, régime de profiteurs, régime de guerre". The text then completes the political message by introducing the opposition – "Le Communisme c'est la paix".

This same method is evident in the party's relatively rare posters using photomontages, of particular interest because they indicate the chief difference between the French Communist use of this technique and those of the far more developed German or Russian varieties. Unlike the biting satire produced by the juxtaposition of inherently unrelated images and text, which characterised German photomontage, in particular that of John Heartfield, and unlike too the visionary utopianism combining symbolic images with images of concrete realities by the Russian Constructivists, montage techniques were used by French militant artists purely to combine numerous images with the same semantic sense, reinforcing a single message. The entire right side of the poster *Défense de la propiété paysanne* from the campaign for the cantonal elections in 1937 is occupied by a collection of superimposed photographic images – a cow, a wagon, a haystack, farm buildings and people (specifically a woman and a child). All the objects represented are necessary elements of peasant life and property, which the party proposes to defend. No attempt is made here to create new meaning from the addition of the various objects. They all reinforce the one central message. Semantic legibility and clarity remain the propagandist's paramount objective.

The second important consequence brought about by this evolution is that it led to a simplification of the graphic concept of the poster. From the reduction of the content to focus on a single message, this method evolved towards the crystallisation of the message in the representation of a single element. This approach reached its apogee in 1936 in the series of posters produced for the legislative elections which culminated in the election of the Popular Front government.

The widened audience for Communist propaganda provided by the pact signed in 1934 between the French Communist and Socialist parties, later extended to include the centrist Radical Socialists, to form the Popular Front and the urgency to win the adhesion of the masses faced with the menace of Fascism (from the *ligues* within France, and from Italy and Germany without) also caused the Communist party to re-evaluate its strategy. The desire to produce material accessible to a public larger than the traditional working class base of Communist support led to a simplification of propaganda at all levels. In addition the party concluded that a new approach was necessary and that Communist propaganda should in future endeavour to "touch the sentiments" because "avec la raison seule on n'arrivera pas à ébranler les positions de l'adversaire" (Pey 402-6). Communist posters in this period concentrated therefore on the creation of images with immediate visual impact, creating new visual symbols related to the political context.

The poster *Pour que la famille soit heureuse* from the 1936 election campaign shows an almost photographic style image of a group of three figures (father, mother and child – free, it should be noted, of any iconographic elements specifying class or occupation). The text here again provides the political significance of the image by integrating the identification of the group – as "the family" – into the political *mot d'ordre* of the party's electoral campaign – "Pour une France libre, forte et heureuse". A further poster from the same campaign carries the process even further as text and image become completely interdependent. In *Pour qu'elle soit libre, forte et heureuse* (fig. 3) text and image function like a kind of rebus – the visual recognition of the shape of

Figure 3. French Communist Party poster for
the legislative elections of 1936. (Lan) Paris:
Coll. A. Gesgon.

France providing the necessary element to complete the textual *mot d'ordre*.
This interrelation thus politicises the image by linking (the shape of) the country
to a party political slogan (relating to its moral existence and aspirations). The
force of these images, and the associated text relies on provoking an emotive
response to rallying symbols.

This approach did not survive the difficulties and final disintegration of
the Popular Front. Particularly from 1938 on, opposition to the national government and the increasing menace of Fascism and war, caused the use of
extensive textual argumentation to return to the Communist poster. However, this does not result in a return to the visual argumentation of the earlier
period. Although the posters are invaded with text, the image of a single element remains the norm. Instead the image itself is endowed with more overt
political significance. The role of the image, beyond its initial visual impact,
becomes an essentially documentary one – providing illustration or visual proof
of the claims made in the text.

The use of documentary-style photographs is widely exploited as in the
poster *Mein Kampf* which features a photograph of Hitler, right fist raised,
addressing a rally, beside two extracts from the book whose title serves as the
poster's headline. Here text and image maintain their interdependence in delivering the political message. The author of the quotations is visually identi-

fied by the image. The words of the speech he is clearly delivering in the photo are provided by the text. Text and image together embody the menace German Fascism represents for France. The documentary role of the image is nowhere made clearer than in the poster *Hitler veut l'Alsace,* where the detail of a map which redraws France's borders in Germany's favour is labelled "la preuve". These later posters therefore prove that, regardless of changes in political objective, the evolution in the graphic concept towards single strong propaganda images intended to produce an immediate emotional impact, which lies at the basis of most modern propaganda techniques, had been definitively established.

The Communist concept of rational argumentation as the foundation for all propaganda determined, in the early years of the party's existence, the style of visual image which sought to reproduce visually, complex political argumentation. The inherently militant images, using styles and iconography developed by existing French graphic traditions, were related to topical political issues by the use of text adding contextual interpretations to more global ideological representations. Across the interwar period, as a result of increasing public accessibility to visual media and the Communists' political objective to reach a wider audience, an evolution occurred in the style and concept of propaganda. Firstly there was a move towards a simplification of the subject matter of the poster, focussing on a single issue. Secondly there was a simplification of the graphic image which centers on the presentation of a single visual element. Militant iconography is abandoned in favour of topically legible images, politicised by the addition of textual *mots d'ordres.* The new style of propaganda, adopted by the Communist party which relied increasingly on the visual impact of its images definitively moved the party into the realm of modern propaganda techniques.

REFERENCES

Burrin, Philippe. "Poings levés et bras tendus. La contagion des symboles au temps du Front Populaire". *Vingtième Siècle* 11 (1986): 5-20.

Buton, Philippe, and Laurent Gervereau. *Le Couteau entre les dents. 70 ans d'affiches communistes et anticommunistes.* Paris: Chêne, 1989.

Delporte, Christian. *Dessinateurs de presse et dessin politique en France des années 1920 à la Libération.* Paris, IEP Thèse. 1991.

Ellul, Jacques. *Propagandes.* 1962. Paris: Economica, 1991.

Gervereau, Laurent. *La Propagande par l'Affiche.* Paris: Syros, 1991.

Hobsbawm, Eric. "Sexe, symboles, vêtements et socialisme". *Actes de la recherche en sciences sociales* 23 (1978): 2-18.

Nadaud, Eric. "Le renouvellement des pratiques militants de la SFIO au début du Front Populaire (1934-1936)". In: *Le Front Populaire et la vie quotidienne des français*. Paris: Colloque CRHMSS, 1986.

Pey, Serge. *Structures internes et rythmes de developpement de la section d'agitation et de propagande du Parti Communiste français entre les deux guerres*. Toulouse -Le Mirail, Thèse 3e Cycle, 1976.

Tartakowsky, Danielle. *Ecoles et éditions communistes 1921-1933. Essai sur la formation des cadres du PCF.* Paris VIII, Thèse 3e cycle, 1977.

En grisaille – Painting Difference

Charlotte Schoell-Glass

The term *grisaille* in art-historical terminology has been until recently a catch-all for works of art that can differ widely with respect to technique as well as contexts. Over a long period of time – principally since the late Middle Ages – images *en grisaille* were painted in fresco in connection with large narrative cycles, in tempera and oil as panels and canvasses, or as part of decorative programmes. In late medieval book decoration and illustration as well as on early winged altars, *grisaille* played, for a period of 200 years, an important role, which was frequently overlooked and, when it was not, was never questioned thoroughly. *En grisaille* is a term that is also often used to refer to paintings with a considerable proportion of colours other than grey – paintings that contain other pigments. Being monochrome, or almost monochrome, is the visual criterion which, beyond all other differences, forms a common tradition.[1]

In the context of the study of the relationship of image and language, *grisaille* painting presents us with a particularly fascinating case: it can be said to be almost completely unaccompanied by any sort of verbalising, i.e. it was neither theorized nor was it, as far as we know, an important part of the written studio tradition. This can be said to be true of the entire time-span of its frequent use since the fourteenth century. In other words, *grisaille* goes literally 'without saying'. Painting *en grisaille* is, on the other hand, so obviously a visual marker as almost (but only almost) to speak itself about its function in relation to the much larger body of painting in colour. It can be seen, therefore, as representing another mode of putting forward thought about – and theory on – art, not in words, but in a metaphorical practice. Such practice may be a third element to be added to the word-image duality and as such I would like to introduce it here.

Over the last decade or so, art historians have begun to take more interest in *grisailles*.[2] Compared to earlier scholarship, there is a new direction of questioning, aiming at the *phenomenon* from a less specialized point of view. The existence of a monochrome, grey thread of tradition in the colourful web of the history of painting has become the focus of attention in terms of art theory – historical and contemporary. For Giotto's famous cycle of the virtues and vices in the Arena Chapel, Reinhard Steiner demonstrated the probability of a connection with the evolving art theory of the fourteenth and early fifteenth centuries in Italy; for Jan van Eyck's Annunciation diptych in the Thyssen Collection, Rudolf Preimesberger showed in 1991 that the Eyckian illusionism does not only consist of the painting of a sculpted scene, but, simultaneously, the painting of the theory of representation of the artist's time within the painting. That theory – summed up conveniently as the 'paragone' – is really a negotiation of both the possibility and the role of the representation of space and time in the two-dimensional medium of painting.

Although *grisailles* generally have tended to be overlooked, there have been three exhibitions presenting exclusively *grisailles*. The exhibition – "Gray is the Color" in 1974 in Houston, Texas, for the first time focused on *grisailles,* including modern classics, such as works by Jasper Johns.[3] Two later exhibitions in Paris 1980 and Brussels 1986 mainly concentrated on illuminated manuscripts *en grisaille*.[4] There was and is a plethora of specialized studies, particularly on early Flemish *grisaille* paintings, French manuscript illumination and stained glass of the thirteenth century. However, there is as yet no comprehensive study and history of the phenomenon or 'genre' of *grisaille* painting. Such a history would bring to light, I believe, a kind of painted gloss to the history of the main body of art: painting in colour, architecture and sculpture.

By calling the tradition of painting in greys a *phenomenon,* one of the problems that arises in this context becomes apparent: that of defining what exactly does belong to the tradition and what does not; the question of terminology, and with it the question of continuity and discontinuity of the tradition. Clearly, also, the paintings themselves raise questions about the reality of images, and finally we may ask, whether there is indeed a tradition of painterly statements on the status of painted reality.

The term *grisaille* itself describes widely differing objects, and in our terminology is not restricted to a specific period. It was first used in the seventeenth century, and only applied to twentieth century painting in 1974 by the curator of the Houston exhibition mentioned earlier. It is often used interchangeably with the terms *camaieu* and monochrome. Not much seems to have changed since the eighteenth century encyclopedia of Johann Georg Krünitz (his *Oekonomische Encyklopädie*) which gives a cross-reference from "Grisaille" to "Grey" and states a true chaos of terminology: "Grey in Grey is said of monochrome paintings, be they yellow, red, green etc. Such paintings in only one colour are called by the Greeks *monochromata,* and the French have special names for such paintings: they call them *grisailles,* and the *camayeux* in yellow they call *cirages.* Those pictures which are in fact grey in grey are done with black and white: which is, why the French call such paintings blanc & noir. It is a kind of *al fresco* technique with which the *basso relievo* of sculpture is imitated. It is used to decorate flat walls of buildings to represent architecture, statues and the like. Another kind of grey in grey painting is incised painting in gypsum – see sgrafitto."[5]

One could, of course, for the sake of intellectual clarity and proper classification now try to systematize this terminological jumble. But I believe we should, rather, take this state of disorder as an indication of the underlying unity of the diverse materials, a unity more important than the many forms (and colours) which have been connected in the technical and aesthetic discourses since the seventeenth century. This unity, however, was never commented on in written texts: whereas the theory and practice of *chiaroscuro* painting were debated in theoretical treatises since the sixteenth century,[6] painting *en grisaille* belonged solely to the realm of practical application and was not accompanied by theoretical discourse. The *colour* grey, however, was commented upon at length by Alberti in his treatise *On Painting*. For him, grey is the structuring principle in all colour-painting, as it enables the artist to create the different hues and thus model his forms and figures. However, his considerations pertain to the realm of colour, they do not take into account the restricted palette of *grisaille*.[7]

It is also quite true that the actual colour used – that is, grey – is not always the most important feature of a *grisaille*. In decorative schemes, what matters much more is the *two corresponding modes*. A full range of colour is employed for the central cycle, while the monochrome mode for a different cycle of images is used to relate these to the main themes. *Grisailles* illustrating Old Testament scenes accompany the narrative of the New Testament; *monochrome* emblems supplement the lives of saints in Baroque decorations or, as it was mentioned in Krünitz, the *trompe l'oeil* of architecture and statuary *en grisaille* is pitted against landscape and figures that are rendered in colour.[8] And then there is *demi-grisaille,* particularly in French and Flemish manuscript illumination of the fourteenth and fifteenth century, which includes colours for backgrounds or flesh colour, and finally *grisaille* with varying proportions of other pigments. In French and English terminology in particular we find references to *grisaille* glass – that is, medieval glass which is not coloured, but which relies on varied shades of grey and degrees of translucence to create the pure and unearthly light prescribed by Cistercian rules for building churches and cloisters.[9] The term "stone-coloured" – already in use since the early sixteenth century (Dürer) – refers to *grisailles* that represent statues or bas-reliefs. With it, we are on firmer ground, but it cannot explain at all the large proportion of works which are not attempting to represent plastic works of art. In French fifteenth-century inventories, manuscripts with *grisaille* illustrations are described as having "images de blanc et de noir": we know from extant manuscripts that these descriptions do not refer to drawings but to precious illuminations.[10] The description "black and white", however, seems to be the opposite of all that is customarily associated with grey, as it seems to refer to

contrast rather than sameness and monotony. Such associations accompanying the colour grey, its perception as lacking colour, or as being a state of
discolouring, have for long influenced the scholarship on the *grisaille* tradition.

Uncoloured, colourless, discoloured: the problem is hidden in these pre-
fixes and suffixes. The understanding of *grisaille* is a function of its being perceived as the negation of colourful reality, a lack, a want: reality *minus* colours.
This – modern – perception was rarely questioned because the negative connotation of the colour grey seems to be a constant in European culture. In
German, at least, and English the idiomatic use of grey combines the colour
with "dead", with "dull" and many more negative meanings. This seems to be
one of the reasons why one interpretation, put forward in 1959, explaining
the use of *grisaille* as a "lenten observance" was accepted so willingly, even
though in most cases such a connection cannot be proven or even made plausible.[11] What seems too simplistic as an explanation of the phenomenon *grisaille,*
however, is the assumption of a colour-psychological constant: this becomes
obvious if we consider for instance those fifteenth-century luxury manuscripts
from Flanders and Northern France, where no such negative connotation can
be traced.[12]

The reason for this account of semantic nuances concerning a heterogeneous yet clearly distinguishable group of art-works is twofold: I wish to plead
for giving the objects precedence, to look for their common qualities rather
than eliminating all factors which could be in the way of a clear-cut terminology. I even suggest we should not to exclude those *grisailles* which are really
red or green or yellow monochromes. Secondly, I hope to demonstrate that
from the historical muddle at least one conclusion can be drawn: that our
habits of perception with relation to grey things must themselves be seen critically. Without refuting such interpretations of historical sources that bring
together *grisaille* paintings with the very restricted use – in time and region –
of grey as a liturgical colour, I would like to suggest that we should use categories which will accommodate the diversity of the historical material.

Surely, such categories have to be looked for on the basis of a revision of
the assumption that *grisailles* are wanting colour, are colourless always as a
result of asceticism. The economic argument, often repeated (cheap pigments),
cannot be upheld in view of the precious manuscript with *grisaille* illustrations
by Jean Pucelle for the French queen Jeanne d'Evreux. The renunciation of
stained glass and of luxurious architecture likewise can be seen not as a loss
but a spiritual gain symbolized in the pure light in the space of the church.
And there can be no doubt about Mantegna's sophistication, even irony in his
grisailles, which in fact demonstrate the painter's supreme mastery.[13] The conscious choice of a particular medium or mode in different circumstances is
one of the factors common to all the works of art in question here. This ap-

plies to Jean Pucelle's Book of Hours and the Parament de Narbonne, just as it does to Mantegna's *grisailles* or Rubens' oil sketches. If we emphasize conscious choice of the artist and (or) patron, another quality suggests itself to describe the function and meaning of *grisailles:* difference. This difference results from the context in which *grisaille* paintings invariably must be seen: the manuscript page with its other decorative elements, the winged altarpiece with its coloured main paintings, and, as a special case, painted architecture and sculpture in paintings or in the context of narrative cycles. Independent *grisailles,* like those of Mantegna and from then on until today are nevertheless perceived in the degree in which they differ from a norm and from the environment, the world of colours. This is still the case even in twentieth century painting, with Picasso's *Guernica,* or Jasper Johns' *grisailles,* to name only the best known examples.

Creating difference in this way can be seen as a way of reflecting on the reality of the real world.[14] In terms of art theory it can and will often take on qualities of the ekphrastic mode, but a practical rather than a verbal description or, as was the case of Rubens' decoration of his house in Antwerp, a commentary on the uncertainties of the translation of images into words.[15] As an artistic choice it can be seen, too, as a movement of distancing, the creation and representation of distance. In his 1907 article on the Florentine patrician and patron of arts, Franceso Sassetti, Aby Warburg came to understand the role of *grisaille* in Florentine wall-painting of the fifteenth century in this function: "*Sub adumbratione* classical form and content are held at a typological distance."[16] The recovery of the classical tradition was seen by Warburg as a liberating force in European culture. The "positing of distance *(Distanzsetzung)*" was both a precondition and a result of studying and integrating consciously the artistic heritage of the ancients. To understand the dual function of art as a means of both shaping and thus handing on the expression of passions as a necessary life-force and of bridling them in the creative process, was central to Aby Warburg's thought and work.[17] This process of distancing can be understood in terms of psychology but could also be described in terms of the visual: if images are representations – once removed, then *grisailles* are twice removed, since they are images carrying with them visually a statement about their status as art-works. This has been discussed for Jan van Eyck's Annunciation diptych[18] and Giotto's cycle of virtues and vices:[19] in both cases, "painted art theory" is visualized by the artists. They reflect within their works the condition of their potential and their limitations, the potential and limitations, that is, of mimesis. *Grisailles* are in this sense metarepresentational. It is precisely this fact which seems so worrying to some: the discontinuity of the textual tradition between Flemish art and Classical, (Pliny's) as well as Italian (Alberti's) art theory that one could see as most intriguing about van Eyck's and Giotto's *grisailles.* Van Eyck reflects the problems of optics visually through mirror-

effects of polished stone, he visualizes the tenuous status and character of religious art as "art".[20] Van Eyck's sense of history and tradition is documented by
his restricting his palette to the four pigments which Pliny mentions as those
of the earliest, founding acts of painting and drawing. There is a great distance, in several respects, between these works and illuminated manuscripts of
the fourteenth and fifteenth century, or the *grisailles* of later centuries. However, if we confront them with the framework of assumptions on *grisaille* painting sketched out in this paper, there can be more satisfying answers than just
"fashion" and "goût"[21] which explain nothing but in their turn require explanation.

The reconstruction of the history of *grisaille* painting is a history of the
physically painted, iconic thinking about art and images. There will of course
always be the problem of bridging the gap between historical facts, the paintings, and (Warburg's and many others') discourse about them, saturated with
metaphor. Aby Warburg's characterization of images "sub adumbratione" in
the "shadowy realm of simulated sculpture",[22] could be seen in a tradition
reaching back to the Platonic founding legend of the art of painting itself, as it
is told in Pliny's *Natural History* about the Corinthian Maiden, who traced the
shadow of her beloved's head on the wall, hoping in this way to be able to hold
on to him whom she is to lose. Paintings *en grisaille* remind us of the metaphorical character of all art as a practice and as representation.

Notes

1   For a new comprehensive summary of the history of *grisaille* painting and a short
     bibliography see the *Dictionary of Art,* vol. 13, 672-77.

2   Most importantly: Grams-Thieme, Marion, *Lebendige Steine. Studien zur nieder-
     ländischen Grisaillemalerei des 15. und frühen 16. Jahrhunderts* (Dissertationen zur
     Kunstgeschichte 27), (PhD thesis), Köln, Wien: Böhlau, 1988; Rosenfeld, Jörg, *Die
     nichtpolychromierte Retabelskulptur als bildreformerisches Phänomen im ausgehenden
     Mittelalter und in der beginnenden Neuzeit* (PhD thesis), Ammersbeck: Verlag an der
     Lottbek, 1990; Dittelbach, Thomas, *Das monochrome Wandgemälde. Untersuchungen
     zum Kolorit des frühen 15. Jahrhunderts in Italien* (PhD thesis), Hildesheim, Zürich,
     New York: Lang, 1993; Krieger, Michaela, *Grisaille als Metapher: Zum Entstehen der
     peinture en camaieu im frühen 14. Jahrhundert,* Wien: Holzhausen, 1995.

3   *Gray is the Color. An Exhibition of Grisaille Painting XIIIth – XXth Centuries,* Organ-
     ized by the Institute for the Arts, Rice University, Houston, Texas: Rice Museum,
     1973/74.

4   *La Grisaille,* Cahiers Musée d'Art et d'Essai, Palais de Tokyo Paris, 3. Paris: Editions
     de la Réunion des Musées Nationaux, 1980; *Miniatures en Grisaille.* (Exhibition
     catalogue by Pierre Cockshaw), Brussels: Bibliothèque Royale Albert 1ᵉʳ, 1986.

5   Krünitz, Johann Georg. *Oekonomisch-technologische Encyklopädie oder allgemeines System der Staats- Stadt- Haus und Land-Wirthschaft, und der Kunst-Geschichte.* Vol 20, second ed. Berlin: Joachim Pauli, 1789, 101 (s.v. Grisaille) and vol. 19 [1788] s.v. Grau in Grau, 792.

6   Verbraeken, René, *Clair-Obscur. Histoire d'un mot,* Nogent-le Roi: Laget, 1979.

7   See: Gage, John, *Colour and Culture. Practice and Meaning from Antiquity to Abstraction,* London: Thames and Hudson, 1993, 117-9.

8   Holländer, Hans, "Steinerne Gäste der Malerei", *Gießener Beiträge zur Kunstgeschichte* 2, 1973, 103-31.

9   Jackson Zakin, Helen, *French Cistercian Grisaille Glass* (PhD thesis) Syracuse University, Syracuse, NY, 1979; Morgan, Nigel, "Early Grisaille Windows in England", *Akten des 10. Internationalen Colloquiums des Corpus vitrearum medii aevi.* Stuttgart: Kohlhammer, 1977, 29; Lymant, Brigitte, "Die Glasmalereien bei den Zisterziensern", *Die Zisterzienser. Ordensleben zwischen Ideal und Wirklichkeit (Exhib. Cat.). Schriften des rheinischen Museumsamtes* 10 (1980): 345-56; Hérold, Michel, "La verrière en grisaille de Bermand à Saint-Nicolas-de-Port ou les chemins tortueux de l'italianisme", *Bulletin Monumental* 150 (1992): 223-37. Further research on *grisaille* glass is published in many of the volumes of the *Corpus vitrearum Medii Aevi* and in *Gesta.*

10   See Krieger, Manuela (as in note 2); for an argument connecting Pucelle's *grisailles* with sculpture see Ballas, Edith, "Jean Pucelle and the Gothic Cathedral Sculptures: A Hypothesis", *Gazette des Beaux-Arts* 91 (1982): 39-44.

11   Teasdale Smith, Molly, "The Use of Grisaille as a Lenten Observance", *Marsyas* 8 (1959): 43-54; for a critique see Steiner, Reinhard, "Paradoxien der Nachahmung bei Giotto: die Grisaillen der Arenakapelle zu Padua" in: H. Körner, C. Peres, R. Steiner and L. Tavernier, eds., *Die Trauben de Zeuxis. Formen künstlerischer Wirklichkeitsaneignung,* Hildesheim, Zürich, New York: Olms, 1990, 61-86.

12   Compare *Miniatures en grisaille* (as in note 4); recently, Krieger (as in note 2) has put this notion to rest for good.

13   Christiansen, Keith. "Paintings in Grisaille", in: Jane Martineau, ed. *Andrea Mantegna* (exhib. cat,). London: Royal Academy of Arts, 1992, 394-416.

14   Philippot, Paul, "Les grisailles et les 'degrés de réalité' de l'image dans la peinture flamande des 15ᵉ et 16ᵉ siècles, *Bulletin des Musées royaux des Beaux-Arts de Belgique* 15 (1966): 225-42.

15   Kemp, Wolfgang, "Praktische Bildbeschreibung: Über Bilder in Bildern, besonders bei Van Eyck und Mantegna", in: G. Boehm, H. Pfotenhauer (eds.), *Beschreibungskunst – Kunstbeschreibung. Ekphrasis von der Antike bis zur Gegenwart,* Munich: Fink, 1995, 99-119; for Rubens' ekphrastic paintings juxtaposed to "real" paintings see: Muller, Jeffrey H. "The Perseus and Andromeda on Rubens's House", *Simiolus* 12/2-3 (1981-1982): 131-46.

16   Warburg, Aby, "Francesco Sassettis letztwillige Verfügung" (1907), in: Bibliothek Warburg, ed. *Gesammelte Schriften* Bd. I und II: *Die Erneuerung der heidnischen Antike. Kulturwissenschaftliche Beiträge zur Geschichte der europäischen Renaissance. Mit einem Anhang unveröffentlichter Zusätze,* Unter Mitarbeit von Fritz Rougemont, ed. Gertrud Bing, Leipzig/Berlin: Teubner, 1932 (Reprint in one vol., Nendeln: Kraus, 1969), 127-58 and 353-65.

17 Schoell-Glass, Charlotte, "Warburg über Grisaille: Ein Splitter über einen Splitter", in: H. Bredekamp, M. Diers, Ch. Schoell-Glass, *Aby Warburg. Akten des internationalen Symposions Hamburg 1990: Schriften des Warburg-Archivs im Kunstgeschichtlichen Seminar der Universität Hamburg 1*, Weinheim: Acta humaniora, 1991, 199-212.

18 Preimesberger, Rudolf, "Ein 'Prüfstein der Malerei' bei Jan van Eyck?" in: M. Winner, ed., *Der Künstler über sich in seinem Werk* (Internationales Symposium der Bibliotheca Hertziana Rom 1989), Weinheim: VCH acta humaniora, 1992, 85-100; id., "Zu Jan van Eycks Diptychon der Sammlung Thyssen-Bornemisza", *Zeitschrift für Kunstgeschichte* 54 (1991): 459-89.

19 Steiner, Reinhard (as in note 11).

20 Preimesberger, "Zu Jan van Eycks Diptychon" (as in note 18).

21 See Cockshaw (as in note 4), iii and iv.

22 In his unpublished Library Journal he notes, shortly before his death: "A phase in the battle for a space to think (Denkraum): the *conscious* mnemic function leads to the forging of a "missing link", to the move from the dynamics of the thiasos (of the masses) to the pathos of energy (of the individual) in the form of painting *en grisaille*." *Tagebücher der K.B.W.* (MS), London, Archive of the Warburg Institute, vol. 9. 69.

Books, Typography and Other Media

Le Roi Arthur et la sémiotique visuelle

Francis Edeline

Les histoires des romans de chevalerie ne nous sont connues que par des documents *écrits*, de sorte que les innombrables aspects visuels dont je vais parler ont déjà été traduits en mots, et nous avons à faire le chemin inverse, avec toutes les incertitudes que cela entraîne. Les illustrations et enluminures se sont révélées d'un faible secours. Certes les documents sont nombreux, mais ils sont à examiner avec précaution, car ils sont soit tronqués, soit falsifiés. Le véritable contenu celte a souvent été ignoré, oublié, édulcoré, masqué ou remplacé peu à peu par un contenu chrétien, généralement fade et moralisateur, du genre de celui qui peut aujourd'hui être entendu le dimanche dans n'importe quelle église. C'est pourquoi je me référerai surtout aux textes les plus anciens et les moins suspects: Chrétien de Troyes, les *Mabinogion, Sir Gawain and the Green Knight,* etc.

La culture celte était très visuelle, comme en témoignent les Pictes et leurs étonnantes *Symbol stones,* les Scots et leurs tartans (qui attendent encore une analyse sémiotique valable où se révélerait l'accord subtil avec les plantes tinctoriales du lieu). Dans les romans et les contes arthuriens, toujours les descriptions sont très visuelles. Les châteaux, les demoiselles, leurs vêtements et leurs bijoux, la splendeur des tables, tout est minutieusement décrit avec le désir d'éblouir. Le superlatif est de rigueur, et chaque demoiselle par exemple surpasse en beauté toutes les autres sans qu'on se préoccupe beaucoup d'un classement. De même chaque objet:

> ... fait en or très pur, garni de pierres précieuses de toutes sortes parmi les plus riches et les plus rares qui existent dans la mer et dans la terre; sans nul doute aucune gemme au monde n'égalait en valeur celles qui ornaient ...

Le caractère exceptionnel des lieux, des objets, des circonstances et des personnages est montré visuellement et sert sans doute à marquer que nous sommes dans le domaine de l'imaginaire et du conte.

D'autre part les épisodes successifs ont besoin d'être séparés les uns des autres, dans l'espace, dans le temps, et aussi dans l'imaginaire. La fonction de segmentation est remplie par la Forêt, qui dissout par brouillage l'épisode précédent, introduit par sa sombre densité un bruit visuel qui vide la mémoire, provoque une sorte d'ascèse, efface par son fouillis insignifiant les signes antérieurs, et revirginise le héros, le rendant pleinement disponible pour une nouvelle aventure. C'est un opérateur aléatoire,[1] qui agit sur les auditeurs du conte aussi bien que sur les actants de l'histoire. Ce dispositif est absolument nécessaire. Il se retrouve dans les fondus-enchaînés qui séparent nos montages de diapositives, dans les grilles de nos BD... Et le Graal n'est peut-être aussi bien qu'une quête verbale dans la forêt des mots.

L'analyse de quelques épisodes célèbres fera apparaître une richesse polysémique insoupçonnée. L'existence de plusieurs niveaux de signification est un caractère constant de nombreux corpus. Les auditeurs étaient normalement très entraînés au décodage. L'écriture connaît pour sa part, depuis l'époque patristique, quatre niveaux d'exégèse (Todorov)[2] et les contes de fées en ont trois (Bettelheim). Wittkower pour sa part distingue cinq niveaux de sens possibles dans l'interprétation des symboles visuels. Le public, selon sa sensibilité et son éducation, accède à un seul d'entre eux ou à plusieurs. L'existence d'une signification figurée, indirecte, conventionnelle, emblématique, n'est pas une hypothèse hasardée mais un fait confirmé même dans les parties inéduquées de la population. Les proverbes étaient employés beaucoup plus abondamment qu'aujourd'hui, et l'enseignement d'église, dans ses prêches, faisait un constant usage de paraboles, de reliques, de statues aux gestes conventionnels et aux attributs emblématiques.

Je me propose d'analyser quelques-uns des épisodes (certains très célèbres) dont le contenu visuel dépasse la simple description d'objets réels ou imaginaires, mais met en scène de véritables et complexes systèmes de communication visuelle. De très nombreux autres auraient pu être choisis, justifiant des analyses tout aussi fructueuses.

LES TROIS GOUTTES DE SANG DANS LA NEIGE.

Les trois gouttes de sang devant lesquelles Perceval entre dans une contemplation hallucinée sont un des plus beaux et des plus mystérieux exemples de sémiotique visuelle imaginés par les poètes de la Matière de Bretagne. On nous précise que ces gouttes sont tombées d'une oie sauvage attaquée en plein ciel par un faucon. Perceval ne peut s'en détacher. Tous ceux qui viennent l'appeler, même ses meilleurs amis, sont accueillis rudement et jetés à terre. Seul Gauvain, plus psychologue, parvient à le réveiller de sa contemplation. Finalement il déclare que les trois gouttes rouges dans la neige blanche lui évoquaient le visage de Blanchefleur, sa bien-aimée.[3]

Il ne faut toutefois pas céder à la tentation de se jeter directement dans des interprétations symboliques, mais se poser d'abord des questions élémentaires et fondamentales.

La première est celle de l'étendue du signe (si signe il y a). Lorsque nous interprétons astrologiquement une configuration céleste le noir entre les étoiles n'a aucune signification. De même le vol migratoire des oiseaux sauvages est indépendant du ciel, et la disposition des entrailles d'un animal sacrifié est interprétée pour elle-même. Il suffit que le fond continu offre un contraste perceptif minimum. Or dans le cas des gouttes de sang la neige est aussi pertinente en tant que partie du signe, comme on s'en assure par une épreuve de commutation: les mêmes gouttes de sang tombées sur un champ de blé, une flaque d'eau, une pelouse, une étendue boueuse, n'auraient plus du tout le même sens. La neige n'est donc pas seulement la page blanche qu'elle serait aujourd'hui, et surgit inévitablement la question: jusqu'où, en étendue, cette neige est-elle pertinente? C'est la même question qui se pose pour l'art paysager en général (p. ex. un cadran solaire de Ian Hamilton Finlay), et la réponse est: jusqu'à l'infini, car le propre de ces signes est de servir aussi d'*embrayeurs cosmiques.*

La seconde question préjudicielle est de spécifier la nature un peu particulière du code auquel on a affaire. A nos yeux modernes il s'agit de messages sans émetteurs. Certains phénomènes naturels sont considérés par des récepteurs humains comme du signifiant, derrière lequel se dissimule un émetteur imaginaire. A ce signifiant "donné" nous ajoutons des conventions de renvoi à du signifié, ainsi qu'une sémantique interprétative souvent très complexe. Comme il n'y a jamais de communication dans le sens inverse, sauf à envisager une vérification (bien problématique) de l'efficacité des oracles, nous ne pouvons parler que de semi-codes.

Comme pour la ceinture verte de Dame Bertilak, la signification des gouttes de sang dans la neige est, dans le conte, développée en plusieurs phases successives. Au cours de la *première,* le signifié est connu de Perceval seul: c'est un message privé, dont il refuse de communiquer le sens. Tout ce qu'on peut en deviner, à en juger par ses réactions, c'est qu'il est important pour lui. La scène visuelle agit comme un symbole de contemplation, et la prostration de Perceval peut s'interpréter comme une méditation herméneutique,[4] voire une extase mystique comme il apparaîtra plus loin. Il est "entransé". Frappé ou ému par le spectacle il cherche lui-même la raison de son bouleversement.

La *deuxième* phase le voit expliquer le sens qu'il trouve aux gouttes de sang. L'évocation de Blanchefleur est opérée par iconisme. Le rouge et le blanc étaient à l'époque les couleurs emblématiques (donc codées) de la beauté féminine, mais il y a davantage que la couleur: le nombre trois. On ne nous dit pas comment sont disposées les trois taches de sang, mais cette disposition serait compatible avec le rose des joues et des lèvres. Dans ce cas le récepteur utilise la syntaxe visuelle, c'est-à-dire les relations de coordination entre les trois taches, ainsi que la relation de subordination de ces taches par rapport au blanc.[5] Il y a donc homologation terme à terme de l'opposition rouge/blanc avec l'opposition correspondante dans la carnation de Blanchefleur: c'est la forme la plus réduite de l'iconisme.

Perceval n'en dit pas plus. Mais évidemment l'interprétation est aussitôt renforcée par la blancheur des oies dont provient le sang: *Blanche*fleur, comme Blanche-Neige, a le teint pâle d'une beauté féminine idéale. Mais la blancheur est aussi la couleur de l'innocence et de la virginité. Or l'oie (blanche) vient d'être agressée par un faucon, et le faucon est l'espèce d'oiseau à laquelle on compare le plus volontiers les héros dans les légendes nordiques.[6] Le sang pourrait donc bien, dans une *troisième* phase, être celui de la dé*flor*ation de Blanche*fleur,* et Perceval ne nous a divulgué, de cette isotopie érotique, que le degré euphémistique.[7]

Ce type de signe fonctionne, on le voit, par une succession d'analogies projectives, puisque aucune convention ne vient orienter leur interprétation au départ (sauf peut-être celle des couleurs emblématiques féminines ...).

Mais nous sommes dans le cadre d'un roman soigneusement construit, et une *quatrième* phase se dévoile beaucoup plus tard. Elle n'est pas explicitement formulée mais elle est tellement évidente qu'elle ne peut manquer de surgir dans l'esprit de Perceval aussi bien que dans celui des lecteurs du conte. La scène des oies et des gouttes de sang ne serait qu'un *écho narratif* de la procession du Graal, à laquelle Perceval assistera médusé et, de nouveau, muet. Dans cette procession il y a une lance, portée par un valet, et dont perlent des gouttes de sang. Tout l'épisode peut ainsi être retraduit sur une nouvelle isotopie, proprement spirituelle, selon les équivalences suivantes:

La flèche des oies en migration	La lance qui a percé le flanc du Christ
Les gouttes de sang	Le sang du Christ
Le nombre trois	(La Trinité?)

La valeur oraculaire des oiseaux chez les Celtes est avérée (Graves, 1961), et appartient d'ailleurs déjà par elle-même à une sémiotique visuelle. Le sang du Graal est un liquide précieux et vivifiant, apte à régénérer la Terre Gaste. La longue méditation de Perceval apparaît alors comme une prémonition.

En résumé les trois gouttes de sang se trouvent au centre d'un mécanisme d'interprétation fort complexe qu'on peut résumer par la figure 1. Les trois possibilités retenues par Peirce (Index, Icone et Symbole) y sont présentes, de même que le non-sens.

LE PENTANGLE DE GAUVAIN

Sir Gawain and the Green Knight est un poème anglais du quatorzième siècle, rattaché au cycle des romans arthuriens. Il nous raconte la curieuse histoire d'un défi relevé par Gauvain. Le Jour de l'An, un chevalier tout habillé de vert demande à être décapité, à condition de pouvoir décapiter à son tour son exécuteur un an plus tard jour pour jour. Gauvain relève le défi, tranche la tête, le chevalier décapité la ramasse et s'en va. Un an plus tard Gauvain, fidèle au rendez-vous et muni d'un écu orné d'un pentangle pour se protéger, traverse une "terre gaste", puis passe trois jours chez Bertilak et son épouse. Celle-ci le tente de diverses manières sans parvenir à le séduire, cependant que son mari est à la chasse. Un contrat a été conclu selon lequel chaque soir chacun des deux hommes donne à l'autre ce qu'il a gagné pendant la journée. Le contrat est respecté scrupuleusement sauf le troisième jour où le héros accepte de la Dame une ceinture verte, talisman qui doit protéger sa vie et qu'il omet de rendre à Bertilak. Et effectivement Bertilak, qui n'est autre que le Chevalier Vert, ne fait que lui érafler le cou lors de la scène cruciale. L'affaire de la ceinture cachée est cependant mise au jour, à la grande honte de Gauvain qui l'arbore et s'accuse publiquement lors de son retour chez Arthur. Mais les autres chevaliers de la Table Ronde se moquent gentiment de lui et décident de porter tous désormais un baudrier vert.

Les détails de l'histoire forment un système très serré et cohérent de communication visuelle. La cohérence est encore plus frappante si on considère le substratum pré-chrétien de l'histoire, enrobé d'un contenu chrétien et d'un contenu chevaleresque qui s'y superposent sans vraiment l'annuler. Toutes ces lectures demeurent possibles, mais la première m'intéresse ici davantage.

Les signes visuels employés sont nombreux. Gauvain porte un écu spécial rouge avec un pentangle d'or sur la face extérieure, et la figure de la Vierge sur la face intérieure. C'est de l'"héraldique imaginaire" (Pastoureau). Le pentangle est un signe très ancien qui remonte même, selon Liungman, aux mages chaldéens qui auraient repéré le cycle pentagonal des levers de l'étoile Vénus. Pythagore en faisait un "passeport pour la lumière", le signe de la perfection et un talisman contre le mal. Les Anglais l'appellent *Endless Knot*, marquant ainsi que son tracé continu, bouclé sur lui-même, peut former un entrelac. Chez les chrétiens il dénote tout ce qui va par cinq: les cinq sens, les cinq joies, les cinq doigts, les cinq vertus etc. On a même une analogie projective attribuée à Vitruve selon laquelle le pentagramme est une figure du corps humain (l'"homme pentagonal") avec pour centre le nombril (De Bruyne). Le visage de la Vierge, sur la face intérieure, est en quelque sorte à usage interne et destiné à rendre courage au héros dans l'épreuve, alors que le pentangle est vu de tous et signale à qui on a affaire tout en le protégeant.

Le Chevalier Vert est tout habillé de vert, il a les yeux rouges mais des cheveux et une barbe vertes, et il porte en mains un bouquet de houx, un *evergreen* particulièrement prisé au temps du solstice d'hiver. La deuxième décapitation[8] a lieu à la Chapelle Verte laquelle, souligne Brian Stone (1978), n'est pas vraiment une chapelle: c'est un *barrow* à quatre entrées de type préhistorique, et elle ressemble à une entrée typique de l'Autre Monde chez les Celtes. La ceinture de Dame Bertilak, portée par Gauvain en guise de protection magique, est faite de soie verte. A la fin Bertilak la laisse à Gauvain en souvenir de sa couleur verte. Cette ceinture, dans la scène de séduction, joue d'abord un rôle de métonymie sexuelle, avant de devenir un talisman magique.[9] Elle est en effet clairement désignée dans le texte par les mots *love-token* (2030) et *love-lace* (2226).

Pour achever le tableau des composantes celtiques païennes, rappelons que Gauvain fut d'abord un héros solaire, puis une sorte d'homme-médecine qui, selon Jessie Weston *(From Ritual to Romance)*, dans le rituel de fertilité sous-jacent au mystère du Graal, ramène à la vie "l'esprit de la végétation".[10] Quant à Bertilak, le Chevalier Vert, il n'est qu'une apparition supplémentaire du *Green Man*.[11]

Il ne reste plus qu'à dresser le tableau des deux signes visuels et de leurs oppositions associées:

	bouclier	*ceinture de soie*
Couleur	rouge sang guerrier	verte chlorophylle agriculteur
Activité associée	guerrière masculine	sexuelle féminine
Fonction et forme de l'objet	protection éloignée (à bout de bras) mécanique rigide partielle plaque	protection rapprochée (contre le corps) magique souple totale (encerclante) ruban
Situation dans le récit	départ	retour

Ce tableau fait ressortir plusieurs traits de la symbolique visuelle, se manifestant même dans la diachronie d'une narration, dont ils assurent d'ailleurs aussi la cohérence. Le symbole du retour n'est plus celui du départ. Et surtout la ceinture verte passe par cinq statuts sémiotiques successifs et différents:

1 – elle a la signification métonymique classique de l'abandon sexuel de la femme (cf. "Dénouer sa ceinture", la "ceinture de chasteté", le jet traditionnel de la jarretière lors du mariage ...), c'est un signe social et motivé;

2 – le sens (1) étant refusé par Gauvain, la Dame la fait accepter comme objet magique protecteur, qui ne fonctionne plus visuellement mais magiquement;

3 – Sire Bertilak la donne à Gauvain comme souvenir-témoignage, en raison de sa couleur verte. Elle fonctionne entre eux deux comme un indice (trace matérielle de l'aventure) et comme un signe analogique (la couleur verte du Chevalier, qui est elle-même celle de la végétation);

4 – Gauvain la porte ostensiblement pour marquer publiquement sa forfaiture à l'honneur (mineure selon tous, mais accablante pour lui). Cependant elle n'a ce sens que parce que Gauvain le dit: ce n'est pas un signe convenu et d'ailleurs il est refusé;

5 – la cour d'Arthur inverse le sens de la ceinture, et en fait un baudrier vert porté par tous les chevaliers. Cette fois le signe est jeté dans le corps social et retrouve sa signification au sens saussurien.

Au cours de cette complexe métamorphose de la ceinture verte, le rouge du sang et le pentangle de la perfection demeurent présents pour former l'opposition systématique entre deux couleurs complémentaires. L'affrontement des deux couleurs est explicite dès la première décollation:

(429) Blood spurted from the body, bright against the green.

Les contenus respectifs sont antinomiques, quel que soit le niveau d'analyse relevé au tableau, et ils sont homologués à une opposition tout aussi extrême sur l'axe de la couleur. Pour assurer une visibilité de loin l'axe de la couleur convient mieux que celui de la forme (problème qu'on retrouvera avec la voile d'Yseut). Quant à la polarité de l'homologation, elle obéit à l'iconisme, et les signes résultants sont motivés. On trouve ici une démonstration supplémentaire de la théorie saussurienne selon laquelle les significations tendent à se mettre en place dans des réseaux d'opposition et non isolément. Un problème intéressant, mais que le texte, trop ambigu, ne permet pas de trancher, est la co-présence, dans les vêtements de Gauvain lors de la seconde décollation, du pentangle et de la ceinture. L'un est visible et semble-t-il cache l'autre *(The green silken girdle [...] backed by the royal red cloth ...)*. Tous deux sont protecteurs, mais lequel en définitive a opéré?

L'investissement sémantique de l'opposition colorée est complété par d'autres couples d'opposés:

– le coup de hache sanglant (ou l'effleurement symbolique) est donné par un *homme;* il répand le sang *rouge* et entraîne une *mort* réelle ou symbolique;

– la ceinture *verte* est donnée par une *femme;* elle est un talisman protecteur ou un espoir de *vie,* c'est le symbole végétal du renouveau.

LA VOILE D'YSEUT

On se souvient de l'épisode célèbre où Tristan, marié avec Yseut aux blanches mains, est désormais séparé d'Yseut la Blonde. Malade, à la dernière extrémité, il envoie un homme de confiance supplier Yseut la Blonde de traverser la mer pour venir le guérir par son pouvoir magique. On a convenu que si le messager la ramène il hissera une voile blanche, et une noire dans le cas contraire. Très affaibli, Tristan a fait transporter son lit sur le rivage et demande à son épouse de lui dire la couleur de la voile dès qu'elle l'apercevra. Mais jalouse elle ment, annonce une voile noire, et Tristan meurt avant qu'Yseut la Blonde n'accoste.

On se trouve ici dans la situation la plus élémentaire imaginable: communiquer un oui ou un non, soit une unité binaire d'information, un bit. La nécessité d'être compris de loin impose le choix d'une propriété de surface: la couleur, la texture ou la brillance. Le noir et le blanc sont un choix logique, mais encore fallait-il décider d'une polarité. C'est ici qu'est intervenue une détermination à caractère psychologique et culturel: la mauvaise nouvelle a été associée à la couleur noire. Certaines interprétations (Markale) font d'Yseut une déesse solaire (N.B. "soleil" est féminin en gaélique), dont les cheveux blonds apportent la lumière: la voile blanche lui convenait donc mieux.

Le cas est exemplaire encore en ce qu'il montre que pour fonctionner ce type de signe exige le respect de la convention et du contrat de coopération entre émetteur et récepteur: un des relais situés le long de la chaîne de transmission a menti en inversant la polarité, et il en est résulté la mort de l'interlocuteur.

On trouve dans l'Antiquité d'autres exemples de voiles colorées douées de signification. La voile de la nef de Cléopâtre à la bataille d'Actium était pourpre. Mais surtout Thésée avait fait avec son père Egée une convention assez semblable à celle de Tristan. Les Athéniens avaient la coutume de marquer le deuil par des voiles noires, aussi Thésée, appareillant vers la Crète où il devait combattre le Minotaure, arborait-il des voiles noires pour marquer le deuil lié à l'infâme tribut réclamé par le monstre. A son retour de Crète il devait arborer des voiles blanches s'il avait vaincu le monstre, et noires sinon. Tout excité par sa victoire il oublia de changer ses voiles et Egée, sans attendre qu'il accoste, se jeta à la mer. Le thème de la voile blanche ou noire peut encore être trouvé dans des histoires plus récentes, comme dans le *Barzas Breiz* (La Villemarqué): dans *Bran ou le prisonnier de guerre* c'est une mère qui doit venir soigner son fils prisonnier et malade.

Ici c'est donc par erreur ou négligence que le message provoque la mort, alors que dans l'histoire d'Yseut c'est le mensonge. Sont ainsi illustrés les deux principaux "ratés" de communication, ainsi que la gravité potentielle de leurs conséquences.

Dans les deux exemples il y a une convention explicite, de sorte que le signe peut être arbitraire. Il ne l'est cependant pas car s'y superpose une détermination culturelle: le caractère néfaste du noir.

Enfin on remarquera que le type de code employé est à la fois différent de celui des trois gouttes de sang et de celui d'un alphabet quelconque. Les navires ont des voiles et ces voiles doivent forcément avoir une couleur. Le code consiste ici à exploiter cette couleur comme signifiant, et on parlera de *code greffé*.

CONSIDÉRATIONS D'ENSEMBLE

L'exploration des romans de chevalerie dans le but d'y repérer des épisodes relevant de la sémiotique visuelle se révèle très fructueuse. L'exploitation du visuel s'y est faite avec une grande ingéniosité, car les situations imaginées obéissent à des schémas très divers, épuisant peut-être toutes les possibilités, et en tout cas jamais répétitifs. Sans doute n'est-il pas déplacé de souligner que ces explorations visuelles littéraires étaient contemporaines du développement de l'art héraldique.

Bien d'autres épisodes auraient pu être analysés, tels les suivants qui s'ajoutent à ceux déjà notés incidemment dans les autres sections:

– Le Roi Marc sème de la farine sur le plancher de la chambre de Tristan, et y découvre le lendemain la *trace* des pieds nus d'Yseut.

– Le Roi Marc se dissimule dans un arbre pour épier les amants, mais est trahi par son *reflet* dans l'eau.

– Dans la version du *Book of Days* (suspecte) Yseut envoie à Tristan des messages en écorce flottante, qui consistent en signes gravés de l'*alphabet Ogham*. Les autres versions parlent seulement de brindilles ou de copeaux.

– Merlin confectionne, à l'intention de Guenièvre, un écu de bois représentant la reine et Lancelot. Mais cet écu est fendu et les deux parties, représentant chacune un des deux héros, ne se touchent que par un point; il se soudera magiquement dès que leur union aura été consommée.

– Dans la *Vulgate Lancelot* on met en scène deux Guenièvres, l'une vraie et l'autre fausse, et cette dernière tente de se substituer à la première. Elles sont parfaitement indiscernables, sauf par une *tache de beauté en forme de couronne,* sur les reins de la vraie reine.

– Dans la procession du Graal, le cérémonial réitéré de la *Coupe* et de la *Lance saignante* est présenté déceptivement comme un signifiant dont le signifié est refusé.

– La *Table Ronde* elle-même, avec son symbolisme géométrique, était censée former un couple d'opposés avec la table de la dernière Cène.

– Le messager de Tristan se fait reconnaître d'Yseut grâce à une bague, l'Anel, dont Thomas dit: Prenez cest anel avoc vus / ço sunt *enseignes* entre nus;
... et sans doute bien d'autres.

On peut enfin essayer de grouper les dispositifs visuels arthuriens en fonction du type de codage qu'ils appliquent.

On y trouvera des *codes parfaits,* dont les signifiants et les signifiés sont conventionnellement et univoquement définis (ex. l'écu fendu).

Dans d'autres cas il s'agira de *codes greffés,* dans lesquels une signification conventionnelle est tout simplement ajoutée à un dispositif visuel existant indépendamment par ailleurs (ex. la voile noire). Ces codes ont un effet secondaire intéressant: ils "contaminent" le réel en le rendant signifiant malgré lui. Par exemple si on décrète que la canne blanche signalera les aveugles, on impose du même coup le signifié "non aveugle" à toutes les autres cannes, bien qu'elles n'aient au départ aucun statut de signe relatif à la vision (la canne, en tant qu'indice métonymique le plus souvent, signale plutôt "la personne faible", "le vacancier", "le dandy"...)

Enfin on pourrait nommer *semi-codes* les cas (comme celui des trois gouttes de sang) où on prête une signification à un dispositif visuel dont le producteur n'est pas un émetteur. Ce type est bien familier en dehors des romans, car il englobe tous les cas de divination à partir du vol des oiseaux, des viscères, des configurations stellaires... On peut se demander quels caractères visuels mènent à choisir tel ou tel spectacle de la nature comme signifiant. Bien entendu il y a d'abord une théorie de la correspondance (analogique ou non) entre le macrocosme et le microcosme qui sous-tend toute la démarche. Mais la sélection finale, sous réserve d'un inventaire plus complet et plus strictement analysé, repose semble-t-il sur ces deux caractères: simplicité et discrétude. Tous ces exemples sont, de nécessité, asymétriques: le flux de (pseudo)-information s'y écoule à sens unique.

NOTES

1   Cf. Apostel (1964).

2   Littéral, allégorique, moral et anagogique.

3   Chez Wagner l'épisode est remplacé par celui d'un cygne blessé.

4   Pour la notion de symbole de contemplation, v. Edeline 1995 et 1996.

5   Cf. le modèle de Palmer, tel qu'exploité rhétoriquement dans le *Traité du Signe visuel* du Groupe μ, 1992.

6   Cf.: Jasjon sokol zà gory zaljotival / Dobroj molodec k sénickam privoracival, cité par Jakobson, 1963, où sokol signifie faucon, et dobroj molodec signifie vaillant jeune homme. Selon J. Markale l'étymologie de Gauvain serait également faucon.

7   On rapprochera également ces supputations de l'analyse faite par Bettelheim du sang des héroïnes de contes (op. cit.). Au chapitre *Blanche-Neige,* conte dont il compile plusieurs versions, on retrouve les trois gouttes de sang dans la neige, ainsi qu'un corbeau dont la couleur doit rappeler celle des cheveux de la jeune fille. Un tel corbeau est également présent dans certaines versions de l'histoire de Perceval (directement issues du Peredur des *Mabinogion*), au point qu'un amalgame des deux histoires devient plausible. Bettelheim interprète également le nombre de gouttes: "le chiffre trois [est] celui qui, dans l'inconscient, est le plus souvent relié au sexe". Pour lui le sang est celui de la menstruation, et le long sommeil (Perceval demeure prostré pendant des heures ...) l'attente de l'union sexuelle.

8   La décapitation elle-même est liée aux rites agraires: la céréale est annuellement fauchée et le grain repousse. Citons à ce propos la vieille ballade populaire dorienne mentionnée par Vaughan-Williams: *John Barleycorn.* Pour lui c'est peut-être une "unusually coherent folklore survival of the ancient myth of the slain and resurrected Corn-God".

9   Symboliquement (Chevalier et Gheerbrant) la ceinture est la source de toutes les grâces. La Ceinture d'Aphrodite (le Kestos) est censée contenir toutes sortes de charmes. Chez Hésiode et Homère, c'est un talisman divin conférant à la femme une puissance irrésistible.

10   La même Miss Weston *(The Legend of Sir Gawain)* fait cependant de l'épreuve de décapitation un simple test de la "valeur" de Gauvain. Cette lecture surprenante est difficile à accepter car (1) Gauvain n'a pas été *choisi* par le Chevalier Vert: il a relevé un défi lancé à la cantonade, et (2) l'insistance sur la couleur verte n'est pas expliquée. Ajoutons que Jean Markale conteste le caractère solaire de Gauvain.

11   Voir p. ex. *Green Man* de W. Anderson.

BIBLIOGRAPHIE

A.A.V.V. *Lumière du Graal*. Etudes et textes présentés sous la direction de René Nelli. Paris: Cahiers du Sud, 1951.

W. Anderson. *Green Man*. Londres: Harper Collins, 1990.

Apostel, L. "Symbolisme et anthropologie: vers une herméneutique scientifique". *Cah. Internationaux de Symbolisme* 5 (1964): 7-31.

Bettelheim, B. *Psychanalyse des contes de fées*. Paris: Laffont, coll. Réponses, 1976.

Chevalier, J. et A. Gheerbrandt. *Dictionnaire des Symboles*. Art. Pentangle. Paris: Seghers, 1969.

De Bruyne, E. *Etudes d'exthétique médiévale, T.II L'époque romaine*. Bruges: De Tempel, 1946.

Edeline, F. "Analogie projective et symbole de contemplation". *Cah. Internationaux de Symbolisme* 77-9 (1994): 83-90.

———. "La spirale, un symbole visuel universel". *Signs as Communication and Dialogue*. Intern. Semiotics Instit., IMATRA (Finlande), 1996 sous presse.

Gallais, P. "Les arbres entrelacés dans les 'romans' de Tristan et le mythe de l'arbre androgyne primordial". *Mél. de langue et de litt. médiévale*. Paris: Sedes, 1973. 295-310.

Graves, R. *The White Goddess*. Londres: Faber & Faber, 1961.

Groupe µ. *Traité du signe visuel*. Paris: Seuil, 1992.

Jakobson, R. *Essais de linguistique générale*. Paris: Minuit, coll. Arguments, 1963.

La Villemarqué. *Barzas Breiz*. 1837.

Levi-Strauss, Cl. "De Chrétien de Troyes à Richard Wagner". *Le Regard Eloigné*. Paris: Plon, 1983. chap. XVII, 301-24.

Liungman, C.G. *Dictionary of Symbols*. Santa Barbara, Cal.: ABC-CLIO, 1991.

Markale, J. *Gauvain et les chemins d'Avalon* (Le cycle du Graal, 5). Paris: Pygmalion, 1984.

Pastoureau, M. "L'héraldique arthurienne: une héraldique normande?" *Figures et couleurs*. 1983. Paris: Le Léopard d'Or, 1986.

Stone, B. *Sir Gawain and the Green Knight*. Harmondsworth: Penguin, 1978.

Todorov, T. *Symbolisme et interprétation*. Paris: Seuil, coll. Poétique, 1959.

Vaughan-Williams, R. et A. L. Lloyd. *The Penguin Book of English Folk-Songs*. Harmondsworth: Penguin, 1959.

Weston, J. L. *From Ritual to Romance*. Cambridge, UK: Cambridge Univ. Press, 1920.

———. *The Legend of Sir Gawain*. Londres: David Nutt, 1897.

IMAGinING the Text: Baudelaire's *Parfum Exotique*

Eric T. Haskell

The illustration of poetry presents a lush terrain for verbal-visual studies. Unlike the novel and the play, the poem's polysemic nature, which often allows the reader more interpretive levity, can also afford similar freedoms to the artist. Fragmentation of traditional narrative structures, so characteristic of modern poetry, seems to attract illustrators who may feel less obligated to replicate textual exactitudes of non-poetic literary genres. Thus, illustrating a novel by Dickens or a play by Molière is a significantly different task from making images for a poem by Baudelaire. It is from this premise that we shall investigate issues related to picturing of poetry within the context of its rich theoretical underpinnings.

"Parfum Exotique", one of the most evocative poems of *Les Fleurs du Mal,* has inspired a vast array of graphic interpretations striking in the quality and depth of insight they bring to Baudelaire's poetic universe. These illustrations are worthy of investigation not only because each one constitutes a visual and critical reaction to the text, but also because each proposes new ways of decoding its essential configurations. Although published in 1857, "Parfum Exotique" was not illustrated until 1910. The ways in which twentieth-century artists have pictured this nineteenth-century text affirm the value of illustration as interpretation. How their graphic inventions move beyond representation to the borders of abstraction is the topic of this image-text inquiry.[1]

Critic Robert-Benoit Chérix has framed the opening of "Parfum Exotique" in the following terms: "Baudelaire n'a jamais dépassé, en puissance de suggestion et en adaptation des mots à la pensée et à la musique, des vers comme ceux du premier quatrain" (114). This seamless passage from reality to dream is no doubt what has attracted so many artists to Baudelaire's text. Simplicity is the hallmark of poem's action which is constructed around the three verbs "to close", "to smell" and "to see": "Quand, les deux yeux fermés" (l. 1), "Je respire l'odeur"... (l. 2), "Je vois"... (l. 3). Seeing is essential to the aesthetic dynamics of the sonnet. But Baudelaire's poetic conceit is that real seeing takes place exclusively when the eyes are closed on reality. Only at that moment can they open onto the dream. The eye's transfiguration of landscape into dreamscape is dependent on the presence of the "odeur" (l. 2) – the *agent provocateur* par excellence from which the text derives its title. "Parfum

Figure 1. Georges Rochegrosse, ill. for Baudelaire's
"Parfum Exotique", 1910. © 1998 Artists Rights Society (ARS), New York / ADAGP, Paris.

Exotique" is a verbal catalogue of the dreamscapes that appear before the poet
once he transcends reality. Clearly, the visual nature of Baudelaire's island terrain drenched in idealized notions of exoticism appealed to the creative sensi-
bilities of illustrators early in this century who found in its contours a pre-
industrial paradigm of unspoiled nature as well as a puissant scenario of sensuality.

    "Parfum Exotique" is the first in a cycle of twenty-two poems inspired by
Baudelaire's passion for Jeanne Duval.[2] Fittingly, of the text's six illustrated
versions under examination, more than half feature a reclining female figure
at the center of their compositions. Georges Rochegrosse's illustration for the
poem typifies this treatment.[3] On a hammock that stretches horizontally across
the pictorial plane, the female muse reposes. Her lascivious attitude shores up
the contours of the term "paresseuse" (l. 5), which is the adjective used by
Baudelaire to portray the tropical retreat she inhabits. Her semi-transparent
gown is dappled with sunlight that has pierced through the banana-leaf bower
under which she lies, and the luminescent, sensuous effects are mirrored in
her otherworldly gaze.

    Clearly, this muse instigates the poetic gesture of "Parfum Exotique". Like
a modern-day Helen of Troy, she, too, has launched a thousand ships that lie
waiting in the harbor below, indicated here by the cluster of masts on the

Figure 2. Emile Bernard, ill. for Baudelaire's "Parfum Exotique", 1916. © 1998 Artists Rights Society (ARS), New York / ADAGP, Paris.

horizon. Rochegrosse expounds upon this concept by using the muse and her verdant surroundings to frame the background. Thus, her foreground placement is what allows the graphic vision to come into focus. The textual vision is inextricably linked to the effects of her "odeur" (l. 2) upon the poet and is entirely dependant upon them. Without these effects, both textual and pictorial planes would be confined to the realm of reality in which poetry is stifled and dreams are denied.

Rochegrosse, whose edition of *Les Fleurs du Mal* dates from 1910, was the first artist to illustrate "Parfum Exotique". His positioning of the reclined female figure as the focus of his composition seems to have inspired other artists who followed suit shortly thereafter. This is indeed the case with Emile Bernard.[4] In his *en-tête* illustration, he represents the muse as a Renoiresque nude, voluptuous in stature, and posed in an s-curve that crosses the picture plane on the diagonal. The masts featured in the background of Rochegrosse's image are more prominent here, and they are balanced by the platter of fruit that Bernard introduces in the foreground. These are the "fruits savoureux" (l. 6) of the poem and the icons of its sensual underpinnings. They replicate the exotic intentionality of the text in an illustration that tends to be somewhat stark in comparison to Baudelaire's textual lushness. However, the placement

Figure 3. Raphaël Drouart, ill. for Baudelaire's "Parfum Exotique", 1923.

of the fruit directly under the breasts of the muse suggests the ripened sensuousness of an exotic "elsewhere" which contrasts markedly with the quotidian
reality of the dreaming narrator. Finally, Bernard's repetition of the fruit motif
in his *cul-de-lampe* recalls the seductive contours of the *en-tête* illustration and
prolongs the dreamscape induced by the poem.

Like Rochegrosse and Bernard, Raphaël Drouart also uses the muse to
frame his 1923 illustration of the poem.[5] In this image, exoticism is upstaged
by eroticism as the female moves from a passive to an active pose. Her raised
arm holds the veil which serves as a reminder that the world portrayed in the
illustration is accessible only through the Baudelairian "correspondances" between the senses and that a password, here "l'odeur" (l. 2) of the text, is essential for making the transition from reality to dream. Elements from Rochegrosse
and Bernard, such as the sailor in the background and the fruit in the foreground, are incorporated into this composition. However, the genius of Drouart
resides in his clever conjugation of the two. Indeed, the basket of fruit carried
on the head of the male figure in the distance is so similar to the one lying at
the feet of the muse that foreground and background are visually linked. In
this context, the raised arm of the female is also a signal to the sailors lest they
lose their way up the sandy path from their port to her grassy retreat. Nudity
is central to the intention of Drouart as he carefully recounts in pictorial form
Baudelaire's textual indications: these are the "hommes dont le corps est mince

Figure 4. Edouard Goerg, ill. for Baudelaire's
"Parfum Exotique", 1947.

et vigoreux" (l. 7), and this is the muse of the "sein chaleureux" (l. 2). But his illustration reads beyond the specifics of the text. By suggesting that the men carry offerings to a crowned muse and interact with her, this image captures the erotic undercurrents of the text and, like the scent of "Parfum Exotique", they, too, remain in the air of the graphic entity long after the illustration has been decoded. Once again, the *cul-de-lampe* recalls both *en-tête* image and text by proposing a tropical plant whose suggestive contours sum up the sensuous pleasures of the poem's "charmants climats" (l. 9).

Edouard Goerg's 1947 illustration exemplifies a significant shift in the way artists picture "Parfum Exotique".[6] This image operates less in a representational and more in an abstract mode than the works of artists already examined. Clearly, there is little separation between pictorial and textual planes, and we can talk here of a fusion of the two. Whereas Rochegrosse used an *hors-texte* format and Bernard and Drouart confined their illustrations to *en-tête* and *cul-de-lampe* decorations, Goerg banishes the barriers between image and text. His illustration inhabits the left column of the page and stretches out toward the text across both top and bottom margins. In this novel disposition, verbal and visual planes intersect.

Although there is a vague indication of sea and ship at the lower right of this illustration, Goerg is not interested in transcribing the text in precise graphic terms. Rather, he chooses to focus on the essence of the Baudelairian trans-

Figure 5. Roger Bezombes, ill. for Baudelaire's "Parfum Exotique", 1985. © 1998 Artists Rights Society (ARS), New York / ADAGP, Paris.

figuration from reality to dream. Therefore, the traditional reclining nude is recast into the bust of a muse set zen-like within the dark bowers of a niche above the port. Her closed eyes announce a meditative state fixed on oneiric revelation. In her fingers, she holds a luminescent flower which, placed as it is before her breasts, extrapolates upon the poem's "odeur de ton sein chaleureux" (l. 2) and serves as a reminder that the sense of smell is the instigator of visionary terrains. Curiously, Goerg combines narrator and muse in a single image. For it is not the muse but rather the narrator who must close his eyes in order for the vision to occur – "Je vois se dérouler des rivages heureux" (l. 3). But since the poem's "Je vois" (l. 3) is predicated on "Je respire" (l. 2), Goerg sees the presence of the muse as an integral part in the process of revelation and thus pictures her as holder of the illumination. After all, the floral entity is represented by luminescence more than by form, and this, too, enhances the textual retreat from diurnal reality.

Perhaps the most original graphic representation of "Parfum Exotique" is Roger Bezombes' collage created in 1985.[7] The architecture of the volume is noteworthy. Bezombes sandwiches his double-page illustration between two leaves of printed text in an accordion style binding that enables the reader-viewer to unfold the four-page spread and to see image and text in a single glance. This unique disposition of verbal-visual information allows "Parfum Exotique" to perform as an exhibition.

A large caladium leaf with its unusual crimson nerves appears on the first page of text as a fitting prefiguration of the tropical efflorescence to come. The double-page illustration that follows operates within the aesthetic intentionality of the text by performing a sort of floral explosion intended to proliferate the visual plane with the same intensity experienced by the reader on the verbal plane. Framing the image with a female muse to mitigate foregrounding and backgrounding such as we have seen in other illustrated versions of the sonnet is absent from Bezombes' treatment. Rather, all graphic information is restricted to a single plane which is eminently foregrounded and ultimately present. The viewing experience has an almost disruptive immediacy about it as the beholder is plunged *in medias res* of a visual floriade – the very essence of "parfum" – here represented in the most "exotique" of terms. Hot color is cleverly used to denote fragrance as the artist responds in appropriate graphic terms to the first stanza's use of the verb *éblouir* (l. 4).

Bezombes' illustration is proof of his thoughtful reading of Baudelaire's text. We recall that it is not the woman, but rather her "odeur" (l. 2) that provokes the "rivages heureux" (l. 3) and induces the dream. Therefore, it seems altogether fitting that the artist conceive of a hothouse of species that are as far from horticultural reality as the dream induced by the poem. His *filles-fleurs* are actually antique porcelain doll heads that transcend mimesis and blossom on strange stems in a verdant paradise at once tropical and oriental. The brightly colored parrot on the right insures the former while the chinaman's head at left confirms the latter. These details heighten the otherworldliness of the text's "charmants climats" (l. 9) and propel the illustration from representation towards abstraction.

Bezombes goes a step further than any other illustrator of "Parfum Exotique" by moving from the graphic to the typographic in his visual rendering of the sonnet. Words that he conceives of as central to the textual dynamic are printed in color. While the terms "yeux" (l. 1), "feux" (l. 4), "oeil" (l. 8), "odeur" (l. 9), and "verts tamariniers" (l. 12) appear in blue, "arbres singuliers" (l. 6) and "parfum" (l. 12) are typeset in red. By imprinting these words in color, they leap to the surface of the typographical scheme with the same intensity as Bezombes' illustration. Clearly, these are the key words that serve as the impetus for the artist's visual rendering of the poem and, in this context, they share their typographical function with an illustrative one and thus become part of a common, extended pictorial plane.

Experimentation typifies Bezombes' work. At once exposition and exhibition, his illustration is the very essence of "Parfum Exotique", and his blurring of the lines between typographic and graphic gestures allows the text to be re-read and re-viewed in new ways that point to the intrinsic value of illustration as interpretation. Neither port, nor ships, nor sailors figure in his design and the female entity fails to frame his vision, but the absence of these details does

Figure 6. André Domin, ill. for Baudelaire's
"Parfum Exotique", 1920.

not make this image any less significant than others, only less representational.
In fact, its brand of abstraction ultimately corresponds to Baudelaire's poetic
universe whose aesthetics are so often inspired by the promise of transfiguration and transcendence.

    As a coda for closure, let us consider André Domin's illustration from
1920.[8] Although this image is far less aggressive than Bezombes, Domin's treatment of the text is just as radical. Neither female muse nor visionary landscapes enter into the picture plane. Rather, it is the narrator who dominates
the frame, sharing it with two other pictorial entities: a floral component that
falls from above and a cloud form on the left. Through the pochoir process,
the artist has painstakingly rendered the flowers in gold paint. They shine on
the surface of the plate as icons of "Parfum Exotique". The vision they inspire
is hidden in the cloud pattern which is visible only to the narrator whose eyes
are fittingly closed. Judd D. Hubert reminds us that "En fermant les yeux, le
poète abolit la réalité visuel du moment présent, mais en renforce l'atmosphère
sensuelle".[9] Clearly, Domin's decision to picture the narrator lost in dream
relegates the configurations of the vision to the imagination of the reader and
thus reiterates the essential *modus operandi* of the dreamscape and its fundamental verb pattern of "... les yeux fermés"... / "Je respire"... / "Je vois"....
Simplicity is the hallmark of this image whose abstraction echoes the most

primitive notions of the poetic gesture and places the specifics of the dreamscape within the perimeter of the reader.

In conclusion, the illustrators we have examined incite the reader-viewer to imagine "Parfum Exotique" in new ways. From traditional modes of casting the female muse as the centerpiece of the picture plane to non-traditional, innovative, even radical methods of picturing the text, Rochegrosse, Bernard, Drouart, Goerg, Bezombes and Domin consider the poem from diverse angles and transcribe it onto the pictorial plane in novel fashions. The multiplicity of their thematic approaches to the text shore up its essential configurations in such a way that – like the best of critical inquiry – they, too, shed new light on the often complex yet ever intriguing intersections of verbal-visual inquiry.

NOTES

1   For further information on Baudelaire and illustration, see the author's "Reading the Multimedia Book", "Visibilité/Lisibilité", "Traumlandschafen anderer Welten" and "Illustrations for Baudelaire's *Fleurs du Mal*".

2   For a complete listing of the poems in this cycle and details concerning the life of Jeanne Duval, see Chérix, 112-14.

3   Charles Baudelaire, *Les Fleurs du Mal*, 27 illustrations by Georges Rochegrosse engraved by Eugène Decisy and 16 culs-de-lampe engraved by Ernest Florian. This volume was printed in an edition of 1,200 copies, each numbered and initialed by the publisher.

4   Charles Baudelaire, *Les Fleurs du Mal*, woodcut illustrations by Emile Bernard. This volume was printed in a limited edition of 250 numbered copies.

5   Charles Baudelaire, *Les Fleurs du Mal*, illustrated with original woodcuts by Raphaël Drouart in an edition of 1,000 numbered copies.

6   Charles Baudelaire, *Les Fleurs du Mal*, (Volume I – "Spleen et Idéal", 144 lithographs; Volume II – "Tableaux Parisiens", "Le Vin", "Fleurs du mal", "Révolte", "La Mort", 156 lithographs) 300 illustrations by Edouard Goerg. These volumes were limited to 200 numbered copies.

7   Charles Baudelaire, *Les Fleurs du Mal*, illustrated by Roger Bezombes. This volume, designed by Michael Kieffer, was produced in a limited edition of 150 numbered copies.

8   Charles Baudelaire, *Les Fleurs du Mal*, illustrated by André Domin. This volume, containing a pochoir cover, a title page illustration in black and white and 26 pochoir illustrations, was printed in a limited, numbered edition of 485 copies.

9   Judd D. Hubert, *L'Esthétique des Fleurs du Mal* (Genève: Pierre Cailler, 1952) 175.

REFERENCES

Baudelaire, Charles. *Les Fleurs du Mal.* Woodcut illustrations by Emile Bernard. Ed. Ambroise Vollard. Paris: L'Imprimerie Nationale, 1916.

——. *Les Fleurs du Mal.* Illustrated by Roger Bezombes. Strasbourg: Les Bibliophiles de l'Est, 1985.

——. *Les Fleurs du Mal.* Illustrated by André Domin. Paris: Editions René Kieffer, 1920

——. *Les Fleurs du Mal.* Illustrated with original woodcuts by Raphaël Drouart. Paris: G. Boutitie et Cie., 1923.

——. *Les Fleurs du Mal.* Volume I: "Spleen et Idéal", 144 lithographs; Volume II: "Tableaux Parisiens", "Le Vin", "Fleurs du mal", "Révolte", "La Mort", 156 lithographs. 300 illustrations by Edouard Goerg. Paris: Marcel Sautier, 1947 (Volume I), 1952 (Volume II).

——. *Les Fleurs du Mal.* 27 illustrations by Georges Rochegrosse engraved by Eugène Decisy and 16 culs-de-lampe engraved by Ernest Florian. Paris: Librairie des Amateurs, F. Ferroud, 1910.

Chérix, Robert-Benoit. *Commentaire des Fleurs du Mal.* Paris: Librairie Minard, 1962.

Haskell, Eric T. "Illustrations for Baudelaire's *Fleurs du Mal*: Symbolist Dreams and Decadent Nightmares". *Symposium. Baudelaire and His Artists* 38 (1984): 179-95.

——. "Reading the Multimedia Book: The Case of *Les Fleurs du Mal*". In: Renée Riese Hubert, ed. *Visible Language. The Artist Book: The Text and its Rivals* 2/3 (1991): 272-82.

——. "Traumlandschaften anderer Welten" ("Otherworldly Dreamscapes: August Ohm's Illustrations for Baudelaire's *Fleurs du Mal*"). Preface, *Blumen des Bösen* by Charles Baudelaire. Göttingen: Verlag Bert Schlender, 1985. 5-24.

——. "Visibilité/Lisilibité et la Poïétique de l'Illustration". *Poïétique: Actes du Premier Colloque de Philosophie de la Création.* Paris: Editions Poïésis, (1991): 236-41.

Hubert, Judd D. *L'Esthétique des Fleurs du Mal.* Genève: Pierre, 1952.

The Digital Scriptorium. Towards a Pre-Gutenberg Perspective on Contemporary Typographic Practice

Will Hill

Recent developments in digital media have significantly altered the practice of typography, and relationships of word to image within design practice. Traditional distinctions between the setting of text and the insertion of graphic images, have given way to an integrated practice in which the two previously discrete elements may be developed, modified and manipulated simultaneously within the single workspace of the computer desktop. Digital media have also created a communications environment radically different from the traditions of print publishing. These new conditions imply the possibility of extended graphic vocabularies, and a reappraisal of our relationship to printed language. While it is clear that the history of set type within a print culture does not provide appropriate precedent for this, the wider history of the visual text reveals significant affinities and correspondences between past and present practice.

Digital typography allows for (indeed encourages) modifications of form and structure which have no basis in the development of set type. Traditional typefaces reflect an evolution defined by the material inflexibility of metal or wood, and the adherence of movable type to specific horizontal baselines. We are now able to manipulate these forms, and the space in which they are perceived to exist.

A consequence of this abrupt shift of visual scope is that innovation within this area lacks a defining critical framework. Lacking the cultural density of an identifiable tradition, it tends to be viewed in opposition to the values historically associated with typography, taking on a narrow range of readings concerned with contemporaneity, novelty and iconoclasm.

I will be proposing that this indicates a need to redefine the ways in which we locate tradition, to challenge some assumptions about the past development of typography, and the criteria by which we measure and evaluate that development.

From the computer desktop, we have access to extended options and variations within the act of writing; options as familiar to the medieval scribe as they are problematic to the traditions of print typography. We can interpolate visual imagery within text, introduce non-linguistic or pictographic symbols, modify the structure and form of columns, create overlaid, non-aligning and multi-directional text. The actual letterforms we use can be modified or redesigned. Visual decisions may be made in relation to the characteristics of particular word-groups or letter-groups; visual priorities can be created and modified simultaneously as part of writing itself.

More significantly, we are working directly in the medium of reproduction or distribution. Like a manuscript, but unlike a typewriter, drawing-board or composing table, the computer provides both the visual/textual surface for our words and the medium of their distribution.

As a publishing medium, the electronic document shares significant characteristics with the pre-Gutenberg manuscript. It does not depend upon establishing a mass market in order to be viable, and can be produced in response to individual demand. The graphic signs and letterforms it uses may reflect the visual conditions of a particular localized culture. Its content may involve a mixture of linguistic and non-linguistic values; it may be 'read' visually as an artifact which embodies general truths about itself. And it may take a cumulative form, accumulating marginalia and secondary texts.

Conditions which traditional typography has treated as fixed, have become relatively fluid within digital media, creating different conditions both for the writer and the reader. The history of movable type is defined by the rationalization of forms in relation to fixed horizontals. This can be seen not only as a mechanical but a perceptual bias in the evolution of reading. Literacy has been progressively defined in terms which arise from the conditions and constraints of set typography. Our expectations of text are expectations of singular, linear progression. The computer on the other hand allows us an integrated practice of image-making and text-making. This allows us to incorporate elements of representational material into text, but also to reposition the act of reading as an act of looking; to develop the idea of text as image. In this, digital typography draws upon the associative values of display typography and signage; forms associated with environmental rather than textual spaces, communicating contemporaneity, tradition, cultural associations and tactile values. The non-sequential use of language at varied levels of legibility, reinstates the idea of the word as an object of contemplation.

The computer monitor, and the interactive or electronic document, are not confined by the structure of the bound and numbered page. We can choose a number of progressions from any one point in a text. The digital space in which we create typographic work has no physical surface. It may therefore allow the simultaneous layering of separate levels of meaning. These examples mark some of the affinities between present-day and pre-Gutenberg patterns of practice, and indicate the potential of the computer as 'digital scriptorium'.

In order to consider the effects of the removal of traditional restraints upon typography and the visible text, it is necessary to look briefly at the conditions which existed before these constraints came into being, and also at those areas of practice which have continued to operate independent of them. These can be seen to involve areas of possibility which have been marginalized within the development of printed language, indicating future directions not only for typography, but for a broader area of convergent text-based visual practice.

The medieval manuscript clearly holds meanings and values which extend far beyond its 'use', and beyond its legibility. It can be seen to have significance for a public unable to read it; as an embodiment of meaning; a shrine to the revelation of the word. A liturgical manuscript is simultaneously an object of veneration and use.

The symbiosis of word and image within this period of visual history has striking parallels to our own. Manuscript images provide parallel texts, visual commentaries, mnemonics and reminders, to a partially literate culture. The manuscript page integrates text with symbols and icons, which we negotiate as we negotiate the visual language of the computer screen.

Movable type reinforced the divorce between word and image which began in cuneiform, in the transition from pictography through to fully abstract writing systems. The Carolingian edict standardized a single alphabet, which was further rationalised through the evolution of the printers type case. The transition from script to type revised the agendas and criteria for the evolution of letterforms. Printing established divisions of labour between the origination of text and the published book. It also reinforced distinctions between word and image; between the scribe and the illuminator. It established a value for homogeneity and consistency of form, and provided material arguments for the further standardization of alphabets.

Much of the documentation of type history has taken as central the typography of the printed book, which has led to a reading of this history in terms of incremental progressions towards an ideal of legibility and page economy, (occasionally disrupted by differing interpretations of these ideals). Yet type design has at critical points in its evolution drawn upon models from outside of movable type, invigorating tradition either from sources pre-dating print or from vernacular forms which have evolved separately from it. Baskervilles letterforms are clearly informed by tombstone lettercutting. Goudy used medieval sources for typefaces such as Goudy Medieval and Friar. The capital forms of the Trajan column have been seen as a model by Gill and Goudy, while Stanley Morison identifies the basis of sans serif capitals not as an independent modern innovation but as a conscious pastiche of hellenic monoline letters. Tradition has been invigorated by a dialogue with vernacular forms; forms which have developed outside the limits and values of metal typography: lettercutting, handwriting and other autographic processes. The digital era has provided its own vernacular surface in the low-resolution pixel, which forms an acknowledged element in the work of Zuzana Licko and April Greiman.

Since Gutenberg, the evolution of typographic form has taken place in response to specific economic, political and technological conditions. Typographic conventions are absorbed by a reading public, and gain legibility through familiarity and use. Throughout the print era this has been a 'top-down' process: the development of typography has been rationalised around the material demands of an increasingly massified industry, which has in turn established the basis of familiarity upon which our expectations of legibility are based. Foundry economics have dictated a homogenous and linear value-system, which dictates the values and functions of published writing. (By comparison, both the manuscript and digital cultures show a process of evolution from the bottom up: forms are developed through the writer or designers use and enter the visual currency of the reader, responding to localized conditions of social and cultural demand). Working outside the industrial determinants of print culture, we may question not only the basis of those value-judgments by which specific tendencies within typography have been endorsed, but more significantly, the underlying assumption of single, linear development; the view that greater homogeneity and rationalisation constitutes improvement.

Recent graphic design practice has increasingly called into question the neutrality of the designer, and the corresponding ideal of a transparent typography. The American typographic avant-garde of the 1980s, and specifically much of the work of Cranbrook graduates, was characterized by a reappraisal of the vernacular. Barry Decks Template Gothic, based upon a hand rendered sign in a laundromat, reflects a trend towards acknowledging specificity in type; an awareness that letterforms are informed by specific origins and processes.

The capacity of typographic design to celebrate local cultures rather than internationalism, the environmental rather than the corporate, reflects a user-centered philosophy increasingly prevalent in leading-edge design. Digital media provide a significant area of common ground for the reappraisal of relationships between designers and their audience; a relationship which is increasingly seen in terms of co-participation and socially pro-active strategy.

As typographic technology diffuses down-market into non-specialized programmes, its widespread use by an untrained writing public has far-reaching implications for the practice of writing, and our understanding of that practice.

Under the defining constraints of type history, experimentation within writing has generally focused upon relationships of linguistic, rather than visual structure. Innovations of outward form have been the exception rather than the rule: the familiar examples from Mallarmé, Apollinare, Schwitters are notable precisely because of the rigidity of the orthodoxies from which their work deviates.

Current technology has brought the writer into a direct and unmediated relationship to type. The originator of a text can simultaneously set it to page, bypassing the intervening phases of typescript, typesetting, copy fitting and other stages of specialist involvement.

From our current position we may then need to reconsider the ways in which we evolve and modify our use of letterforms. The capacity to integrate linguistic and non-linguistic material from the keyboard may open up possibilities whose origins predate full writing systems altogether; we may choose to reintegrate mixed languages of pictogram and rebus. The keyboard may now be used to access variant levels of meaning; the ways in which we design the alternate forms of letters may answer a range of functions beyond the conventions of case use. Any historical point of divergence in the linear development of typography may now need to be reassessed, from a viewpoint which reflects stronger affinities with medieval pluralism than renaissance linearity. As we move away from a communications environment defined by singular definitions of literacy in the reading of the written page, towards a multiple literacy in the decoding of messages that are visual, representational, typographic and associative, our experience increasingly echoes the experience of 'reading' an illuminated manuscript.

Much of our everyday experience of language takes this form; we 'read' mass communications not as transparent vessels of verbal content but as multivalent carriers of multiple levels of language and iconography, informed by the word as sign, as cultural artifact, a reading in which the visual particularity of a word carries a range of sub-textual values.

Digital technology creates the conditions and the need for convergent practices, to respond to these convergent modes of reading. While the critical focus of high-end design shifts from the designer as corporate service-provider towards the idea of design as authorship, the experiments of interested writers develop the role of authorship as design.

In conclusion: it would seem that current conditions argue for a reappraisal of the making of written text, for pluralistic approaches to previously accepted conventions of form and structure. Digital typography appears, in many cases, to offer solutions for which we have not identified the appropriate problems.

In a user-centred culture, changes in form are effected by new conditions of use.

The axiom that form follows function is as true of a post-modern typography as within the traditions of Modernism. Where they may differ is in the manner in which function is defined and understood. The development of coherent typographic languages will depend upon identified need from within language use. Significant development in typography will depend upon upward pressure from innovative textual practice.

Precedent for these changes may, as I have shown, be located outside print-based history. In seeking a coherent framework for the use of digital technologies in type, it therefore seems appropriate to look to a model based not upon the historical limitations of print, but upon the historical diversity of letterform: the typographic prehistory of mixed systems, the secret histories of autographic vernaculars, the text as image, the image as sign. From the digital scriptorium of the computer, we may consider a neglected inheritance; the resumption of a tradition broken 500 years ago: the interrupted history of the illuminated word.

REFERENCES

Backhouse, Janet. *The Illuminated Manuscript.* Oxford: Phaidon, 1979.

Bologna, Giulia. *Illuminated Manuscripts: The Book Before Gutenberg.* Trans. Jay Hyams. New York: Weidenfeld & Nicolson, 1988.

Crawford, Neil. *The Spirit and the Letter: Poetry and Print.*

Gray, Nicolete. *A History of Lettering: Creative Experiment and Letter Identity.* Oxford : Phaidon, 1986.

Goudy, Frederick W. *The Alphabet and Elements of Lettering.* Rev. and enl. ed. Berkeley: University of California Press, 1952.

Huizinga, Johan. *The Waning of the Middle Ages: Study of the Forms of Life, Thought and Art in France and the Netherlands in the xivth and xvth Centuries.* London : E. Arnold & Co., 1937.

Kinross, Robin. *Modern Typography: An Essay in Critical History.* London: Hyphen Press, 1992.

Lewis, John. *Anatomy of Printing: The Influences of Art and History on its Design.* New York: Watson-Guptill, 1970.

McLuhan, Marshall. *The Gutenberg Galaxy: The Making of Typographic Man.* Rpt. Toronto (etc.): University of Toronto Press, 1992.

Morison, Stanley. *Politics and Script: Aspects of Authority and Freedom in the Development of Graeco-Latin Script from the Sixth Century B.C. to the Twentieth Century A.D.* Ed. and compl. Nicolas Barker. Oxford: Clarendon Press, 1972.

Vanderlans, Rudy, et al. *Emigre: Graphic Design into the Digital Realm.* Van Nostrand Reinhold, 1993.

From "Things as They Are" to What They Become:
From Illustration to Bookwork

Renée Riese Hubert

David Hockney and Clifton Meador, artists usually associated with post-modernism notably because of the numerous metacritical comments prominently displayed in their works as well as their obvious concern for declining contemporary values, have succeeded in transforming, each in his own way, the esthetic conceptions and practices of book art. In spite of the innovative transformations to which he subjected Wallace Stevens' poetic text, Hockney continued to adhere to many of the traditions of the 'livre de peintre', a genre perfected by such modernist painters as Georges Rouault, Henri Matisse, Pablo Picasso, Georges Braque, Fernand Léger, Joan Miró, Max Ernst, André Masson, and Roberto Matta. Clifton Meador, on the contrary, pays little if any attention to the conventions of the illustrated book, notably by his radical rejection of a canonical text and his refusal to adopt a standard book format. In fact, he has substituted for *The Book of Revelations* seven reductive lines of his own invention and replaced the codex form with a highly complex version of accordion folds. In short, both book artists have transgressed the norm in different but nonetheless complementary ways in producing exemplary postmodern artifacts.

In "The Man with the Blue Guitar", Stevens meditates on the place of poetry in a dysfunctional world while paying homage to Picasso's social minded artifact. And Hockney in his twenty etchings entitled *The Blue Guitar* provides readings of the poem and a visual commentary not only on the representation of an old guitarist, but on Picasso's œuvre in general. Thus, the reader must hold in check three different performative projects, each one a deliberately deviant "fictionalizing act". The cover indicates in blue and red letters: "Etchings by David Hockney who was inspired by Wallace Stevens who was inspired by Pablo Picasso". In his *Blue Guitar*, Hockney appropriates by indirection, for he repeatedly lifts his titles from the text and, through the contours of the recurrent image of the guitar, he produces flexible images of the poet's reiterated references to that musical instrument. However closely they may relate to the poetic text and the visual images, Hockney, both in his titles and his etchings, avoids description and narrative. Thus, mimesis plays a very reduced role.

The voices of the poet and the guitarist merge early in the text as though to obliterate the traditional persona to whom the reader can ascribe the articulation and unfolding of metaphors. The poet has focused on a single painting of the "blue period": *The Old Guitarist.* In a sense, he has retained a color, a voice, and vibrating strings while bracketing the painter's subsequent development. Thus, this single work sufficed for Stevens' indefatigable cogitations about art and reality, imagination and nature. The poet pushes his dialectical inquiry so far that it results in a state of tension and crisis. Picasso's old guitarist appropriately serves as a tragic figure, for we can hardly expect that this emaciated old man in tatters will ever find regeneration through his music. The poet moves alternately from resignation to aggression, offering at moments almost a counterpart to the Picasso painting. Although these traces of social preoccupations marginally serve a thematic purpose during the early cantos, the poem's general relation to Picasso focuses even more on concerns of artistic value and medium.

Critics have stressed that a certain line in Stevens' text:

Is this picture of Picasso's, this 'hoard of destructions', a picture of ourselves

has its source in a statement by the artist which had appeared in a 1935 volume of *Les Cahiers d'Art:* "In the old days pictures went forward toward completion by stages. Every day brought something new. A picture used to be a sum of additions. In my case a picture is a sum of destructions. I do a picture – then I destroy it. In the end though, nothing is lost: the red I took away from one place turns up somewhere else". The term "destruction" pinpoints the poet's artistic allegiance. The necessity to destroy, to oppose reality rather than espouse it, and to overcome a legacy rather than stand by it, refers to the creative struggle with the objects of reality which forces the artist to sidestep any direct appropriation. Stevens' "a hord of destructions" shifts Picasso's esthetics toward a more overt form of violence, the sort of violence featured in *Guernica,* painted in 1937, the year of publication of "The Man with a Blue Guitar" in a volume bearing that title. Each canto brings about its own tensions and its own hopeless confrontations. However, destruction hardly ever runs its course because the repeated rhyming "things as they are" and "the man with the blue guitar" points to endless reversibility.

The first etching of the *Blue Guitar* shows a modified version of Picasso's *Old Guitarist* with the name of the Spanish painter, the title, and his date of birth inscribed in the frame (fig. 1). It thus tries to pass for a mere reproduction rather than a performative representation. While ironically providing reliable documentation, Hockney imposes his own distorting variations. Substantially darkened, the plate appears almost monochrome, and because the

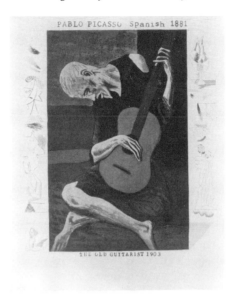

Figure 1. David Hockney, "The Old Guitarist" from
The Blue Guitar, 1976/77. Etching and Aquatint, 20
½"x18". © David Hockney.

old guitarist has somehow organically coalesced with his guitar, player and
instrument have become inseparable. Nor can we ascribe psychological meanings to its dark blue shade, featured thoughout the book. Rather, Hockney
emphasizes and simultaneously subverts the painterly and lyrical aspects of his
art while proclaiming his commitment to his medium, etching. Throughout
the series, Hockney borrows specific images from Picasso, usually producing
variations, if not disclaimers, of objects or fragmenting them. From the beginning, Hockney insists on parodying Picasso, sometimes with freedom and
abandon.

In his *Blue Guitar,* Hockney refers to works by Picasso from several periods. The *Old Guitarist* on Hockney's page emerges from a light colored frame
in which red and green lines predominate. This frame includes several
miniaturelike pictures "inspired" by Picasso and appropriated from various
stages of his career. Still-lifes and portraits predominate throughout the series.
They have invariably undergone manipulations. This relegation to the margins and this reduction to the status of frame as opposed to center-piece suggest that a liberating process has taken place. Hockney lends a hand to Picasso's survival and asserts his own originality while respecting in his renditions

Stevens' multiple references to the blue guitar. Often inscribed with a double outline, this musical instrument refers to the poet's somewhat wavering arguments, which open up a position and then restrict it, and, more directly, to a stylization of Cubist representations. The painter's blue guitar with its vibrations and its experimental perspectives can float, rise, stand apart from, or remain juxtaposed to, other contours or objects. It can generate other shapes without the intervention of anecdotal connections, for only visual allusions such as colors, strings, musical scores really matter. In Stevens' text, the network of signs relating to the blue guitar differs from that of the essentially self-referential presence in the etchings.

Although Hockney's choice of titles, most of which correspond to recognizable lines or cantos, shows a careful reading of the text, we can hardly claim that he focuses on the poem's literary qualities. We may even wonder whether the British artist attempted to translate graphically Stevens' anguished inquiry into poetry and his critical awareness accompanied by doubts. In various etchings, four or five isolated colors, blotches, drippings, or lines sometimes look like brushstrokes and sometimes resemble the brushes themselves as though to evoke a still unarticulated artistic production. Other elements, notably a precisely outlined pen and a nearby inkwell, bring to the surface the problematics of creation. Grids emerge in several etchings, if not completely subservient to geometry at least shaped into highly structured objects. By stylizing, dismantling, or painting over "things as they are" in order to restore or redeem them, the artist obliquely acknowledges Stevens' process of reconstruction and deconstruction. Hockney goes even further insofar as he pinpoints the creative process. Color becomes a self-sufficient entity, lines move in and out of contours, and the frame – screen, wall, or window – frequently asserts its self-sufficiency – frame within frame, frame confronting or disregarding frame, but rarely ever a frame cosily fitting within a frame.

Nonetheless, an etching such as "Franco-American Mail" evokes quite a different notion of cohesion (fig. 2). Each of the uneven thirteen squares contains an image (two in one case), often echoing other representations in the series such as still-lifes and portraits obviously derived from Picasso. Two opposing views of the blue guitar with and without a musical score and two discrepant versions of blue clouds bring into the open latent conflicts that even the old guitarist's melodies may fail to conciliate. The multiple image grid with its clearly recognizable allusions comes close to, while distancing itself from, pop art practices.

By quotations from the poem in some of his titles, Hockney ironically acknowledges the possibility of a mimetic approach that he will never follow. Whether quoted, distorted, or invented, his etchings remain at the same vast remove from mimesis. Titles such as "Franco-American Mail" or "Made in April" provide popular allusions that bypass Picasso only to clash with Stevens'

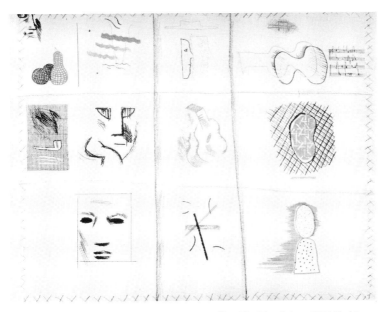

Figure 2. David Hockney, "Franco-American Mail" , *The Blue Guitar,* 1977. Etching.
© David Hockney.

meditative lyricism. Festivities, celebrations, and popular productions play an important part in Hockney's iconography. When Stevens refers to the actor and his masks the tone strikes us as helpless and sad:

> The color like a thought that grows
> Out of a mood, the tragic robe
>
> Of the actor, half his gesture, half
> His speech, the dress of his meaning, silk
> Sodden with his melancholy words

Stevens' figure belongs to the same family as Laforgue's melancholy Pierrot while Hockney turns performance into a parade, the stage in his "non-space" transgresses all borders, and motion runs circles around the universe. The performers include still-life objects, chairs, walls, and undefinable assemblages. Clearly, Hockney's suite with its display of bright color splashes side by side with geometrically designed grids or carpets barely makes any attempt to harmonize with the elusive certitudes Stevens so vainly pursues. Far from treating Stevens as a symbolist poet who shies away from reality to seek a hidden spiritual unity, Hockney realized that these almost obsessive returns to "things as they are" meant that artistic creation was rooted in an unrepresentable reality.

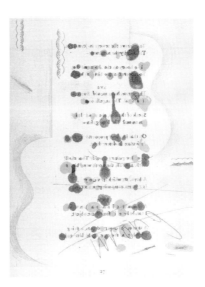

Figure 3. David Hockney, "Made in April", *The Blue Guitar,* 1977. Etching. © David Hockney.

Could Hockney have exemplified this awareness in any better way than in the final etching entitled "What is this Picasso?" Does he not ironically admit that in his final reference to Stevens he turns his own work into a "wrong" Picasso?" The thick blue pleated curtain, almost absurdly "real", reveals Dora Maar's portrait recreated by Hockney.

The title "Etching is the subject" substitutes for Stevens' "Poetry is the subject of the poem". But the parallel is not as systematic as it seems. With his displays of brushes, inkwells, blotches, frames, grids, still-lifes, and portraits, Hockney refers to etching mainly as a craft whereas Stevens seeks a different awareness in his effort to define poetry and to situate it between two opposing forces. In addition to his truncated borrowings from Picasso, Hockney, who has included a portrait of Wallace Stevens entitled "The Poet", thus reveals that his task as illustator, while showing his allegiance to the writer, should display his technical prowess as an etcher.

"The Poet" reveals the duality pervading the series, such as the shifting within the object providing double contours, the opposition between formal and figurative elements, between motion and immobility seemingly reconciled in such a title as "A Moving Still-life", and finally the dichotomy between invention and borrowing, between painted-over frames and clear outlines. Perhaps the most telling example of duality appears in "Made in April", which shows, on a splashed guitar-shaped double easel, a reversed or mirror image of

Figure 4. Clifton Meador, *Book of Doom,*
1984. Stenciled Image. Reproduced by permission of the artist.

the text printed on the left side (fig. 3). Stevens' canto in its original textual existence undergoes a double transformation at the hands of the painter: the unchanging words function as a musical score in a 'tableau-poème' by means of the text's inscription in red and blue notations which, in spite of multiple specks, never mix. In no way reducible to an April Fool's joke, the handwritten "wrong" functions as a signature allowing the painter to appropriate the text as his own.

From the standpoint of bookwork, Hockney may very well have gone beyond the illustration of a poem and the parody of an admired artist. A master of space and color, he has created his own pages and his own art gallery by unframing the pages of the book as well as Picasso's canvases. The so-called curtains, rugs, windows, and grids function as walls displaying works of art. As such, they impose a format all their own in a museum of their own making.

Clifton Meador combines the various roles of book designer, artist, and, mimimally, of author. In order to show to best advantage his struggle with spiritual forms of survival, the artist had to perform complex feats. When we remove the *Book of Doom* from its greyish box where the black title emerges amidst bright red zones, we see an almost flat diamond shaped brightly colored paper surface in stunning contrast with its enclosure. The paper surface consists of several vertical strips instead of the expected single sheet. Occupying the center, the streamlined yellow silhouette of a human figure emerges from blue zones (fig. 4). The two sidestrips display fairly similar though by no means identical patterns. Paradoxically, this overwhelmingly jubilant surface must function as a title page even though it refrains from displaying a text of any sort. Nor can we induce the entire surface to turn to the left in a single gesture as would any proper title-page in a conventional book. When a section of the surface does consent to turn or, rather, fold over, it changes into a narrow rectangle lying diagonally. It would seem that the artist has systematically rejected proportions and shapes that might remind the reader of a standard page. A second operation induces the narrow diagonal strip to turn or unfold once more, extending the outlines of the two sides into a single triangle displaying at long last a one line text in lieu of the missing title.

Because each of the seven single line texts of this seven layered book follows the straightline rims of a triangle, the marginal and perhaps marginalized inscriptions suffice to provide the textual component of the volume. The space below each inscription becomes ever broader, layer after layer. Almost entirely sprayed, the image has completely taken over, in keeping with other recent bookwork productions. And as one would expect, each of the seven stenciled layers follows the model just described. The triangle on which we have focused our attention will, thanks to a third operation, turn once again, unfolding this time into a rectangle. This triple unfolding or development expands the modest sized book we had removed from the shelf to truly impressive dimensions. Only when the volume has reached its full development do we notice its straight and zigzag contours with a diamond shaped double enclosure surrounding a void or, better still, an abyss in the center. Figures, statuettes, silhouettes of men, placed at regular distances from each other, also suggest an encirclement precluding any possibility of escape. The color patterns remain bright throughout while the paradoxical presence of a vitiated circle manifests itself anew each time the viewer unfolds the successive layers of the book (fig. 5). Instead of mechanically turning a series of even pages to contemplate passively confrontations of texts and images, we have to struggle in order to assure the unfolding of a simultaneously pleasurable and threatening spectacle, but without ever losing sight of the gaping hole in the middle.

As I have already stated, the volume comprises seven layers, seven rectangles seven times surrounding the inevitable void. The number seven refers, at least implicitly, to the seven days of the week and, explicitly, to the Seven Seals of the Apocalypse, dictated by the title. With its folded pages *The Book of Doom* imposes new ritual gestures on readers and thus transforms them into participants, if not accomplices, by inducing them to displace and display the world of (dis)order. As Johanna Drucker has stated in her *The Century of Artists' Books,* this systematic unfolding and overlapping conveys the impression of "a deceptively ordered universe" whereas "the rough but relentless patterns

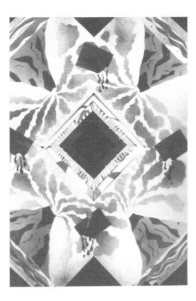

Figure 5. Clifton Meador, *Book of Doom,*
1984. Stenciled Image. Reproduced by permission of the artist.

(influenced by African textiles) create a vision in which reason collapses, un-
sustainable under the sheer force of hypocrisy and superficiality of modern
consumerism" (148). Meador's orderly invention deviates much more from
accepted norms than most accordion books, which also rely on folding and
unfolding as well as on the simultaneous display of several pages.

Identical in shape though not in size when unfolded, the seven layers share
the central abyss. The dark center, that at least obliquely relates to hell, could
also allude to the womb that generated the book as object as well as to the
seven days of creation even though these happenings have nothing to do with
the subject matter of *The Book of Doom*. The volume's potential for expansion
impinges on the reader, and even the absence of a spine contributes to the
transformatory nature of this work in which all the elements lead to extension.
Have we not implicitly noted that the book sacrifices uprightness in favor of a
horizontal sprawl featuring a sink hole in the middle? Each layer provides its
own self-sufficient spectacle and event, unavoidably superseded by the next,
but without ever undergoing a total eclipse since the margins never cease to
protrude. From the first to the last, the reader moves progressively to ever
broadening strips conveying the impression of curtailed distances.

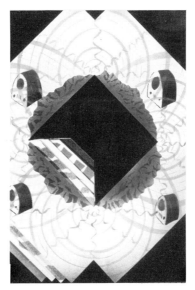

Figure 6. Clifton Meador, *Book of Doom,*
1984. Stenciled Image. Reproduced by permission of the artist.

Different parts of the book interact in varied and multiple ways involving the back and the front of each sheet, the half-unfolded and the completely unfolded commenting all the while on the same event or object. The doubly folded diagonal sections provide a pattern perpetuated by the fold of the next page with variations and intensifications: yellow sun arches and green waves link one layer and one strip to the other. The folded strip extends beyond its own paper surface, promising a continuity of happenings, spectacles, geographical scenes, and movements of elements. Yet we have to take into account the strongly decorative quality of the design, based on symmetrical repetitions of colors and shapes, which transforms extension and expansion into a woven tapestry while maintaining the appearance of flatness and precluding any suggestion of psychological depth concerning the dark hole.

From the point of view of bookwork, Meador has introduced an innovative way of exploiting both the back and the front of the same page. The viewer does not leave behind one section in moving to the next. The artist has superseded the conventional system of eclipsing a page by substituting a new one in a manner quite different from other accordion volumes. In more than one way its physical presence – its materiality – makes the reader aware of the simultaneous presence of the pages in their acquired flexible divisions. As the pages fold and unfold instead of turning to reveal their imaged patterns, the inside and the outside no longer relate in the expected manner. When the book unfolds into a flat surface where all sections participate we can hardly claim that we look from the outside toward what lies within, because in the course of the book's unfolding we have already viewed each section from several perspectives: visual memory definitely plays a part in our reading.

The first layer presents stylized images of men, houses, waves, and stars; ordinary commercial objects such as radios and lit cigarettes emerge later (fig. 6). These nondescript and apparently harmless consumer items will ignite or contribute in their way to the struggle between order and disorder, peace and eruption, a struggle perpetually inscribed though not always in the most disturbing manner. The apocalyptic narrative follows its course: a volcanic eruption clearly makes its presence felt and heavy clouds ominously but gracefully modulate their shapes. Plastic objects, as humorous as those in Tati's *Mon Oncle,* reach the dripping stage. Objects continue to blend in with atmospheric scenery, and we can hardly make clear distinctions between sunbursts and sound waves. By taking the place of trumpets blown by angels, boomboxes bring the biblical event up to date. Substituting for horses, automobiles of every vintage and model disappear into yawning crevices. Blossoming modern consumerism enters into the throes of its final struggle in the *Book of Doom* whose last layer suggests darkness and disappearance. However, the paradoxical situation already noted has by no means subsided. Let us consider the full text of the book:

> Men became aware of a strange dark star in the sky
> Sudden vast tides inundate coastal cities putting out all cigarettes
> Loud low rumbling emanates from below drowning out pop radio
> Fires from volcanoes and lightning sweep the land melting all plastic
> Crevices open up, swallowing all late model and used cars
> Direction is lost and confusion is King.
> Doom random Doom

A single announcement of one stage or happening suffices for each full page, an announcement directly referring to the graphic display on the corresponding fully-opened side. Beginning with the second page, clearcut discrepancies between the significant and the insignificant, between the cosmic and the everyday, the permanent and the ephemeral reveal the parodic and satirical intent of *The Book of Doom*. Objects corresponding to the text emerge; they reappear in an orderly manner at regular distances. They seem to respect the order of pages already enforced by triangularity, circularity, and rectangularity. Indeed, the presence of geometric proportions and shapes counts heavily in spite of a prevalence of chaos within the text: "Direction is lost, confusion is King" "Doom, random, Doom". Prompted by the title, we as readers recognize the upheaval progressively reported, creating associations with an Apocalypse cut off from the Last Judgment. At the same time, Clifton Meador flattens out events in a condemned world schematically modeled on representations of events made familiar by painters. "Direction is lost". This postmodern formulation concerning higher forces leaves only doubt and disarray. The final textual statement: "Doom, random Doom" heightens the paradoxes. "Random" may appear like a follow-up of a lost direction, but framed by doom on both sides, it reveals the downgrading of traditional beliefs, disbeliefs, and values, so that Meador's resulting postulate marks the final thrust into the absurd. "Doom, random Doom", with its analogies of sounds, with its variations suggests a game similar to the folding of pages.

We may wonder why Meador in his brief texts has reduced Saint John's Apocalypse to consumerist insignificance while producing a masterpiece of book art. Whereas the apostle's imaginative vision has both terrorized as well as edified countless generations of believers, Meador's beautiful rendition can only please esthetically inclined viewers without frightening even the most timid souls. It would seem that the discrepancy between so short a text, in which the world ends its final abridgment with a whimper, and compelling bookwork that leads to a splendid unfolding and expansion produces a disproportion that can only accrue to the stunning effect of the whole. In thus downgrading a religious work familiar to most readers, Meador has lifted the production of books to heights definable as dizzying because of the omnipresent abyss.

I have examined two books where the visuals have avoided any form of mimeticism. From *The Blue Guitar* with its famous text I have moved to *The Book of Doom,* a book sculpture supplemented by the artist's minimal text. I could of course show this development or, better still, jump from Hockney to Meador, by providing examples from other books, notably *Anecdote of the Jar* based on a poem by Stevens. The emergence of new genres such as installations and videos could support the hypothesis of increasing visual encroachments on the verbal and perhaps lead to many provocative Word Image studies.

REFERENCES

Benamou, Michel. *Wallace Stevens and the Symbolist Imagination.* Princeton: Princeton
     University Press, 1972.
Drucker, Johanna. *The Century of Artists' Books.* New York: Granary Books, 1995.
Henry E. Huntington Library and Art Gallery. *13 Ways of Looking at Wallace Stevens.* A
     Special Exhibition, 1975.

Hockney, David. *A Retrospective.* Organized by Maurice Tuchman and Stephanie Barron, Los Angeles County Museum of Art, 1988.

———. *The Blue Guitar.* London: Petersburg Press, 1977. [A limited number of large format copies are available].

Hogben, Carol and Rowan Watson, eds. *From Manet to Hockney: Modern Artists' Illustrated Books.* London: Victoria and Albert Museum, 1985.

Livingston, Marco. *David Hockney.* London: Thames and Hudson, 1981.

MacLeod, Glen. *Wallace Stevens and Modern Art from the Armory Show to Abstract Art.* New Haven: Yale University Press, 1993.

Meador, Clifton. *Book of Doom.* New York: Space Heater Multiples, 1984.

———. Interviewed & on his books. *JAB* 7 (1997): 2-12.

Zervos, Christian. "Conversation avec Picasso". *Cahiers d'Art* 10 (1935): 73-8.

Matérialités de l'immatériel.
Vers une sémiotique du multimédia

Yves Jeanneret

Dans sa prime jeunesse, le terme: "multimédia" exhibait les charmes de la complexité. Il a désigné des formes de spectacle associant plusieurs médias, puis des campagnes publicitaires réalisées sur divers supports. Aujourd'hui, la référence au multimédia évoque l'idée de simplicité, caractérisant les dispositifs capables d'intégrer, sur un support unique, des messages de nature diverse.

Intégrer: le terme n'est commode qu'en apparence. A trop vite transférer cette notion technique dans le champ sémiotique, on risque d'escamoter la différence entre les médias et de ranger au magasin des antiquités communicationnelles la complexité de nos langages. L'annonce d'une nouvelle ère anthropologique ne saurait dispenser de l'éclairage d'une histoire, matérielle et culturelle, de l'échange entre les médias. A ce titre, le développement du multimédia est à coup sûr une provocation, et pour les créateurs, et pour les théoriciens des rapports entre texte et image.

1 - L'AVENIR D'UNE ILLUSION

En quoi consiste cette "révolution" annoncée? S'agit-il, comme on le dit souvent, de "dématérialisation" de la communication (Théofilakis)? Cette idée séduisante mérite d'être élucidée. La technique ouvre à la communication des espaces nouveaux: les réseaux s'étendent et s'interconnectent; une masse d'informations est disponible en des temps et des lieux les plus divers; les écrans reconstruisent les formes les plus variées de messages; des documents de nature très différente sont numérisés, et donc traités et transportés par le jeu du calcul. Inscrites dans la continuité d'innovations plus anciennes, ces avancées techniques posent en termes nouveaux la question de la médiatisation des signes.

Le thème de l'immatériel n'en est pas moins un excès de langage, qui constitue pour la sémiotique un objet d'analyse plutôt qu'un concept opératoire. C'est en effet un double signe (indiciel): du désarroi que nous éprouvons vis-à-vis d'une sémiose dont la nature nous échappe; du désir qui travaille le projet technologique de transparence communicationnelle.

Le second de ces aspects est le plus facile à décrire, pourvu qu'on y prenne garde. L'idée d'immatérialité a une histoire, travaillée par l'idée d'une communication sans corps. Il y a un siècle on évoquait: *"les routes de la pensée"* (Hélène), on admirait le *"sortilège télépathique"* de la télégraphie sans fil "éveillant *[...] la pensée à distance"* (*L'Année scientifique*, 1897), on créait le terme "télécommunication" pour désigner *"la transmission de la pensée à distance, au moyen de l'électricité"* (Estaunié). Il y a quelque chose de constituant dans cet escamotage, une nécessité de nier la matière des signes afin de mieux se proposer un but thaumaturgique. Le projet de résoudre la question de la communication par la technologie est profondément idéaliste, quelque pragmatique que puisse être la conduite de ses bâtisseurs.[1]

Cette tentation d'ignorer le corps des signes connaît aujourd'hui une virulence renouvelée. A en croire le discours commercial, la communication multimédia nous plongerait dans un bain intellectuel homogène, exhaustif et transparent. Homogène puisqu'on numérise pareillement toutes les formes de message; exhaustif puisqu'on ménage l'accès à toutes les "données"; transparent puisque chacun dispose de l'initiative. Bref le rationnel triomphe du divers, le contact de l'ignorance et le dialogue de la censure.

La sémiotique ne peut accepter ces équivalences, sous peine d'évacuer tout simplement la pensée du signe. Un monde sans signifiants matériels – à supposer qu'on puisse s'en former l'idée – serait un monde où l'interprétation ne pourrait advenir. Le travail sémiologique consiste précisément à faire des hypothèses sur la façon dont les signifiants, dans leur forme singulière et dans leur matérialité, peuvent suggérer et autoriser l'interprétation. On voit bien, symétriquement, pourquoi cette question a tant de mal à advenir au sein de la pensée technologique de la communication: c'est une question qui empêche de tourner en rond, qui dénonce l'illusion de pouvoir rendre transparente la communication, d'espérer lui apporter une … solution finale. Elle indique que la communication ne saurait être débarrassée, par quelque prothèse que ce soit, du risque et de l'opacité qui la constituent.

Toutefois, cette question refoulée fait retour aujourd'hui d'une façon vive, et ceci, paradoxalement, du fait même des avancées de l'entreprise technologique. C'est bien parce que les messages de la nature la plus diverse peuvent aujourd'hui être convertis en séries de 1 et de 0 et peuvent se combiner librement, que l'attention trop distraite à leur forme matérielle et la négligence du contrat de communication produisent des effets intolérables. Le listing qu'exhibent certaines pages de l'internet et les plagiats de livres en CD-ROM attirent l'attention sur cette nécessité criante: une fois l'intégration des informations annoncée, le recours à une culture du signe, du texte, de l'image, devient impérieuse, si l'on veut échapper à la confusion – et au fiasco éditorial et économique qui menace d'accompagner cette dernière. Car même lorsque le calcul peut circuler sur tous types de supports, le message doit s'actualiser sous une forme matérielle et historique: celle d'un objet concret que des lecteurs peuvent reconnaître comme susceptible de porter du sens, constituer en vecteur de culture, s'approprier par la réécriture. La technologie ne saurait donc déboucher sur un au-delà du signifiant, mais plutôt sur d'autres configurations signifiantes.

Bien entendu, l'idée d'immatérialité, illusoire, n'est pas inopérante. Elle affecte notre façon de percevoir les signes que nous échangeons et suggère que la technologie dissipe la question sémiotique: d'où des régressions spectaculaires, lourdes de conséquences, dans certains savoir-faire de l'écriture et de l'image.

2 - Une nouvelle phénoménologie de l'écrit

Cela dit, reconnaître cette idéologie constitue la part la plus aisée du travail sémiotique. Car il faut aussi comprendre ce qui rend plausible une telle conception des objets écrits contemporains. Si l'écrit multimédiatique nous donne l'impression qu'il est immatériel, c'est parce qu'il déstabilise à la fois notre conception de l'écrit et notre perception de la matière.

L'imaginaire de l'écrit que nous avons acquis repose sur la stabilité du couple support-signe. L'écrit est pour nous une trace attachée à la surface qui la porte (gravée, tracée, imprimée etc.). C'est d'ailleurs pourquoi on s'obstine encore aujourd'hui à opposer l'écrit et l'écran, comme si un mode d'expression et un support pouvaient être mis en opposition.[2] A l'inverse, il s'agit de percevoir en quoi l'écrit est affecté par ses nouvelles manifestations, sur un écran constitué d'éléments d'images (pixels). L'informatisation de l'écriture et, *a fortiori,* le développement du multimédia, ont conféré à l'écrit un mode de manifestation labile, polymorphe et dynamique, dans lequel le rapport entre l'écran et l'écrit est fait à la fois d'interdétermination et de dissociation: interdétermination parce que l'écrit est appréhendé dans l'écran qui lui donne forme, dissociation parce que cet écran ne porte que furtivement la trace de l'écriture.

Cette dynamique ne tient pas à une immatérialité, mais à une physique de l'invisible, ne tombant pas sous nos sens. Les particules électroniques nous apparaissent comme des objets imprimés qui se succèdent devant nous, comme par magie. Forme d'illusionnisme que justifie la nécessité, pour lire l'écran, de le voir comme métaphore d'une page ou d'un mur. Par un processus inverse de celui qui a été décrit plus haut, la conscience sémiotique ne peut se déployer que dans une certaine ignorance de la physique, dans un certain aveuglement. Sans doute les autres formes de l'écrit, comme l'imprimé ou le manuscrit, n'obéissent-elles pas à une physique plus simple. Mais elles ne contre-

disent pas notre perception de la matière comme une collection d'objets sta-
bles, pleins et architecturés, conception sur laquelle repose notre phénoménologie acquise de l'écrit: *"verba volant, scripta manent"*.

Aujourd'hui, les écrits volent (Melot), ou presque: ils glissent. Le mode de
présence de l'écrit sur l'écran et, alternativement ou simultanément, sur le
papier ou sur écran de "démo", donne au texte un caractère éternellement
provisoire , doté de la mobilité que permet son "activation". Il est là et, en
même temps absent, virtuellement (selon l'opposition aristotélicienne entre
"dunamis" et *"energeia"*) caché au-delà ou en-deçà de l'écran, dans l'espace
mystérieux d'où il paraît pouvoir être tiré à tout instant. Ainsi, perpétuellement disponible, le texte devient perpétuellement invisible, il fuit littérale-
ment: d'où la prolifération des systèmes d'écriture qui permettent de "pêcher"
quelque part ce que le regard du lecteur ne saurait trouver.[3]

Une telle phénoménologie de l'écrit touche au plus essentiel, le mode d'accès
au texte. Les catégories, si essentielles pour l'écrit, de l'inscription, de la localisation et de la conservation ne peuvent plus être envisagées que de façon métaphorique. L'écriture ne s'inscrit plus à proprement parler dans son support:
l'impression que nous avons d'une telle inscription tient à une illusion. Aussi
la distinction si essentielle entre l'écrit de l'écriture (le brouillon, l'épreuve),
l'écrit de la lecture socialisée (l'imprimé) et l'écrit de la conservation (écrit
protégé, effacé, etc.) disparaît-elle désormais. Le texte est en permanence
candidat à sa propre pérennité, tandis que le support, redevenu éternellement
vierge, ne porte nulle trace des textes qui l'ont habité. Qu'on songe à l'idée
absurde d'un *brouillon* informatique ou d'un *palimpseste* électronique … .

Se trouvent cependant alors paradoxalement réactivées les spécificités les
plus anciennes de l'écriture, aussi bien le caractère hybride et instable du signe
écrit que son aptitude à évoquer un au-delà de sa propre présence (Christin).
Comme les hiéroglyphes égyptiens, qui glissaient entre les possibilités signifiantes et tiraient leur richesse expressive de cette incertitude en réclamant sans
cesse l'engagement du lecteur,[4] les signes de l'écriture multimédia sont en permanence actifs et comme texte et comme image. Et ces ambiguïtés, qui ont été
toujours présentes dans l'interprétation des écrits, deviennent aujourd'hui tan-
gibles dans le mouvement des signes sur l'écran. C'est pourquoi la poétique du
texte multimédia exige l'invention de nouvelles formes d'écriture, capables de
jouer de cette richesse possible des signes, dans les dimensions du texte, de
l'espace visuel, de la figure, du concept.

Parallèlement, comme les inscriptions scrutées autrefois par les devins, ces
figures donnent à penser qu'elles surgissent d'un au-delà du visible, où réside-
rait la perfection de leur ordre et la totalité de leur sens. Elles placent en tout
cas le lecteur ordinaire devant une forme nouvelle de transcendance. En somme,
nous sommes en permanente relation avec le Dieu caché d'un texte virtuel,
situé dans un au-delà de l'écran mais pouvant sans cesse s'y manifester.

Mais le plus important sans doute, pour nous qu'a formés la tradition alphabétique, qui veut que l'écriture soit pure trace d'une parole, c'est que l'écriture multimédia requiert une réelle conscience de la nature visuelle de l'écrit. En effet, dans un "titre" multimédia, la lettre n'existe que comme image, animée, au sein d'une forêt d'autres signes visuels indispensables pour donner accès au texte lui-même.[5] Ceci exige une nouvelle approche du texte comme objet construit dans l'espace visuel, tout en autorisant des formes de pensée liées à la manipulation du signe visuel non linguistique, signe un peu vite nommé aujourd'hui: "icône", en un terme qui rend mal compte de la richesse de ce registre visuel de communication.[6] Et si certains auteurs ont déjà souligné que les possibilités offertes par l'association de signifiants hétérogènes, y compris la manipulation d'images vectorielles dites "virtuelles", appellent l'émergence de nouvelles écritures (Balpe, Lévy, Quéau), la transformation des utopies concrètes en réelle approche sémiotiquement armée – reliée à une histoire de l'écriture – reste à faire. En particulier, le projet séduisant de représenter n'importe quelle information par n'importe quelle substance impose une approche réductrice du processus de signification. Il suppose résolue une question qu'il ne pose pas, celle de savoir si une pensée identique portée par deux substances différentes de signification peut avoir un sens. Croyance qui peut déboucher, soit sur le fiasco, soit sur la violence: c'est affaire de rapport de forces dans la confrontation du dessein technologique avec la profondeur d'une culture.

3 - MATÉRIALITÉ PLURIELLE

Le multimédia ne nous fascine donc pas par son immatérialité, mais plutôt par une prolifération de matérialités: en tant qu'objet offert à l'interprétation, le signifiant graphique des messages numérisés est quelque chose comme un signifiant pluriel. Comment décrire rigoureusement ce signifiant?

Cette question autorise une première réponse simple, s'agissant de la plupart des produits commercialisés sur CD-ROM ou accessibles en réseau. L'information y est 1/ stockée sous forme d'impulsions électroniques analysables comme un code binaire 2/ représentée par des éléments d'images (pixels) sur des écrans à deux dimensions. Ainsi se définit une certaine platitude de ces objets, qu'on a pu justement proposer de nommer *unimédia* plutôt que *multimédia*.

Mais cette uniformité n'est pas pure fluidité. Il faut récuser la fiction d'un objet hypostasié, prétendument dupliquable à l'infini: ces dispositifs techniques s'inscrivent dans l'espace, constituent, comme tout support des écritures, des objets en trois dimensions, fabriqués avec des matériaux dont l'histoire culturelle n'est pas neutre, installés dans des espaces professionnels, sociaux et privés. Les batailles commerciales autour de l'ordinateur et du téléviseur comme écran multimédia témoignent de ce que les hommes ne sont pas indifférents à la nature des objets sur lesquels les signes leur sont donnés à voir. En outre, rien ne circule qui ne soit supporté par un vecteur matériel de l'énergie. Comme le montrent les petites fenêtres actuellement dévolues aux images vidéo, les possibilités du matériel constituent une contrainte analogue à celles que connaît le livre: c'est parce que la capacité des mémoires conduit à compresser les images jusqu'à une définition médiocre qu'ont été créées ces "vignettes" vidéo. Peut-être faut-il d'ailleurs se féliciter d'avoir ainsi été préservés d'une invasion des clips vidéo dans le multimédia…

A partir de là, il convient d'envisager la relation auteur-lecteur et de se demander ce que peut être, non plus seulement un écran, mais un texte multimédia. En effet, la notion même de message devient problématique et même inadéquate. Dans un grand nombre de cas le scripteur ne voit pas le message qui sera lu par le lecteur. Ceci tient à plusieurs contraintes technologiques: l'affichage de ces documents nécessite des équipements complexes, en perfectionnement constant, et les liaisons et les modes de réception sont hétérogènes. Aussi bien la lecture de documents lacunaires, allant jusqu'à n'actualiser parfois qu'une catégorie de signes, n'est-elle pas un accident rare. Ce polymorphisme des messages, parfois monstrueux, devrait être durable. En effet, l'une des valeurs essentielles de la communauté électronique est le droit au perfectionnement permanent, à l'initiative des individus techniquement les plus aguerris (Caby et Flichy) et, en outre, l'idéologie de l'immatérialité donne à penser que le développement des réseaux suffit, en rendant l'écrit accessible, à résoudre le problème de sa socialisation.

Mais il y a surtout, par-delà ces perspectives, les réalités dont les messages se nourrissent par citation, exhibition et leurre. Bien avant le succès du terme "multimédia", il y avait des corbeilles sur les écrans des Macintosh et des ongles vernis sur les distributeurs de billets. De tels trompe-l'œil sont indispensables pour que l'idée de multiplicité des médias devienne crédible sur un support unique. C'est pourquoi l'histoire du multimédia est bien loin d'être celle d'une dématérialisation. Lorsqu'on compare, par exemple, les barres de "menu" des versions successives du traitement de texte *Word,* on voit s'agglutiner les marques d'épaisseur, d'objectalité. De dessins réduits à quelques lignes géométriques, on est passé à des figures ombrées, à des "boutons-poussoirs" dessinés en perspective et en volume: on trouve même des boutons en faux relief portant eux-mêmes des objets en faux relief. Surmatérialité en abyme du leurre … .

Ce n'est pas seulement affaire d'ergonomie, mais d'esthétique: un hyperréalisme qu'on pourrait nommer "grotesque", par comparaison avec l'imitation des fouilles romaines dans les palais Renaissance, un goût pour l'apparence du solide, du patrimonial, qui obsède les praticiens du "virtuel". On trouve dans le "cyberspace" une citation constante de l'épigraphie, les textes gagnant quelque multimédialité à apparaître sur un support architectural. On affiche des barres de menu en granit, on expose les tableaux sur tissu. Ces textes semblent nous dire, luttant contre leur propre labilité diaphane: *"Exegi monumentum aere perennius"*[7]... Tel dispositif de visite virtuelle d'un musée réagit au toucher de l'utilisateur en affichant une empreinte digitale, comme si le multimédia pouvait changer en l'occurrence le pictogramme en trace (et même en stigmate).

Ces exemples témoignent d'un *complexe de matérialité* qui travaille l'imaginaire graphique. Mais il s'inscrivent aussi dans l'effort pour rendre lisibles dans notre culture des objets nouveaux, qui ne s'y diffusent qu'en s'inscrivant dans ses schèmes de perception de l'image, de l'écriture et de l'architecture. C'est ainsi qu'on réalise des "pages" Web. C'est ainsi que la métaphore du livre (Victor-Puchebet, *Le Livre de Lulu*) pourrait être un filon de rentabilité éditoriale. C'est ainsi que la perspective de la Renaissance se retrouve sur bien des écrans, donnant accès à un espace de promenade ou d'initiation. Ces formes iconiques sont des citations de toute notre culture de l'inscription matérielle des signes, hommage rendu au poids de l'histoire, celle notamment des matières du savoir.

La question gagne en complexité si l'on ne réduit pas l'analyse à l'objet achevé, mais qu'on considère le processus social d'élaboration et de circulation de l'écrit, ce complexe travail de l'écriture multimédia, dans lequel de multiples ressources graphiques hétérogènes (sur papier et sur écran) sont mises en œuvre afin de "saisir" la structure des messages en élaboration. Elle doit prendre en compte également les moyens de nommer et de penser ces écrits, les riches métaphores matérielles qui habitent le discours commercial, savant et technique. Par exemple, le passage du *labyrinthe* désorientant mais structuré qui obsédait les encyclopédistes (Benrekassa) à la *navigation* fluide qui caractériserait le cyberespace ne saurait être dépourvu de signification et d'effets. L'idée de piscine de données *(Data pool)* ou de dérive informationnelle *(NetSurfing)* porte secrètement un imaginaire destructeur pour le signe. Elle nous donne à penser que nous serions face aux atomes d'un élément naturel: métaphore délétère contre laquelle il pourrait être utile de parler d'aspérité et de discontinuité. Les effets de cette métaphore sont constatables tous les jours: elle conduit les auteurs à penser les documents comme des ensembles d'atomes reliés par diverses valences et non comme des formes textuelles ayant leurs propres conditions de lisibilité. Aussi bien la critique de cette métaphore invite-t-elle à un double travail: s'interroger réellement sur ce que peut être un texte multimédiatique et imaginer d'autres langages pour nous représenter la structure de ces messages.

Enfin, nous ne devons pas oublier que les dispositifs multimédia peuvent être mis en contexte, bien autrement que les fantasmes de l'autoroute ou les routines naissantes de l'écran arborescent nous habituent insensiblement à en appauvrir la charge potentiellement novatrice (Barret et Redmond). Poser la question de la forme matérielle des dispositifs multimédias, des lieux dans lesquels ils peuvent être installés, des contextes de lecture individuelle et sociale dans lesquels ils peuvent faire sens, de la façon dont ils peuvent se conjuguer avec d'autres formes de communication, est une condition impérative pour que ces nouvelles ressources de l'écriture donnent matière à socialisation, à pensée et à création. L'une des tâches d'une sémiotique du multimédia est en effet d'élaborer une pensée de la communication dans laquelle le réseau ne se substitue pas à la question de l'appropriation sociale des œuvres et des savoirs, mais demande au contraire une intelligence plus grande de la culture triviale et de ses enjeux.

NOTES

1   L'étude de Philippe Breton met précisément en évidence, par le commentaire des textes techniques liés à la naissance de l'ordinateur, le projet de modéliser directement les processus de la pensée supposés résider dans le cerveau vu comme un outil formel, sans aucune référence aux modalités d'échange entre les sujets.

2   Sur la critique de cette opposition et le programme d'une sémiotique de l'écrit d'électronique (cf. Souchier). La catégorisation à la fois conceptuelle et historique de la "graphosphère" et de la "vidéosphère" chez Régis Debray est la forme la plus savante de cette opposition.

3   Le nom d'un système célèbre de recherche des données sur l'internet, *AltaVista*, montre bien comment l'impression de l'altitude conjure le sentiment de l'enfouissement du texte.

4   L'analyse de Pascal Vernus montre, grâce à un commentaire précis des rapports entre texte et image dans les inscriptions égyptiennes, que si le système hiéroglyphique ne se réduit pas au phonétisme, ce n'est pas par insuffisance de maîtrise, mais par souci de conserver à l'écriture toute sa force iconique.

5   L'inscription de l'écrit dans une temporalité, éventuellement accompagnée de la parole, caractérise également le multimédia, comme d'ailleurs le cinéma et la vidéo. Mais les nouvelles possibilités offertes aujourd'hui au multimédia tiennent avant tout à la façon dont le lecteur peut voir l'espace possible de sa propre intervention. C'est par le biais de cette lecture de l'écran (espace visuel habité par l'image et le texte), et des interventions autorisées par les interfaces sur cet espace que le document virtuellement complexe se traduit en un parcours de lecture singulier, pour chaque lecteur. Il faudra voir dans quelle mesure le développement annoncé des commandes vocales pourra déplacer cette problématique. Mais le lien est fort entre

oralité et linéarité, d'une part, et entre visualité et approche pluridimensionnelle des messages d'autre part.

6   En particulier, dans la terminologie Peircienne, ces signes visuels ne sont pas systématiquement des icônes.

7   *J'ai édifié un monument plus durable que l'airain* (Horace, *Odes*, III, 30).

BIBLIOGRAPHIE

Balpe, Jean-Pierre. "Accessibilité de l'architecture". *Hyperdocuments, hypertextes, hypermédias.* Paris: Eyrolles, 1990. 165-82.

Barret, Edward. *Contextual Media. Multimedia and Interpretation.* Mary Redmond, ed. Cambridge (Massachussets): MIT Press, 1995.

Benrekassa, Georges. "Penser l'encyclopédique: l'article 'Encyclopédie' de *l'Encyclopédie*". Dans *Le Langage des lumières. Concepts et savoirs de la langue.* Paris: Presses universitaires de France, coll. Écriture, 1995. 232-62.

Breton, Philippe. *A l'image de l'homme. Du Golem aux créatures virtuelles.* Paris: éditions du Seuil, 1995.

Caby, Laurence et Patrice Flichy, eds. "Les Usages d'internet". *Réseaux* 77 (1996): 7-113.

Christin, Anne-Marie. *L'Image écrite ou la déraison graphique.* Paris: Flammarion, coll. Idées et recherches, 1995.

Estaunié, Edouard. *Traité pratique de télécommunication électrique.* Paris: Dunod, 1904.

Hélène, Maxime. *Les Nouvelles Routes du globe.* Paris: Bibliothèque de la nature, 1883.

Melot, Michel. "Scripta volant". *Le Débat* 86 (1995): 165-72.

Lévy, Pierre. *L'idéographie dynamique. Vers une imagination artificielle?* Paris: La Découverte, coll. Textes à l'appui, 1991.

Quéau, Philippe. *Le Virtuel, vertus et vertiges.* Seyssel: Champ vallon, coll. Milieux, 1993.

Souchier, Emmanuël. "L'Ecrit d'écran. Pratiques d'écriture et informatique", *Communication et langages.* 107 (1996): 105-19.

Théofilakis, Elie, ed. *Les Immatériaux.* Paris: Autrement, 1985.

Vernus, Pascal. "L'écriture de l'Egypte ancienne". Dans A.M. Christin, ed. *L'espace et la lettre.* Paris: Union générale d'éditions, 10-18, 1977. 61-77.

Victor-Pujebet, Romain. *Le Livre de Lulu*, CD-ROM. Paris: Flammarion multimédia, 1995.

———. "La Télégraphie sans fils". *L'Année scientifique* (1897): 47.

Beyond Mere Word and Image

Ektopias: Two Landscapes of the Ideal

Burattoni & Abrioux

We have created the word *ektopia* as a generic term for an on-going series of projects which finds itself formalised here for the first time. Formed along the lines of "*u*topia" and its contrary "*dy*stopia", or again Michel Foucault's recent coinage "*hetero*topia", the word *ektopia* is also calculated to rhyme – dissonantly – with "*topo*graphy", in its older sense of landscape description, and with "*ek*phrasis". An ektopia is the inverse of an ekphrasis: not a picture translated into words but rather text translated into landscape. Ektopias will not only foreground visual, as opposed to discursive, knowledge in the field of word and image studies. As practical exercises in image-making on an environmental scale, they will explicitly introduce the body and its movements into the field of visuality, thereby insisting on the significance of somatic knowledge.

Ektopias are premised upon the observation that elements of landscape description frequently recur in the most diverse contexts – aesthetic, philosophical, theoretical, scientific, political, etc. – so that a landscape sensibility, more or less consciously figurative in nature, commonly underlies the most disparate patterns of thought. Ektopias set out quite literally to landscape these more or less ephemeral descriptions, fictions and figures; and thus to landscape aesthetics, philosophy, theory, science, politics, etc. They necessarily take the form of landscape proposals, which may initially be fictitious but must (at least theoretically) be realizable.

An ektopia has its point of departure in topography (in the sense noted above). Ektopias are "found" verbal landscapes, "translated" into actual (or at last potential) physical landscapes. Found landscapes of obvious promise, which we may some day turn into ektopias, include the following:

- "the specter of Vietnam has been buried forever in the desert sands of the Arabian Peninsula" (George Bush) – premise for a memorial garden ;
- "the antinomy of word and image is something like a historical *a priori*, cropping up like an unruly weed whenever some attempt is made to stabilize and unify the field of representation and discourse" (W. J. T. Mitchell, after Gilles Deleuze) – premise for a landscape project crossing land art and ecological gardening;

- "heat is *par excellence* the communist of our universe" (P.G. Tate & Balfour Stewart [1875]) – premise for an entropic hothouse garden;
- "the butterfly romance" (H. Rider Haggard) – premise for an allegorical garden in an exotic mode;
- "Jonagored" (name on a sticker peeled off an apple bought in a French supermarket, July 1996) – premise for a *paysage* dé*moralisé* evoking the unholy alliance between science and agriculture : an elaboration on the name "jonagold", given to a variety of apples which jonagoreds have joined (or perhaps replaced) on supermarket shelves, "jonago*red*" invites transformation into the phonologically more satisfying "jona*g*ored".

Any landscaping projects to which such examples of topography may give rise would be required to demonstrate the cultural, intellectual and indeed political potential of landscape as an instrument and medium of simultaneously critical and creative practice. We thus envisage ektopias as a step "beyond" the new-historical demystification of landscape. The two landscape proposals which follow, and which constitute our first ektopias, explore the potential of the mode by confronting two landscapes of the ideal. As a concept – or perhaps merely a genre – the ideal seeks to regulate the tension between reason and sense, body and mind, abstract and concrete, etc., in a manner which our ektopias can only vigorously contest.[1] Each of our *landscapes of the ideal* will thus proceed by engaging a close reading of (respectively) Plato's myth of the cavern and a recent article by the Canadian artist Jeff Wall "About Making Landscapes", followed by an ektopic landscape proposal sketched out in words and images.

I : LANDSCAPE WITH *skeue pherontai* AND *desmotai.*

In order to represent the state of our nature in relation to instruction and ignorance, one must, according to Socrates in a debate staged by Plato (*Republic*, book 7), place a group of men in the heart of a vast landscape. Its most familiar feature is a cavern with a broad entrance to allow light from a bonfire blazing on high ground opposite to penetrate into its darkness. Other men move to-and-fro along a high road intersecting an imaginary line drawn between the fire and the cavern. Since these men are hidden by a wall, presumably running parallel to the road, only the objects, lit by the bonfire, will cast shadows on the back wall of the cave far below. These shadows constitute the only knowable objects perceivable by the men in the cave, since the poor creatures are chained by the neck and legs and consequently have no other choice than to constitute a captive audience for the shadow-show on the back wall. Since these prisoners can only escape by climbing the steep slope leading to

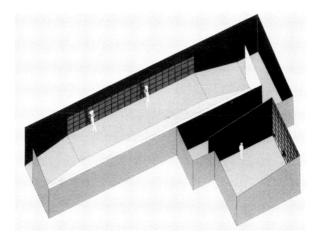

Figure 1. Landscape with *skeuē pherontai* and *desmotai:* layout.

the heights with the fire, road, wall and porters, there is no reason to suppose that they will be prepared to transform themselves willingly into philosophical tourists. It thus becomes necessary to pick one out, in order to drag him up to the heights, which we now learn to be bathed in sunlight. Having reached the top, the unwilling climber will obviously be dazzled by the light, which prevents him from contemplating the objects he previously knew only through their shadows. Fortunately, it would seem that the road used by the object-bearers runs along the bank of a river – unless, that is (and we confess to finding this hypothesis more realistic), one postulates the landscape to have been changed by magic while the forcibly freed prisoner was striving to make his way to the top. Be that as it may, the fire is no longer the chief source of light, since if that were to be the case the climber would only find before his eyes the shadows of the porters projected on to the wall which formerly hid them, and not those of the objects, which were projected on to the back wall of the cavern at the foot of the climb. However, what the prisoner now sees is a general set of shadows, followed by the reflections of men and other objects in the waters and still later the objects themselves. Finally, he will be able to confront the various heavenly bodies after nightfall – something he will always find easier than staring at the sun during the daytime.

If this strange landscape and the actions which take place within it constitute the primal scene of idealism, one can only conclude that the ideal presupposes a complex, disturbingly violent form of land settlement. Indeed, both the setting and the esoteric rituals of the Platonic myth recall nothing so much as the sundry sects whose collective violence all too frequently hits the headlines of our late twentieth-century press.

Figure 2. Landscape with *skeuē pherontai* and *desmotai:* walkway.

Furthermore, the optics of the Platonic shadow play are problematical, since obvious problems of magnification and distortion are not even touched upon by the author. Indeed, it is only with the advent of modern technology that the difficulties of transmitting images have really been overcome.

Our proposal for a landscape with object-bearers *[skeue pherontai]* and prisoners *[desmotai]* places in the foreground the object-bearers, who play an essential part in the Platonic scenario but pass almost unseen in most commentaries. The project also restores the overall landscape described in the *Republic,* which is too often reduced to a gloomy cave and a climb into the sunshine. Finally, it highlights the technological and disciplinarian dimensions of the ideal.

In a large indoor space (which might equally, and perhaps more appropriately, be the hall of a shopping centre as an exhibition area in a museum or gallery a ramp will be installed. This will lead up to an elevated walkway passing in front of a wall of video screens bathed in an orange-red glow evocative of firelight. The top row of screens will be blank (black). Images of perfectly proportioned Greek statues will pass in silhouette along the massed screens, the tops of their heads flush with the top edge of the highest row of red-tinged screens. As visitors pass in front of the screens, they will find themselves preceded by their shadows, captured by video cameras set into the wall. Since few of our contemporaries are endowed with a physique comparable to the Greek ideal, most will have either to crouch or walk on tiptoe if they want to measure up to the Grecian shadows.
Visitors will be invited to balance (or hold) an object on the top of their head as they proceed along the walkway. Cut-outs of Greek artefacts will be provided; other objects may, however, be used. Visitors who succeed in striking the right pose will find that the objects they bear do not appear above them on the banked screens.
At the far end of the walkway, a second ramp will lead down towards a darkened room, open at the front. Video screens banked along its back wall will blankly emit red light. Along the bottom row of screens, there will pass a series of silhouettes of Greek artefacts, perfectly proportioned and filling each screen. Images of whatever

Figure 3. Landscape with *skeuē pherontai* and *desmotai:* cavern.

protrudes above the wall of video screens along the walkway as visitors go by with objects carried aloft will also be transmitted to this bottom row of screens. A time-device will delay the transmission of these images long enough for visitors to reach the subterranean cavern in time to contemplate their own performance as they proceeded along the high road a few moments earlier. The degree to which they succeeded in imitating the bearing of the Grecian shadows will be measured by the extent to which the objects they carried – and these objects alone – now fill the screens.

Visitors will be able to pass backwards and forwards through this hi-tech landscape of the ideal, so as to experience – rather than observe – its configuration and to conform themselves physically to its demands. Fetters will be dispensed with in the cavern, since these are manifestly nothing more than a metaphor for the fascinating power of images.

II : Landscape with the Tomb of the Ideal Landscape.

In a recent article on "Making Landscapes", the Canadian artist Jeff Wall declares that he makes landscapes "to study the problem of settlement as well as to work out for [him]self what the kind of picture (or photograph) we call a 'landscape' is" (140). We have ourselves demonstrated with reference to Plato (cf. Proposal I) that the concept of "settlement" – i.e. land seizure and occupation – is of central importance to the understanding of landscape.

Re-coding "settlement" in stylistic terms, Wall opposes "overdevelopment", described as "a sort of mannerist-baroque phenomenon of hypertrophy and exaggeration", to underdevelopment which, he suggests, implies "a poetics of inconclusiveness, filled with secessionist rural pathos". The norm against which

Figure 4. Landscape with the Tomb of the Ideal Landscape (after Poussin).

each of these departures is to be measured is, classically, the "harmonious mean" or "notion of measure", concepts which define the "pleasure experienced in art" in terms the artist readily acknowledges as "idealist", referring the "ideal standard" back to Plato. Measurement against a "harmonious and indwelling mean" is, Wall suggests, "a valid way of thinking about the typology of pictures, which, unlike some other art forms, are radically devoted to the semblances of the human being. This is just one of the senses in which we have not gotten 'beyond' idealistic aesthetics".

Taken together, the concept of measure in aesthetics as "indwelling" and the suggestion that "we have not gotten 'beyond' idealistic aesthetics" give an unexpected twist to the notion of land occupation. Whether or not Wall is holding out hope for the existence of virgin – i.e. unsettled – terrain beyond the frontiers of idealism, his vision of landscape is itself seemingly unwittingly inscribed within a landscape; more precisely, in the kind of landscape he is concerned with – the landscape of "settlement" (dwelling). Curiously, Wall puts scare quotes round "beyond" but not "indwelling", a gesture which may be suspected of illegitimately naturalizing the supposedly indwelling aesthetic mean. Does the ideal standard indeed "dwell" naturally within our landscapes? Should it not rather be suspected of having in all vulgarity staked out its empire by a process of "settlement"?

Our investigation of this question draws on two earlier texts by Jeff Wall. In "Unity and Fragmentation in Manet" (1984), the artist declares the French artist to be the "tombstone of the Salon", before going on to explain that, as such, he is "outmoded by the developments in the new realms of modern art,

Figure 5. Landscape with the Tomb of the Ideal Landscape.

the 'independent spaces' which reach their first maturity in the 1870s and 1880s, and which, in the intervening century, have become our site of absolute inversion, of 'pure culture'" (89). It is scarcely necessary to insist on the manner in which the spatial images used here – "realms", "independent spaces", "site" – are caught up in the politics of "settlement"; nor on the fact that the "tombstone" of the Salon anticipates Wall's later views of cemeteries: "a picture of a cemetery is, theoretically at least, the 'perfect' type of landscape. The inevitably approaching, yet unapproachable, phenomenon of death, the necessity of leaving behind those who have passed away, is the most striking dramatic analogue for the distant – but not *too* distant – viewing position identified as 'typical' of the landscape. We cannot get too distant from the graveyard" ("About Making Landscapes" 144).

Wall follows a different line when, in a brief series of remarks on one of his most convincing works centred on an exploding container of milk (not therefore a landscape), he associates "the phenomenon of the movement of a liquid" with "the means of representation" employed in creating the work – i.e. the camera, whose instantaneous action represents for the artist the epitome of mechanical dryness ("Photography and Liquid Intelligence" 90). Water, Wall goes on to say, "plays an essential part in the making of photographs, but it has to be controlled exactly and cannot be permitted to spill over the spaces and moments mapped out for it in the process, or the picture is ruined". Consequently, the "archaism of water, of liquid chemicals, connects photography to the past"; it provides a "speculative image in which the apparatus itself can be thought of as not yet having emerged from the mineral and vegetable worlds" and gives a "sense of immersion in the incalculable", which Wall associates with "liquid intelligence" (90-93).

Jeff Wall's remarks on photography entertain complex, contradictory relations with his idealised aesthetics of landscape. How can the rhythm of liquid flow suggest landscapes other than those of "settlement"? In "About Making Landscapes", Wall argues that "In modernity's landscapes, figures, beings, or persons are made visible as they vanish into their determinations, or emerge from them – or more likely, they are recognized as both free and unfree; or possibly misrecognized, first as unfree, then as free, and so on" (145). We are impelled to ask how landscapes might pass from this dialectic of freedom and unfreedom, recognition and misrecognition, into a sense of "immersion in the incalculable?" Our project suggests that, whatever ideological function the picturesque may have filled when, in the eighteenth century, it came to supplant the idealist *imperium*, its aesthetics have the power to fluidify landscape and render incalculable relations upon which the ideal had sought to impose its own particular "measure".

We propose to produce a free-standing monumental slab of white marble intended to be set in a variety of landscapes. From a slight distance, it will look like a tombstone of some importance and act as a classic repoussoir *(a role still played by the monument in the right foreground of Jeff Wall's* The Holocaust Memorial in the Jewish Cemetery*). From closer up, the surface of the marble structure will be seen to be imbued with the flowing movement of a piece of cloth, akin (say) to those which can be seen stretched out to dry on tenter frames in panoramas of Leeds done by Turner and others during the glory years of the textile industry in England. The textile fluidity of the marble slab will only become apparent as the viewer approaches, so that it will emerge as the white structure begins to fill up the foreground, causing the values of lines, features and figures in the landscape behind it to fluidify incalculably.*

The tombstone will not mourn the improbable demise of idealist landscape; it is not intended to take stock of our manifest estrangement from the ideal, which Wall dates back to Manet, arguing that "Estrangement experienced in the experience of the picture has become our orthodox form of cultural lucidity" (UFM). For the viewer who circulates between the divergent focal functions of our white marble structure, the notion of a single "distant – but not too distant – viewing position identified as 'typical' of the landscape" will lose its relevance, as he or she explores "the interrelation between liquid intelligence and optical intelligence" (PLI) stimulated by the peripatetic dimension of the picturesque.

NOTES

1.   Preliminary work on these two *landscapes of the ideal* was presented in Burattoni &
     Abrioux, "Paysager, dépayser", lecture given at the Pompidou Centre, Paris, May
     1996, and in Yves Abrioux, "Landscaping Myths", lecture given at a symposium on
     "Myth and Landscape", Delphi, June 1996.

REFERENCES

Wall, Jeff. "About Making Landscapes". In: *Jeff Wall*. London: Phaidon Press, 1996. 140-
     5.
———. "Photography and Liquid Intelligence". In: *Jeff Wall*. London: Phaidon Press,
     1996. 90-3.
———. "Unity and Fragmentation in Manet". In: *Jeff Wall*. London: Phaidon Press,
     1996. 78-89.

Touching Gender: The Word, the Image and the Tactile.
Barbara Hepworth's "Stereognostic" Sculpture

Penny Florence

Sculpture has changed since Barbara Hepworth was working out the basis of her art in the 1920s and 1930s, naming it and describing it as process, as meaning, as abstract structure. From then until the end of her life in May 1975 at the age of 72, she continued to deploy her considerable skills as a writer strategically, putting what she did into the artistic and political discourses of Modernism. What I have to say uses some of this writing, but it does not focus on it. Nor does it explore the specific relation between her written and her visual production, whether two or three-dimensional. Rather, what interests me here is the ways her work reflects on some of the underlying issues common to all word-image, and perhaps all interart, studies. What happens if touch is taken account of as well as the visual and the aural? This is a question that now has to go well beyond any idea that sculpture is "about" touch. The minimalism and conceptualism that overlapped with Hepworth's last years in the 60s and 70s related to the verbal in complex and structural ways, arguably changing three-dimensional work completely. But those changes connect in important ways with what Hepworth was doing. They are part of the recent developments in reconceptualising language that have put much into question that she is assumed to have accepted, and that enable the contemporary viewer of her work to read it against the Modernist grain – or, at least, what has become the dominant version. This is illuminating on several counts, not least that of the persistence of the bodily trace in language and vision, and of materiality in abstraction.

I begin, then, with some of Barbara Hepworth's words, which I shall take (more or less, and at first) at face value. She is writing about her work:

> This is not an optical sensation: It's a matter of a physical relationship. (Thistlewood 90)

Next, a further remark, which I do not take at face value:

> As a woman I've nothing to say – only as a sculptor. (Williams 129)

According to these two observations, Hepworth defines her activity as an artist in terms of a physical relationship, an articulate physical relationship, since it is "one which has something to say". It is, furthermore, one of reciprocity; the sculptor carves – and the stone reveals or admits the carver. I am not suggesting any simple explanation of her practice through her writing.[1] I would, however, suggest they form a richly revealing intertextuality of great relevance to establishing the genealogy of contemporary debates concerning "sexed" subjectivity. It is in this sense that I am interested in the force-field between word, image and tactile symbolisations. This is not to attempt to diminish the important work that has been done on many levels since Lacan concerning the scopic drive,[2] but rather to supplement it: how far the interrelations between the visual and language might be radically changed by any more fully "corporeal" model is as yet unclear and, furthermore, beyond the scope of this essay. But some light can be cast on the kinds of questions that arise in relation to word-image studies.

Carving was not at any time in Hepworth's life an unremarkable activity for a female individual, whatever terms are adopted. Hepworth is widely known for piercing the stone, an action for her which is a much about revealing the relation between interior and surface, kinds of depth and tensile revelation, as it is about penetration. Yet to claim a physical relationship which is nothing to do with the sex of her body is untenable. Such a claim may however be read in fruitful ways which are relevant to an historicized understanding of her complex practice. Hepworth was above all a carver, which is, of course, about penetration, and it symptomatizes the unspeakable position she occupied as a woman and as an artist. While it may be (typically masculinist) denial to desex artistic activity – either unconscious or deliberately motivated – denial is only necessarily delusion if your model of reality is unitary.[3] According to a more complex model, it may be a move towards resolution of a different order. The paradoxes of Hepworth's self-positioning may be read as a complexly sexed ontology according to which she rejected the symbolizations implied in defining work as "sexed", which would historically have meant limited, because not transcendent and therefore universal, while at the same time elaborating a distinct and embodied artisitic practice.

In an article in "Unit One", for example, Hepworth comments that a horse or a dog are not stone forms, and her love of them can only be expressed in abstract terms. "I do not want to make a machine that cannot fulfil its essential purpose; but to make exactly the right relation of masses, a living thing in stone" (*Pictorial Autobiography* 30). In the particular Western philosophical terms that frame her modernist milieu, this is a strangely contradictory remark: it is love, and it is a relation of mass; it is stone, and it is animate. She goes on: "... it is not simply the desire to avoid naturalism in the carving that leads to abstract work. I feel that the conception itself, the quality of thought that is embodied must be abstract ...."

This notion of abstraction and embodiment is symptomatic, not of Hepworth's confusion, but of her attempts to negotiate impossible positions, alone, with courage; and many hated her for it.

What I want to do is try and come at this material relationship, this abstraction and embodiment, as one of contiguity, and to point towards how it might impact on understandings of the sign in and across language. For example, in the many works through which Hepworth explored the implications of piercing, there is of course no material break between the hole and the form – as there is where she used colour, which is an applied surface, sometimes signalled as such in the title – as in *Pierced Monolith with Colour* of 1965 (not illustrated). Yet they (the hole and the form) are not identical in language; I have just differentiated between them, and not merely as aspects of each other. I want to relate this undivided difference to a broader philosophical notion of proximity, and finally to open out into some speculations about the sign, whose conceptualization is founded in a philosophy that distorts these proximous or conterminous [sic] relationships by interposing a break, or, where there might be such a break, by prioritizing that division over an equal osculation. Those familiar with the debates about sexing the symbolic, and the maternal symbolic, will recognise how this relates to them.[4] (Parenthetically, though, I do not equate female and maternal here or anywhere else; the female symbolic requires the maternal in a sexspecific manner. So does the male.) Understandings of the visual, of language, and of the intersections between them, have clearly been altered by the recent shifts within some feminist thinking, and gender theory, towards embodied conceptualizations of subjectivity and of cultural processes. Taking the complex of issues around space, which is crucial in the formation of sexed subjectivities, bringing the tactile into consideration means that space can no longer be thought primarily in terms of optics. A certain "distortion" is introduced between the experience of one sense and another, since location by touch is often "inaccurate", even on the subject's own body. This suggests a relation of non-identity between tactile and visual interpretations not only of space but also of internal and external realities. This will inflect understandings of Oedipal asymmetry between sexes (cf. Chodorow, de Lauretis) all important elements in the elaboration of a female or sexed symbolic.

In this way, Hepworth's work and practice can be clarified in itself and made useful in the wider project of explicating the implications of a reworking of "the subject of semiotics" (in Silverman's phrase) according to a broader understanding of the semiotic field in which all sensory experience would be understood as constitutive of subjectivity. The visual and the auditory senses, in that order, have been accorded privileged positions, not least because of their demonstrable relation to language, which last is understood as the primary and structuring signifying system. The tactile seems clearly to diminish greatly during the maturation of the subject and her/his acquisition of language. But it does not cease, and, furthermore, will leave legacy or trace to mark sexual difference, as consistent with Freud's model of ego formation (Grosz 204).

These are the kinds of questions raised by Hepworth's practice and theory, though discovering ways of making them explicit are still part of its work. So, too, are the diachronics, issues of historicization and development in and beyond Hepworth's work in itself. Sculpture as distinct from and triangulated with the image and with language, is about a materiality that returns to the body, Hepworth's woman's modernist body, even in the moment of abstraction. This rewrites distinctions between geometric and organic abstraction, even though Hepworth contributed to confusing the matter in her desire to distance herself from the omnipresence of Henry Moore; as when she sought to differentiate her work from Henry Moore's biomorphic abstraction (Florence 33).

In her finely judged writing about carving, Hepworth uses the word "stereognostic", which means, "pertaining to the mental apprehension of the forms of solid objects by touch" *(Oxford English Dictionary).* The first question this raises for me brings together Hepworth's forms and her practice, and it is whether the mental apprehension of the forms of solid objects by touch actually shifts towards a disembodied abstraction or only appears to. The kind of shift entailed in mental apprehension may inevitably be towards abstraction, both at the levels of signifier and signified – a distinction which here traverses the differing yet unseparated materialities of language and sculpture – yet according to the philosophical frame and the specific linguistic event it may entail a counter movement. The same shift can equally be syncretic, or, maybe what would have been called in the nineteenth century, synaesthetic.

Breaking down Hepworth's word into its constituents reveals how exactly she understood the power of relating her work to verbal discourse, even though she would have articulated the point far differently. Both "stereo" and "gnostic" are entirely apposite. Taking "gnostic" first, since I do not intend to stay with it, it can mean "pertaining to knowledge" quite simply, relating to knowledge; cognitive, intellectual. This art is epistemological. It also can mean "believing in the reality of transcendental knowledge, possessing esoteric, spiritual knowledge", which is also consistent with the cognitive and libidinal economy into which I am inserting the work

"Stereo" derives from the Greek meaning "solid". In its various uses, it has come to indicate some bipolar arrangement or relationship which reveals depth. The connotative spatial meanings that now predominate derive from the other senses, optics and especially sound. It is an apparent shift which would seem to imply moving away from touch. Vision and sound are the dominant senses of the culturally mature, the language-based, of semiosis. But abstract science has broken away from conceptualizing the solid as opaque and impenetrable towards a more molecular apprehension of atoms held in spatial tension with inner space between. The solid is a provisional state, like stasis; it is movement in suspension, transparency in abeyance. This may be clarified through a comparison of *Sea Form (Porthmeor)* 1958 with *Oval Form (Trezion)* of 1962/3 (figures 1 and 2), the first deriving from the sea, liquid, and the second from a geometric and stable form, usually solid; both are equally mobile and alive to internal tensions and relationships. Nor is this an isolated example. It is a preoccupation which may also be seen in her drawing, as in the gouache *Forms in Movement* of 1943 (figure 3), where the dynamism of the lines is subtly increased by the use of muted colour. The asymmetry of the blue, beige and white rectangles and the recurrence of these colours within the forms sets up relations between interiority and exteriority that tension the drawing in a manner complementary to the lines. Finally, such internal dynamics are made explicit in *Red in Tension* of 1941 and the very similar *Red and Grey* (figure 4).

I cannot really cite these works and their expansion into inner space without reference to the Constructivist, Naum Gabo, living nearby in Cornwall at the time and an admirer of Hepworth. Gabo was undoubtedly important to Hepworth as an artist and friend, and their relationship is as illuminating for the contradictions it reveals as it is for the (clearly significant) analogues. For Hepworth would seem to be doing something very different from Gabo. They certainly differ at the level of method, and in terms of fundamental spatial conception it looks to me at the moment as if she encompassed and went beyond Gabo. I do not yet, at this stage in my researches, know with any great degree of certainty. But if I did, I might speculate in the following way.

Gabo also used a "stereo" word, or phrase rather: "stereometric construction", which was to be distinguished from a solid; a solid is "a volume of mass" whereas a stereometric construction "represents the space in which the mass exists made visible" (Hammer and Lodder, "Monoprints" 8). A good example would be *Construction in Space with Crystalline Centre* of 1938-40 (figure 5). But Hepworth's stereognostic carvings and Gabo's stereometric constructions approach the problems of space from opposite ends. As abstracting movements they are indicative of compatible conceptualizations of space; but because Hepworth sought the relations beween planar, linear and mass elements of form, where Gabo sets them in opposition, her understanding is potentially broader and more radical in application than what appears at present to be Gabo's dualism.

Gabo made sculpture according to Constructivist principles which are usually defined in opposition to Hepworth's method ("form is constructed from distinct planar and linear elements, as opposed to being carved or modelled", Hammer and Lodder, "Monoprints" 7) though she herself up to the early 1940s said she identified with Constructivism (Florence 33, Hammer

Figure 1. Barbara Hepworth, *Sea Form (Porthmeor),* 1958. Bronze, length 46 ins. (116.8 cm), edition of seven. © Alan Bowness, Hepworth Estate.

Figure 2. Barbara Hepworth. *Oval form (Trezion), 1962-3.* Bronze, length 57 ½ ins. (146 cm), edition of seven. © Alan Bowness, Hepworth Estate.

Figure 3. Barbara Hepworth. *Forms in Movement,* 1943. Gouache and pencil, 13 x 13 ins. (33 x 33 cm), private collection. © Alan Bowness, Hepworth Estate.

Figure 4. Barbara Hepworth. *Red and Grey,* 1941. Gouache and pencil, 9¼ x 11¾ ins. (23.5 x 29.85 cm), Collection David Lewis. © Alan Bowness, Hepworth Estate.

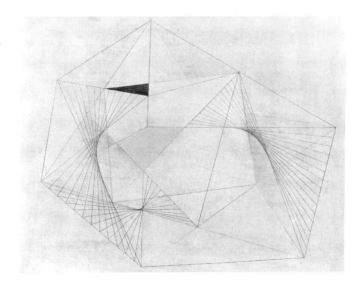

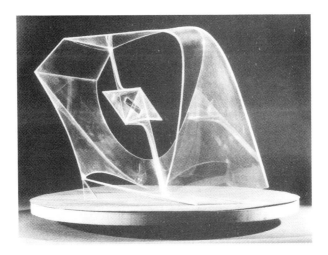

Figure 5. Naum Gabo. *Construction in Space with Crystalline Centre*, 1938-40. ©Nina and Graham Williams / Tate Gallery, London.

and Lodder, "Hepworth and Gabo" 180). The adoption of direct carving was a very particular issue for Hepworth in her early work of the 1920s, and it remained vital to her practice, including the bronzes or cast forms, since she often cut and chiselled the plaster. How as a spectator to deal with such questions of method, when the artists saw them as definitional, remains problematic. Carving was not taught in Hepworth's day, and while direct carving later became associated with "biology and geology" (Curtis 11) – scientific abstraction in other words – it was then presented within the non-Western tradition alongside so-called ethnographic examples (Curtis 11). This gnostic epistemology, if I may call it that, is still perceptible, for example, in a work such as *Two Ancestral Figures* of 1965 (not illustrated), so it cannot be seen as just a phase on the way to "purer" abstraction.

Sexing the abstract probably has to be connotative and methodological in this way. The difference in method between Hepworth and Gabo may readily be sexed or gendered, in the by now relatively clear way that artists may be read as differently positioned in Western culture according to sex or gender; socially, contextually. But how the forms and the conceptualization of space can be read as sexed has been explored far less. And in fact, rather than sexing the forms as such, I see the task as reconceptualizing how they are embodied. In so doing, androgyny has no place; it should become clear why. Both artists here are in some senses directly concerned with matter, the materiality of their work. This is already difficult to talk about in the terms I am seeking; for example, according to Irigaray, the concept of matter both constitutes and

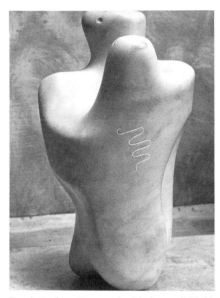

Fig. 6   Barbara Hepworth. *Mother and Child,*
1933. White marble, height 12 ins. (30.5 cm),
Collection T. D. Jenkins. © Alan Bowness,
Hepworth Estate.

hides "la coupure" (Burke et al. 159), which is "a break with material contiguity", a break on which philosophical systems are founded. This has, inevitably,
implications for ethics, for psychoanalysis and for language/symbolization.
Ethically, proximity replaces reciprocity, for example; intimacy implies a contiguity without the erasure possible and implied in reciprocity. But it is the
psychoanalytic and language implications that concern me most here. Contiguity restores the uncertainty of boundaries between individuals that originate in the maternal bond. These uncertainties appear in language in metonymic
proximity which counters the substitutions of metaphor or unified concept
which enable erasure. They imply rethinking matter, partly because they are
in excess of it, and equally because they effect a rapprochement between matter and symbolization. This is *de facto* in excess of a purely abstract notion of
the concept or symbol. It is a question of restoring to the philosophical medium through which sensory experience is filtered the maternal-derived, which
may or may not be recognised as such. Either way they are currently erased or
denied. With this aim in view, it is important not to allow subject-matter to
dominate; the mother-infant contiguity is not restricted in signification to
subject-matter. This can be demonstrated through an example, the marble
piece *Mother and Child* of 1933 (figure 6). It is important not to sentimental-

ise what is a finely tensed abstract form. If anthropomorhic terms are avoided altogether, perhaps perversely, since the piece is titled *Mother and Child,* the rhythms and structural dynamism both of the piece and of the relationship they embody – the subject-matter – can be brought out because their abstraction is foregrounded: the exactitude with which the smaller rectangular protuberance is cut to lean away from the larger which is vertical and monumental, the two forming an open hollow between them. This allows for a more generalized corporeal representation than the obvious "large mother with smaller, though still large child" – and note it is not an infant – in which that originary pairing may be seen to subsist in a single individuated form. This is, to use Rosi Braidotti's term, a gendered universal; it is a general and fully abstract statement, out of female generation – I avoid "origin" because that word conceals the temporal mobility I have been pointing towards. The reinstatement of sexed origin as present – temporally and ontologically – in the general or universal moves towards reconceptualizing the forms, and by extension, other heterogenised collectivities, if that is not too awkward.

Very similar things could be said about several works, including *Ancestral Figures* previously mentioned, where as always the dual meaning of "figure" is fully at play; they are human bodies and geometric figures, animate and inanimate motion. With regard to the fully abstract, Hepworth's use of what she calls "forms in echelon" is a recurrent exploration which would repay thematic study, covering as it does at least 30 years. All the meanings of "echelon" in English concern formation, whether it be ranking, V-flight patterns or segmented groupings. Once again it is the dynamics of interrelation which interest her ontologically, formally and thematically, if they may be so separated out.

What happens if we take this recurrent structural exploration as a gendered universal? I would suggest that it is worth considering as a way of approaching as sexed not only her particular kind of abstraction, but abstraction in general. As a sexed understanding of contiguity it also impacts in turn on sex itself. Whitford has pointed out that these relations of contiguity also subsist between the masculine and feminine economies. They are not fully separable therefore (Burke et al. 159). Contiguity may originate in the maternal, but infant is of any sex. And in any case, contiguity is by definition non-exclusive. Judith Butler indicates that it is problematic to return to a materiality of sex because of the sex of materiality (166), which she demonstrates in relation to Plato to be male – a specific and possibly founding example of the probably familiar and certainly pervasive logic of othering, whereby definition is established by exclusion and/or negation. But I do not see why she does not read contiguity as problematizing this "always already". If it is accepted that the contiguity that subsists between the male and female economies means that they are not fully separable, and that the contiguous economy is therefore not sexed as female in some logically pure sense, then materiality cannot be sexed male in any pure sense either. By the same metonymic logic, however, in the signifying economy, based in material fluidity, their cultural accretions are sexed; and it is here that materiality becomes male. "La coupure" does not have to be short and sharp, sudden and complete in a moment, to be a terrible severance.

The tactile shifts the linguistic – it does not abolish, but rather displaces and re-forms it. It also repositions psychoanalytic "moments" such as the so-called pre-linguistic or pre-oedipal. Touch of course persists. It informs all phases of experience and artistic labour. It is like Irigaray's "obscure sort of commemoration" (Florence 31), implying a disruptive temporality; can it be located in other temporalities, or should tactile time be used to inform other temporal modalities, such as perspective in painting and in forms of writing that mobilize visual temporalities, especially poetry? But this is to become diverted towards the contiguous effects of differential time; in the contiguous economy, time is a three- or four-dimensional reticulation in which tradition cannot be broken, partly because breaks are incorporated already and construed as provisional. But this is an indication of further work to be done. Thinking about contiguity brings abstract speculation back to the interchange between the real, the sign and subjectivity, and to the materiality that goes beyond the physical at that point of slippage-between.

It is now 13 years since Bryson pointed out that "we have, as yet, no unified theory either of signifying practice or of the body" (167). Much has been accomplished since then, and though it is still true that the pathways between the sexed body and signifying practice that I have been exploring through Hepworth are multifariously perplexing, their outlines do at least begin to emerge.[5]

NOTES

1   Hepworth was a gifted writer and a considered self-publicist. Clearly it is never a simple matter to bring an artist's written statements to bear on their work in whatever medium, and Hepworth's need as a woman to situate herself makes this all the more important as an issue. See my essay "Odd Man Out?" (24-42).

2   It would be, in this context, either over-long or arbitrary to try to signal adequately the range of this work, which will, in any case, be familiar to many readers. However, readers new to it will find excellent starting points in Grosz and Bowie.

3   Denial here is to be differentiated from disavowal in the strictly Freudian sense, though the terms can be interchangeable. If a dynamic and continuous process of ego-formation is adopted as a model, any clear separation of levels of realities can

become blurred. It is in these transitional spaces that the ego can perhaps change its realities through semiotic or social interaction. The issues are complex; suffice it to say here that my emphasis is more on adjustment and negotiation than trauma and defence.

4   The same applies as in note 2 above; Burke et al. is most helpful.

5   One of the difficulties is that work is being done in very different areas and contexts, so that considerable familiarity with particular discourses, and with the pitfalls of moving between them, is necessary. The work of Mieke Bal and of Teresa de Lauretis is exemplary here, perhaps especially in this specific context de Lauretis' last chapter of *Practice of Love* (305 ff).

REFERENCES

Bowie, Malcolm. *Lacan*. London: Fontana, 1991.

Braidotti, Rosi. *Patterns of Dissonance*. Oxford and Cambridge: Blackwell and Polity, 1981.

Bryson, Norman. *Vision and Painting*. London: Macmillan, 1983.

Burke, Caroline, Naomi Schor and Margaret Whitford. *Engaging with Irigaray*. New York: Columbia University Press, 1994.

Butler, Judith. *Bodies that Matter: On the Discursive Limits of Sex*. New York and London: Routledge, 1993.

Chodorow, Nancy. *Femininities, Masculinities, Sexualities. Freud and Beyond*. London: Free Association Books, 1994.

Curtis, Penelope and Alan G. Wilkinson. *Barbara Hepworth: A Retrospective*. London: Tate Gallery Publications, l994.

de Lauretis, Teresa. *The Practice of Love*. Bloomington: Indiana University Press, 1994.

Florence, Penny. "Barbara Hepworth: The Odd Man Out". In: David Thistlewood, ed. *Barbara Hepworth Reconsidered*. Liverpool: Liverpool University Press, 1996. 23-42.

Grosz, Elizabeth. *Jacques Lacan: A Feminist Introduction*. London: Routledge, 1990.

Hepworth, Barbara. *A Pictorial Autobiography*. London: Tate Gallery, 1985. (First published - Bath: Adams and Dart, 1970).

Hammer, Martin and Christina Lodder. "Hepworth and Gabo. A Constructive Dialogue". In: David Thistlewood, ed. *Barbara Hepworth Reconsidered*. Liverpool: Liverpool University Press, 1996. 109-33.

Hammer, Martin and Christina Lodder. "Monoprints in the Life and Work of Naum Gabo". In: Graham Williams, ed. *Naum Gabo Monoprints*. Ashford: The Florin Press, 1987.

Thistlewood, David, ed. *Barbara Hepworth Reconsidered*. Liverpool : Liverpool University Press and Tate Gallery Liverpool, 1996.

Williams, Graham, ed. *Naum Gabo Monoprints*. Ashford: The Florin Press, 1987.

Jasper Johns, Richard Hamilton et "le critique", 1959-1980

Dario Gamboni

Un préjugé implicite tend à réserver la fonction de métalangage, avec la dignité et les privilèges qui lui sont attachés, au langage verbal. C'est avec des mots seulement que l'on pourrait et devrait réfléchir aux images et *a fortiori* aux rapports entre les images et les mots. Cette division du travail de représentation et cette répartition des rôles de sujet et d'objet ont évidemment partie liée avec les relations de hiérarchie et de pouvoir établies entre producteurs d'images et producteurs de discours. Parmi les très nombreuses œuvres d'art qui contredisent ce préjugé et contribuent, par les moyens qui leur sont propres, à notre réflexion, il n'est donc pas étonnant d'en trouver qui protestent contre la domination des praticiens du verbe et dénoncent son fondement, son arbitraire ou ses effets. C'est le cas des œuvres auxquelles est consacré cet article, qui participent d'une critique artistique de la critique d'art tout en commentant plus largement les rapports entre art et langage, œuvre d'art et spectateur. Elles sont dues à deux artistes, l'Américain Jasper Johns (né en 1930) et le Britannique Richard Hamilton (né en 1922). Comme elles forment un enchaînement, il est nécessaire de les présenter tout d'abord dans l'ordre chronologique.

En 1959, Jasper Johns exécute un dessin au fusain (Rosenthal 148) qu'il intitule *The Critic Smiles* (le critique sourit). Une brosse à dents y porte cinq molaires en guise de poils. La même année, ce motif est réalisé en trois dimensions à l'aide de sculpmetal, matériau ductile durcissant après usage proposé aux amateurs de modelage (ill. 1). Le titre est inscrit sur une base. En 1961, Johns applique du *sculpmetal* sur un parallélipipède de plâtre dont une face présente des lunettes à travers lesquelles on voit, au lieu d'une paire d'yeux, deux bouches inégalement entrouvertes (ill. 2). L'œuvre s'appelle cette fois *The Critic Sees* (le critique voit). En 1962, un dessin (Rosenthal 149) remplace les matériaux de la sculpture par des inscriptions: "sculpmetal", "glass", "plaster cast (mouth)". En 1966, outre trois dessins et deux gravures consacrés au même sujet, Johns introduit *The Summer Critic* (le critique d'été) sous la forme d'un dessin et d'une gravure par embossage et sérigraphie dans lesquels l'image d'une bouche est remplacée par le mot "mouth" se détachant en lettres blanches comme des dents sur le fond noir représentant le verre fumé (Field 40). Parmi les variations ultérieures, qui s'échelonnent jusqu'en 1977, on peut signaler en

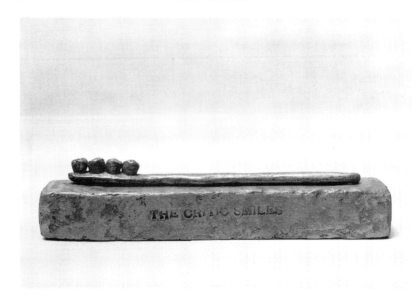

Illustration 1. Jasper Johns, *The Critic Smiles*, 1959. *Sculpmetal*, 4.1 x 19.7 x 3.8 cm. Collection de l'artiste.

Illustration 2. Jasper Johns, *The Critic Sees,* 1961. *Sculpmetal* sur plâtre avec verre, 8.3 x 15.9 x 5.4 cm. Localisation actuelle inconnue.

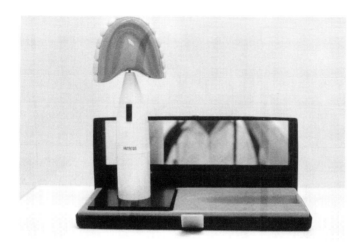

Illustration 3. Richard Hamilton, *The critic laughs*, 1971-1972. Brosse à dents électrique avec dents, étui et mode d'emploi, 27 x 11 x 6.5 cm. Collection de l'artiste.

1969 un relief en plomb de *The Critic Smiles* dont les diverses parties sont distinguées par la matière et la couleur (Field 73).

A une date non précisée mais antérieure à 1968, Richard Hamilton reçoit de son fils qui revient de vacances passées à Brighton un bloc de sucre en forme de mâchoire supérieure géante (Tate 1992, 172). Hamilton fixe l'objet au sommet de sa brosse à dents électrique et, songeant à la sculpture de Jasper Johns, baptise le tout *The critic laughs* (le critique rit), à cause du mouvement grotesque produit par l'appareil en marche. En 1968, pour une gravure que lui commande le galeriste berlinois René Block dans le cadre d'une campagne de financement pour la quatrième *documenta* de Cassel, il consacre à cet assemblage une œuvre mêlant photographie, lithographie et peinture (Tate 1970, 74). Le bloc de sucre subissant mal l'épreuve du temps, il en fait ensuite exécuter une réplique en plastique dentaire par Hans Sohm, dentiste et archiviste du mouvement Fluxus. L'objet ainsi perfectionné sert de base à la réalisation, en 1971, d'un "multiple" en petit tirage pour la galerie Block (ill. 3). La marque "Braun" est remplacée par la marque "Hamilton", une boîte *ad hoc* est fabriquée sur le modèle de celle du rasoir électrique Braun Sixtant. Le tout est complété par une carte de garantie et un livret de mode d'emploi qui donne en quatre langues les instructions suivantes:

"*Mise en marche et arrêt de l'appareil* / Tenez l'appareil fermement dans la main avec le pouce sur le bouton (4). Mettez l'appareil en marche en poussant le bouton vers le haut (en direction de la denture). Le multiple donnera alors un rire comme effet. Arrêtez l'appareil. / *Exposition* / Retournez le porte-appareil qui deviendra alors le socle du multiple (5). Placez la partie inférieure de l'appareil dans le creux circulaire du socle et observez la réflexion dans le miroir du couvercle de l'étui".[1]

En 1980, la série télévisée *The Shock of the New,* écrite et présentée à la BBC par Robert Hughes (342-64), permet à Hamilton de réaliser un spot publicitaire pour *The critic laughs,* dont l'artiste résume comme suit le scénario:

> This is the plot. A svelte and beautiful young lady bears the gift-wrapped multiple to the bathroom where her partner is about to shave. She carries the box ceremonially, as an Egyptian high priestess might support a sacred talisman, and presents it to her lover. Surprised, and slightly awed, he lifts the lid of the exquisitely wrought case to disclose giant teeth and an electric toothbrush. They are assembled, a look of amused disbelief crosses his features as he switches on, and realizes that the vibrating object is more for Her than Him. She smiles slyly as the tip of her tongue glides sexily along her lip. / The 'voice-over' says this: / For connoisseurs who have everything ... at last, a work of art to match the style of modern loving ... *The critic laughs* ... a perfect marriage of form and function ... created for you and yours by Europe's caring craftsmen in an exclusive edition of only sixty examples ... *The critic laughs* ... Feel the thrill of owning ... *The critic laughs.* / Hamilton is proud to present its new multiple ... / *The critic laughs* ... by Hamilton.[2] (Hamilton 73-74)

Ces œuvres de Jasper Johns et de Richard Hamilton se caractérisent par un humour offensif. Elles procèdent par déplacement, condensation, et inversion, individuellement comme les unes par rapport aux autres. Dans *The Critic Smiles,* point de départ de la série, le patient de l'opération du brossage (la dentition) devient agent (la brosse); la brosse-mâchoire, à la manière d'un mot-valise et d'une synecdoche, personnifie "le critique" et son sourire. Dans *The Critic Sees,* la substitution des yeux par la bouche s'accompagne d'un dédoublement de l'appareil buccal, le tout représentant cette fois le regard du critique. *The critic laughs,* quant à lui, est doublement un objet trouvé. La mâchoire en sucre a été achetée toute faite, "ready made". L'artiste dit qu'elle "exemplifie le côté noir de l'humour anglais":[3] elle donne en effet non seulement à un objet de consommation alimentaire la forme d'un agent ou instrument de cette consommation, mais prête aux dents la matière de leur pire ennemi, le sucre. L'interprétation de la combinaison mâchoire-manche de brosse à dents que donne le titre *The critic laughs* dérive quant à elle explicitement de *The Critic Smiles.* L'œuvre de Hamilton a ainsi pu être définie par Richard Morphet comme sa "mise à jour, pour une époque de technologie dentaire et domestique avancée" (Tate 1970, 73). En modernisant la sculpture de Johns, elle renchérit sur elle, faisant passer de l'objet artisanal à l'objet industriel, de l'immobilité au mouvement, du "sourire" au "rire".

A en croire les titres, la cible de cet humour est "le critique", soit l'ensemble des critiques d'art ou encore "la critique d'art". Plusieurs déclarations de Jasper Johns vont dans le sens de cette hypothèse. Michael Crichton rapporte ainsi les explications suivantes au sujet de *The Critic Smiles:*

> I had the idea that in society the approval of the critic was a kind of cleansing police action. When the critic smiles it's a lopsided smile with hidden meanings. And of course a smile involves baring the teeth. The critic is keeping a certain order, which is why it is like a police function. The handle has the word 'copper' on it, which I associate with police. I imagined the sculpture to be done in various metals–base metal, handle silver and teeth gold.[4] (Crichton 43)

Max Kozloff écrit par ailleurs que *The Critic Sees* aurait été "inspiré par une visite de trois minutes faite par un critique à l'une de ses expositions" (10). *The Critic Smiles* a été conçu et réalisé l'année suivant la première exposition personnelle de Johns chez Leo Castelli, c'est-à-dire au cours d'une période marquée par un succès fulgurant et donc par un contact fréquent avec des critiques, dont l'intérêt pour son travail ne pouvait être que d'une profondeur variable. A propos de *The Summer Critic,* conçu au Japon pendant l'été de 1966, Johns a manifesté à l'égard des critiques une sorte de sympathie non dépourvue d'ironie ou de condescendance en déclarant à Richard Field que les lunettes de soleil étaient celles des critiques qui étaient à la piscine au lieu de demeurer cloîtrés dans leur chambre à écrire comme le souhaitaient leurs éditeurs (Bernstein 56).

Les exégètes de Johns ont relevé la dimension polémique de ces œuvres, en particulier de *The Critic Sees,* et ont cherché à la traduire verbalement par des formules qui adoptent significativement une allure de proverbe: "a critic sees with his mouth" (Kozloff 9), "critics often put their mouths where their focused eyes ought to be" (Rosenthal 148), "critics are blind, they see with their mouths" (Orton 153).[5] Richard Hamilton, quant à lui, n'a fait aucune allusion aux critiques d'art dans ses commentaires à *The critic laughs,* et la mention du critique y paraît surtout reprise de l'œuvre de Johns. L'essentiel réside pour lui dans l'imitation du mode de production et de promotion industrielles d'objets de consommation de luxe, une imitation parodique qui n'exclut d'ailleurs pas l'admiration (Cooke 65).

En fait, ce n'est pas seulement par leurs titres que ces œuvres participent de la problématique des rapports entre artistes et critiques. Elles s'inscrivent aussi dans la tradition peu connue de l'image de la critique d'art, et des parallèles les relient à d'autres représentations apparues dès la fin du XVIIIe siècle, sans doute davantage par l'effet d'une continuité structurelle qu'en raison d'une véritable filiation iconographique. On peut repérer ainsi deux de leurs thèmes principaux, celui du critique prédateur et celui du critique aveugle.

Illustration 4. Friedrich Dürrenmatt,
Kritiker, 1968. Dessin à la plume.
Grenchen [Switzerland], collection
Hans Liechti-Lienhard.

Johns faisait allusion au critique prédateur en évoquant le sourire qui "découvre les dents"; Roberta Bernstein l'a explicité en reliant ce sourire hypocrite à l'attaque préparée par le critique et à la souffrance de l'artiste soumis à sa "morsure" (55). En 1896 déjà, l'artiste belge James Ensor poussait la métaphore plus loin dans une toile intitulée *Les cuisiniers dangereux* (Gamboni 48). Deux des principaux promoteurs de l'avant-garde artistique en Belgique à la fin du XIXe siècle, Edmond Picard (critique et collectionneur) et Octave Maus (secrétaire de la société "les XX" et organisateur d'expositions) y sont montrés apprêtant divers artistes et les servant à une tablée de critiques, qui en éprouvent d'ailleurs des problèmes de digestion. Porté sur un plat par Maus, Ensor lui-même, réduit à une tête humaine accolée à un corps de poisson, évoque non seulement un hareng saur – selon le jeu de mots "ART/ENSOR" qui figure sur une étiquette – mais encore la tête martyrisée de saint Jean-Baptiste. Ensor a consacré une part non négligeable de son œuvre à la critique de la critique, et ses attaques coïncident avec la mise en place de ce que Harrison et Cynthia White ont appelé le "système marchand-critique" (Gamboni *Plume* 229-39). Mais l'idée du critique dévorant ceux qu'il commente apparaît à d'autres moments et au-delà du domaine de la seule critique artistique, comme en témoigne un dessin de l'écrivain suisse Friedrich Dürrenmatt intitulé *Kritiker* ([le] critique), qui vise sans doute au premier chef la critique littéraire (ill. 4).

Quant au thème de la cécité du critique, on peut en mentionner entre autres deux occurrences datant respectivement de la fin du XVIIIe et de la fin du XIXe siècle. Dans une caricature postérieure à 1797 (Gamboni 48), le

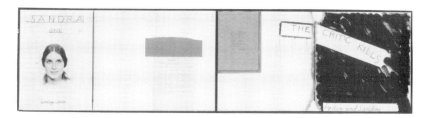

Illustration 5. Ronald B. Kitaj, *The Critic Kills.* Huile et collage, 20 x 80 cm. Collection de l'artiste.

Français J.-J. Espercieux reproche à Amaury-Duval, critique de *La Décade philosophique,* d'être incapable d'appréhender les objets soumis à son autorité. En dépit de la longue-vue que lui tend une personnification de l'Ignorance aux yeux bandés, une inscription sur le socle supportant l'Apollon du Belvédère qu'il examine dénonce: "L'ignorant ne nous aperçoit pas". En 1888, le peintre suisse Frank Buchser se met quant à lui en scène dans une "allégorie réelle" (Soleure, Kunstmuseum; Gamboni 47) intitulée *Kritik* ([la] critique). Un modèle à demi-nu y jette au peintre un regard admiratif tandis qu'un vieux critique pointe un doigt vindicatif vers la toile à laquelle il travaille. L'incompétence du critique est affaire de vision: au contraire du peintre dont les yeux cerclés de métal prennent le spectateur à témoin, le vieillard laisse pendre inutilement ses lorgnons et a rejeté sur son front ses lunettes de tir – car ce critique, qui revient le fusil en bandouillère d'une fête de tir, est aussi une sorte de prédateur.

Une critique de la critique apparentée a été avancée récemment par Ronald B. Kitaj, peintre américain né en 1932 et installé en Angleterre depuis 1958, dans un envoi (ill. 5) à l'exposition d'été 1996 de la Royal Academy à Londres intitulé *The Critic Kills* (le critique tue). Il s'agit d'une image complexe dans laquelle les inscriptions jouent un rôle important, et que l'une d'entre elles présente comme le premier numéro d'un magazine artistique inspiré de la revue polémique *Die Fackel* de Karl Kraus. Son rapport à *The Critic Smiles* et *The critic laughs,* mentionnés dans l'"instruction" de gauche, paraît linguistique et thématique plutôt que visuel. L'accusation adressée aux critiques repose sur la simultanéité de deux événements douloureux survenus en 1994 dans la vie de l'artiste: la réception hostile de son exposition rétrospective à la Tate Gallery et la mort tragique, à l'issue d'une grave maladie, de sa femme Sandra – représentée par la photographie de couverture et par le titre du "magazine". Dans la partie droite, à côté du "tableau" portant l'inscription "THE CRITIC KILLS", une citation d'Adolf Hitler annonce que "les prétendues œuvres d'art qui ne peuvent être comprises en elles-mêmes et nécessitent des modes d'emploi prétentieux pour justifier leur existence ... ne trouveront plus jamais le chemin du peuple allemand".[5] On peut supposer que Kitaj évoque la persécution de l'"art dégénéré" par les nazis comme modèle de l'action mortifère qu'il attribue aux critiques, bien que dans le texte en question, Hitler s'en prenne significativement aussi à l'étroite collaboration entre artistes et exégètes caractéristique de l'art moderne.

La critique de la critique ne saurait cependant épuiser *The Critic Smiles, The Critic Sees* et *The critic laughs.* Johns et Hamilton ne figurent d'ailleurs pas parmi les défenseurs puristes de la spécificité des arts visuels, tout au contraire. A la fin des années 1950, Johns explore systématiquement les rapports entre mots et images. Dans plusieurs toiles dont *False Start* (faux départ) de 1959 (Orton 35), les couleurs sont remplacées, dédoublées ou contredites par leurs noms. A partir de 1961, une tension émotionnelle nouvelle dans ses œuvres (Bernstein 75) fait participer les mots à un processus de communication ambigu. Dans *No* (Orton 36), les deux lettres de la négation, taillées dans le *sculpmetal,* sont à la fois suspendues au-devant de la toile et imprimées dans la surface de peinture à l'encaustique. Cette négation s'adresse-t-elle au tableau, au spectateur, ou encore au peintre? La même question vaut pour *Liar* (menteur), également de 1961 (Orton 57). Citant une phrase des *Sketchbook Notes* de Johns ("'Looking' is and is not 'eating' and 'being eaten'"),[6] Roberta Bernstein voit dans le motif de l'ingestion une métaphore de la "consommation" visuelle de la peinture (80). Ce motif apparaît explicitement sous la forme d'ustensiles (fourchette, cuillère, couteau) que l'on remarque dès 1961 dans *In Memory of My Feelings – Frank O'Hara* (en souvenir de mes sentiments – Frank O'Hara; Orton 34). Il s'exprime de la manière la plus directe et la plus violente (Bernstein fig. 31) dans *Painting Bitten by a Man* (peinture mordue par un homme). Tandis que "le critique" n'est plus mentionné explicitement, l'ambiguïté demeure: l'empreinte de dents visible en creux est peut-être l'indice de la morsure effectuée par le peintre mais en est-elle l'icone ou symbolise-t-elle, par anticipation, le regard du public?

Au-delà de la critique du critique, les principaux commentateurs de Johns ont ainsi proposé des interprétations plus complexes, voire plus consensuelles et en tout cas moins offensantes pour tous ceux – dont eux-mêmes – qui discourent sur l'art. Max Kozloff, ouvrant en 1969 sa monographie sur Johns par l'examen de *The Critic Sees,* y trouvait "une illustration, ou presque un paradigme, de la situation" du spectateur face aux œuvres de Johns, une synthèse de la vision et de l'articulation verbale conçues comme se renforçant mutuellement, ainsi qu'une allégorie de ce que Paul Valéry considérait comme "la cause première d'un ouvrage ... un désir qu'il en soit parlé, ne fût-ce qu'entre un esprit et soi-même".[7] En 1990, Nan Rosenthal avançait deux autres hypothèses: par le rendu illusionniste des bouches dans le dessin de 1962, Johns aurait voulu suggérer qu'"un examen attentif est une idée raisonnable"; par la représentation des bouches dans deux attitudes légèrement différentes,

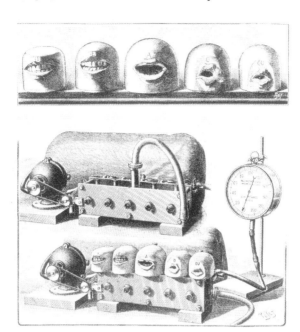

Illustration 6. L. Poyet, appareil du Dr Marage pour l'étude de la parole et moulages en plâtre de la bouche prononçant les voyelles, gravure sur bois reproduite dans *La Nature*, 1908.

qu'"il y a au moins deux vues de toute œuvre d'art" (148). Fred Orton, enfin, pour qui tout l'art de Johns est de nature "allégorique", a souligné en 1994 le phénomène de personnification ("le critique") déjà relevé par Kozloff et noté que *The Critic Sees* "renverse les termes habituels de la perception visuelle de sorte que le regardeur devient l'objet vivant de ce qu'il regarde" (183).

Les hypothèses de l'"examen attentif" et d'une bifocalité exprimant la polysémie ne paraissent guère convaincantes, en particulier lorsqu'on les confronte avec une déclaration faite par Johns en 1961: "A painting should not require a special kind of focus like going to church. A picture ought to be looked at the same way you look at a radiator".[8] Le dédoublement non identique des bouches évoque plutôt une séquence temporelle de l'activité verbale, comme en témoigne une ressemblance fortuite avec les moulages en plâtre d'une bouche prononçant les voyelles réalisés au début du siècle par le Dr Marenge (ill. 6). Il est plus difficile de se prononcer sur l'idée d'une complémentarité entre vision et discours, mais il est certain que Johns propose dans *The Critic Sees* une interrogation sur les rapports entre visualisation et verbalisation qui ne se limite pas à la dénonciation de cette dernière. L'inversion de la relation entre œuvre et spectateur, enfin, me semble constituer une observation d'autant plus judicieuse qu'elle participe de la revendication métadiscursive de *The Critic Sees* (c'est l'œuvre qui critique le commentateur) et que le thème du retournement est récurrent chez Johns, en relation avec l'une des références artistiques qu'il partage avec Hamilton, celle de Marcel Duchamp.

Dans le coin supérieur gauche de *No*, une trace résulte de l'impression de *Feuille de vigne femelle* (Schwarz n° 332), une œuvre de 1950 de Duchamp dont Johns avait acquis un tirage de bronze édité en 1961 par la Galerie Rive Droite à Paris (Bernstein 76). Cette œuvre, représentant l'empreinte négative d'un sexe féminin, est elle-même un retournement. Duchamp avait d'ailleurs poussé ce procédé plus loin encore, dans le registre érotique ou obscène, avec *Objet-dard* de 1951 (Schwarz n° 335), dont le titre établit une sorte d'équivalence entre art et pénétration. Au moment où il réalisait le "ready-made aidé" qu'est *The critic laughs,* Richard Hamilton venait précisément de consacrer plusieurs années à l'œuvre de Duchamp, réalisant entre autres une réplique de *La mariée mise à nu par ses célibataires, même* et organisant l'exposition rétrospective de la Tate Gallery en 1966. On peut supposer que cette fréquentation assidue n'est pas étrangère aux métaphores sexuelles de la relation entre œuvre et spectateur qu'il a ajoutées aux métaphores orales et alimentaires proposées par Johns.

La publicité pour *The critic laughs* incorporée à *The Shock of the New* et le récit qu'en donne Hamilton sont en effet très clairs à cet égard. Il y a bien quelqu'un qui rit dans cette histoire, donc un "critique": c'est l'amant, censé être le destinataire du cadeau, lorsqu'il comprend que celui-ci "est destiné davantage à Elle qu'à Lui". Faut-il voir dans cette représentation du "style d'amour moderne", faite de séduction et d'exclusion, suggérant voyeurisme et onanisme mécanique, la parabole d'une communication esthétique moderne vouée aux "machines célibataires"? La critique de la critique y est-elle tempérée et compliquée par une conscience de la complicité et de l'interdépendance – plus ou moins perverse – des artistes et des critiques? En conformité avec l'ambivalence et l'ambiguïté fondamentales de *No, Liar* et *Painting Bitten by a Man,* peut-être faut-il voir dans cette série métalangagière moins une affirma-tion dénonciatrice à l'endroit des critiques qu'une interrogation à portée plus générale: dans le ménage à trois que forment l'artiste, l'œuvre d'art et le regardeur – que ce dernier soit "critique" ou simple amateur –, qui regarde qui? qui mord ou dévore qui? qui séduit ou repousse qui? qui rit de qui, ou de quoi?

NOTES

1   Je remercie Nigel McKernaghan, assistant de Richard Hamilton, de m'avoir aimablement communiqué une copie du mode d'emploi de *The critic laughs.* La

version anglaise de ce passage est: "*Turning in and off*/ Hold the unit tightly in your hand, with your thumb on the switch (4). It is turned on by pushing the knob up (towards the set of teeth). The multiple will then present the effect of laughter. Turn off the unit. / *Exhibition*/ The holder is turned over and thus becomes a pedestal (5) for the multiple. Place the lower part of the unit into the circular recess of the holder and watch the reflection in the mirror of the case cover".

2   "Une belle et svelte jeune femme apporte le multiple, emballé comme un cadeau, dans la salle de bains où son partenaire s'apprête à se raser. Elle porte la boîte cérémonieusement, comme une prêtresse égyptienne pourrait tenir un talisman sacré, et l'offre à son amant. Surpris et légèrement effrayé, il soulève le couvercle de la boîte exquisement ouvrée et découvre un dentier géant et une brosse à dent électrique. L'appareil une fois assemblé, il le met en marche; un air d'incrédulité amusée se peint sur son visage tandis qu'il réalise que l'objet vibrant est destiné davantage à Elle qu'à Lui. Elle sourit finement et passe avec sensualité le bout de sa langue sur ses lèvres. Une voix *off* déclare: 'Pour les connaisseurs qui ont tout ... enfin, une œuvre d'art qui convienne au style d'amour moderne ... *Le critique rit* ... un parfait mariage de la forme et de la fonction ... créé pour vous et les vôtres par les meilleurs artisans d'Europe dans une édition exclusive de soixante exemplaires seulement ... *Le critique rit* ... Ressentez le frisson de posséder ... *Le critique rit*. Hamilton est fier de présenter son nouveau multiple ... *Le critique rit* ... par Hamilton".

3   "A confection to be found in the English seaside resort, Brighton, which exemplifies the darker side of English humor" (Guggenheim 61).

4   "Je pensais qu'en société, l'approbation du critique était une sorte d'action policière d'épuration. Quand le critique sourit, c'est un sourire en biais plein de sous-entendus. Et bien sûr, sourire implique de découvrir les dents. Le critique est le gardien d'un certain ordre, c'est pourquoi cela ressemble à une fonction de police. Le manche porte le mot "cuivre" ["copper", proche de "cop" c'est-à-dire "flic"], que j'associe à la police. J'imaginais la sculpture réalisée en divers métaux – la base en plomb, le manche en argent et les dents en or".

5   "Le critique voit avec sa bouche"; "les critiques mettent souvent leurs bouches là où devraient se trouver leurs yeux"; "les critiques sont aveugles, ils voient avec leurs bouches".

6   Inscription de gauche: "'*Instruction*'/ *This painting is a magazine.* / It is the first issue of an irregular art journal called *SANDRA*. / At the left is a version of the cover. / At the right is a picture called *THE CRITIC KILLS* which, of course, ows debts to *THE CRITIC SMILES* (1959) by Jasper Johns and *THE CRITIC LAUGHS* (1979) by Richard Hamilton. / The new journal, which will sometimes feature Guerilla Action Painting (and writing), was inspired by Karl Kraus, who published *DIE FACKEL* (The Torch) in Vienna for 40 years until the rise of Hitlerism. / The second issue of *SANDRA* may be published in Paris in the Fall of 1996"; inscription de droite: "'Works of art' that are not capable of being understood in themselves but need some pretentious instruction book to justify their existence – until at long last they find someone sufficiently browbeaten to endorse such stupid or impudent twaddle with patience – will never again find their way to the German people! / Adolf Hitler". Je remercie Geoffrey Parton de Marlborough Fine Art, Londres, pour les informations qu'il m'a obligeamment fournies au sujet de cette œuvre.

7   "'Regarder' est et n'est pas comme 'manger' et 'être mangé'".

8   Kozloff 9-10. La citation de Valéry provient de "Autour de Corot", préface à *XX Estampes de Corot*, 1932, repris dans *Pièces sur l'art*, Paris: Gallimard, 1934, 125.

9   "Une peinture ne devrait pas demander un type de concentration particulier comme pour aller à l'église. On devrait regarder un tableau de la même façon qu'on regarde un radiateur" (cité in D. R. Rickborn, "Art's Fair-Haired Boy", *The State*, 15 janvier 1961, reproduit dans Susan Brundage, dir., *Jasper Johns / Leo Castelli*, New York: Harry N. Abrams, 1993, non paginé).

BIBLIOGRAPHIE

Bernstein, Roberta. *Jasper Johns' Paintings and Sculptures 1954-1974. "The Changing Focus of the Eye"*. Thèse, Columbia University, New York, 1975. Ann Arbor/Londres: UMI Research Press, 1985.

Cooke, Lynne. "Art Comes Usually without a Guarantee". *Richard Hamilton. Exteriors. Interiors. Objects. People.* (cat. expo.: Winterthour, Kunstmuseum; Hannovre, Kestner-Gesellschaft; Valence, IVAM Centre Julio Gonzalez). Londres/Stuttgart: Edition Hansjörg Mayer, 1990. 65-8.

Crichton, Michael. *Jasper Johns* (cat. expo.: New York, Whitney Museum of American Art). New York: Harry N. Abrams, 1977.

Field, Richard S. *The Prints of Jasper Johns 1960-1993. A Catalogue Raisonné.* New York: Universal Limited Art Editions, 1994.

Gamboni, Dario. "L'image de la critique d'art, essai de typologie". *Quarante-huit/Quatorze. Conférences du Musée d'Orsay* n° 5. Paris: Réunion des musées nationaux, 1993. 44-52.

————. *La plume et le pinceau. Odilon Redon et la littérature.* Paris: Editions de Minuit, 1989.

Guggenheim: cat. expo. *Richard Hamilton.* New York: The Solomon R. Guggenheim Museum, 1973.

Hamilton, Richard. *Collected Words 1953-1982.* Londres: Thames and Hudson, 1982.

Hughes, Robert. *The Shock of the New* (éd. révisée). New York: Alfred A. Knopf, 1995.

Kozloff, Max. *Jasper Johns.* New York: Harry N. Abrams, 1969.

Orton, Fred. *Figuring Jasper Johns.* Londres: Reaktion Books, 1994.

Rosenthal, Nan, et Ruth E. Fine. *The Drawings of Jasper Johns* (cat. expo.: Washington, National Gallery of Art). Londres: Thames and Hudson, 1990.

Schwarz, Arturo. *The Complete Works of Marcel Duchamp, with a Catalogue Raisonné.* Londres: Harry N. Abrams, 1969.

Tate 1970: cat. expo. *Richard Hamilton.* Londres: The Tate Gallery, 1970.

Tate 1992: cat. expo. *Richard Hamilton* (Londres, The Tate Gallery; Dublin, Irish Museum of Modern Art). Londres: The Tate Gallery, 1992.

White, Harrison C. et Cynthia A. *Canvases and Careers: Institutional Change in the French Painting World.* New York/Londres/Sidney: Wilney & Sons, 1965.

Generic Specificity and the Problem of Translation in Galvano Della Volpe

Kenneth G. Hay

> In all language and linguistic creations there remains in addition to what can be conveyed, something that cannot be communicated
>
> —Walter Benjamin, "The Task of the Translator"

INTRODUCTION

From Horace's day onwards there have been many attempts to categorise the various forms of art into distinct 'genres' and to individuate their specific competences (Lee) . One of the most straightforward methods of conceptualising the specificity of these genres is to attempt a translation from one genre to another and, as Benjamin points out, to thereby observe what gets lost 'in transit'. The danger in so doing is to reassert the old idealist chestnut of the 'ineffability' of art – that there exists, in some abstract realm, what Goethe called an *Urphänomen*, a potential phenomenon waiting to be given form through art; such a notion sponsors an ideal, ultimately inexplicable art, one which 'passeth our understanding'. Such is not my project here.[1]

Roman Jakobson argues for a distinction to be drawn between three types of translation ("Linguistische Aspekte der Übersetzung"). There is, firstly what he terms "*intra-lingual translation*" or simple paraphrase, where we interpret one verbal sign by means of other verbal signs of the same language. For example when we give an explanation of an unknown word. Secondly there is what he calls, "*interlingual translation*" or translation in the normal sense, and the practice in which Benjamin himself was involved. – The interpretation of a verbal sign with the aid of another language. But thirdly, and most relevant for my discussion today is what Jakobson called "*Intersemiotic translation*": the interpretation of a linguistic sign with the help of a non-verbal sign system (or vice versa: the interpretation of a non-verbal sign with the help of a verbal sign, such as the verbal description of a ballet or a painting) (cf. Ogawa).

In addition to these cultural and linguistic differences common to most translations, the task of the translator who would attempt a translation *between genres* also has to take on board the more complex incongruities of different semiotic structures each with its own histories and traditions.[2] It is particularly this type of 'translation' and these sorts of difficulties which preoccupied the Italian philosopher Galvano Della Volpe (1895-1968) throughout his aesthetic reflection, some of whose aspects I shall attempt to examine in what follows.

This century, Benedetto Croce's *Aesthetic* (1905) represents the last major attempt on the part of idealism to build on the legacy of Lessing and Diderot and codify what it saw as the proper competences of the abstractly separate realms of art, ethics and logic, although this idealist tendency reappears with any kind of formalist criticis (cf. *Aesthetic as General Linguistic and Science of Expression*). In Croce's *Aesthetic*, as indeed in any formalist criticism from Clive Bell's to the later Clement Greenberg's, the visual is conceived as irretrievably separate from the verbal, the logical or the ethical. Consequently, its 'meaning' can be grasped by intuition alone. For Croce, it is a fundamental feature of art that it is not reducible to rational thought (logic), but takes the form of mental 'images' which have to be intuited 'internally' (in ways which are forever mysterious) by the receiver / viewer. It is easy to see this as a return of the alienated bourgeois subject (or isolated existential monad) which materialism had effectively banished in the 1840s. As with Hegelian idealism, Croce's romantic idealism stressed the primacy of (timeless) mind or spirit over what he saw as the "brute" materiality of the real (socio-historical) world.[3]

In contrast, the Italian philosopher Galvano Della Volpe produced a radical critique of both romanticism and idealism (whether of Hegelian or Crocean origins), and a critique of 'vulgar' materialist approaches which underestimated the formal-semantic autonomy of art, relying either on a crude socio-economic determinism or a form of 'contentism' (such as Lukàcs' theory of realism)(cf. Aristotle, *Poetics*). I outline below some of those aspects of Della Volpe's rich and unjustly neglected aesthetic theory relating to the problem of generic specificity and the problem of translation, with specific reference to his anti-Croceanism and his work on film.[4]

Il verosimile filmico (Filmic Realism): a materialist anti-Croce.

In August 1954, Della Volpe published a collection of ten essays on aesthetics in the "Piccola biblioteca dello spettacolo" series, published by the Italian journal, *Filmcritica*. To these were added a further five studies in the second edition, published as a special section of *Filmcritica* in the summer of 1962 *(Il verosimile filmico)*. The book carried two epigraphs from Diderot and Lessing, relating to the classification of the arts by 'genres' and the difficulties of *'translating'* one genre into another.[5] The essays, on film, ideology and the inter-relation of the arts, centre around the 'problems of a scientific aesthetics', which involve the critique of Crocean idealism and all forms of 'a-priorism', as well as of the shortcomings of post-Crocean materialist aesthetics, whether in Gramsci or Lukàcs, the specificity of filmic language in Pudovkin, Chaplin or Ciné-vérité and the relationship between ideology and art. Declaring the need for the "rigorous development of an anti-romantic, anti-idealist" aesthetic, or "an aesthetic of the means of expression", to counter critics like Moravia for whom the film was a 'crude' instrument compared to the pen, Della Volpe proposes a "new Laocöon" which would recognise the availability of semantically heter-onomous means of artistic expression and their "peaceful co-existence" as means of expression.[6] The classic hierarchy of the genres which stressed their inter-changeability, seemed even less sustainable in the light of specifically 'filmic' (i.e. *'untranslatable'*) elements in Eisenstein, Groucho Marx or Chaplin. Della Volpe reiterates his opposition to Croce's idealist theory of 'cosmic intuition' and argues instead for an aesthetic which recognises the "full intellectuality" of art by acknowledging its "full cognitive value" (cf. *Il verosimile*). His is thus an an anti-Kantian theory which rejects the principle of the beautiful as disinter-ested "aesthetic idea" and which reasserts the positivity (and ultimately, pri-macy) of the material (political) world (cf. Hay, *Italian materialist aesthetics* and *Bertrando Spaventa*).

FILMIC LANGUAGE AND TRANSLATION

The central essay in the book, from which it derives its title, takes up a sugges-tion of Pudovkin's, that the content or script of a film provides only the overall concept to the director not the final filmic form. *(Film Technique and Film Acting)*. From this apparently simple observation Della Volpe deduces an en-tire aesthetic, based on the recognition of the generic specificity of the 'filmic' image, as distinct from the 'literary', 'pictorial', 'musical' or whatever, image. For Pudovkin, the filmic image is essentially plastic and concrete; qualities which enable it to operate as metaphor and symbol, and thus as carrier of complex ideas about the real world. In a film, it is thus not necessarily the specific wording of the script which communicates meaning but the uniquely filmic way this is handled or 'inflected' as a filmic image by the director. In-deed, the director's main function is precisely to elaborate this filmic plasticity.

Eisenstein, taking up Rudolf Arnheim's suggestion of a 'new Laocöon', never-theless notes the difficulty of individuating the generic specificity of filmic metaphor as against that of painting:

> In painting the form is born from the abstract elements of line and colour, whereas in the cinema the material concreteness of the image-frame as an element presents the greatest difficulty of [formal] elaboration". (*Film Form* 60)

To Della Volpe, for filmic metaphor to exist it must operate through a montage or juxtaposition sequence, rather than in terms of single frames, and he cites the juxtaposition of the images of the workers being killed and the slaughtered cattle in Eisenstein's "Strike" (1924) or the 'awakening lion' sequence in "Battleship Potemkin" (1925). In the first, the concrete, rational meaning of the filmic metaphor is the equation of the cold, methodical slaughter of the ox with the gunning down of the workers in the square; in the second the juxtaposition of the images of the 'awakening' stone lions, interspersed with images of the broadsides being fired from the battleship convey a sense of the awakening of the 'spirit' of rebellion in the Russian people. These images, while being precise in the filmic sense, are yet difficult to 'put into words' or translate into another expressive medium. Defining art as an 'a-priori' synthesis of intuition and expression as Croce did, negates the aspect of 'technique' which in film is all the more evident. Croce himself saw that technique could not be separated form the artistic process but failed to acknowledge that it also played a determinate part in that process, thus forming part of the specific meaning of the art-work.

Della Volpe conceives of the filmic image as a material discourse, constituted of determinate forms and ideas, just as the literary image is constituted. Only here, the traditional roles of 'form' and 'content' are reversed such that the term 'content' comes to refer to art's concrete historical-discursive 'form' (its symbolic-communicative aspect) whereby the 'image' is constituted. The universality or objectivity of the artistic image is an attribute of the form of the concept, not of the image, and the term 'form' implies a determinate discriminate, rationally intelligible image. A 'form' which is 'unintelligible' is in fact a contradiction in terms, being a reversion to the neo-Platonic 'mystic oneness' of Plotinus, or the mystical unity of Schelling's 'mystic black night'. Moreover, the "content" of the filmic / artistic must be none other than the concrete rationality of matter: the real and the social.

A further conclusion can be drawn from this that, just as the form always directs us towards the content, the content is nothing if it does not direct us towards the form, to the idea, for its full objectification or expression. The structural circularity of form and content which Della Volpe theorises here leads him to conclude that there can be no successful formal 'transcendence' of a content which is banal, academic or stereotypical, (and therefore 'un-truthful') because the content cannot *but* influence the form: where there are only stereotypes and untruths, there can be no artistic (formal) value. Della Volpe notes that the reasons for this type of failure, need not lie in the personal originality of the individual-artist and in his/her application of formal, technical norms, but rather:

> in the non-dialectical use of expressive models, and that is of symbols or ideals, or ideas (forms), which have been historically (i.e. really) superseded or consumed. *(Il verosimile)*

This, for Della Volpe, is the modern, post-Romantic problem of artistic originality. Once the mystical and irrational definitions of form and content have been rejected, one is free to see that the diad 'form-content' is none other than 'idea-matter' or 'empirical concept'. Artistic empirical concepts are distinguishable from empirical concepts in the normal or scientific sense by their different expressive means and by their different semantic techniques: where film uses a dynamic-visual language, literature utilises verbal symbols and images, painting adopts static-visual-'abstract' symbols and images, etc. The specific genres of art (film, painting, literature, music etc.) can thus be individuated and their differing techniques analysed. Aristotle's definition of 'similitude' as a nexus linking 'distant and different things' such as happens in philosophy and science, proposes that metaphor (art) is thought (although not only thought) since it is in fact a 'transposition' (metaphor) from the genus to the species. An image, insofar as it is 'truthful' (i.e. coherent) will have a 'life-like' or realistic quality, even if the realism is 'impossible' in the Aristotelian definition (such as Eisenstein's stone lions 'awakening'); i.e. it is preferable to have an 'impossible' but 'believable' image (i.e. successfully expressed) than an incredible (i.e. incoherent) but possible one. Aristotle argues that 'impossible' or 'unbelievable' images in art are 'errors' when directly connected to the technique of the artist, but not when they only have an 'accidental' relationship to this technique. Thus the notion of "probability", (and thus 'realism') as nexus of distant and distinct, as internal coherence, or as internal rationality of the image, takes on a central role as a constitutive condition of art, whether filmic, literary or pictorial etc. In this way Pudovkin can distinguish between the concrete nature of the 'filmic idea' as against the literary idea. The distinction can be seen at its clearest in the often crude attempts to 'translate' one form (a novel) into another (a film) which lack artistic coherence because they have been conceived in a different form. The literary idea, however brilliant, is to the director nothing more than 'abstract content' i.e. another material which has only an accidental relationship to the art of the director. This is a clear declaration, of *the cognitive independence of different species of artistic form-*

making, which applies equally to the relationship of 'apparent' ('literary') and 'real' (concrete/material) content within the visual arts, (and music, etc.) which has, as Della Volpe remarked, waylaid most 'engaged' social critics.

Translatability in the *Critica Del Gusto*

The *Critica del Gusto (Critique of Taste)* is Della Volpe's major contribution to the field of art theory. Its composition occupied him for around eleven years, from the first outlines of 1955 prior to its first publication in 1960, to the two subsequent reworkings of 1964 and 1966 *(Critica del gusto /Critique of Taste)*. Space here will allow me only to outline one or two themes.

In the *Critica del Gusto* Della Volpe develops two fundamental ideas from the *Verosimile Filmico*. Firstly, that it is useless to try and structure the arts in terms of an expressive hierarchy (the only tenable position being to recognise the legitimacy of the various arts as 'peacefully coexistent equals'); and secondly, that, in opposition to the romantic/idealist notion of the 'ineffability' of art, that its full cognitive status be recognised as being on a par with that of history or science, from which it should be seen to differ only in its semantic, means not its epistemological import.

The claim for art's equal cognitive value alongside science and history, derives from the Aristotelian distinction between the genres of poetry and history (between the expression of what is possible and what is merely actual, cf. *Poetics*). If Aristotle's solution is no longer sufficient, and poetry can no longer be seen as "superior" to history (because even that which has happened could not have occurred if it were not possible), then the specific differentiating feature can only be individuated in the technical-semantic field – with the epistemological specificity of genres which this implies.

Language, being a social product, cannot but utilise forms and structures which are both socially functional and rational, (rather than arbitrary or inherent); thus, for Della Volpe, the dialectical relation of form and content is firmly rooted in everyday language, and each branch of the arts must consequently possess its own unique 'language' or expressive, technical-semantic sign-system, comprehensible only through the existence of socially shared common logical language:

> The theory of the rational character of the sign, and the grounding of reason and meaning in ordinary, natural language, was developed definitively in the *Critica del Gusto*. (Fraser)

Taking his starting point from a suggestion of Goethe's that the "pure and perfect content" of a poem is what remains when this is 'translated' into prose, Della Volpe develops his notion of *'critical paraphrase'* as a means of identifying the logical core of the art-work *(Critica del gusto)*. This rational core remains after the "dazzling exterior" of 'musicality' or rhythm (which pertain to the signifier and are thus external to the meaning as such) has been removed, and is thus synonymous with 'formed content' or poetic form in Della Volpe's analysis. The criterion of *translation* must therefore only be one of fidelity to the letter of the poem. This is because even the literal translation is expressively and semantically an historical product so that fidelity to the objective spirit of the poem is at the same time fidelity to its subjective spirit. Poetry is thus always capable of being translated since it is this 'prosaic' aspect which alone corresponds to the discursivity of polysemic discourse. That which remains 'ineffable' or untranslatable is not the poem itself (as the Romantics or Croce would have us believe), but its euphony. For Leopardi, a perfect translation is one in which the author, translated from say French to German, is the *same* author in Italian or English, for which he maintains that poetry can only be translated by poets (Leopardi). The difficulty or limitation in the accomplishment of this is due to specific semantic differences between languages, such that "it is not always possible in all languages" (Leopardi). The difference lies in what Saussure termed the linguistic value of the word as distinct from its meaning. The 'value' refers to the function of the word in the linguistic structure, and applies not only to words but also to grammatical entities and syntax. Since different languages have different syntactic structures and characteristic grammatical norms, it follows that a 'true' translation (i.e. one which captures the logical core of the work) will not necessarily mimic the syntactic structures of the original, and may need to depart quite far from them *(Critica del gusto)*. Ultimately the greatness of an author lies precisely in his/her ability to transcend these 'incidental' aspects of language – to become eminently *'translatable'* in effect.

Cinema

For Della Volpe, cinema was not a 'visual art' nor less a sub-species of painting'. As he argued in "Il verosimile filmico" Della Volpe considered the two dimensionality of film to be extrinsic or accidental to the nature of 'filmwork'. The intrinsic feature of the frame (the basic film sign) is that it is a photographic reproduction of a three dimensional real, world, hence essentially documentary in character. Even montage is a counterpointing of frames in a sequence. A film is thus composed of "edited photo-dynamic image-ideas" *(Critica del gusto)*. And colour, like the literary film score, was seen as a 'contamination' of film's essential black and white essence. These filmic im-

ages, such as Eisenstein's stone lions in "Battleship Potemkin", can be "reproduced in words only with difficulty", as Pudovkin observed. Any attempt to
'describe' them, like the similar attempt to describe a dream, will be banal and
impoverished by comparison with the vividness of the original, because they
possess a superior "optical-expressive force" *(Critica del gusto)*. A similar banal-
ity would result in trying to 'translate' a peculiarly poetic image like that of the
lion in Dante's "Inferno" (I, lines 47-48) into an essentially filmic image. In
both, what should be kept in mind is the criterion of semantic difference, by
which each expressive (art) form has its own autonomous range of expressive/
formal/technical possibilities (and no others).

THE LEGACY OF LESSING

As I have argued elsewhere *(Italian Materialist Aesthetics),* what Della Volpe
had been attempting in the *Critica del gusto* and the *Verosimile filmico* was, in
a certain sense, a modern semantic and materialist reappraisal of the categori-
cal differentiation of artistic 'genres' first outlined by Lessing.

Della Volpe argues that because the different arts utilise different technical
and semantic expressive structures which are unique to each medium, they are
not readily translatable (if at all) from one genre to another. Whilst the various
arts contribute to knowledge (real, historical etc.) in concrete and determinate
ways, the notion of approximate equivalence in Della Volpe's "critical paraphrase" is an indicator only of what gets lost in the process of trying to 'equate'
one genre to another. Instead, critics should be careful to give due care and
attention to:

> the differences in expressive techniques arising from the structural differences of
> the signs. *(Critica del gusto)*

which in turn highlights their superstructural functions:

> Instead, what is needed is a clear articulation of the differences in the
> superstructural collocations of art according to the different genres and their
> respective semantic techniques. *(Critica del gusto)*

Della Volpe's analysis amounts to an extremely useful recognition of the diversity of expressive means and a clearly articulated critique of hermeneutic over-
simplification, to which critics of visual art and film, in their attempt to match
form with content too closely, are particularly prone. His intellectual mentor
in this, Antonio Gramsci, similarly argued against the equal but opposite dan-
gers of an overemphasis on a work's content, which he termed, the 'contentist

fallacy' and the formalist or 'calligraphist fallacy' which overemphasised its form.

Like the Maori chieftain unable to distinguish between painted and real fruit, whose example Della Volpe cites in the motto which heads the 'Laocöon 1960', such confusions between genres, common to critics and artists alike, amount quite simply to:

> impatience with analysis, or more simply with distinction (*Critica del gusto* 232).

APPENDIX: JOHN HUSTON'S *THE DEAD,* ADAPTED FROM *THE DUBLINERS,* BY JAMES JOYCE: SKETCH FOR A PROVISIONAL MATERIALIST READING.[7]

Figure 1. *The Dead,* dir. J. Huston.

To Della Volpe, an appropriate 'transcription' of the 'literal material' (subject matter, inspiration, original) into another form (translation or genre), requires a concrete understanding of the limits and specificities of each language such that the crudities and oversimplifications resultant from overestimating either form or content are avoided. He is as opposed to 'formalism' as he is to 'contentism'. Della Volpe's critical procedure operates through the agency of a close verbal transcription of the artwork in question, (what he terms a 'critical paraphrase') which brings out the literal content whilst simultaneously high-lighting the gap between this literal transcription and the formal specificity of the artwork in question. Such an approach, being rigorously materialist, can-not but focus on the formal-semantic nature of the artwork, but it is a concep-tion of the formal-semantic which implicates the historico-social 'humus' from which it is formed, and in which it is embedded. What follows is a provisional attempt to see how an appraisal informed, rather than directed, by such an approach might help our understanding of filmic metaphor.

John Huston's film *The Dead* is an adaptation of a short story from James Joyce's *The Dubliners*. As in any filmic adaptation, the verbal original (the 'literal material' in Della Volpe) is re-presented to fit the specific requirements of filmic form. Thus, interior monologue becomes voice-over, verbal description becomes the product of panning shots, stage set, costume and lighting design; verbal narrative becomes filmic sequence and dialogue etc.

What makes Huston's *The Dead* such a masterful semiotic translation, however, is the degree to which Huston's understanding of the inherent necessities of film form, his mastery of the filmic medium, has been mapped onto an equally profound understanding of the 'look and feel' of Joyce's verbal original. *The Dead* is a story of contrasts – of togetherness and solitude, cold and warm, light and dark, beauty and sadness, memory of lost love versus knowledge of present compromise affection. As is usual with Joyce the text is rich with word-play, allusion and nuance: he had taken the surname of the elderly hosts, the Misses Morkan from his knowledge of Danish, where Mørke means 'darkness', Gabriel is the angel of death and darkness; the dialogue is peppered with allusions to death and mortality – "three mortal hours", the old ladies "toddle" (from the German der Tod = death), "she must be perished alive" with the cold etc.[8] Where these subtleties are verbal, Huston has managed to preserve most of them in dialogue. Where Joyce utilises his famous 'ventriloquist' style, to reveal character, Huston has relied on probing close ups and the characterisation of the actors. Where descriptive detail is included, Huston dwells on slowly panning location shots. After a slow and measured build up of single characters and couples, fragments of conversations and political vignettes around a Christmas dinner table, conversation, memories, party pieces, recitations and politics mingle in the comfortable glow of the Misses Morkan's apartment, then disperse into the cold December night. Throughout, there are contrasts of cold exterior and glowing interior, black night and white snow, black suits and hats and white dresses shirts, and scarves, movement and stillness, present and past, noise and silence. The contrasts slowly focus in and revolve around the two central figures Gabriel (Donal McCann) – (careful, self-conscious, a little pompous, gentle, responsible, aware of not being loved), and his wife Gretta (Anjelica Huston), (more spirited, natural, aware of being loved but unable to return it). These themes are common to both story and film and Huston has been careful to stick as closely to the mood of the original as he can.

But Huston's mastery of filmic metaphor becomes evident in the penultimate sequences of the film, when, the party over, Gabriel and Gretta return in a black carriage through the snow-clad streets of Dublin. Here the contrasts become polarised, the silence of interior brooding, versus the chatter of inane storytelling and the clatter of the horses hooves; the togetherness of the confined space of the carriage versus the mental and emotional distance of its occupants, and the immensity of the sky and landscape. One sequence comes to epitomise the whole narrative and psychological structure of the film, and it is an essentially *filmic* metaphor, which does not and could not exist in Joyce's original. It is an extremely contrived shot, formally, which yet flows with complete naturalness (what Della Volpe meant by 'filmic realism') in terms of the filmic structure. From directly overhead a perfect diagonal is formed across the screen, comprising an upper triangle of black Liffey, with a white triangle of snowclad bank. The composition is held briefly in silence, and then the black shadow of the carriage enters the white triangle from top right, accompanied by the clopping of the horses hooves and the rattle of the carriage over cobbles. The composition is held precisely until the moment at which the carriage exits, bottom left. What we have here is a perfect filmic moment. Perfect formal composition, perfect metaphoric appropriateness, a consummate use of visual, psychological and aural contrast; a perfect filmic condensation of narrative sequence. The time it takes for the carriage to traverse the scene is real time, but because of its investment of psychological significance, and the simplicity and stillness of the formal composition, the moment seems suspended, 'frozen' even; and further, we grasp the double triangle conceptually very quickly – the shot is held, suspended, for an instant – a moment of perfection – and is gone. No sooner have we grasped it visually/conceptually/psychologically as the turning point of the film – as the axis along which slip the emotional separateness of the characters, than the carriage interrupts it. Triangles, as we know from formalist criticism, are both stable in themselves and imply movement. Diagonals tend to lead the eye out of the frame. The perfect moment cannot be frozen – time and distance slide against each other, the carriage exits, stage left, bearing its occupants away to their lives of distance-in-togetherness.

The final sequences reveal the nature of this emotional gulf. Contrasting physical proximity and affective loss; blackness/whiteness, life and death, ending with another consummate filmic metaphor, (which this time derives directly from Joyce's own descriptive passage) of soft white snowflakes descending against a black night sky, as the voice over reflects on the forecast that "snow is widespread over Ireland ... falling faintly through the universe, and faintly falling, like the descent of their last end, upon the living and the dead".

The appropriateness of Huston's use of filmic metaphor, which derives from an intimate understanding of both the verbal original and the filmic medium, enables the successful 'translation' from one genre to another whilst allowing both words and images to follow their own (formal-semantic) logic, permitting Huston's film to exist in its own epistemological space without overshadowing, competing or crowding out, Joyce's original, the poignancy and strength of which is preserved in the new format.

NOTES

1   But cf. Hay, "Introduction". It is one of Benjamin's many paradoxes that while asserting a materialist aesthetic of production, he yet believed in the existence of a Cabbalistic version of Goethe's *Urphänomen*, but that is another story.

2   Tadashi Ogawa, in a recent article on translation argues that "[a]ny translation presupposes two sorts of invariance, which we might refer to as intercultural and interlingual respectively – these two sorts of invariance have to be brought to light in the process of translation" (19).

3   For a more detailed discussion of this in relation to Italian materialism from the Neapolitan Hegelians to Della Volpe, cf. K. G. Hay, *Italian materialist aesthetics* and *Bertrando Spaventa*. On Della Volpe's Aesthetics, cf. Hay *Della Volpe's Critique of Romantic Aestetics*. For a discussion of Della Volpe's materialist logic see Geymonat.

4   In English the only publication devoted to Della Volpe is John Fraser's (Geymonat); only three volumes of Della Volpe's writings have been translated into English *(Critique, Logic* and *Rousseau and Marx)*. For his aesthetics, the most valuable sources are his *Crisi*, the *Poetica, Il verosimile, Schizzo* and *Critica*.

5   The epigraphs read: (1) "Why should a description which is admirable in a poem become ridiculous in a painting? ... why should the God [Neptune] whose head is so majestic in the poem [in Aeneid I, 126-7 – rising above the waves] look like decapitated head in a painting of the scene? How is it that something which is pleasing to our minds is yet displeasing to our eyes?" (Diderot, *Lettre sur les sourds et les muets*) and (2) "when the Laocöon of Virgil shouts, who would consider that in order to shout he must have his mouth wide open and that this would render the figure ugly? It is enough that the 'clamores horrendos ad sidera tollit' appeals as a noble image to our ears and minds, and the visual aspect can be left to your imagination" (Lessing, *Laokoon*).

6   *Il verosimile* (12). The expressions derive from Rudolf Arnheim and Umberto Barbaro respectively.

7   Starring Donal McCann as Gabriel and Anjelica Huston as Gretta.

8   For these and more elucidations see Wyse Jackson and McGinley (157-99).

REFERENCES

Aristotle. *Poetics*. Trans. W. Hamilton Fyfe, London, 1960. 1451b, 1ff.

Benjamin, Walter. "The Task of the Translator". *Illuminations*. Trans. Harry Zohn. London: Fontana, 1976. 69-82.

Croce, B. *Aesthetic as General Linguistic and Science of Expression*. Trans. D. Ainsley. London: P. Owen, 1953.

Della Volpe, Galvano. *Opere*. 6 Volumes. Ed. Ignazio Anbrogio. Rome: Editori Riuniti, 1972-73.

————. *Crisi critica dell'estetica romantica*. D'Anna, Messina, 1941. *Opere, 3*.

————. *Poetica del cinquecento*. Bari: Laterza, 1954. *Opere, 5*.

————. *Il verosimile filmico e altri scritti di estetica* . Rome: Filmcritica, 1954. *Opere, 5*.

————. *Schizzo di una nuova storia del gusto*. Rome: Riuniti,1971. *Opere, 5*.

————. *Critica del gusto* . Milan: Feltrinelli, 1960. (Second, enlarged edition, 1964; third Italian edition, Feltrinelli, 1966.)

————. *Critique of Taste*. Trans. Michael Caesar. London: New Left Books, 1978.

————. *Logic as a positive science*. Trans. Jon Rothschild. London: New Left Books, 1980.

————. *Rousseau and Marx*. London: Lawrence and Wishart, 1978.

Eisenstein, S. *Film Form*, Trans. Jay Leyda, London, 1949. 60.

Fraser, John. *An Introduction to the Thought of Galvano Della Volpe*. London: Lawrence and Wishart. 1977.

Geymonat, Ludovico. "La positività del molteplice". *Rivista di filosofia* xlii, vi (1951): 303-11.

Goethe, "Uebertragungen ... ". *Werke*, XV. Zürich, 1953. 1085.

Hay, K.G. "Introduction to Walter Benjamin and Wolff Zucker, 'Pay rise? You must be Joking! – A short Radio play". Trans. S. Alagapan. *The Tempest* 1 (1992): 36-43.

————. "Picturing Readings: Della Volpe and Lessing". *Paragraph* 19 (1996): 272-85.

————. *Italian materialist aesthetics*. Unpublished Ph.D Thesis. The University of Wales. 1990.

————. *Bertrando Spaventa and Italian Hegelianism* Graduate Research Seminar paper. Department of Cultural Studies, The University of Derby, 1995.

————. "Della Volpe's Critique of Romantic Aesthetics". *Parallax* 1 (1996): 181-90.

Jakobson,Roman. "Linguistische Aspekte der Übersetzung". *Übersetzungswissenschaft*. Ed. Wolfram Wilss. Darmstadt, 1981. 189-98.

Lee, R. W. "Ut Pictura Poesis: The Humanistic Theory of Painting". *Art Bulletin* XXII (1940): 196-269.

Leopardi, "Zibaldone". *Tutte Le Opere* . Ed. W. Binni and E. Ghidetti. Vol II. Florence, 1969. 564.

Lessing, Gotthold Ephraim. *Laocoon*. Trans. W. A. Steel. London, 1930.

Ogawa, Tadashi. "Translation as a Cultural-philosophic Problem: Towards a Phenomenology of Culture". *The Monist* 78 (1995): 18-29.

Pudovkin, V. I. *Film Technique and Film Acting*. London: Vision Press, 1958. 116.

Wyse Jackson, John & Bernard McGinley. *James Joyce's Dubliners: An Annotated Edition*. London: Sinclair-Stevenson, 1993. 157-99.

Word & Image in the Garden

John Dixon Hunt

'Tis in every feature
I would make it shine.

— Richard Alfred Milliken, "The Groves of Blarney"

This topic presents various challenges, but they can be expressed as the double need to argue for the garden as a sufficiently important site to merit inclusion in the various learned discourses of word and image studies gathered in this volume and, no less, to contrive for the study of gardens itself a sufficient discourse.

Any concentrated study of trade publications on the making of gardens will confirm the casual impression that they mostly lack intellectual or conceptual rigour. This scepticism was expressed, courteously enough, by James Elkins in the pages of the *Journal of Garden History:* he argued that many writings on the garden incite to reverie, where expected coherence or scholarly reference is abandoned.[1] While this is not the occasion for any strategic answer to Elkins' implied challenge to those who make gardens their study, a consideration of the respective roles of word and image in the garden will yield an opportunity to set out how that study, as a critical enquiry, might be conducted.

There are probably three aspects of the enterprise: first, the role played in the design of gardens by verbal and visual languages; second, their dual role in the experience of actual gardens (or, if you like, their "reception"); third, the ways in which different media represent gardens, or rather the *idea* of the garden. My examples in this essay are drawn mainly from poetry and paintings; but the enquiry could obviously be extended also to advertisements, film, novels, and the many other media which word and image students consider. Beyond these, and drawing them into closer connection, is the larger, but crucial question, whether the theme of word and image is truly endemic to the garden, whether it marks something essential and even unique in this design art. By this I intend not just a dual involvement of word and image, but a symbiotic one, without which the design, experience and idea of a garden are incomplete.

II

We encounter words in gardens in different ways. But it is important to register from the start that sometimes words in a garden may not always function as they do, say, in a newspaper: they can be as much part of the garden's visual world – an additional texture in a stone, that lichen and erosion may make even more interesting; an inscription can simply be a visual supplement (Latin characters to augment a temple's classical tonality or "authenticity") or a simple sign of cultural control that is also apparent in topiary or gravel walks; further, if we read aloud as we decipher an inscription, which many site-specific ones explicitly invite us to do (drawing upon the rhetorical strategy of *prosopopeia*), then we add our own to the plenitude of garden *sounds*.[2] I shall return later to this aural dimension of gardens.

Some words are explicit – that is to say, relevant ones actually appear before us, because the designer or owner has been concerned to direct our attention in a particular fashion: for example, the mottoes and names on the Temple of British Worthies at Stowe, which identify its busts and recapitulate biographies. Others, however, are only implied – so it is left to us to articulate features that have names (generic or proper), which are not spelt out *in situ:* for instance, the name of that Temple of British Worthies is nowhere legible upon it. This absence could be because it was never thought necessary – the original users of the gardens at Stowe all knew the name of a temple or section of the garden and they never thought that "outsiders" would need to be oriented. When visitors did start coming, it is significant that the naming of garden parts was made available, first, through a poem written by one of the inner circle of initiates, then through a series of commercially produced guides.[3] Even the Lord God, you will recall, never felt it necessary to repeat in an inscription what he had told Adam and Eve in conversation about not eating from the Tree of the Knowledge of Good and Evil – with disastrous consequences that might have been avoided if only he had put up a notice.

The simplest motive for verbal intervention is to provide information. Sometimes this is of a highly practical nature (directional notices for those who do not know the territory; injunctions on how to behave – the *lex hortorum* of Roman and Renaissance custom (see Coffin), and its continuance in the public notices that confront visitors to many European public parks. Sometimes words are inserted for instructional reasons (botanical labels) or purposes of identification (memorial labels on graves or monuments within gardens – a function hugely extended, obviously, into the cemetery movement).[4] Yet, even the simplest of these modes implies that the garden is thought to need this verbal supplement – that you will get lost or miss a special experience by not visiting the grotto or the "Surprise View" to which therefore a notice directs you; or that botanical labels necessarily extend the sensual pleasure into what is nowadays known as a learning experience. All this implies that the fullest potential of a garden, whether its identity, use or function, will only be achieved by explicitly announcing some extra-visual significance. But it is also likely to be extra-territorial.

For beyond the need or urge to identify, explicate, educate and generally guide or control the garden visitor within its spaces and through its immediate concerns, explicit or implicit verbal supplements also gesture beyond those fairly precise events to matters that are not on the face of it essential to the garden nor, indeed, often within the garden. Sometimes the actual or implied naming of a garden feature takes us into this larger territory: to register at Stourhead that there are two buildings known as the Pantheon and Alfred's Tower is to embark upon a wider, discursive meditation that goes somehow beyond the immediate garden context (see Kelsall). From the earliest known examples of real or imagined gardens (and I doubt whether imagined ones invent a wholly new dimension for gardens), words have linked, however tenuously, the immediate world of the garden with a larger world elsewhere.

III

The site of gardening has been contested, especially since the nineteenth century, between the horticulturists and the intellectuals. This is nicely illustrated by the two panels from 1912-13 by Roger de la Fresnaye – in *Arrosoir* a watering-can signals the active theme of gardening, in *Mappemonde,* a globe, violin and books feature the intellectual life.[5] But the world of the garden was never always thus bifurcated: even its very practicalities – digging, sowing, clipping and general maintenance – have always made and still make the garden seem a very special place (to those who do it, as to those who wouldn't be caught dead doing it). The garden as a place of work, hard work, is constituted as a site of special significance simply by that activity. Ralph Austen, a puritan gardenist of the mid-seventeenth century in England, is not really such a special case when, as his title-page of 1653 announces, he extends his practical *A Treatise of Fruit Trees* into a discourse on "The Spiritual Use of an Orchard". And this recognition of the garden as something special effectively transcends practical exigencies, local situation and names. To derive a pun from Roland Barthes' famous distinction, the work of the garden itself, the garden as work, generates its status as text.

This textuality of the garden has many reasons and causes, but I suggest that a prime one derives from the garden's site as a place of memory. The recent focus upon *lieux de mémoire* as a theme in French writing has inevitably caught the garden up in its deliberations (see Pierre Nora and the volume edited by Mosser and Nys): in design, in experience (or reception) and in representation the garden has been privileged as a place where we recall other things. But in a recent essay, "Les mots, les images et la mémoire des jardins" (published in Mosser and Nys), Michel Baridon has suggested an extension of this memorial activity by examining the linguistic means by which two fundamentally different types of garden design engineer the instinctive, endemic gesture of gardens outwards beyond their own scope. What is particularly useful about his etymological meditations is that they return us to the garden's fundamental and unique play with space and time.

Most obviously, picturesque gardens, or what Baridon calls *jardins de la sensibilité,* were constructed with an apparatus of associationism, to which words chiefly gave expression, that specifically recalled their ephemeral nature. This association of the garden with time and temporal process derived (as Baridon shows here and elsewhere) from a whole congeries of human enquiries and interests, but it was a unique *démarche* for the garden to be associated with transcience as never before (think – Baridon suggests [192] – of the emergence of meteorological time as an integral part of eighteenth-century garden experience). He therefore implies how strong a case could be made for associating this *jardin de la sensibilité* (otherwise known as the "English", "natural", "informal" or "picturesque" garden) primarily with verbal supplements. By contrast, it might therefore be inferred that the earlier (or "formal" or geometrical") garden resisted verbalization in its primary concern with space; however, this was not the case, and Baridon shows how its linguistic connections gestured towards larger spatial concerns. What is important about this demonstration (although only incidentally for our purposes) is that gardens are not distinguished according to their formal properties but because of the different human experiences – time and space – to which their verbal supplements refer.

Baridon shows how the various verbal languages of Renaissance and baroque garden treatises relate to the perception and representation of space outside gardens; through the agency of words like symmetry, perspective, proportions, quadrature, etc., which attach to and sustain the physical forms of which gardens were composed, we are recalled to spaces both physical and metaphysical that stretch far outside them. Thus these gardens also are marked as *lieux de mémoire* by their verbal insistence on the principles of spatial perception which sustained design, principles a *priori* to any actual layout, even if they were reified within it: indeed, Diderot would later register (wrongly) how these principles were "point dans la nature".[6]

Though Baridon begins his essay by suggesting that "Certains jardins ... sont ... concus comme des lieux ou s'incarne la mémoire" (184), it seems doubtful whether any garden can in fact evade its role as a site the very design of which alludes to spaces and times larger than those of the garden itself. And, furthermore, since the two modes of gardening are both shown to rely upon verbal supplements to indicate their different relations with – or representations of – time and space, it could be argued that we need to rely less upon those formal distinctions in our taxonomies of garden art and instead register the extent of their concern with space or time. And for us at the end of the twentieth century gardens are doubly places of memory, even those created yesterday: we encounter them as places where a certain society or culture sought to recall space and time, while by our own visit or study we recapitulate that particular time and place and make them palpable here and now.

IV

But gardens recall things outside not simply because they are places of memory. Any successful garden engages in acts of representation, re-presenting within its achieved and calculated spaces less finished or coherent worlds elsewhere (this is a theme that cannot be recapitulated here, but see, variously, Hunt "La représentation", "The Idea of the Garden" and "Imitation"). And an implicit element in that garden act of representation is what I should call an idea of the garden (by analogy with Matthew Arnold who argued for holding on to an idea of the world so that we are not overwhelmed by the world's multitudinousness).

Any fine garden sustains within its formal and physical effects an idea of the garden, which grows, like the fatal tree at the heart of the first garden, in the centre of every place that is made a garden. And like that Edenic tree – at once flowering, fruitful, *and* harbouring the serpent – the idea of a garden is an awkward concept for many people who only think of gardens in terms of gardening; yet the coexistence of metaphysical with physical is but one of the many paradoxes that thrive in the garden. Placemakers may ignore or deny the contributing or sustaining role of the idea of a garden in their designs; garden owners, keepers or visitors may also evade or bypass any recognition of intellectual intent or subtext; even the metaphysical notion of evil is carefully transposed into slugs, chipmunks, weeds, couchgrass, etc. But the conceptual realm flourishes in the garden notwithstanding.

The garden is supremely self-conscious – spatially and temporally, as Baridon led us to recognize; and this self-conscious determination feeds upon, just as it brings to the fore, the *idea* of the garden. To carve out a local space that is a refinement, abstraction or concentration of others – both the organic and inorganic natural world (the garden as "nature methodized") and the culture that temporarily colonizes that world; both to thwart and to capitalize upon time – by seeking to create an artful space within a changing natural world that is ever in process, even when that very process is accepted as endemic to the endeavour and not something to be repressed ("time shall make it grow, a work to wonder at"); to entertain these ambitions is to mark the special place that place-making has in the space and time of human society and in its turn to stress the sustaining role of the idea in the garden's actual being.

That sense of special place-making necessarily initiates or thrives upon verbal articulation. Jacopo Bonfadio, one of the earliest Renaissance theorists of the garden, saw that a proper experience and understanding of landscape required not only a "diligent eye and much consideration", but a constant dialogue between eye and mind (see Hunt "Paragone in Paradise"). Merely naming something a garden constitutes its specialness, its difference from orchard, field, woodland or wasteland (witness the down-playing of garden in the American usage, yard). Among the more eloquent demonstrations of this are the ubiquitous baroque engravings of European country seats which certainly found visual, indeed spatial, ways to mark gardens as especially privileged among other kinds of human territory. These engravings do so through an iconic resemblance to the varied face of the landscape itself, though the fact that they are always raised into a bird's-eye view in order to represent a sufficiently wide range of spatial handling underlines at once (before the days of hot-air balloons) the ideal nature of this vision.

But throughout the same period, indeed from the mid-sixteenth century onwards, verbal references also indexed this human recognition of gardens as special spaces. I have written extensively of the neologistic formulation of the term "third nature" (terza natura) for gardens by two Italian humanists, Jacopo Bonfadio and Bartolomeo Taegio. The concern of these two writers, independently of each other (as far as I can see), was to distinguish the place-making of garden art from the "second nature" (or *alterna natura*) of the cultural landscape, this being the term with which Cicero in *De natura deorum* had designated a world of agricultural and urban infrastructure, which in turn he implicitly distinguished from their prime, unmediated source in "first nature" (for him, the territory of the Gods).

These concerns with the garden as one of several different natures were at their most intense around the year 1700. For various reasons subsequent painting and writing about gardens neglected to emphasize the garden in this way, or felt no need to represent it within a scale or continuum of interventions – though these still existed, of course; when we think of it, a garden has always to be distinguished from, say, orchards or fields or "wilderness". But a consideration of gardens as a different, special place within the varied fabric of human cultural institutions and infrastructures was obscured if not even lost by the end of the eighteenth century; this may have been for ideological reasons – after all, William Kent was supposed to have leapt the fence and found that all nature was a garden; or maybe the declensions of natures were so taken for granted as to become invisible. (It can be noted that proponents of the picturesque garden deliberately worked to blur the distinction between different kinds or zones of "nature": thus, say, British sites like Hawkstone and Hafod aim both to be "unmediated" wildernesses and yet to declare the art that has worked to make them so).

V

In the West we do not tend to name gardens other than by their ownership or topographical location; though that is not true of some contemporary garden artists such as Ian Hamilton Finlay or Bernard Lassus; otherwise the word "garden[s]" is forced to bear by itself an extra weight of significance. But the Chinese have traditionally gone to some trouble to invent site-specific names like the *Nursery Garden of Autumn Vapours* or *Green Vine Study;* indeed, they consider the naming of gardens, or parts of them, even more difficult than the physical making of them because more is at stake than the formal arrangement of rocks, and stones and trees; it was Jia Zheng in the eighteenth-century *Story of the Stone* who said that "these prospects and pavilions – even the rocks and trees and flowers will seem somehow incomplete without the touch of poetry which only the written word can lend a scene".

Western attitudes are a little more casual; but we can all think of spaces or objects in gardens that, named, constitute a special meaning for them that transcends the local and immediate, a meaning that the locality in fact could not by itself contribute (Rousham's *Praeneste;* Versailles' *Parterre de Latone*). Of course, actual inscriptions in both eastern and western gardens perform that function deliberately and conspicuously: some simply name themselves; some stimulate memories or initiate associations both trivial and momentous, but always taking us outside the garden itself; some catch us up into games by conundral formulations, hidden clues or deliberately omitted references, making us work to win from the garden experience some larger meaning. Ian Hamilton Finlay is a master here, but both Stowe's British Worthies with a Virgilian line about priests deliberately dropped from its central inscription or the Chinese delight in inferring but never directly stating is another mode of this interactive verbalizing in gardens. Indeed, so logocentric is the world of gardens that inscriptions are clearly deemed an indisputable part of a garden experience – so "natural" even that we accept easily how some garden creators constitute a "garden", that is to say a significant, circumscribed zone or space, by the simple insertion of words into the larger, usually natural scene.[7] But not all those who value gardens are so attentive to the vital role of words in supplementing the garden's imagery (which cannot, of course, be presented adequately here).

VI

Yet, if the verbal supplements to garden design and garden experience have been overemphasized to this point, it is in part because garden art needs to be rescued from the horticulturists and ecologists. Place-making has been throughout history a significant expression of human nature – its own combination of nature and culture accurately mirroring the same complex synthesis in the human being, its designer, owner and visitor, and the only animal known to make gardens. And that significance draws upon, as it gives expression to, our double facility with words and images, although it is a dual faculty that has (certainly) its historical and cultural declensions and variations.

But we must equally resist the temptation to make landscape architecture analogous to the art which, in Tom Wolfe's *The Painted Word,* appears as merely an aftereffect of the verbal. Wolfe's jaundiced diatribe reminds us, if nothing else will, to maintain the intricate balance of gardens, what I have called their essentially paradoxical nature. If we promote the word over the image – to adapt Wolfe's formulation: "first you get the Word, and then you can see [the garden]" (60) – we are liable not only to lose touch with the gardeners and horticulturists, which constitute after all a substantial part of the concerned constituency, but also to jeopardize that intricate experience of all great garden art which is a combination of the sensual and the spiritual (I am not happy with the term "spiritual", but I use it as a means of suggesting the continuing role for gardens, even in our secular times, as sites of the sacred).

Fine a poem as it is, W. H. Auden's "Their Lonely Betters" wittily or wickedly manipulates the garden in favour of its verbal supplement: sitting in a deck-chair and listening "To all the noises that my garden made", the poet translates into words what "vegetables and birds" have been denied and only their "lonely betters" vouchsafed. Auden's logocentricity brushes aside the garden world in its fulness: we are indeed "better" for our verbal skills than the materials and unhuman inhabitants of the garden – we can lie, mark time, fall in love, laugh and weep eloquently, and discourse of concepts like loneliness and superiority. Yet, that very linguistic facility cuts us off, not just from a world of forms, smells, colours, spaces that have no obvious verbal equivalents (nor need of them), but also from an instinctive apprehension of the natural world that Auden condescendingly allows to the Robin and the pollinating bee. Our "loneliness" is an inadequate acknowledgement of that isolation.

The non-linguistic aspects of gardens are hard to isolate and/or analyze: the smells; the sound of birds, of water (in all its metamorphic playfulness and energy) or of different surfaces beneath our feet (recall how different sized gravel makes different noises, let alone making the experience of walking different); the feel of things – either underfoot (whether gravels or grass, damp or dry) or as we touch or brush against things. Even the exploration of garden spaces escapes verbal commentary. Yet, each of these and more are an ineluctable element of garden design and experience (reception), which we ignore at our peril.

Some of these elements, largely insusceptible to adequate linguistic discourse, may be accessed through painting. No period has been without garden pictures, and there even appears to be a revival of the tradition of country house portraiture in Britain (see Harris, both titles). Some of the excitements of garden paintings should not be surprising. The best reveal how place-making is a spatial art: not just the definition of space by walls, hedges, ha-has, water-courses, but the role in place-making of connections and juxtapositions. Paths, openings, transitions, edges, textures, scale – all determine how we negotiate and so experience garden space. Some show it, so to speak, at ground level, placing us below a flight of steps, or about to pass through an opening; some raise us above the site so that we appreciate scale, distance and juxtaposition – the old baroque engraving recharged with a fresh sense of different treatments of organic material and their proportion to the inorganic.

Another strong tradition in garden paintings, because of course it has been such a strong tradition in gardens, is the display of them as stages, as theatres. As I have discussed elsewhere, this can take formal shape – the exedras, the platforms viewed from quasi-auditoria, even the inclusion of actual green theatres in the design. But often in scenery that does not even suggest the physical forms of *caveae* or *auditoria*, artists have depicted people performing – social roles in the hot-houses of Victorian conservatories, roles that social protocols or fashion demands in certain public situations like garden ceremonies or visits, or the more mundane presentation of the selves of garden owners or visitors in the everyday world of the garden. We may be trembling here on the edge of extrapolating verbal scenarios, scenarios which the painting can at best infer or imply and for which novels or plays may prove the better evidence. But what fascinates me in this class of imagery is the artists' keen apprehension of how the garden invites, even requires or compels its visitors to "perform". We talk casually of garden settings or scenes; the etymological connection to the theatre is no accident and transpires before and after the verbal supplement.

Garden paintings also show us work in gardens (more so, at any rate, than the photographs of any modern coffee table book on gardening ever do). This is made especially significant in what we are liable to call "formal" gardens, where labourers recall the effort required to maintain the forms and patterns that, though they may derive from the natural materials themselves, are still abstracted and reified by human agency. But there are other, modern paintings which immerse us in the fecund tangle of garden planting; here the dialogue between human and plant order is reversed, either to celebrate the ultimate victory of the vegetable world (the abandoned or ruined garden) or to hint at the mysterious efficacy of human control over even the most resolute fecundity of things.

It is also perhaps surprising how much the corpus of poetry about gardens, if we read it attentively, has reached beyond its formal mode to stress the same non-verbal elements of garden design and experience as paintings have done. This is more difficult to indicate briefly: but it is not just the emphasis on work, the physical struggle to maintain even horticultural order, which is a dominant note in contemporary poems on gardens, but the spatial discoveries – the gardens as adjacent to other social spaces, views outside from inside a house or shed, from one part of a garden to another, and, via the mnemotic process that we have discussed, the palpable physical sense of somewhere else impinging on a specific garden moment and location. I am also struck by the almost perverse attempt of writers to treat of shapes ("intricate mesh of trees, / Sagging beneath a lavender snow / of wisteria, wired by creepers"), textures ("the minted flesh of leaves / against the garden wall"), smells (Thom Gunn sniffing "at the bergamot / the fruit-sage smell") or sounds that are beyond the recall of even a Tennysonian onomatopoeia ("The broad ambrosial aisles of lofty lime / Made noise with bees and breeze from end to end" [for these and other examples see the *Oxford Book of Garden Verse*]).

VII

But in the end we have, I believe, to acknowledge that in our efforts to understand the "discourse" of the garden, it escapes both visual and literary modes. Neither alone nor in conjunction can they wholly present those elements of garden design and experience that constitute its special effects. Unlike other objects of enquiry in this volume, the garden is not an illustrated text nor an advertisement; it is not a series of pictures with words inscribed upon them, nor the appending of poetry to visual imagery. Garden designers may have been, traditionally at any rate, expert in many fields; but we cannot discuss place-makers as we would those artists who work in various media – William Blake, Dante Gabriel Rossetti, or Hans Arp. Some of the approaches and methods of other word and image studies, therefore, cannot serve the turn of place-making.

The garden is *sui generis* as a spatial art, surpassing both architecture precisely in its inclusion of living materials (colloquially termed "nature") and sculpture in its territorial scope and (usually) variety of materials. If they are texts, gardens are dramatic not discursive, and their dramas are in the order of what Henri Gouhier has termed "les arts à deux temps"; that is to say, their "scripts" are endlessly subjected to fresh "performances". In affecting the resources and achievements of other non-spatial arts, gardens may often constitute themselves as "loci of utterance" (quoted in Angeline 2), as texts; but their narratives and their iconography lend themselves awkwardly to literary or art historical analysis. Given the fragility of gardens, it is often only through the approaches of literary scholars and art historians, respectively working in their habitual domains of texts and images, that gardens have been held up for consideration; therefore verbal and visual approaches have been over-privileged.

There therefore still needs to be developed an analytical language of garden analysis, hospitable to how the garden visitor translates his or her experience, how that translation (as well as the experience) is culturally conditioned, how those conditions of place-making and place-exploring are constituted by more than meets the eye (or the ear) in the garden, yet, must also be present explicitly or implicitly within the garden, and if implicitly, how and why they have earned their place in the world of the garden.

We have not, I suggest, begun to figure the garden yet, and it remains an exciting challenge for the future. Just as too many garden books and landscape architects fail utterly to grasp the strong conceptual dimension of gardens and how place-making speaks fully and richly of cultural purpose and ambition, so many scholarly analyses read as if their authors had never walked through a garden, never exposed themselves to its mix of demands and sensations. The problem in part, of course, is that sentimentality and the tangled convolvulus of the pathetic fallacy cling to gardens; accepted, even cherished, by garden writers in their green-fingered prose, they are eschewed in horror by the intellectuals and rooted savagely out of their footnotes.

Paradox is as endemic to gardens as to no other art form. Place-making comprises both nature and culture, product and process, praxis and theory, object and subject, physicality and metaphysics; it is an art (by necessity) ever-renewing itself, yet the most atavistic. Recently, such a landscape architectural theorist as Bernard Lassus has considerably augmented our sense of these paradoxes to include vertical/horizontal, measurable/immeasurable, environment/landscape, homogeneous/heterogeneous.

To these gardenist paradoxes we must insist on adding that of word & image, even if their collaborative approach does not deliver the garden to our analysis. It will be as much by their rivalry or *paragone* as by their collaboration, that they will lead us into the paradoxical nature of gardens at all stages of their being – from their design, through the experience of them, to the idea of them that guides everything from their creation to their conservation.

NOTES

1   I have also made one, somewhat different, attempt to respond to Elkins's essay in "La représentation dans l'art du jardin". It should also be noted that the ekphrasis of gardens is not in question here: for which see my "Ekphrasis of the Garden".

2   See the exemplary discussion of this by Geoffrey Hartman, and my own brief discussion of memorial inscriptions, Hunt (forthcoming).

3   See George Clarke, *Descriptions of Lord Cobham's Gardens at Stowe 1700-1750.* Buckinghamshire Record Society 26 (1990); Gilbert West's poem of 1731 (36-51) is the "insider's" perspective and its verses often fail to name names, leaving it to explanatory footnotes to label the references.

4   See Erasmus in *The Godly Feast,* where the labels identifying plants in Eusebius' botanical garden also issue ethical injunctions: see *The Colloquies of Erasmus,* ed. Craig R. Thomson (Chicago, 1965), 50-5 & 76-8.

5   These are illustrated in Germain Seligman, *Roger de la Fresnaye. With a catalogue raisonné.* Greenwich, CT., 1969. 166.

6   Cited Baridon, 192; Diderot was wrong of course – Boyceau's celebration of symmetery, for instance, is premised upon nature's own efforts in this line, and modern ecology has also propelled itself into a recognition of the amazing abstract effects of nature herself (see in this respect the photographs in Pat Murphy & William Neill, *By Nature's Design.* San Francisco, CA., 1993).

7   A useful example is the work of the Montreal-based artist Gilbert Boyer: on whom see John Angeline.

REFERENCES

Angeline, John. "Gardens for the People: Gilbert Boyer and 'The Urban Paradise'". *Journal of Garden History* XVI (1996): 298-309.

Coffin, David. "The *lex hortorum* and Access to Gardens of Latinum During the Renaissance". *Journal of Garden History* II (1982): 201-32.

Elkins, James. "On the Conceptual Analysis of Gardens". *Journal of Garden History* 13 (1993): 189-98.

Gouhier, Henri. *Le théâtre et les arts à deux temps.* Paris, 1989.

Harris, John. *The Artist and the Country House. A History of Country and Garden View Painting 1540-1870.* New Haven, CT., 1979.

——. *The Artist and the Country House from the 15th Century to the Present Day.* London, 1996.

Hartman, Geoffrey H. *Beyond Formalism: Literary Essays 1958-70.* New Haven, CT., 1970. [Especially the essays on inscriptions and *genius loci.*]

Hunt, John Dixon. "'Come into the garden, Maud': Garden Art as a Privileged Mode of Commemoration and Identity". In: Joachim Wolschke-Bulmahn, ed. *Places of Commemoration. Search for Identity and Landscape Design.* Washington, D.C., forthcoming.

——. "Ecrire le jardin: la quatrième nature". *Le temps des jardins.* Fontainebleau, 1992. 12-15.

——. "Ekphrasis of the Garden". *Interfaces. Image Texte Langage* 5. Dijon: 1994, 61-74.

——. "The Idea of the Garden, and the Three Natures". In: Joachim Wilke, ed. *Zum Naturbegriff der Gegenwart.* 2 vols. Stuttgart-Bad Cannstatt, 1994.

——. "Imitation, Representation, and the Study of Garden Art". In: Susan C. Scott, ed. *The Art of Interpreting. Papers in Art History from the Pennsylvania State University* (IX), 1995. 198-215.

——. "Paragone in Paradise: Translating the Garden". *Comparative Criticism* 18 (1996).

——. "La représentation dans l'art du jardin". Bernard Lassus, ed. *Hypothèses pour une troisième nature.* Paris, 1992.

——, ed. *Oxford Book of Garden Verse.* Oxford, 1993.

Kelsall, Malcolm. "The iconography of Stourhead". *Journal of the Warburg & Courtauld Institutes* 46 (1984): 133-43.

Lassus, Bernard. *The Landscape Approach of Bernard Lassus.* (Forthcoming from the University of Pennsylvania Press, 1998).

Mosser, M. and Philippe Nys, eds. *Le jardin. Art et lieu de mémoire.* Besançon, 1995.

Nora, Pierre. "Between Memory and History: les lieux de mémoire". *Representations* 26 (1989): 7-25.

——, ed. *Les lieux de mémoire.* 3 vols. Paris, 1992.

Wolfe, Tom. *The Painted Word.* New York : Farrar, Straus and Giroux, 1975.